AMERICA AND THE CHINA THREAT

AMERICA
AND THE
CHINA THREAT

From *The End of History*
to the End of Empire

Paolo Urio

Clarity Press, Inc.

ISBN: 978-1-949762-50-1
EBOOK ISBN: 978-1-949762-51-8

In-house editor: Diana G. Collier
Cover design: R. Jordan Santos

Library of Congress Control Number: 2021947284

Clarity Press, Inc.
2625 Piedmont Rd. NE, Ste. 56
Atlanta, GA 30324, USA
https://www.claritypress.com

Table of Contents

CHAPTER 2

The Ideological Divide / 116

American Ideology, Past and Present / 118

If America Is Back, What Kind of America Is It? / 338

Acknowledgments

I<small>T IS NOT POSSIBLE</small> to quote all the people who have helped me in my research on China's reforms—scholars, researchers, students, senior civil servants, and ordinary Chinese people I had the opportunity to meet during my numerous visits to China. I have recognized their invaluable contributions to my understanding of China in my previous books. But allow me to cite a few special contributions. My colleague Hu Angang of Tsinghua University, whom I met for the first time in 1997, has encouraged me in my research, providing advice, access to unpublished research papers, introduction to colleagues, logistic and academic support from assistants of his team. Among them, I should like particularly to thank Wang Qizhen, who worked on the preparation of my books when I was at Tsinghua in 2016 and has continued to provide assistance since then. While in the UK for a PhD, she has updated the statistical tables of this book and has given invaluable comments and suggestions on my analysis of China's ideology for Chapter 2. My former assistant, Chen Yali, has worked with me from 2012 to 2017, when she started to work on the integration of Chinese women who emigrate to Switzerland. She has just obtained a PhD from Geneva University in gender studies. She also provided very interesting insight on my analysis of Chinese culture.

My former publishers have granted me permission to use parts of my books published by them in 2018 and 2019: Routledge for *China Reclaims World Power Status. Putting an end to the World America Made* (2018), and Springer Nature for *China 1949-2019. From the End of History to the End of Empire* (2019). This allowed me, by using and starting from what I had written for them, and adding new insights, especially for the analysis of American and Chinese myths, to produce a more refined interpretation of Chinese ideology, adding new comments, and the update of statistics I had already used for my previous books.

Last but not least, my English wife has done, as usual, the difficult job of putting my prose in a form acceptable for an English-speaking audience. On top of that, Diana G. Collier, editorial director of Clarity, has provided several comments and suggestions that have allowed me to significantly improve the manuscript.

It goes without saying that I am responsible for errors, omissions and misinterpretations that an attentive reader may find in this book.

Geneva, August 27, 2021

Introduction

I should not be surprised if my book were to be considered by many, both scholars and laymen, as anti-American. Well, it is not. But it is certainly very critical of the American establishment, based not upon a superficial, emotional reaction to the behaviour of the U.S. leadership during the last decades, but upon a careful enquiry into the origins of the extraordinary self-confidence that has underpinned practically all the aspects of the U.S. foreign policy since the Declaration of Independence. This is why, if my book is not anti-American, it is certainly anti-American establishment.

My generation of Europeans (I was born in 1940) was positively impressed by America. The victory over Nazi-fascism against the Axis powers, American films, music, jazz, Glenn Miller, Count Basie, Duke Ellington, Benny Goodman, skyscrapers, highways, Coca Cola, Abbott and Costello, freedom, democracy—these were just a few features of American culture that impressed us. Only communists and left-wing socialists, a small minority, at least in my small hometown in the south of Switzerland, were anti-American. As a child, I have seen the American soldiers in their uniform, crossing Switzerland unarmed, as the Swiss government required. Impressive! As a teenager in the 1950s I welcomed with enthusiasm rock-and-roll, Elvis Presley, Frank Sinatra, Gerry Mulligan, the Modern Jazz Quartet, and anti-racist films such as Giant, Shadows, and Imitation of Life.

I visited the U.S. for the first time in 1971, attending a summer program in political science at the University of Michigan, Ann Arbor. I discovered that a former colleague, like me previously an assistant at the University of Geneva, was also attending the program. He was married to an American lady, and they lived in California. At the end of the program, we drove, in his iconic Mustang, from Ann Arbor to California, crossing the Middle West to Denver, down to Taos, Santa Fe, and the Painted Desert, up to the Grand Canyon, west to Las Vegas, to Los Angeles and Santa Barbara. I fell in love with California and Santa Barbara. In 1979 I sent our older son to a one-year exchange programme in the U.S. He lived with a Republican family. The father was a lawyer

1

who campaigned for the post of Attorney General of the County against the incumbent of the Democratic Party and won. My son experienced the extraordinary American electoral campaign process, placing posters, stickers, visiting citizens and families, etc. Quite an experience. The following year we went to the U.S. to fetch him. The whole family—father, mother and our 4 children aged 17, 14, 12 and 10—crossed the U.S. from Washington D.C. to California, passing through Denver, Santa Fe, the Painted Desert, Grand Canyon, Lake Powell, Capitol Reef, Bryce Canyon, Las Vegas, Death Valley, then proceeding North to Yosemite, West to San Francisco, South on the N. 1 to Los Angeles. We ended the journey in Santa Barbara with one week's rest. An unforgettable holiday for the whole family. Everywhere we were welcomed with sympathy, a helping hand when in need, and we experienced how much Americans appreciate families and children.

In the 1990s and until the beginning of the 2010s my wife and I spent many of our summer holidays in Santa Barbara. There we were able to become friends with a number of middle-class Americans. They were great people. None of them were left-wing. We found the Americans to be good people, who were used to travelling abroad, including Europe, proud of their country, but with no aggressive posture, and no need to teach lessons. Generally, I do not discuss politics with friends. But I understood that some of them were Republicans, some others, Democrats. All in all, they provided a good sample of the American middle class: a university professor, two City College professors, two nurses, a geological engineer, a pastor, two estate agents, an artist painter, a former cadre of a private enterprise, a writer specialized in Mexican traditional architecture and his wife. So, what went wrong?

Of course, there have been several warnings of matters taking a disturbing trajectory. The Korean war could have been one, but it was successfully presented as a just war. There was also the regime change in Iran in 1953, one of the first successful endeavours by the CIA, but again, the Iranian president, Mossadegh, was misrepresented as a trojan horse of communism. Then there was the Vietnam war that was strongly criticised, even in the U.S. But mainstream opinion countered: was it not a just war to stop the spread of the communist dictatorships? Paradoxically the fall of the Soviet Union may be the historical moment when the problem with U.S. foreign policy became evident: its *raison d'être* was not just the necessary fight against the Stalinist dictatorship.

After the fall of the Soviet Union, the U.S. leadership felt it was 'on top of the world' that the end of history had at last been achieved, and the rest of the world would shortly adopt American-style liberal democracy and capitalism—under the leadership of the U.S, without a doubt, reflected in George H.W. Bush's pithy four-word pronouncement: What We Say Goes. This was a clear manifestation of an extraordinary self-confidence, that too often took the form of arrogance and disrespect for other peoples, states and cultures.

After the "Vietnam Syndrome" was successfully countered by the assault on Iraq of 2003, going to war far away from the sacred land became a habit, an addiction. The risk was almost null. The economic and military powers of the U.S. were unmatched, by far. But Americans had never experienced a big war on their own sacred land, except for their now distant civil war. In 1945 the U.S. had fought and won the war against Japan in the air and on the sea, not on soil, being over-confident if its nuclear superiority, that did not last long. By doing so, it ended the war without having the need to send its infantry onto Asian soil where Japan had a formidable army. Should it have done so, it would have been able to efficiently support China Kai-shek in his fight against the communists of Mao. By avoiding bringing its infantry onto the continent after defeating Japan with the atomic bomb—after all an easy win—the U.S. 'lost China.' And after WWII the U.S. lost all the wars it fought, and most of them were unnecessary.

The result has been the development of a Cold War mentality that has plunged the world into situations of permanent chaos, uncertainty, animosity, distrust, aggressivity and has increased the occasions not only for economic war, regime change, and covert armed actions, but also for 'a new world war' that may be fought with all the modern terrifying weaponries which all the great powers are developing, including nuclear weapons. Of course, countries such as Russia and China are developing their armaments at a steady pace. The West generally considers that it is their behaviour that causes fear, chaos, uncertainty and aggressivity. But one can also sustain, with good reasons and documentation, that these countries develop their armaments as a response to the threat and possible use against them of the U.S.'s extraordinary military arsenal. Compare what happened to Libya and what did not happen to North

Korea.[1] Faced with this situation, the response of the West is systematically the same: we are the Good, they are the Evil. The evil countries are presented as a danger to liberal democracies, because they want to change the rule of the international system the West has implemented reflecting its ideas and interests, and has imposed upon the rest of the world. Does this orientation constitute a danger for the realization of the interests of liberal democracies, themselves? But whose interests? Those of the people or those of the elites? Is it not possible to see that, in spite of serious problems within these revisionist countries, they have also been able to provide many positive outcomes for their own people? Would it not be better to respect the sovereignty of these countries, while promoting our values—and their actual implementation both within our countries and within the international system and counteracting, whenever necessary, the behaviour of those countries when, and only when, they really harm democratic countries and their people?

The events I have recalled above, needed to be explained with an in-depth analysis, and not with a superficial and emotional reaction to the many times the U.S. acted, and is still today acting, with confidence in its democracy and in its economic and military power, as well as with an unbearable arrogance toward foes and allies. This book aims to respond to these questions.

The foreign policy the U.S. implemented to deal with the China threat has been built with the purpose of keeping its status of sole great power, proclaimed to be the only way of assuring peace, stability and prosperity of an international system converted to liberal democracy and capitalism. The first chapter shows that the U.S. foreign policy has often been based upon several myths that have obscured the reality and have forbidden the U.S. to rationally analyse the relationship between the U.S. and China in the 21st century. Therefore, the aim of this chapter is to debunk these myths, such as the myths of the existence of universal values, and the myth of the dictatorial character of today's China governance.

The second chapter explains the division between the U.S. and China through the analysis of their ideologies going back to the

---

1 Libya abandoned its nuclear programme under pressure from the U.S., and its regime was deposed by an international coalition supported by the U.S. The North Korea regimen under heavy pressure from the U.S. still has its nuclear programme and, so far, it is still in place. One would say that China supports North Korea, and the U.S. are well advised not to militarily attack North Korea. But still. History shows that it is better to count on one's own weapons than on one's allies.

foundation of the U.S. Republic and the Chinese Empire. It shows the remarkable internal consistency of the American ideology and its unshakeable stability through time. But at the same time, it shows the extraordinary difficulty the U.S. experiences to adapt to the changes that have occurred in the international system. By contrast, the Chinese ideology, while also possessing a remarkable internal coherence through time, has achieved this by integrating values imported from the West and several Confucian values, to form a new ideology, more flexible and better apt to adapt its public policies to the changes of the national and the international environments. It also explains the remarkable resilience of the Chinese Party-State. The third chapter is an empirical demonstration of the suggestions derived from the analyses of Chapters 1 and 2.

As all the dimensions dealt with in the three chapters are linked to each other within a kind of structural interdependency, there will be many cross references within and between chapters that have made repetitions necessary. The sinologist may find this way of presenting my argument rather tedious. My purpose in doing so was to facilitate the reading for laymen, so that each chapter may stand on its own. Each chapter can be read independently of the others, and should readers wish to find more detailed explanations, they may refer to the other chapters as suggested in the text.

CHAPTER 1

Debunking American and Chinese Mythologies

Myths are a negation of reality. It is absolutely necessary to debunk them before trying to analyse rationally and '*sine ira et studio*' the interaction between China and the U.S. in the chapters that follow. In his *Annals* Roman historian *Tacitus* considers that in order to narrate events with impartiality and objectivity it is necessary to do so without anger, and with neither sympathy nor prejudices. This is not easy, but if we do not first debunk the more frequently used myths related to China and the U.S., we will have difficulties in understanding and analysing their relationship '*sine ira et studio.*'

In summary, a myth is (1) a simplified representation of events, social phenomena, or persons that is based, at least in part, on elements that do not exist in reality, and therefore the myth is a lie, an illusion, a dream or a utopia; but (2) when it is expressed over and over again with force may be accepted as true by members of a social group, or by the majority of a population or even by an entire population; (3) it thus may influence social life, individual and collective behaviour, contribute to social cohesion, and legitimate the existing authority and power—in this sense the myth can be considered as equivalent of, or contributing to the dominant ideology, and thus it can secure consensus for the status quo—and finally (4) it may be expressed as a set of values universally valid, and therefore those who believe in it, and who in principle orient their behaviour accordingly, may be tempted to impose it on other groups, people, or countries.

Some myths are a total negation of reality, such as the myth of eternal youth. But other myths are only a partial negation of reality, such as the myths of progress, of liberal democracy, of free trade.[1] The latter are the most insidious. As they are based partially upon reality, they

---

1 The political science literature is full of myths, for example: Ha-Joon Chang, *Bad Samaritans. The Myth of Free Trade and the Secret History of Capitalism,* New York, Bloomsbury, 2008. Paolo Urio, *China, the West and the Myth of the New Public Management,* London & New York, Routledge, 2012.

are more likely to obtain acquiescence, especially if they correspond to ideological biases predominant in the audience. In fact, when evaluating whether a myth is a total or partial negation of reality, we are confronted with what I call the Venus de Milo dilemma. In the ancient Greco-Roman world the *Venus de Milo* was the model of feminine beauty.[2] She is beautiful without the slightest trace of ugliness. But is Caesar's wife also beautiful? It is likely that she does not perfectly match Venus's beauty, but nevertheless she may retain a certain level (or kind) of beauty. So, the dilemma is: what is the extent of difference in the beauty of the *Venus de Milo* and Caesar's wife that we are ready to accept in order to qualify Caesar's wife as a beautiful woman? Of course, we will need to establish some generally accepted criteria for defining feminine beauty. Not a simple task. But the task is even more difficult when dealing with the myths of American democracy and the myth of Chinese dictatorship. As these two examples illustrate, some myths such as American democracy have a primarily positive connotation, while China dictatorship, as an instance, is primarily negative. Furthermore, quite often such positive myths as American democracy are contradicted by several negative features, inter alia the reality of the political process as it is actually practiced in the U.S. Similarly, some features of the political process as it is practiced today in China do not correspond to the myth of China Dictatorship.

The reader should not expect to find in the following pages a quantitative analysis of the gap between the myths and reality. Rather, the intent here, based on available empirical evidence, is to demonstrate that there is often a considerable gap between these myths and reality, with a view to encouraging, if not the Western pundits, including mainstream professors, think tanks experts and journalists who may have other reasons than the pursuit of truth for staking out their positions, then at least the concerned general public to manifest a less arrogant posture towards countries that, at least so far, have chosen to organise their polity, economy and foreign policies in ways that may considerably differ from the Western model, or in fact from the Western myths. In the gaps between myths and reality the open-minded reader may discover some positive aspects that are generally obscured by the overwhelming flow of Western short-sighted ideological criticisms.

---

2 Of course, I may as well take the *David of Michelangelo;* the reasoning would be the same. I hope that the reader will pardon me for taking the *Venus of Milo* instead.

In this chapter I will analyse three types of myths according to whether they are specifically Western (i.e., European and American), typically American or typically Chinese.[3] Moreover, the myths are interconnected, sometimes reinforcing each other, sometimes contradicting each other. The consequence is that repetitions have been necessary, as well as cross references both inside this chapter and with the following chapters.

AMERICAN AND EUROPEAN MYTHS

THE MOST THREATENING MYTH: THE CHINESE ARE COMING!

Although the 'China threat' has been a common theme in the West for a long time, its most recent manifestation appeared toward the beginning of the 21st century with the astonishing development of China's economy, inevitably linked (as has always happened in history) to the concomitant development of science and technology, as well as of military resources. This development has been acknowledged by the U.S. (and more generally by the West) as offering a mixture of opportunities (the development of trade and investments in the vast Chinese market) and invoking a new form of fear, a new form of the 'China Threat.' More particularly, the U.S. started to understand that China's development risked putting an end of the world America made, the foundation of the dominant U.S. role in the world. And the latter is, certainly for the U.S. establishment, the major threat.[4]

Moreover, the reaction of the U.S. to the rise of China is a clear indication of fear, more than of any other sentiment. This is not new for America. The fear that some 'OTHER' (uncivilised, or 'not normal' countries—in the words of Mike Pompeo referring to Iran) may jeopardize the realization of U.S. national interests, was present from

---

3 The British historian Lucy Worsley has undertaken a similar endeavour by unmasking the fibs of British and American history often presented by mainstream historians as 'what really happened.' She has produced several TV programmes broadcasted by the BBC; some of them are available on YouTube.

4 Urio 2018 and 2019, chapter 6.1. Nevertheless, another country is often presented by mainstream pundits as formidable threat: Russia. The Russia threat is even more worrying since Russia and China have established a de facto alliance, or at least a partnership, covering trade, international finance, and military. See for example Jeremy Kuzmarov and John Marciano, *The Russian Are Coming, again. The first cold war as tragedy, the second as farce*, New York, Monthly Review Press, 2018.

the very beginning of the U.S. Republic, i.e. around the last quarter of the 18th century. I remember that as a schoolboy, while at elementary school between 1947 and 1951, I used to go to the movies every Sunday afternoon, at what was at that time the 'Oratory for Boys' in my home town in the South of Switzerland. The great majority of films came from the U.S. They were primarily of two categories: war films about the epic fights between the American and the Japanese pilots during WW2; and Western films about the not less epic conquest of the American West. One of the very frequent scenes depicted the difficult march of the pioneers' caravan towards the promised land. At the end of the afternoon, they stop for the night and form a circle with their covered wagons. They eat, chat, and flirt. Good, decent, peaceful people hoping for a better life. At nightfall, they put out the fires and go to bed. Then, suddenly we hear, in the middle of the night, a frightful cry: *The Indians!* The first time I saw this scene, I did not understand the meaning of that cry. But immediately afterwards I understood, since on the screen a horde of savages appeared, with feathers on their heads, bows and arrows in their hands, and anger on their frightening faces. I was terrified ... but not for long as the pioneers with rifles and pistols managed to repel the attackers, and sometimes, the U.S. cavalry arrived just in time to rescue the migrants.

The meaning was quite clear: *The barbaric Indians are attacking us!* This was irrefutably the message the filmmaker gave us to understand. It was only later at the beginning of the 1960s, while studying U.S. history at university, that I understood the underlying message conveyed by that scene: 'We consider that the Indians merely squat our Promised Land, they have no rights to be there, they have no formal rights, at least according to our Law'; such as the Doctrine of Discovery, the law the European West had written and implemented since at least the Renaissance, starting from the invasion of Latin America by Spain and Portugal. Such was the legal justification: *Terra nullius*. There was nobody even there. Of course, the 'Indian threat' is a myth, i.e., something that does not correspond to reality, or whose reality has been distorted, a blatant falsification of history, in order to explain and justify the settler reaction to it. True, the Indians were in fact attacking the European settlers, but they did so because the latter attacked them in the first instance. Moreover, for the native peoples of the Americas, the violent occupation of their territory represented an existential threat, which explains why they were so determined to fight against the 'civilized invader' ... in their 'savage manner.' The U.S. continued to attack the Native Indians during the 19th century, expelling them from their land, until 1890 when the U.S. Government officially declared, after the massacre of Wounded Knee, that the conquest of the West had been accomplished.

When I was revising this chapter in June 2021, I came across a text by Thomas M. Engelhardt, the founder of the *TomDispatch* website, introducing an article by Aviva Chomsky with the title 'Making Native Americans Strangers in Their Own Land.'[5] Engelhardt, born 1944, grew up in the heart of New York City, whereas I, born 1940, I grew up in a small town in the South of Switzerland. It is interesting to note that we had the same experience with the Western films of that time.

Clearly, already between the end of the 1940s and the beginning of the 1950s, the planet had become a small world. Engelhardt writes:

> Those films] were, of course, filled with Indians (…) and the blue coats, the stagecoach drivers and their passengers, the cowboys, and the pioneers I identified with, were regularly ambushed by those Indians. In the end, with rare exceptions, the native predictably fell as they circled the wagon train or stagecoach or attacked those cavalrymen, whooping and shooting their arrows. They went down, naturally enough, before the implacable power of 'our' weaponry, 'our' marksmanship. And here's the thing: they deserved it. After all they were attacking us. We never ambushed them. They, that is, were 'the invaders' and we, invariably, the aggressed upon.'

The 'Indian threat,' and the fear associated with it, were followed by a succession of other threats posed by countries that constituted an obstacle to the realization of U.S. national interests: Spain, Mexico (remember Alamo!), Cuba, Germany, Soviet Russia, Japan, Russia, North Korea, Vietnam, Iran, Iraq, Syria, Libya, Venezuela, and … China. Let me explain why I deal first with the 'threat myth': it allows us to see some very special characteristics of Western/American behaviour towards other countries. In fact, by taking into consideration the aggression against the Native Indians and the long sequence of threats that followed, we can see how the U.S. has manifested an extraordinary capacity to reverse attribution of its own aggressions in the form of verbal, economic and military threats onto those it has first deemed inimical, insofar as they represented barriers to its pursuit of its interests—as has since been the

---

5 Aviva Chomsky, 2018.

case for example in its relations with Russia after the collapse of the Soviet Union. The notion of the Indian threat (and those that followed) allowed the American establishment to justify its behaviour, quite often of an extraordinary violence and hypocrisy, to realize U.S. interests.

Moreover, in pursuing our understanding of how the U.S. puts the blame on the 'Other' who is attacking it, even if it has been the one who started the conflict one way or the other, we discover the frequent American ways of *pushing the Other to attack us*. This is achieved by implementing different kinds of provocations, whether by the U.S. or by its allies, so that in the end, the 'Other' is left with little choice: either to accept American conditions or to respond in ways that will be unacceptable not only the U.S. but also to the so-called 'international community' that it claims to speak for. Among the many examples, let me briefly deal with the 1950–53 Korean War. Here, the predominant Western narrative is that the war began on 25 June 1950 when North Korea invaded South Korea (for example: Wikipedia 'Korean War'). This was a fact, documented and recognized by the overwhelming majority of countries, and it facilitated the U.S. effort to obtain from the UN Security Council the right to lead an international military force in a legal war against North Korea.[6] But a fact acquires its full meaning only when placed within the flow of history, taking into consideration the events that precede it. In fact, the U.S. was well aware that an attack was imminent but did nothing to prevent it. Moreover, the conflict actually started with a series of attacks by South Korean forces, aided by the U.S. military.[7] The international community was either not aware of these facts or it considered them to be outweighed by the pressures that the U.S. could bring to bear by way of persuasion.

Let us move on from the "threat" myths to other major myths that obscure the way Americans (and more generally Westerners) interpret, and advertise as exemplary, the major dimensions of their own economy, polity and society, as well as their view of the international system and their role within it.

---

6 This was also made possible because the Soviet Union was boycotting the Security Council by not attending its meetings as a protest against the U.S. veto not allowing Mao's communist China to take its seat within the Council rather than Chiang Kai-shek's Nationalist Republic that lost the civil war in October 1949. This serious mistake deprived Russia of using its right of veto. The U.S. recognized Communist China only on January 1, 1979.
7 Stone, 1952–1970, Cumings 2005 and 2011, Bovard 2020, Leebaert 2011, Conway-Lanz 2006, Hanley et al. 2001.

Western civilization developed through at least two and a half millennia to reach its present day form via Greek philosophy, Roman law, Christianity, the scientific revolution, the passage from the economy of the Middle Ages (using a form of slavery, the serfs of the glebe) to a new form of economy where slavery would be abolished, the market economy (not to be confused with capitalism, as we will see hereafter with Fernand Braudel 1979a, 1979b), and the Industrial revolution to the liberal revolution with its ideas of democracy, human rights, individual freedom and responsibility, and the socialist revolution with its idea of state responsibility for collective wellbeing. It is a great civilization, especially for many of the ideas and values it has developed for itself and for the rest of the world. Much less great (to say the least) have been Western civilization's deeds: the Roman circus games, the martyrdom of Christians, the Crusades (which still persist today in other forms), the Inquisition, the slaughter of Native American civilizations and the annihilation of their culture, the organization of the African slavery trade and the inhuman integration of slaves into a Western plantation-based economy at the service of the development of Western empires, the domination and exploitation of Africa, the Middle East and large parts of Asia, the imposition of colonial dictatorships and imperialism, and two world wars that killed and displaced dozens of millions of people. Impressive. For the last five centuries European countries, and then the U.S., have dominated the world. Practically no other civilization or people has been able to resist Western domination, at least until very recently.

In these countries Europeans found an 'empty world,' or a world that we have emptied, or at least that has not been able to resist us.8 Not much remains today of the original cultures of those countries. For example, today the inhabitants of the Americas, including those non-Anglo-Saxons who came from Europe and participated in the founding of the U.S., and also the descendants of the local 'Indians,' now speak English, Spanish or Portuguese. The same cultural assimilation was applied to the Africans who were deported to the Americas in dreadful conditions, to be sold as slaves like merchandise and used as a cheap workforce deprived of any sort of rights. Moreover, racial laws forbade intermarriages between the Africans and the Europeans, and the children born after extra-marital intercourses between black women with white men were considered as Blacks and therefore as slaves—an innovative way to create a class of cheap labour reproducing itself, ideally for ever.

---

8 Jullien 2005, pp. 9–11.

Should the descendants of Indians and Africans want to get on well in life, and eventually reach the top of the social hierarchy, they must be fully integrated into Western culture, as are General Colin Powell, former U.S. President Barack Obama, and former U.S. Secretary of State Condoleezza Rice, for example. On September 1, 2020, Rice assumed leadership of the Hoover Institution as director of one of the nation's top policy research centres. Hoover proudly writes on its website that Ms Rice is the first African American woman to hold both senior cabinet positions as adviser to the President (2001–2005) and secretary of state (2005–2009). On the other hand, African American leader Minister Louis Farrakhan, speaking to the interests of American blacks, and a primary instigator of a succession of three peaceful "Million Man" African American marches on Washington in the 1990s, a mobilization unsurpassed by any other U.S. leader, remains in political and historical obscurity.

This relationship between the West and the rest of the world has given Westerners the feeling, and for many even the certitude, that on every count, their culture is superior to the other cultures: better government, economy, military, legal system, social relations, and even a better God. The West has emptied their world and filled it with its own image. But not so for this remarkable exception: when we arrived in China, we found a world that was full. The missionaries and artists who arrived in China had to learn the Chinese language, respect the Chinese rites, and honour the emperor. Some of them dressed in the Chinese way and took on Chinese names; for example, the Italian, Milanese, Jesuit and painter Giuseppe Castiglione (Lang Shining), who was entrusted by the Emperor with the task of conceiving the Western-style palaces in the Eastern part of the Summer Palace Park.[9] In short, somewhere they were 'sinicized.' Since the end of the Empire, and even more so after 1949, China has considerably increased the standard of living of its population; has lifted from extreme poverty 800 million people; has favoured the development of a middle class of about 450 million people endowed with a remarkable freedom in the economy; and has developed science and technology, including high tech. At the end of these developments, China has been able to reclaim world power status. It has done this

---

9 Pirazzoli-T'Serstevens (2007), *Giuseppe Castiglione;* see also, for instance, the title of the following book, which underlines the fact that Castiglione is considered as a Chinese painter: Michel Cartier (ed.), *Giuseppe Castiglione dit Lang Shining, 1688–1766, Jésuite italien et peintre chinois,* Paris, Favre, 2004.

without invading and subjugating distant countries as the West has done, and by limiting the use of military power to its periphery. China has done this by integrating within its traditional culture some new values imported from the West to form a new ideology different from the ideologies of both Imperial China and the West—by far, an achievement whose trajectory is absolutely different from what the West has done since the discovery of the Americas based upon an ideology of conquest that has remained basically the same until today. So, the first means to determine the difference between the U.S. and China is to be found in an analysis of their system of values (see below, and also chapter 2).

THE MYTH OF UNIVERSAL VALUES

The myth of universal values is probably the central myth of the West, as several other myths converge onto it, and reinforce it to form a powerful ideological system: the myth of liberalism as the foundation of liberal democracy, which in turn gave rise to the myth of the free market; the myth of Western-style (liberal) democracy and its related myths: the myth of the independence of the polity and the myth of the independence of the media. Let us start with the case for Universal values as imbedded into liberalism.

Universal values and the myth of liberalism

The origin of the Western universal values myth dates to how Europeans envisaged and conducted their conquest of the rest of the world, starting with South America in the 16th century. This has been further confirmed not just by the sense of superiority manifested by both Europeans and Americans during the processes of colonization and imperialism, but by its actual and overt legal and political manifestations. All this being supplemented by the legal Doctrine of Discovery, coupled with the politic of the 'civilized world,' the 'white man's burden,' in particular. Liberalism is presented in the West as the '*Weltanschauung*' that provides universal values that should orient behaviour not only in the West but also all over the world. Moreover, Liberalism is considered to be the best ideological basis for realizing the ideal of democracy, itself another myth, as we shall see below. In fact, democracy as is practiced in the West is qualified as 'liberal democracy' in opposition to 'illiberal democracies.'[10] Moreover, the U.S. qualifies the international order it

---

10 Zakaria 1997.

dominates as 'a liberal international order' or, more precisely 'a U.S.-led rules-based liberal international order.'

One of the most radical critiques of liberalism has been developed by the Italian philosopher and historian Domenico Losurdo not only *per se*, but also as the ideological basis of the American Republic and its imperial foreign policy.[11] In short, Losurdo shows that Liberalism, as it has been implemented all over the West, and in the European colonies, has taken the form of what Pierre van Den Berghe termed a *Herrenvolk democracy*, typical of their political systems.[12] In German, *Herrenvolk* means 'master race,' and *Herrenvolk democracy* means 'democracy of (or for) the masters' or 'master-race democracy.' More precisely, it refer to a system of government in which only one ethnic group participates in government, while the other groups are disenfranchised. This posture was the foundation of Western colonialism in their colonies: there, the superior white people were regarded as (pre)destined to govern over the other ethnic groups.

This was certainly the case in the 13 English colonies in the New World as well, and persisted after the Declaration of Independence and the creation of the United States of America. The white people governed over the enslaved Africans and the savage dispossessed Native Indians, who were forced to cede their territories to the white *Herrenvolk*. The situation persisted until the end of the civil war when the Africans' descendants were nominally freed, soon to be subsumed under segregation, a kind of American apartheid, until the mid-1960s when they were granted equality before the law—an equality never paralleled in indicators of social well being. Moreover, in the early centuries even within the white Anglo-Saxonized ethnic group there was a partition similar to the one based upon race: that between the white ethnic components (between those of British-Scottish descent and those of German, Italian, Greek, Irish, etc. descent) and that between religious groups (Protestants and Catholics, Jews, etc.). But what has been a constant is the partition between the upper class that benefited from the political rights (e.g., owners of plantations industrialists, etc.) with the lower classes deprived of them (e.g., farmers, workers, servants) until the 20th century.[13] In this case 'aristocratic republicanism,' 'elite democracy,' 'oligarchy democra-

---

11 Losurdo, 2011, Losurdo 2007.
12 The term was first used by Pierre van Den Berghe in his book *Race and Racism. A Comparative Perspective,* New York, Wiley, 1967.
13 See the social status of the signatories of the Declaration of Independence. For more detail on these aspects see Losurdo 2011, pp. 102–125, 323–344.

cy,' or 'plutocracy' would be more appropriate. The values of freedom, equality, the rule of 'one man one vote,' etc. were enjoyed by the elite (whatever its composition) that made all the decisions orienting public policies to its advantage and dominated the rest of the people.[14] While in the mid-20th century, unionized workers were able to obtain greater political power and economic benefits, the eroding of this brief period of their countervailing power has led more recently to a new orientation of the Democratic Party towards America's lower class, now identified by presidential candidate Hillary Clinton as 'deplorables,' tarnished as presumptive Trump supporters, with the implication being that they were unworthy of participating in the democratic competition. Clearly, *Herrenvolk democracy* is still alive in the U.S. under the form of 'elite democracy' or 'plutocracy,' as we shall see below. Moreover, Western liberalism has gone on to project this posture in the international system, as it has done not only under the form of colonialism, as it did for the 13 English colonies, but also under the form of imperialism of which the U.S. Empire is the last, and probably the most significant manifestation. It is now the superiority of the *American* people 'chosen by God,' and of its 'democratic institutions,' that gives to the U.S. the right and the duty to lead and dominate over the rest of the world.[15]

While those who implement liberalism inevitably tend to use it for organizing the polity and the economy to their benefit, political liberalism in the polity is said to be based *inter alia* upon the value of equality, sustained by the rule of 'one person–one vote.' Therefore, it appears to place the equitable satisfaction of the needs of all the citizens as the focus of the analysis and intent of public policies. On the contrary, economic liberalism, in the form of capitalism, places economic efficiency at the centre of the analysis, based upon what are touted as the rational behaviours of economic actors competing in free markets with a view to maximising market shares and thereby profit.

---

14 It is interesting to note that whilst legislation moved towards universal male suffrage for whites, it also further entrenched the prevention of black people from participation in government and upheld their disenfranchisement until the passage of the Voting Rights Act of 1965

15 I will develop this point in the first part of Chapter 2. See also the works of Pankaj Mishra as commented by Daniel Immerwahr, under the revealing title of 'You Can Only See Liberalism From the Bottom. Why Pankaj Mishra sees the ideology's limits more clearly than its most powerful fans" (Immerwahr 2020). See especially: Pankaj 2020 and 2013.

The inevitable consequence is the appearance of disparities between the two. In fact, the emergence of the disequilibrium between these two ideologically based aspects of liberalism constitutes the major challenge facing countries simultaneously practising economic and political liberalism. If governments give too much space to the requirements of a capitalist economy, they will lose legitimacy as it concerns political equity; but if they give too much space to the polity they will lose in economic efficiency.[16] In other words, within this paradigm, the challenge is to find an equilibrium between capital and labour acceptable to the organizations (political parties and pressure groups) representing capital and labour.

Since the beginning of the simultaneous implementation of liberal democracy and capitalism, economic efficiency has nonetheless tended to prevail, as the numerous economic and financial crises leading to the crisis of the 1930s very well demonstrate. After the introduction of Roosevelt's New Deal in the U.S. and the economic and social policies implemented in Europe after WW2 (giving more space to the polity), the West entered a phase where the consensus on the new equilibrium between labour and capital led to a golden era the French call 'the glorious thirty years' ('*les trente glorieuses*'). Progressive and equitable taxation of income and wealth, and re-distributive public policies favouring the rise of disposable income for the lower and medium classes, complemented by the development of social services provided by the State (the Welfare State), led to a decrease in inequalities. It looked as if the approval of a new 'social contract' was at last allowing the pacific cohabitation of the contradicting logics of political and economic liberalism. But it did not last long.

After the Second World War, a group of liberal intellectuals met at Mount Pèlerin, a Swiss resort above Montreux, in April 1947 and founded the Mount Pèlerin Society. They represented several approaches to liberalism, and some participants were even very critical of capitalism, such as Karl Polanyi.[17] Some other liberal economists who did not support the most radical forms of liberalism (neoliberalism) quit the Society.[18] Soon the neoliberals, such as Friedrich von Hayek and Milton Friedman took over the direction of the Society and established

---

16 Stone 1997.
17 Polanyi 2001.
18 For example, Wilhelm Röpke, who, with Walter Eucken, is considered to be the founder of the *Soziale Marktwirtschaft* (social market economy).

the theoretical and ideological foundation of neoliberalism.[19] At that time they were not heard, as the West was busy building the new 'social contract' between capital and labour mentioned above. Friedman bitterly complained about this situation in the second edition of his *Capitalism and Freedom*.[20] What Friedman did not say is that the neoliberals were supported, ideologically and financially, by the political and economic Right, which financed university chairs and research, congresses, and publications. The neoliberals were waiting for the outbreak of the next crisis. That happened between the end of the 1970s and the beginning of the 1980s, with the so-called crisis of the Welfare State and the elections of Margaret Thatcher (1979) and Ronald Reagan (1980) that brought neoliberalism in to stay.

Milton Friedman called for the role of the state to be limited to maintaining the framework necessary for the functioning of market economy. The market, in turn, is based upon the notion that competition will provide the most efficient allocation of economic resources and therefore of the outcomes of the economic process. If this is taken as true, then best way to improve the management of public affairs is to 'marketize' state and society, i.e. to deregulate the markets to boost competition (such as taxation and anti-trust policy) and to privatize state activities that have nothing to do with the state's foreordained role of establishing capital-friendly rules to sustain the functioning of the market. This means that practically all the other state's activities can be privatized, including social policies. Failing this, states should introduce, at least partially, market elements into the management of the public sector by means of contracting out to private entities and/or by introducing competition inside the state.

This new form of liberalism clearly had the strategic goal of freeing the economy from the constraints of state interventions, and above all from the constraints on capital, as supported by Keynesianism. Therefore, not only had management techniques to be transferred from the private to the public sector with the aim of improving the efficiency of public management, assuming the superior efficiency of the former, but the state should also retreat from all sorts of domains in which private entrepreneurship was supposed to provide better services at lower cost than what the state had been able to provide in the past. The road was then ideologically opened to extensive privatization, contracting out,

---

19 Urio 1999.
20 Friedman 1982.

public–private partnerships, and deregulation in all domains, including (and above all) the financial sector.

In order to disqualify arguments that might reasonably have shed some light on the weaknesses of neoliberalism, its promoters claimed that in any case globalization was inevitable, and consequently national states should 'rationally' adapt their management to this inevitable development by participating in the opening up and deregulation of the global economy. This would have been the final attack on the State. Let us see how.

The ideological basis of neoliberalism was then used to strengthen its two armed wings: the Washington Consensus aimed at developing countries and the New Public Management (NPM) aimed at the developed ones.[21] The ideological foundation being the same, it was inevitable that these two wings would promote the same policy reform both in developing and in developed countries. The proof came when the financial market attacked a developed country, Greece. The troika (IMF, European Commission, and the European Bank) imposed on the leftist Greek government the same panoply of reforms and austerity programmes typical of neoliberalism that had already devastated developing countries in South America and Africa. It was then the turn of the Greek economy and the Greek citizen. The two armed wings of neoliberalism proved their formidable capacity to devastate not only the economy of these countries, but also the lives of their citizens.

The Greece case is a good example to demonstrate the remarkable coherence of neoliberalism whose policies are the same regardless of the historical, political, economic, and cultural situations of the countries concerned. This indicates another characteristic of neoliberalism: it is totally a-historic and in fact, is totalitarian. The fate of countries that would not conform their policies to the dictates of the neoliberal ideology was already becoming evident at the beginning of the neoliberal era. François Mitterrand won the French presidential election in 1981 with a programme based upon left-wing policies agreed upon with the communist

---

21 The main features of NMP: primacy of economic efficiency ; secure property rights; people are treated as customers and not as citizens ; fiscal discipline; large scale privatizations, including social policies; deregulation of markets, national and global, including and above all financial market; eliminate barriers to foreign direct investment; limiting taxation of high revenues of people and enterprises to stimulate business investment (trickle-down economics); marginalization of trade unions. See, e.g. Urio 2012, significantly entitled 'China, the West and the Myth of New Public Management.'

party. The implementation of the programme did not last long. After a series of nationalizations, in 1983 Mitterrand adopted the so-called '*tournant de la rigueur*' (turn towards austerity) and soon started the first wave of privatizations. The communists left the government in 1984. It was thus proven that it is difficult (or even impossible) to implement left-wing political programmes within a capitalist economy, especially when the national economy is increasingly embedded into the global neoliberal capitalist economy that dictates the rules of the game. This was the first sign of a slow but steady movement of the social-democratic parties towards the centre (and consequently towards the right), as confirmed by the policies implemented in Germany by Gerhard Schröder, in the UK by Tony Blair, and later in France by François Hollande and in Italy by Matteo Renzi. These 'socialist' parties effectively accepted capitalism as the only possible choice, or according to the infamous TINA statement by Margaret Thatcher: "There is no alternative."

In their will to open the world economy to the movement of capital in search for profit, the neoliberals also had to deregulate the global economy. This trend had already started at the end of WW2 when the U.S. emerged as one of the two world powers and succeeded in instigating the globalization movement thanks to several new economic institutions—the World Bank (WB), the International Monetary Fund (IMF) and the General Agreement on Tariffs and Trade (GATT, the predecessor of the WTO) — and also thanks to the upgrading of the U.S.D as the international reserve and trade currency supplanting the British Pound, At the end of this process, the U.S., under the presidency of Barack Obama, promoted the implementation of two mega trade and investment treaties: the Transatlantic Trade and Investment Partnership (TTIP) and the Trans-Pacific Partnership (TPP). These treaties were supported by the American, European and Japanese multinationals. Should they have been adopted, the world would have entered an era dominated by what Joseph Stiglitz has named 'free trade fundamentalism.'[22] The objective of these treaties is to eliminate practically all the obstacles to trade and investment other than tariffs and quotas, which had been already reduced to a very low level.

Morcover, the deregulation of financial markets would make the export of capital completely free, while heretofore governments were able to limit the entry of foreign capital. For the purpose of making this

---

22 Stiglitz 2013, with the significant title: 'The free-trade charade.' In fact, the formula should be changed into: 'free trade and investment fundamentalism.'

freedom as large as possible, these treaties sought to enable multinationals to sue states before a private court if their public policies would reduce not only the profits investors could contend they would have achieved in the absence of these policies, but also the profits they expected to reap in the future. This included even public policies in the domain of health and environmental protection. Moreover, the decisions to be taken by these private courts would be final, i.e., not subject to appeal by neither companies nor governments.[23]

If those two treaties had been approved, they would have legitimized the domination of multinationals (including those of the financial sector) supported by the U.S., the European Union (through the leadership of the European Commission) and Japan over states in a vast area, and would have been able to dictate and enforce these treaties' conditions beyond their borders. The ideological and policy goals of economic neoliberalism would have been fulfilled beyond the most optimistic expectations.

These treaties also had a geo-political goal, as they were conceived by the Obama administration as a means to contain Russia and China. The aim of the TTIP was to strengthen the containment of Russia by further integrating Europe into an Atlantic area dominated by the U.S. and by Western multinational companies, in addition to the NATO military alliance.[24] The TPP was an important part of the Obama 'pivot to Asia' strategy.[25] In fact, the aim of the TPP was to strengthen the containment of China by integrating the economies of 12 countries of the Pacific region into an economic area to be dominated by the U.S.[26] These two treaties, if approved, would have constituted two formidable tools for containing the rise of the two major competitors of the U.S.[27] It is not

---

23 Stiglitz 2002, 2010, 2013, 2016, Wallach 1998, 2013, 2017, Kelsey 2011, Jäcklein 2014. For a critique of the procedure called 'Investor-state dispute settlement (ISDS),' Eberhardt 2016.

24 Le Corre, and Pollack 2016.

25 https://en.wikipedia.org/wiki/East_Asian_foreign_policy_of_the_Barack_Obama_ administration (accessed 22 May 2017). On the U.S. pivot to Asia, see Kenneth Lieberthal (2011) and Clinton, Hillary (2011)

26 The 12 countries of the TPP: Australia, Brunei, Canada, Chile, Japan, Malaysia, Mexico, New Zealand, Peru, Singapore, the U.S. (until 23 January 2017) and Vietnam. On the strategy for containing China, see McCoy 2015.

27 The project of the Transatlantic Agreement has long been supported by the Trans-Atlantic Business Council (TABC), created in 1995 under the sponsorship of the European Commission and the U.S. Department of Commerce. Similarly, the Trans-Pacific Agreement is supported by multinationals, especially American, for example, those in the pharmaceutical and tobacco industries.

clear yet whether the Biden administration will abandon or pursue the finalization of these treaties.

In my 2012 book[28] I evaluated the damages made by the implementation in the West and in China of one of the two armed wings of neoliberalism, the New Public Management: the deterioration of labour market conditions as a source of income and increasing income inequality; rising poverty, crime and incarceration rates; and deterioration of health in an overly competitive and insecure market.[29] Notwithstanding, the neoliberal euphoria continued until the 2016 American presidential election, in spite of the fact that the negative consequences of free-trade fundamentalism had been recognized by critical scholars, investigative journalists and alternative think tanks, and despite the concomitant decline of U.S. power that supported that fundamentalism.

The next president had to manage that decline. Trump did so by putting a halt to the neoliberal globalization. He withdrew from the TPP and postponed *sine die* the negotiations for the TTIP, while starting—or more precisely—intensifying the trade war against China in which his predecessors had already engaged.

Then came Covid-19, unmasking the negative consequences of the global deregulation, such as the delocalization of large sectors of its industrial base by the West (especially by the U.S.) and the consequent dependence of the West on other countries, especially China. Moreover, by devolving parts of their supply chains to countries such as China, the West discovered the extent to which it was dependant on its major competitor. When parts of a product are made by China, the assembly of the final product in the U.S. can be interrupted (this became extremely noticeable as it concerned pharmaceuticals).

And then came the illusion (another myth): the decoupling of the U.S. and the Chinese economies. Trump is probably the first American President who viscerally understood that the U.S. had lost its capacity to impose its will on the rest of the world as it had in fact done for a long time. As I wrote in 2019, Trump was the first President who had the difficult task of trying to lead his country through the labyrinths of the new multi-polar world.[30] But this effort was undertaken in a chaotic way, due in part to the hostility (to say the least) he experienced from large parts of the establishment. Now President Biden will have to take over

---

28 Urio 2012.
29 Urio 2012, pp. 109–44.
30 Urio 2019, p. 245.

from where Trump has left the U.S. foreign policy at the beginning of 2021. It will be difficult to come back to the dominating overtones of the Obama presidency, despite the bellicose posture Biden has shown in his presidential campaign confirmed by the choice of his team.[31]

Where do universal values come from?

It is their cultural structures that provide peoples with the intellectual means for understanding the world and the global society in which they live, as they establish the fundamental values, beliefs and behavioural norms with which actors should comply at home and abroad. In a liberal democracy, this is accomplished through the agents of socialization: family, schools, social clubs, organizations such as political parties and pressure groups, churches, mass media, and social media.[32] The major values the West has adopted via the socialization processes, are those of human rights, freedom, democracy, free markets, etc. A reputation for acting in conformity with these stated values at home and abroad is necessary to attract and convince the other actors in the international system of the moral standards of the country purveying them. This enables these actors to approve the international policies of the country entrusted with that reputation and eventually to let it lead the world. This is one of the strongest beliefs of the American establishment itself,[33] and was certainly the case for the trust achieved by the U.S. in relation to other state actors after the end of WW 2.

From the beginning of the twentieth century, the U.S. started to promote at home and abroad the values of democracy, human rights and free trade through its activities by a variety of means: radio and TV broadcasting companies such as the Voice of America, Radio Free Asia and CNN, mainstream media, governmental agencies such as the U.S. Agency for International Development (USAID), the 'American Cultural Centres,' think tanks such as the Council on Foreign relations and the Brookings Institution, not-for-profit foundations dedicated to the growth and strengthening of democratic institutions around the world, non-governmental organizations (NGOs), some of them in fact government-funded organizations such as the National Endowment for Democracy and its subsidiaries. Moreover, the U.S. acquired the habit of attracting foreign students to American universities (especially in

---

31 I will develop this point in Chapters 2 and 3 below.
32 Almond and Powell 1966, Almond and Verba 1963.
33 Nye 2004, 2008, 2011, 2015.

economics and business administration) so that when they returned to their countries, they would diffuse American values (more details follow in Chapter 3). The overall purpose of these activities is to have American values accepted by the international community as possessing a universal and therefore unimpeachable character. The U.S. has persistently called on these values and it still does so today for justifying its foreign policies, particularly embargos, regime changes, the training of military forces of allies, supplying of arms to the 'rebels' fighting a 'dictator,' covert military interventions by Special Forces, or even overt war operations. Moreover, the full use of military means is always there, as an explicit or implicit threat.[34]

However, since the Vietnam War, the reputation of the U.S. has suffered several setbacks, due to violations by the U.S. establishment of the values it proclaims to support, such as alliances or partnerships with autocratic regimes, economic embargos on both enemies and allies (as occurred during the Trump administration, but not exclusively), the financing of terrorist organizations (e.g. to oppose the Russians in Afghanistan in the 1980s or, more recently, against the Syrian regime), the training of military and security forces of allies and repressive client states, and last but not least, the organization of regime changes of governments not supporting the realization of American interests, the most emblematic examples being Iran in 1953 and Chile in 1973, and more recently Georgia, the Middle East (especially Syria and Iran), Libya, Somalia, Ukraine and Venezuela. Largely all these activities have enjoyed the support of the other Western states.

Moreover, some features of the American model of democracy are also subject to severe criticism: the excessive importance of money in the political arena (especially in the electoral and legislative processes) which some do not hesitate to consider as examples of corruption; the increasing power of interest groups (especially multinationals in the fields of taxation, banking, insurance, agro-business, pesticides and genetically modified organisms, oil, medical drugs, etc.). The question of civil and political rights for the African-American minority, as well as their exclusion in large numbers from equal standing in wellbeing indicators remains, as it does for the descendants of the Native Americans. The

---

34 During the Trump administration this menace has often taken the form of a public declaration: 'all the options are on the table.' This is not typical of the Trump administration. In his 2016 State of the Union Address, quoted below, Barack Obama made it clear that military power is an essential part of U.S. power.

wealth gap is ever widening; increasing numbers of people are living below the poverty line; the incarceration rate is the highest in the world, while all classes are beset by the opioid epidemic. And, last but not least, since the presidential campaign of 2016, the U.S. political elites present a sad spectacle unworthy of a mature democracy: a democracy that has retained its name but not its substance.

So, in many cases the U.S. behaves in ways that contradicts the values it proclaims to comply with. Despite these setbacks, it is interesting to remark that the U.S. elite believes, still today, that the large majority of countries accepting the U.S. leadership do so because of the attractiveness of its values, its democratic government and its moral behaviour in the international system,[35] though this may well change, post the January 6th, 2021 assault on Congress, widely billed in the press as an insurrection, and the ongoing and sizeable domestic scepticism regarding the trustworthiness of election outcomes, sheds a negative light on U.S. democratic processes worldwide and its claims to serve as a role model.

Irrespective of the usefulness of U.S. standing as a model for democracy, on many occasions American politicians and ideologues have and in future will insist on the fundamental importance of military means.

One of the most influential neo-conservatives, Robert Kagan, in a 2012 article has pointed out the fundamental importance of military means in the international arena:

---

35 See the articles by Blinken and Kagan 2019, and Biden 2020. For an excellent analysis of the Biden article see Bandow 2020a. Bandow is Senior Fellow at the Cato Institute and a former Special Assistant to President Ronald Reagan. As for the 2019 Blinken-Kagan article it is interesting to note that Blinken was to become the new Secretary of State in the Biden Administration, and Kagan is one of the most influential neo-conservatives. In this article they write: "Doubling down on 'America First,' with its mix of nationalism, unilateralism and xenophobia, would only exacerbate these problems. But so would embracing the alternative offered by thinkers across the ideological spectrum who, concerned that our reach exceeds our means, advise us to pull back without considering the likely consequences, as we did in the 1930s. Back then, the result was an even greater global conflagration. But after World War II, when Americans stayed engaged, built strong alliances with fellow democracies, and shaped the rules, norms and institutions for relations among nations, we produced unprecedented global prosperity, democracy and security from which Americans benefited more than anyone. It wasn't a perfect world, but it was far better than the alternative." (Blinken and Kagan 2019).

People are rightly mesmerized by the rise of China, India, and other Asian nations whose share of the global economy has been climbing steadily, but this has so far come almost entirely at the expense of Europe and Japan, which have had a declining share of the global economy. [...] Military capacity matters, too, as early nineteenth-century China learned, and Chinese leaders know today. As Yan Xuetong recently noted, "military strength underpins hegemony." Here the United States remains unmatched.[36]

President Obama also made it clear that military means were an essential part of the U.S. power. In his 2016 State of the Union Address Obama declared that the 'The United States of America is the most powerful nation on Earth.' But immediately after, to sustain this claim, he proudly reminded the audience that America spends 'more on our military than the next eight nations combined. Our troops are the finest fighting force in the history of the world.' Clearly the message is for both the American and the world audiences, as this statement is part of the 2016 State of the Union Address:

I told you earlier all the talk of America's economic decline is political hot air. Well, so is all the rhetoric you hear about our enemies getting stronger and America getting weaker. Let me tell you something. The United States of America is the most powerful nation on Earth. Period. (Applause.) It's not even close. It's not even close. (Applause.) It's not even close. We spend more on our military than the next eight nations combined. Our troops are the finest fighting force in the history of the world. (Applause.) No nation attacks us directly, or our allies, because they know that's the path to ruin. Surveys show our standing around the world is higher than when I was elected to this office, and when it comes to every important international issue, people of the world do not look to Beijing or Moscow to lead—they call us. (Applause.).

President Biden has been welcomed, with some exceptions, as the one who could reverse the aggressive foreign policy posture of Donald Trump. It is interesting to note that he wrote in a 2020 article that 'the

---

36 Kagan 2012a.

use of force should be the last resort, not the first. It should be used only
to defend U.S. vital interests, when the objective is clear and achievable,
and with the informed consent of the American people.'[37]

Nevertheless, Biden did not make it clear what the U.S. vital interests were, nor if that statement meant a departure from the practice of
his predecessors who waged wars with the consent of the 'Blob' (i.e. that
part of the establishment that orient and support the President's foreign
policy options) but not with the explicit consent of the American people,
who elected previous candidates who promised peace (Obama, Trump)
but did not deliver—another indicator of the actuality of U.S. democratic
practice. In fact, Biden reaffirmed the U.S. leadership belief in the central role of the U.S. military in international relations which, moreover,
requires further funding for the war industry:

> I will never hesitate to protect the American people, including,
> when necessary, by using force. Of all the roles a president
> of the United States must fill, none is more consequential
> than that of commander in chief. The United States has the
> strongest military in the world, and as president, I will ensure
> it stays that way, making the investments necessary to equip
> our troops for the challenges of this century, not the last one.[38]

The centrality of Biden's military orientation was evident in the
fact that he should conclude his 2021 inauguration speech with the
words: 'May God bless America and may God protect our troops.'

This faith in the superiority of the American values is translated
into the will to lead the world, not only as a will to obtain and retain
power, but also as a necessity for avoiding chaos. A primary belief of the
U.S. leadership, largely accepted in the West, and indeed as is taught in
American political science, is the necessity of the existence of a global
hegemon to maintain global stability. In an article published in 2017
Robert Kagan says that it is absolutely necessary to maintain the 'dominant position the U.S. has held in the international system since 1945,'
otherwise 'the existing world collapses and the world descends into a
phase of brutal anarchy.' Should this occur, the values likely to be damaged are free market capitalism, democracy, and political freedom(s),

---

37 Biden 2020
38 Biden 2020.

associated not just with American national interests, but with those of international system itself.[39]

The right to lead the international liberal system is often linked to the right to define the rules that should govern the behaviours of states, enterprises, and other organisations such as NGOs in the international arena. This is the opinion not only of influential neo-conservatives such as Robert Kagan, but also of the leaders of the Democratic party. For example, Barack Obama has on many occasions affirmed the 'natural' leadership of the U.S. and its right and duty to define the rules of the international system ... otherwise China will take the lead. For President Obama, in doing so, the U.S. is the 'indispensable nation' that has the role to lead the world, as he said in the commencement speech at the U.S. Air Force Academy in 2012:

> the U.S. is exceptional and will always be the one indispens-
> able nation in world affairs. [...] I see an American century
> because no other nation seeks the role that we play in global
> affairs, and no other nation can play the role that we play in
> global affairs. That includes shaping the global institutions of
> the XX century to meet the challenges of the XXI century.[40]

More specifically, let us take as a concrete case of international policy one of the major components of Obama's international strategy for maintaining the U.S. as the world hegemon: the Trans-Pacific Partnership—TPP mentioned above. In his 2016 State of the Union Address, Obama made it very clear that the U.S. has the responsibility, and very likely the right, to set the rules governing international trade and investments:

> With TPP, China does not set the rules in that region; we do.
> You want to show our strength in this new century? Approve
> this agreement. Give us the tools to enforce it. It's the right
> thing to do. (Applause).[41]

---

39 Kagan 2017b. Other publications by Robert Kagan that are worth reading are: *The Return of History* (Kagan 2008); *The World America Made* (Kagan 2012b); 'Superpowers don't get to retire: what our tired country still owes to the world' (Kagan 2014).
40 Kent 2012.
41 State of the Union address 201, (Obama 2016). The other mega-treaty having the same policy goal in the Atlantic area is the Transatlantic Trade and Investment

More recently several American scholars, experts and politicians have pointed to the failure of the U.S. foreign policy to deal with the surge of China as a world power and the resurgence of Russia as a powerful regional actor, as its intervention in Syria has clearly demonstrated. As did Nadia Schadlow, an American academic and defence-related government officer who briefly served in 2018 as Assistant to the President and Deputy National Security Advisor for Strategy in the Trump Administration. In an article significantly entitled "The End of American Illusion," Schadlow has taken stock of the decline of U.S. power. She points to the illusions at the foundation of U.S. foreign policy toward China, i.e., that by integrating China into the U.S.-led liberal international order, China would become 'a responsible international actor' under U.S. leadership, arguing that, to the contrary, China and Russia have long manipulated the rules of the liberal order to their own benefit. As a consequence, Schadlow notes, the world has moved beyond the 'unipolar moment' and she concludes that 'to properly navigate this new era, Washington must let go its illusions, move past the myths of liberal internationalism, and reconsider its views about the nature of the world order.'[42] One could not be more lucid.

This is clearly not the view of the American establishment, which regards the China threat as growing because China is developing its strength both internally and internationally. Worse, China is doing this according to its own cultural, political, and economic values and choices, and not by imitating the Western model. And there are no signs that China will change in a foreseeable future. The acknowledgment of this failure should have driven the U.S. leadership to envisage a different international system and within it a different role. There is no movement in this direction.

President Joe Biden, whom many in the U.S. see as a promising change after the 'terrible Trump years,' seems to be willing to go back to foreign policy as we have known it for a long time. In his 2020 *Foreign Affairs* article "Why America must lead again," whose title lays out the basic premise loud and clear, Biden mentions the necessity to return to a world led by the U.S. at least twenty times.[43] This is presumed to

Partnership (TTIP) whose goal is the containment of Russia.
42 Schadlow 2020. Nadia Schadlow is an American academic and defence-related government officer who briefly served in 2018 as Assistant to the President and Deputy National Security Advisor for Strategy in the Trump Administration.
43 Biden 2020. See also: Joseph R. Biden and Michael Carpenter, How to Stand Up to the Kremlin,' *Foreign Affairs,* January/February 2018. On Vice-

represent a position contrary to Trump's foreign policy. But that is another illusion. Trump's foreign policy remained a policy of 'the U.S.
leading the world' but under the disguise of 'America first,' as its policy
towards China, North Korea, Iran, and Venezuela clearly demonstrated.
The style and the means are different, but the goal remains the same. It
appears therefore that a new multi-polar world is clearly not forthcoming
under what is likely to be a brief interlude, the presidency of Joe Biden.
The persons he has chosen to form his team clearly show that he will at
least go back to 'the wonderful years' of the overt-covert military interventions, sanctions and regime change policies of Nobel Peace Laureate
Barack Obama. One is forced to conclude that in spite of the rhetoric of
liberal universal values, the 'ultimate value' of American foreign policy
prized by American elites is the realization of U.S. national interests—irrespective of the impact of that on the rest of the world. The U.S. foreign
policy aimed at leading the world according to American national interests is the result of an informal coalition of actors sharing ideological and
material interests. It comprises a large number of both Republican and
Democrat members of the U.S. Congress, the industrial-military complex, the so-called 'intelligence community' (about a dozen agencies,
including the CIA), mainstream university scholars, think tanks and the
media.[44] The U.S.'s behaviour since at least WW2 shows that whenever
it had to choose between universal liberal values and U.S. national interests, it has almost always chosen the latter.[45]

President Kamala Harris see Caleb Maupin, *Kamala Harris and the Future of
America: An Essay in Three Parts,* Center for Political Innovation, 2020. On
Biden Team see: Jake Johnson, 'Biden Quietly Adds Goldman Sachs, Big Tech
Officials to Transition,' *Consortium News,* 22 December 2020; Jonathan Guyer,
'How a Biden Adviser Got a Gig With Uber,' *Prospect.org,* 8 July 2010; Medea
Benjamin and Marcy Winograd, 'Why Senators Must Reject Avril Haines for
Intelligence,' *Common Dreams,* 29 December 2020. For a more balanced analysis
of the relations between the U.S. and China from a mainstream journalist: Fared
Zakaria, "The New China Scare. Why America Shouldn't Panic About Its Latest
Challenger," *Foreign Affairs,* 6 December 2019.
44 Kluth 2020. These are the generally admitted components of the
'establishment.' Space does not allow me to discuss in detail the composition and
meaning of the 'establishment,' versus the 'blob,' the 'deep state,' the 'shadow
government,' and the 'foreign policy establishment.' See e.g. Lofgren (2016),
Scott (2017), Engelhardt (2014).
45 See for example the statements of other influential politicians, senior civil
servants, scholars and think tanks: the former Assistant Secretary of State for
European and Eurasian Affairs (2013–2017), who played a decisive role in the
2014 coup d'état in Ukraine, Victoria Nuland, 'Pinning Down Putin,' *Foreign*

Finally, it is interesting to remark that even those Americans who accept that the rules of the international system should be changed, are reluctant, to say the least, to abandon or reform its liberal features, and above all, they consider that if reforms are necessary, they must nonetheless still occur under the leadership of the U.S.[46] This clearly does not portend a posture favouring the passage from a U.S.-led liberal unipolar Western-dominated world to a collectively-led multi-polar world, where non-liberal and non-Western countries would be free of U.S. meddling and regime changes interferences, enabling them to determine their own futures, to the extent that might be possible. Nonetheless, this transition toward a multi-polar world is strongly suggested as forthcoming by the changes in the global balance of power that has been going on since at least the end of the 20th century, in favour of what the U.S. establishment deems 'revisionist powers,' such as Russia and China. Moreover, several minor regional powers, such as Iran, Syria and Turkey seem to be similarly unwilling to bow to American dictates.

In fact, insofar as Biden's 2020 article mentioned above as well as his public statements to U.S. public policy are a clear sign that the new administration is advertising to the world that America is back, Japanese *Nikkei* asks this crucial question: Is Asia ready to welcome it?[47] A few

Affairs, July/August 2020; the United States National Security Adviser Robert C. O'Brien, 'How China Threatens American Democracy. Beijing's Ideological Agenda Has Gone Global,' _Foreign Affairs,_ 21 October 2020; the Senior Fellow at the Hoover Institution and professor at Stanford Univ. Michael McFaul, 'How to Contain Putin's Russia,' _Foreign Affairs,_ 19 January 2021; the professor of Politics and International Affairs at Princeton University, Aaron L. Friedberg, 'An Answer to Aggression,' _Foreign Affairs,_ September/October 2020; from one of the most renowned sinologists, Rana Mitter, 'The World China Wants,' _Foreign Affairs,_ January/February 2021; from the website of one of the most influential think tanks: Constanze Stelzenmüller, 'Stronger together: A strategy to revitalize trans-Atlantic power,' _Brookings,_ 14 December 2020; Andrea Kendall-Tylor, Erica Frantz, and Joseph Wright, 'The Digital Dictators. How Technology Strengthens Autocracy,' _Foreign Affairs,_ March-April 2020 (Kendall-Taylor is Director of the Transatlantic Security Program at the Center for a New American Security, Frantz is Assistant professor of political science at Michigan State University and Wright is Professor of political science at Pennsylvania State University).

46 See for example the article by one of the most influential American strategists, Zbigniew Brzezinski, significantly entitled 'Toward a global realignment. As its era of global dominance ends, the United States to take the lead in realigning the global power architecture.' (Brzezinski 2016).

47 Alex Fang et al., 'Team Biden says America is back. But is Asia ready to welcome it?'(Fang et al 2020).

weeks later another crucial question received an answer, when at the end of 2020 the European Union signed an important trade and investment deal with China. This took the establishment totally by surprise, as if such a deal would have been unthinkable. True, at the beginning of the Biden administration, the EU Parliament has blocked the ratification of this deal. However, the economic interests of several European countries to deal with China will not fade away. Moreover, several influential American observers have considered that this agreement constitutes a defeat for the new Biden administration. Just an example: the influential Bloomberg has without hesitation qualified this deal as a big mistake.[48] The Empire and its media do not like international deals of which it is not the artisan or at least one of the contracting parties.

The world is certainly ready to cooperate with the new elected President, hoping that he will be more respectful of his allies, not to mention America's competitors. Welcome, certainly, but not as a country who treats his Asian and European allies more as vassals than allies. To paraphrase a sentence too often used by the Trump administration (even if he was not the first one to use it) let us hope that the message has been clearly understood by the new administration. Europe is less ready to be told what its interests are, and how to safeguard them. For example, there is the case of the Nord Stream 2 pipeline between Russia and Europe (terminating in Germany), over which the Trump administration bullied Europe for several years, in fact forbidding Europe to finish the construction of the pipeline by sanctioning enterprises working on the pipeline, putting construction to a halt and causing one of the enterprises (a Swiss one) to withdraw from the construction. The official reason: this Pipeline will make Europe dependant on Russia for its energy resources, and this is against Europe's own strategic interests. The real reason: not simply the specific that the U.S. wants to sell to Europe American gas, which is 30–40% more expensive and obtained by fracking, that has devastated the environment of several American regions. The old trope remains in play: Keep the Russians out, the Americans in, and the Germans down.

Nevertheless, at the moment of finalizing the writing of this book we learned that Joseph Biden had just concluded a deal with Angela Merkel.[49] Under the four-point deal, which will see America drop sanc-

---

48 A few days later, 4 January, the influential American Economic Institute published a blog by Claude Barfield significantly entitled 'Biden's first defeat: the China-EU trade agreement' (Barfield 2021).
49 *Washington Post:* 'Why the world Worries About Russia's Nord Stream 2 Pipeline,' 22 July 2021; *BBC:* 'Nord Stream 2: Biden Waives U.S. Sanctions

tions against Nord Stream 2, Germany and the U.S. will seek to promote investments of at least $1 billion in a so-called Green Fund to help Ukraine's transition to cleaner sources of energy. Germany has committed to an initial $175 million investment in the fund. Germany would also appoint a special envoy—with $70 million in funding—to support bilateral energy projects with Ukraine. It will also pledge to push Russia into extending the current gas pipeline arrangement with Ukraine, which provides Kiev with $3 billion in annual transit fees. Moreover, if Russia attempted to use energy as an economic weapon or commit aggression against Ukraine, Germany would take action itself while also pressing for measures at the European level, including sanctions to limit Russia's energy exports.

Reactions to the deal, as one could have easily forecasted, have been mixed, to say the least. U.S. official Victoria Nuland said Nord Stream 2 was "a bad pipeline," but said the deal envisaged sanctions against Moscow if it tried to blackmail Ukraine. German officials also welcomed the sanctions waiver as "a constructive step" from the Biden administration. Foreign Minister Heiko Maas told reporters: "It's an expression of the fact that Germany is an important partner for the U.S., one that it can count on in the future.." Russia has also expressed satisfaction: Deputy Foreign Minister Sergei Ryabkov was quoted by the state-run Tass news agency as welcoming "a chance for a gradual transition toward the normalisation of our bilateral ties."

Negative reactions, sometimes quite violent, came from both Democrat and Republican hawks such as Jim Risch, the top Republican on the Senate Foreign Relations Committee, Michael McCaul, the top-ranking House Republican on foreign affairs, and the New Jersey Democrat Bob Menendez, Senate Foreign Relations Committee chairman. Negative reactions included accusations such as that it was a "gift to Putin that will only weaken the United States," and the deal will "render Ukraine more vulnerable to Russian aggression and provide billions of dollars to Putin's coffers." Negative reaction came also from Ukraine and Poland, not surprisingly, as they are two good allies of the U.S. in its crusade against Russia.[50]

---

on Russian Pipeline,' 21 July 2021; *Russia Today:* As U.S. Finally Drops its Opposition to Nord Stream 2, it's Clear plans to Block the Pipeline Were Always About Money, not Security, 24 July 2021.

50 The *Washington Post* article is interesting not only for its usual hostile tone towards Russia, but also for how it describes the relations between Russia and Ukraine (and incidentally also with the U.S.): the relations 'between Russia and

Clearly, the deal is in favour of Germany and Russia. It is true that Germany has agreed to put pressure on Russia, should Putin engage in committing aggressions against Ukraine. But this eventuality is only in the narrative of the U.S. hawks. Putin has no interest in increasing the already conflictual relation with Ukraine, he just wants to keep Ukraine out of the NATO alliance. A reasonable stance. How would the U.S. react if Russia organized a regime change in Mexico favouring a hostile foreign policy right at the border of its Northern neighbour? The bottom line of the agreement is clearly that after years of bullying, the U.S. had to step back. As the *Russia Today* article quite rightly commented: "America has come back down on Earth.' In the framework of the Biden foreign policy, based on assembling U.S. allies to contain Russia and China, giving Germany 'its' pipeline in exchange for its support of the alliance may be considered a good deal. Nevertheless, the fundamental interests that orient Germany's foreign economic policy will not fade away. Already today, they are oriented eastwards, and they are likely to further develop in this direction.[51] So, overall, the old trope has been slightly, but significantly, changed: the American are still in, but a little less, the Russians are kept out, but also a little less, and the Germans are not down as before. Changes are on their way, as we shall see when dealing with the U.S. foreign policy in Chapter 2 and 3.

Notwithstanding, the writings of President Biden mentioned above and the foreign policy statements by politicians, think tanks researchers and even academics, as well as many members of the Biden team, do not give the impression that the U.S. is ready to share with other countries the management of peace and conflicts in the international system, let alone the definition of their own national interests. The will 'to lead again' so often put forward, is unfortunately a sign that the U.S. is not ready to fundamentally revise its foreign policy, and that it will remain faithful to a narrow and unilateral conception of 'its values and national interests' to which the world has been accustomed for a very long time. Moreover, the Biden Administration continues the existing propensity of government officialdom to permit 'revolving doors' between positions in

---

Ukraine have worsened, culminating in the Ukrainian popular revolt that kicked out the country's pro-Russian president and led to Russia seizing the Crimean Peninsula.' A distortion that is hardly surprising, when one knows how the U.S. mainstream media are keen on writing the history *ad usum delphini* and have never heard about the 2014 coup d'état, the regime change orchestrated by the U.S.

51 More on the U.S. foreign policy in chapters 2 and 3.

the public sector and in private investment companies and think tanks, many of them with clear links with military procurement companies and with the military-industrial complex. It seems that President Biden is quite at ease with these conflict of interest realities.[52] This is certainly far from an indicator of any significant change in U.S. foreign policy. On the contrary, it seems that U.S. unilateralist thinking entrenched both psychologically and systemically in its will to lead the world is totally in contradiction with the rise of new world and regional powers who are no longer willing to accept the dictates of the Empire.

At the end of the analysis presented above it is necessary to remind that the main features of the American ideology and its fundamental values are not different from the ideology developed by Europe since the Renaissance, even if Europe itself now has to contend with U.S. vassal-ization. The empirical proof is the contribution of Europe to the imperial foreign policy of the U.S., either by individual states (especially France and the UK, but also some Eastern European countries), or collectively through the NATO military alliance dominated by the U.S. After all, the first immigrants who came to North America were Europeans who took with them the European ideology structured according to a mix of reli-gious and secular beliefs. Indeed, these features were already embedded into a variant of Protestantism, i.e., Puritanism, that the first immigrants took with them to the New World. From the time of the Renaissance, Europe had developed the ideological foundations of its relationships with other cultures that can be defined as follows:

1. the sense of superiority and belief in the exceptional char-acter of European culture;
2. the belief in the values of the Christian religion and in the values and laws of capitalism;
3. the definition of European values as universal;

---

52 You can easily make up your mind about the career and policy orientations of members of the Biden team by searching on the internet, especially for key positions such as: Victoria Nuland (Under-Secretary of State for Political Affairs), Anthony Blinken (Secretary of State, see also his very revealing testimony before the U.S. Senate available on YouTube), Gen. Lloyd Austin (Defence Secretary), Avril Haines (Director of National Intelligence). It is better to complete information given by mainstream media by consulting alternative and critical websites such as: Politico, Consortium News, American Prospect, Truthout, AntiWar; and the traditional conservative websites such as: Ron Paul Institute, Lew Rockwell, The Future of Freedom Foundation.

4. the right to diffuse these values and therefore to civilize the barbarians and the savages;
5. the belief in economic growth and progress based upon European values;
6. the right to take possession of the land of the barbarians as it is not protected by legally binding property rights;
7. the right of the 'civilized world' to intervene in the 'non-civilized' world to end practices that violate universal values as defined by Europe—this right would be developed in the 1980s and used to justify interventions in several places, for example, in Bosnia and Kosovo; and
8. the belief that the diffusion (and expansion) of European values is beneficial to mankind and historically inevitable. As Wallerstein put it, 'The expansion [of Europe] has involved, in most regions of the world, military conquest, economic exploitation, and massive injustices [...] justified on the grounds of the greater good that such expansion has had for the world's population.'[53]

This ideology has been operating since the beginning of the European conquest of the rest of the world, starting with South America. Wallerstein summarizes the debate in favour of and against the brutal conquest of South America by Spain at the beginning of the sixteenth century, between Juan Ginés de Sepúlveda justifying the conquest, and the Catholic priest Bartolomé de Las Casas criticizing it. In particular, it is interesting to note that already in the sixteenth century, 'Las Casas was implacable against what we would call today collateral damage: it is a sin meriting eternal damnation to harm and kill innocents in order to punish the guilty, for it is contrary to justice.'[54]

The case for universal values: Both Western and universal?

Unsurprisingly, it is the American politicians and ideologues that have expressed this posture since the end of WW2 and even more so after the fall of the Soviet Union. Fukuyama's "end of history" in fact refers to the purportedly final triumph of Western values, albeit in their renewed

---

53 Wallerstein 2006, p.1.
54 Quoted by Wallerstein 2006, p. 9, quoting Las Casas 1974, see also Las Casas 1992, chapters 31, 32 and 33, in particular pp. 204–20.

American form.[55] Robert Kagan, one of the most influential neo-conservatives, clearly expressed this view again in 2017, writing that: 'the liberal enlightenment project elevated universal principles of individual rights and common humanity over ethnic, racial, religious, national, or tribal differences.'[56]

No wonder that some Chinese neoliberals have adopted the same view and the same values—in particular, Liu Junning who, according to the Singaporean professor Zhang Yongnian, has established the philosophical basis of Chinese neoliberalism. Chinese neoliberals consider that liberalism is universal, and stresses universal rights and values such as representative democracy, indirect democracy, constitutionalism, rule of law, limited government, and basic human rights. While the state often deprives people of these rights, the market helps people to realize these rights. These values are considered to be universal, and therefore, 'individual freedoms resulting from market-oriented economic reforms and capitalist development cannot be regarded as a process of "westernization." They contend that if China wants to be "civilized," it has to accept liberalism.'[57]

A historical analysis shows that the thesis of the existence of universal values is not sustainable. What the West calls 'universal values' are in fact values that appeared in the West during the formation of Western civilization and acquired force especially after the end of WW2, to counter criticism of colonialism that was, at least apparently, recognized by the West as an unsustainable foreign policy posture. By an act of unilateral and arbitrary decision (to which the West has been accustomed for a long time) they promoted these Western values as universal. The intent was not only that that they should be considered as such by the rest of the world, but that the West should therefore be accorded the right and even the duty to diffuse them all over the planet, by all means, including overt warfare.[58]

This posture is fundamentally a-historic and negates practically all worth to other cultures and civilizations, and to the values they have developed through time. This is not to say that Western values could not be recognized one day as universal by other cultures, but to contend that this should be done by these countries in accordance with their own

---

55 Fukuyama 1989 and 1992.
56 Kagan 2017b.
57 Zheng 2004, pp. 167 and 169.
58 Wallerstein 2006.

consideration and will. The West should limit itself to advertising its values, and even more so, to conforming its behaviour accordingly at home and abroad. History shows that this has not been generally the case. In fact, the belief in the superiority of Western values has been, and is still today, one of the main drivers of colonialism and imperialism, based on the following notions and pretexts: We in the West have the right to conquer other countries for two non-exclusive reasons: first, because 'they do not know how to organize their polity and, especially, their economy' so we will do it instead of them; second, we will teach them how to do it … provided that they remain, one way or the other, under our rule.

This is what in fact happened with the passage from the classical colonial rule typical of the 19th century, to the formal independence acquired by these countries after WW2, when the Washington Consensus took over the process of facilitating European countries' exploitation of their former colonies. The novelty is that Europeans have not just been joined by the U.S. but rather fallen under its domination as well. This was achieved thanks to the role of the U.S.D as the major reserve and trade currency, sustained by the requirement to purchase oil in U.S. dollars, as well as by the neoliberal international economic organizations the U.S. has managed to establish at the end of WW2, as mentioned above. Add to this the threat and deployment of economic sanctions against enterprises that thwart its demands—the fines against French and German banks, the takeover of companies, and the fear of loss of access to U.S. market. The U.S. has retained this posture until today, without any change, and, on the contrary, is still invested with the will to maintain the 'world America made,' according to the title of a Robert Kagan book.[59]

Daniel Bell has brilliantly summarized the persistence of U.S. ideology through time:

> this blind faith in the universal potential of liberal democracy would not be so worrisome if it had not taken the form of U.S. government policy to promote human rights and democracy abroad, regardless of local habits, needs, and traditions. Notwithstanding the rather huge gap between liberal democratic ideas and the reality at home, the repeated history of misadventures abroad due (at least partly) to ignorance of local conditions […], nothing seems to shake the faith in the

---

59 Kagan 2012b.

universal potential of Western democracy in [U.S.] official circles.[60]

Universal values and the Universal Declaration of Human Rights

Quite often, liberals refer to the Universal Declaration of Human Rights, subscribed to by practically all the members of the United Nations, that enumerates the values that every country should be responsible for implementing, at least morally.[61] Referring to the *Declaration* for sustaining the universal character of Western liberal values is contra-productive, to say the least, insofar as many of the rights mentioned in the *Declaration* have little to do with liberalism, at least as it is practiced today, and for the Italian philosopher and historian Domenico Losurdo even since its beginning.[62] It is true that the Declaration mentions political and civil freedoms, which are most of the time exclusively used by Westerners to criticize countries such as Russia, China, Iran, etc. But the Declaration also mentions rights and values that most of the time are not implemented satisfactorily, or not at all, by Western democracies: For example, Article 23:

1. Everyone has the right to work, to free choice of employment, to just and favourable conditions of work and to protection against unemployment.
2. Everyone, without any discrimination, has the right to equal pay for equal work.
3. Everyone who works has the right to just and favourable remuneration ensuring for himself and his family an existence worthy of human dignity, and supplemented, if necessary, by other means of social protection.
4. Everyone has the right to form and to join trade unions for the protection of his interests.

---

60 Bell 2006, pp 4–5. In the Introduction, paragraph entitled significantly: 'The uniquely parochial development of liberal democracy.'
61 The *Declaration* is not an international treaty. Therefore, the signatories are not legally responsible for not complying with the human rights mentioned in the document, but the signatories are at least bounded by a moral duty to comply with them. The Universal Declaration of Human Rights is available at www. un.org/en/universal-declaration-human-rights, in many languages.
62 Losurdo 2011.

And Article 25:

1. Everyone has the right to a standard of living adequate for the health and well-being of himself and of his family, including food, clothing, housing and medical care and necessary social services, and the right to security in the event of unemployment, sickness, disability, widowhood, old age or other lack of livelihood in circumstances beyond his control.
2. Motherhood and childhood are entitled to special care and assistance. All children, whether born in or out of wedlock, shall enjoy the same social protection.

Maybe, the sole right (and value) generally recognized universally is the one mentioned in paragraph 2 of the Preamble of the Universal Declaration: the right [to realize] 'a world in which human beings shall enjoy freedom of speech and belief and freedom from fear and want.' This allows variations amongst cultures to define what level of freedom of speech, and of freedom from fear and want they intend to safeguard within their borders, according to the historical moment they are in. History shows that even within Western democratic countries the level of freedom has been quite different from one historical moment to another. One has to look at the astonishing level of censure existing today (though this has been going on for a long time) in Western countries, especially in the U.S. Dissenting opinions and even verified facts are disqualified as fake news or conspiracy theories, a term innovated by the CIA itself to dispose of such annoyances. One has to have the will, the skill, and the time to have access to alternative information, opinions and facts outside mainstream media, academe and think tanks.

Moreover, if one is ready to accept that rights are not listed in a hierarchical order in the Universal Declaration, one should also accept that a culture may implement some rights before some others, as it is not possible to implement them simultaneously. This is exactly what China has done and is still doing by dealing first with economic and social rights instead of civic and political ones. Several Western pundits consider that China has attained today a satisfactory level of economic and social rights, and therefore it should now implement the political and civic rights of the Universal Declaration. There is some logic in this argument. Nevertheless, it is up to the Chinese leadership and to the Chinese people to evaluate if the time has come to implement those rights and under what form.[63] Moreover, China is now under an overall pressure to open up its economy to the movement of ideas, goods, and capital. This pressure takes different complimentary forms: an impressive string of military bases set up by the U.S. and its allies; economic war, often under the form of illegal extra-territorial sanctions; and, last but not least, the overt and covert support to internal subversion and independentist movements by the U.S. in Tibet, Hong Kong and Xinjiang. I will develop this point in chapter 3 below. The West has been accustomed to penetrating countries with a variety of means (no matter if the country is democratic, authoritarian, or dictatorial) when that country does not comply with Western interests. It is much easier to penetrate a democracy than an authoritarian or dictatorial state as the cases of Iran (1953), Chile (1973) and Russia in the 1990s demonstrate—indeed, for the West, yet another point favouring the promotion of democracy—the electorally-based, representative government version. It is therefore easily understandable that today may not be an ideal time for China to open up its political system and its economy.

Universal values and cultural identity

To conclude the analysis of the validity of the thesis of the existence of universal values let me briefly refer to the French philosopher and sinologist François Jullien who has probably developed the most radical critique of the existence of universal values (Jullien 2017). Jullien deals with this pretence through the concept of cultural identity, of which universal values are a component. Through a historical analysis Julien shows that Culture is not a static phenomenon but is constructed and reconstructed through time. Therefore, there is no place for 'Fukuyama's end of history.' Jullien reminds us, European culture was constructed from Greek philosophy, then Roman law, then Christianism. To which we can add: the scientific revolution of the Renaissance, the passing from a medieval economy practising a form of slavery to a free economy, the liberal revolution, and then the socialist revolution. European culture holds all this, reviewed as per today. And clearly, for Jullien the movement will not stop there. Moreover, insofar as European culture took form and developed in a particular geographic area, its values cannot

---

63 We have seen above that for the time being Chinese citizens are satisfied with the way the Party-State has managed the transition from a rural country to a relatively well-off urbanized society.

be considered as universal. Unless one thinks that with European (or Western) civilization and its values, humanity has reached the end of history and therefore the clash of non-conforming civilizations is not just inevitable as per Huntington, but justifiable.[64]

Is this a TINA situation—or indeed might other civilizations have differing value systems which are equally worthy of consideration or support? Instead of the apocalyptic vision of the clash of civilizations, François Jullien provides a more promising and optimistic approach.[65] In particular, he strongly believes that Values should not be considered as something that a country possesses, and even less, that a country should try to impose upon other cultures, including not, to say the least, by destroying them by means of forced assimilation. Those who think that Western values are universal should remember that this is exactly what the West has done in the Americas, in Africa and in Asia. On the contrary, values should be considered as resources at the disposal of any country, any culture. So, Jullien proposes a strategy of cross-fertilization between cultures and not a clash of civilizations, which for Jullien is the result of a superficial analysis of the relations between cultures.[66] Unless, again, one state or civilization believes that its culture has all the worthy values, and that the other cultures, from whom it has nothing to learn, have none.

THE MYTH OF THE FREE MARKET

This is one of the myths most frequently used by the West, and especially the U.S. establishment, to proclaim the superiority of the Western liberal economy. Associating the market economy with 'freedom' should do the trick. But nothing is more mythical than this. The market can be simply described as a playing field in which the economic actors compete to realize their interests. By referring to Adam Smith's

---

64 Huntington 2011.
65 In 2015 Jullien put forward the idea of a 'dialogue between cultures' (Jullien 2015).
66 It is interesting to note that one of the most renowned Chinese Neo-Confucians, Joseph Chan, uses 'resources' when dealing with the contributions Confucianism can provide to democracy: 'What needs to be done, I think, is for democracy to be supplemented with a strong ethical foundation and alternative institutions, and *Confucian resources* can be drawn upon to supply these' (emphasis added), Chan 2014, Chapter 5, p. 90 of paragraph 'Combining Democracy and Confucian Values,' pp. 90–94. I will come back to Chan's work below.

The Wealth of Nations liberals and neoliberals appeal to the authority of one of the most prestigious theoreticians of the market economy. They conclude that a free market is a market free of state intervention that would jeopardize the rational functioning of the market. For radical liberals (neoliberals) such as Milton Friedman, the state should limit itself to maintaining the framework necessary for market functioning.[67] But Adam Smith did not advocate an economy free of state intervention. In fact, he meant a market free from the realization of rent (in his time, the rent from land) that is not the result of work, which is the only acceptable and legitimate source of income and wealth. Moreover, the notion that the market is, or should be, free of state intervention meets with no protest when it concerns state mercantilist support for corporate endeavors, whether by law, by funding, or by a myriad forms of intervention (economic warfare) in relation to other states.

When the market makes some grave mistakes (as those resulting in the 2008 financial crisis or during the Covid-19 crisis), the actors dominating the market expect, and even demand that the state intervene to save from bankruptcy the very enterprises that in fact have been at the origin of the crisis.[68] Certainly, rules in today's markets exist but since the 1980s they have been considerably relaxed, under pressure from neoliberalism. History shows that when rules are not strict enough to avoid counterproductive behaviour on the part of the major economic actors, economic crises occur.

Unfortunately, the last two economic crises have impacted the poor and even the middle classes very heavily in all the Western countries. This is because, in fact, the world no longer has a real market economy

---

67 Friedman 1982.

68 Prins 2011 and 2018; Stiglitz 2010. According to Nomi Prins (2011 and 2018), 'Standard & Poor's "rubber-stamped" $14 trillion of toxic assets in the five years leading up to the crisis of 2008. This green light enabled Wall Street to thrive while it manufactured these assets and sold them globally.' Joseph Stiglitz 2010 is useful for identifying those who were responsible for the 2008 crisis; he mentions in first place leaders of the financial sector (head of central banks—especially the U.S. Federal Reserve—banks and investment companies, and traders), mainstream economists and leading mass media who approved the neoliberal project, politicians who listened to both the above-mentioned leaders of financial institutions and economists, and last but not least rating agencies that have long attributed the highest ratings to financial institutions up to the eve of their collapse. Chief executives of multinational companies and banks, and traders, continue to draw enormous salaries and bonuses. The same is happening at the moment of writing (July 2021) for managing the Covid-19 crisis.

but rather one that allows a small vastly wealthy minority to take advantage of the absence of state rules to make the economy work to their almost exclusive advantage. The resultant massive inequity creates social and political unrest, often in violent forms. This, of course, is generally condemned by those social layers in charge of managing this type of polity and economy—government and the media. Violence, except in some rare pathological cases, does not burst out without cause. On the contrary, violence due to economic crises such as the one that devastated homeowners, among others, in 2008 or those due to the effects of the Covid-19 pandemic, should be considered as very serious wake up calls for the internal social and political actors managing the cohesion of the countries concerned, and as a formidable threat to peaceful coexistence in the international arena. Let us try to see where the major problem is.

Although the extent of state intervention in the market has been subject to very passionate debates, it is generally admitted that for Adam Smith, the term free market does not mean a market free from state intervention, but rather free from all forms of economic privilege, monopolies, e.g., the rent of the land, and artificial scarcities. If Smith is to be the guide, this drives us to take into consideration the creation of wealth that is not based upon work, but on positions of rent, as today is the case with financial markets. Clearly, here we can ask whether we are still in presence of a real market economy (even with its inevitable weaknesses) or another type of economy that does not comply with the two basic requirements of a rational market: competition and transparency. Based upon his analysis of the historical development of the way societies have organized the interface between production and consumption, Fernand Braudel has made a clear distinction between market economy and capitalism.[69]

Braudel posited 'three worlds' that he treats not as theoretical models but as real phenomena that have emerged through history: first, material life (in which markets do not exist, yet); second, markets; and finally, capitalism.[70] Significantly, the first world tends to persist after the appearance and the development of market economy and capitalism, as does the market economy after the development of capitalism. Furthermore, these three worlds are organized within a hierarchy in

---

69 Braudel 1979a, 1979b.
70 Material life can be simply defined as the kitchen garden economy, where there are no prices, not demand nor supply as they will play in the market economy and to a lesser extent in capitalism, but existential needs that have to be fulfilled by the cooperation between the members of the family.

which, at the end of the process, capitalism becomes the upper and dominant layer.

Braudel is persuaded that his findings show an opposition between 'normal economic activity' on one hand, the real market economy, and the upper dominating layer, that he qualifies as a 'sophisticated, superior economy,' on the other. Moreover, the economic agents, actions and mind-sets are not the same within the three layers, and even more interestingly, the laws of market economy, especially free competition as described by classical economics, operate more rarely within the upper layer, which is where calculations and speculation abound, and massive concentrated wealth resides. Here there is a 'zone of shadow,' and of insiders' activities, which Braudel considers to be the root of the phenomena covered by the word 'capitalism'—which is not the true market economy, but too often its clear contradiction.[71]

So in this view, we should consider the market economy (whatever its scope of freedom) as an economic system quite different from capitalism, an economy that for Braudel lacks transparency and competition. How far we are here from the dominant discourse of liberals and neoliberals in universities, mass media and political debates!

Finally, in this time when many pundits announce the end of capitalism, it is noteworthy that Braudel reminds us that capitalism has managed to stay alive in spite of numerous crises that could have driven it to its end, thanks to its capacity to resort to all sort of 'tricks' which allow it to remain, in the end, faithful to itself. In Braudel's own words:

> capitalism has always been monopolistic, and merchandise and capital have always circulated simultaneously, for capital and credit have always been the surest way of capturing and controlling a foreign market. Long before the twentieth century the exportation of capital was a fact of daily life, for Florence as early as the thirteenth century . . . Need I observe that all methods, dealings, and tricks ['ruses' in the French edition] of the financial world were not born in 1900 or in 1914? Capitalism was familiar with them all, and, yesterday as today, its uniqueness and its strength lie in its ability to move from one trick to another, from one way of doing things to another, to change its plans ten times as the economic

---

71 Braudel 1979a, vol. 2, pp. 8–9; see also pp. 542–546.

conjunctures dictate –, and as a result, to remain relatively faithful, consistent with itself.[72]

The actors who dominate the capitalist economy have succeeded in dominating the democratic process. While publicly glorifying democracy, they hide the real nature of the political process, protecting it and their real goals under the smoke of propaganda, concealing their activities under the mask of democracy, conceiving their activities behind closed doors, where they can define the strategy for implementing their 'tricks.' In fact, they have emptied democracy of its substance. The name remains, but it has simply become the mask for the oligarchy.[73]

THE MYTH OF DEMOCRACY

The analyses developed above converge into a critique of liberal democracy as such, where in reality the values of freedom, human rights, equality, and prosperity for all, are not fairly distributed within and among countries. Luciano Canfora, the Italian classicist and historian, is one of the most radical critics of liberal democracy.[74] Canfora reminds us that Liberal democracy developed in countries such as France, Britain and America, that were considerably smaller than China in terms of population and territory. The size of China certainly has an impact on the way it has chosen to manage the country since the foundation of the Empire. Referring to the PRC, Canfora quotes Deng Xiaoping as saying: 'in any country, at any time, there is at least 1% of the population of citizens who contest state authority, no matter which. But here in China with a billion and 200 million of people, 1% means 12 million of rebels in the squares.' Westerners do not understand this point because they have the habit of interpreting events in China with the evaluation system and the parameters of their world instead of studying China on the basis of its own local conditions, principles, historical experiences and culture and instead practice what Canfora has termed "democratic fundamentalism."

A further issue with democracy (especially the electoral process) is that it depends on the intellectual capacity of citizens to evaluate the

---

72 Braudel 1979b, pp. 113–114.
73 For example, Chayes 2020a and 2020b; on Chayes 2020a see Parramore 2020. See also Schweizer 2020, Prins 2018, Grundvig 2016, Angell 2005, Craig 2005.
74 Canfora 2002, 2006, 2008, 2009, 2010, and 2017; Canfora and Zagrebelsky 2014.

programmes of political parties (both governmental and opposition), as well as the outcomes of the public policies adopted and implemented by the government. This is particularly worrying when we know how frequent the use of propaganda is for obtaining the support of the majority. Politicians make promises, then break them once in office, whether due to regarding their electoral promises as mere propaganda to win office, or to encountering the difficulties of achieving their promises due to the pushback of deep-seated interests deployed against it. And that this has in fact occurred is evident by the fact that election results do not respond to the constant public desire for change, witness the continuity of policies from one administration to the next.

And this leads us to the major problem of democracy in capitalist countries: the interferences of the economy, and of its major actors within the polity. In fact, the liberal democratic criteria for evaluating what is to be considered 'good behaviour' is quite different from, and even contradictory to what occurs when it is impinged upon by a capitalist economy. In a liberal democracy which rests primarily on the systemic elements of representative government and elections, the participation of people in the political domain is based upon the principle of equality, i.e., the rule of 'one person one vote' in an open electoral competition, supported by freedom of speech and information (a free press), as well as free and equal (or at least fair) access to the decisional process. However, for capitalism as represented by financial and corporate elites, large vested and future interests are what is at stake, so their efforts are directed not just toward elections, where they bring their unequal power resources to bear by way of campaign funding, media access, party platform control, etc., but also outside of this democratic exercise by ongoing investment, in particular, in information-competencies, control of the production of means to understand the world (ideology and choice among political options), i.e., schools, mass media and preferential access to the decision-making processes. In order to avoid a too negative outcome of this contradiction, should the economic interests prevail over the polity to an excessive extent, countries have tended to implement some rebalancing policies in order to compensate those who have lost the competition in the economy, without fault. So, the question is: have the dominant Western countries succeeded in this endeavour? Are they still even trying?

Taking the case of the U.S. (but the same could be said of other Western liberal democracies) the coherence of the present system is due to the prevalence of the interests of a small group of actors that do not in fact democratically represent the majority of the American people. Rather, these actors have managed to develop a coherent informal alliance composed of stakeholders that share ideological and material interests. This is the 'establishment' comprising the majority of Republicans and Democrats elected members to the U.S. Congress, but also several major special interest sectors that are appointed and not democratically elected: the industrial-military complex, the so-called 'intelligence community' (about a dozen agencies, including the CIA), academia, mainstream think tanks, and the mainstream media. The impact of money on politics is well documented: no one can hope to win an electoral competition (both at the local and national levels) without the support of money coming from very rich people and big companies. An astonishing number of lobbyists are at work to convey to the state the interests of both the domestic establishment and foreign interests, and huge sums drop in deluges into campaign coffers. The members of the establishment not only are keen on preserving the present structure of the power system that allows them to realize their interests but can put forward a coherent vision of how the polity and the economy should be organized in relation to sectors of their concern. They promote the drip-down hypothesis: "Let us run it, because we know what we're doing, and you'll all get some."

After the end of the Cold War, the American establishment considered that the world had reached the end of history; thus, no other way of organizing the polity and the economy could be considered as a valid alternative. Small and medium-sized powers who may try to resist will be forced to comply by economic and/or military means. Countries with technological, economic, and military means approaching the level of the U.S., and willing to change the structure of the U.S.-led international system, would be considered as 'revisionist,' an existential threat to the U.S. dominance.[75] Initially, their competition in the international economy was tolerated, under condition that they accept to behave according to the rules the U.S. has established. However, since the beginning of the 21st century several countries have acquired sufficient strength to force a change in the international structure. This is leading to the intensifica-

---

75 There is a vast literature on this point, both from authors such as Robert Kagan and official U.S. documents. Examples of authors: one of the most influential neo-conservatives: Kagan 2008, 2012a, 2012b, 2014, 2017a, 2017b. Official U.S. documents: U.S.A 2016a, U.S.A 2016b, Trump 2017, U.S.A 2018a, U.S.A 2018c; as well as documents by influential think tanks, e.g. for the Brookings Institution: Chollet et al. (2017).

tion of already aggressive U.S. foreign policies towards many countries: economic wars (e.g. sanctions against China and Russia), regional overt or covert military operation (e.g. against Iran, Syria, and Venezuela), covert operations aiming at regime changes: e.g. the interferences in Hong Kong, Xinjiang and Tibet targeting China, and in other countries such as Belarus and Thailand, thus attacking and weakening Russia and China in their periphery—to say nothing of conducting NATO military exercises close to Russia's borders. Should the U.S. persist in this posture, the outburst of an overt war between major powers cannot be underestimated. The only way out, considering that the balance of power in terms of economic and military resources is constantly, perhaps inexorably, changing in favour of countries such as China and Russia, would be a reorientation of U.S. foreign policy, and its accepting the emergence of a multi-polar world. But is the U.S. ready for this epochal change? Not very likely, if we consider the publicly proclaimed goals of Joe Biden before and during his presidential campaign and the choice of several hawks to constitute its team.[76]

Coming back to the two dimensions of the U.S. (and more generally of the West) vision of the way to organize polity and economy and the real nature of the U.S. political system and its failure to comply with the features of a genuine democracy, account must be taken of the fact that the U.S. governing structures have several systemic features that are put forward as underpinning its proclaimed democratic character– but these are no longer operational in actuality. First, it has deleted the operational distinction between the roles of the three powers (legislative, executive and judiciary). This is in theory one of the major positive features attributed to liberal democracies. But in reality, there has never been a clear-cut separation of powers. In liberal democracies, most of the time parliaments have some executive functions and the governments some legislative ones. This is more evident when the legislative sector limits itself to defining general principles in law, leaving the government to complete the legislation by decrees under the policy advice of interested sectors, i.e. the pharmaceutical sector weighs in on health care; yesterday Monsanto, today Bayer weighs in on agricultural policy, etc. Moreover, while most of the time judges are chosen by the government, the parliament or even the citizen, the recent appointments to the Supreme Court by the President and the Senate are rife with ideological and political debates and competition, given the awareness that the faction (liberal or

---

76 Biden and Carpenter 2018, Biden 2020.

conservative) that dominates the Court will have an additional political means for safeguarding its own ideological and political preferences, as is, for example, the case with family planning and abortion. Moreover, both parties have the publicly affirmed goal of obtaining a majority in the two branches of the American Congress. This further weakens another theoretical feature of the American democratic system: the institutionalization of checks and balances in order to avoid the domination of one actor over the others.

That said, for many public policies no clear difference exists between the two major American parties, especially for foreign policy, in any event. The consequence is that competing political ideas that contradict the dominant positions within the establishment are marginalized; they do not emerge into the open. The majority of citizens do not have access to these political fora; true political debate is thus restricted, and the policy options competing with those defined by the establishment are not even discussed most of the time or are immediately disqualified as non- or even anti-American. This is particularly the case for policy options that have a mild socialist connotation, ones that would not be considered as socialist in European continental democracies. The same can be said of the options put forward by the Libertarian party and its main leaders. When one knows that while the traditional Right, represented by Libertarians, is against American wars of aggression and 'big government'[77], Libertarians and their ideological enemies on the Left, the social-democrats, have little chance of being heard in U.S. mainstream media and in the political debate. When they are quoted, quite often their analyses are disqualified as 'fake news' or 'conspiracy theories.'

The consequence is that public policies are mainly evaluated and approved insofar as they satisfy the major interests of the establishment as represented in the American Congress by Democrats and Republicans, a de facto bi-partisan alliance as demonstrable in the continuity of both domestic and foreign policies, irrespective of administration. As capitalism is the economic basis of the strength of the establishment, these policies are inevitably favourable to the market. i.e., to capitalism. Only the military-industrial complex can outweigh the interests of capitalist

---

77 See for example the site of the Libertarian Party (https://www.lp.org/), the Ron Paul Institute (http://ronpaulinstitute.org/) and the Lew Rockwell (https://www.lewrockwell.com/) that proudly announces its *credo:* anti-state, anti-war, pro-market.

companies when they are forbidden to do business in countries under U.S.'s sanctions.

While liberals claim that there exists a 'free press' that can monitor the work of the elites, most of the mainstream media that have a large circulation nationally and internationally is under the control of powerful companies and billionaires, members of the economic elite, and sharing its ideological values and economic interests. It is not likely that these media can exert an efficient and impartial control over the ruling elite. Examples abound, such as its lies concerning and support for the invasion of Iraq, the regime change coup d'état in Ukraine in 2014, and to the ongoing coup d'état efforts by the U.S. in Venezuela. It is little wonder that when Donald Trump labelled the mainstream media 'fake news,' so much of the American public applauded. This means that in the West economy dominates politics, thus making it difficult to implement policies that 'put people first.'

If we also take into consideration the increasing use of censorship, propaganda and spying not only on foreign countries but also on American citizens, we come to the conclusion that references to democracy, as the new President Biden has so frequently done in his speech, can be seen a window-dressing masking the rule of the oligarchy.[78]

In fact, politicians have abandoned one of the major characteristics proclaimed as a key value of liberalism: the prominence of the individual, and have opted instead for the prominence of profit, which is the goal of capitalism. By doing so they have systematically favoured the interests of the establishment, a small percentage of the American population. This abdication of politicians, also evident on Europe, has resulted in a change of the domain where political competition takes place. For several decades, political competition had developed on a horizontal axis opposing the Right and the Left. In the age of neoliberalism, left-wing parties started to converge towards the centre since the beginning of the 1980s, so that by the end of this process, there was no significant difference between the Right and the Left, the latter having accepted the major ideological and policy options of the former. The final result has

---

78 Canfora and Zagrebelsky 2014. For censorship see for example for censorship MacLeod 2020, Johnstone 2021a and 2021b and Cashill 2020, Lauria 2021, Kendall and McKinnon 2020; for propaganda Alford and Secker 2017, McGovern 2020, Pike 2020, Norton 2020a, Norton 2020b, and Singh 2020; for spying Zuboff 2019b and 2021, Starr 2019, Walker 2020, Vos 2020, Napolitano 2020, Koepke et al. 2020.

been that poor and lower middle-class people had the feeling that they were not represented on the horizontal Right-Left axis.

The foreseeable consequence has been that the place of political competition has shifted to a vertical axis in which anti-establishment (or anti-system) movements oppose the traditional elite. It suffices to point to the violent social unrest that burst out in France in 2019 by the 'gilets jaunes' (which is still going on today), the unrest in many American cities in 2020 after the murder of a black citizen that saw such a huge component of white people, or even the violent protest movements in Hong Kong since the spring of 2019. The protest movement in Hong Kong is generally presented in the West (by both mainstream media and politicians) as a desperate demand for democracy due to the interferences of the Chinese dictatorship. There is certainly some truth in this, but I will show in Chapter 3, under 'The Folly of Regime Change and Subversive Activities,' that the main cause for these movements is not so much the lack of democracy, but the very liberal (i.e., capitalist) nature of the Hong Kong economy as managed by the local capitalists supported by their international allies. The consequence has been that Hong Kong today has the highest level of income inequality in capitalist economies, a lack of affordable and decent lodgings for the masses, and the lack of reasonable employment prospects for students coming out of schools at all levels.[79]

It is true that in America there has been a reaction from the left, that started during the presidential campaign of 2016 which saw a further surge of support for Bernie Sanders, a moderate social-democrat, and the emergence of a new generation of young politicians. Notwithstanding, the establishment has proven that it still has the capacity to marginalize them, as the case of Tulsi Gabbard very well shows.[80] Moreover, it has

---

79 Hong Kong's standing on the Gini index measuring social inequality had risen to 54 in 2016 (it was 45 in 1986) according to the Hong Kong Social Indicator site (http://www.socialindicators.org.hk/en), which is considerably higher than the index of all other capitalist countries. According to the UNDP 2020 Report, the China Gini index was 45.4 approximately at the same date (UNDP date for Gini indexes are mentioned as 'most recent date in the period 2010–2018'), considerably less than Hong Kong, i.e. ten points less. The U.S. index was 41.4, demonstrating that in Hong Kong, inequality exceeded even that in the United States, where it is widely acknowledged as excessive.
80 Tulsi Gabbard, Representative of Hawaii in the U.S. House of Representatives, had taken a clear position against the perpetual wars and regime change of the U.S. government. Having served in the U.S. military in Syria, she even met President Bashar Al Assad with the purpose of gathering

been able to narrow the number of options facing the citizen by offering the choice between Clinton and Trump in 2016 and between Trump and Biden in 2020. Four candidates, three clearly from the establishment and another, Trump, with an unusual profile and who, during the presidential campaign has put forward several foreign policy options clearly incompatible with the interests of the establishment.[81] Some aspects of his proposed international policy were clearly against the interests of large parts of the establishment, such as the declared will to negotiate with Russia and North Korea, and to limit intervention abroad (e.g. in Syria and Afghanistan). Had these policies actually been implemented, this would inevitably diminish military spending and international presence, thus hurting one of the major components of the establishment, the military-economic complex, to say nothing of those advocating U.S. hegemony. That said, some other policy options were clearly favourable to large sectors of the establishment, such as reduction of taxation for the wealthiest and the multinationals.

The only significant force for electoral change, Bernie Sanders could not even obtain the Democratic Party nomination, despite having demonstrated he had the strongest popular following. He was eliminated

---

information on the spot about the situation in that country. As a candidate in the Democratic Party primaries, she performed quite well during the first debates, in particular by exposing some of the negative aspects of the activities of Kamala Harris when she was prosecutor in California. Many media considered that she had 'destroyed' Kamala Harris and had thereby put an end to her presidential ambitions. That was without counting on the reactions of the establishment: you do not attack the traditional belligerent posture of U.S. foreign policy, and you do not meet its enemies. Moreover, Gabbard was often mentioned as an interesting candidate by the English broadcast of the Russia television 'Russia Today.' That was clearly too much. A formidable mainstream media campaign was orchestrated against Gabbard with the support of the major representatives of the establishment, among which Hillary Clinton played a nasty role, to say the least. Gabbard dropped out of the race and Kamala Harris became the Vice-President of the U.S.
81 Urio 2019, pp. 230–283. Trump's foreign policy options were contrary to the interests of the establishment: negotiate with Russia and North Korea, NATO is obsolete (clearly suggesting that it should at least be reformed with a reduction of U.S. spending and increasing contributions from European members), diminish U.S. debt, reducing spending in the military, diminish military interventions abroad, withdraw from Afghanistan and Syria; he also criticized international treaties for trade and investment. This would have meant a reduction of military spending in favour of the military-industrial complex. The only proposal favourable to the establishment was to point to China as the main U.S. competitor. And perhaps some of his actions with regard to Israel, not yet rescinded.

twice in the primaries and forced to support the Democratic Party's official nominee: first rightist warmonger Clinton in 2016 and then the
self-defining centrist, but in fact rightist, Joe Biden in 2020. Biden's
long career and his declared domestic policies are not fundamentally different from the pro-establishment policies of the democratic presidents
of the past, and his proposed foreign policy options are totally in line
with the traditional imperial policy the U.S. has implemented for a very
long time.[82] The consequence of this 'pseudo choice' is that even people
who traditionally are very critical of the establishment have more or less
clearly called upon the American people to vote for Clinton in 2016 and
Biden in 2020 citing the Trump menace: such is the actual utility of the
freedom to vote. In fact, no American politician with national ambitions
can launch a career based upon policy proposals different from the interests of the establishment. Look at what happened to Bernie Sanders and
Tulsi Gabbard. And indeed, to former President Trump.

The mainstream media techniques used for manipulating the minds
of people in favour of the establishment, while long in place, have now
been developed into a formidable machinery of pro-establishment propaganda. Some of these media are often briefed by the military-industrial
complex, and by the intelligence community (comprising the CIA and
other security agencies) or indeed have taken them on as pundits, leaving no room for those such as William Arkin of NBC, who resisted.[83]
Propaganda has been used since ancient times. But its modern form
has been significantly developed since the seminal works of Gustav Le
Bon, Edward Bernays and critically updated in the brilliant synthesis
by Shoshana Zuboff.[84] Propaganda tools are used today for influencing

---

82 Biden 2020, with the significant title: 'Why America Must Lead Again.
Rescuing U.S. Foreign Policy After Trump,' *Foreign Affairs,* March-April 2020.
Moreover, his choices for constituting his team comprise a number of hawks,
many of them former members of the Obama administration; see references in
notes above.

83 'In his resignation letter, Arkin says that at NBC he found himself in the
"peculiar position of being a mere civilian among THE GENERALS," the ex-
military commanders that it and all of the broadcast and cable networks hired as
their talking heads to spout out the official position on multiple U.S. wars. He
may well have added that the other prominent "civilian" employed as an expert
commentator by NBC was the former director of the CIA, John Brennan.' https://
www.wsws.org/en/articles/2019/01/05/arki-j05.html

84 Le Bon (1905), Edward Bernays (1928), Zuboff (2019b). Three books
significantly entitled: Le Bon: *Psychologie des foules;* Bernays: *Propaganda;*
and Zuboff: *The Age of Surveillance Capitalism: The fight for a human future at*

the behaviour of citizens in the polity, and consumers in the economy. During WW1, they found an ideal place within the U.S. bureaucracy in a newly created agency called the U.S. Office of War Information, whose goal was to convince the reluctant American public opinion that the U.S. should enter in WW1. Its director, George Creel.[85] writes: 'Our effort was educational and informative throughout, for we had such confidence in our case as to feel that no other argument was needed than the simple, straightforward presentation of facts.' Mark Crispin Miller, professor of media studies at New York University, comments that 'the passage itself, of course, is a stunning bit of propaganda, as it bluntly reconfirms the Manichaean plot that Creel&Co. had hammered home throughout the war: Germans always lie, Americans always tell the truth.'[86]

Just replace 'Germans' with 'Russians,' 'Chinese,' or 'Iranians,' and you will have an idea about how and why propaganda today may be used for selling a political party, a candidate, a form of economy, a type of democracy, the expansion of a country (or a coalition of countries) abroad, the dismembering of a country, all this in the name of the fight for democracy and against dictatorship, i.e., against today's 'Huns,' in an endless fight between good and evil. The establishment thus plays an important role in 'informing' the U.S. citizens about whichever situation that, according to them, requires a military intervention. This is easily swallowed, given 'the provincialism of an electorate with minimal knowledge of the outside world'[87] particularly when confronted with the mainstream media bullhorn, as has been the case concerning U.S. actions against Iran (1953), Chile (1973), Iraq (2003), and Ukraine (2014) to name just a few.[88]

---

the new frontier of power.

85 Creel 2012, p. 3 Creel significantly entitled: *How We Advertised America: The First Telling of the Amazing Story of the Committee on Public Information That Carried the Gospel of Americanism to Every Corner of the Globe Corner;* see also Ponsonby, Arthur (1928), *Falsehood in War-Time: Propaganda Lies of the First World War;* Ponsonby is often quoted as the author of the dictum "When war is declared, truth is the first casualty," in quotation marks as an epigram at the start of this book.

86 Creel 2012, p. 14.

87 Anderson 2015, pp. 1–2.

88 See for example these articles and their significant titles: Louise (2020): 'These 6 corporations control 90% of the media outlets in America. The illusion of choice and objectivity'; and Vinton (2016): 'These 15 Billionaires Own America's News Media Companies.'

As other liberal democracies present similar features to those of the U.S., we can now generalize to address the case of Western democracies per se, even if one of the major components of the U.S. establishment, the military-industrial complex, is considerably less powerful in Europe. Democracy as it is practiced today in Western countries is characterized by an inextricable symbiosis between the political elite that performs official public roles within the state's organs on one side and, and on the other, the economic elite that dominates the market economy. It is within a complex game between military-intelligence, economic, political, and intellectual elites (including influential university professors and journalists) that policy options are examined, choices are made and then presented to the public with finality. Apart from some limited cases of semi-direct democracy (as these do exist in Switzerland) the people cannot directly interfere with or from within these processes; they are limited to electing their representatives every 4–5 years.

Of course, in Europe too it is claimed that there exists a 'free press' that can monitor the work of the elites. Nevertheless, as we have seen in the case of the U.S., the majority of the mass media that have a large circulation within and amongst Western countries as a whole are under the control of a very few powerful companies, including some very rich people who themselves belong to the economic elite, with whom they share ideological values and economic interests. It is not likely that these mass media could exert an efficient and impartial control over the ruling elite. This collusion between economic, political and intellectual elites is clearly demonstrated by the way European mass media have covered important events like the Vietnam war, the Iraqi war, the intervention of the NATO alliance in former Yugoslavia, and the more recent cases of Georgia (2008) and Ukraine (2014) when European establishments took side with the U.S. Moreover, some critics of Western democracy also consider that trade unions and left-wing parties that should defend the interests of the weakest sector of society have little by little, at least since the beginning of the 1980s, failed in this mission, and have embraced the major options of the liberal economic elite.

Furthermore, European governments too have abdicated in favour of the interests of financial institutions and organizations by giving autonomy to their Central banks and renouncing the possibility of better regulating financial markets.[89]

---

89 Governments have instituted regulators with the task of supervising these sectors (and the same has been done with supervising the privatized SOEs).

Democracy can work only if citizens are very well-educated and can therefore assess the validity of the policy options put forward by elites in the public space.[90] Otherwise they are forced to believe what the elites say, which is in fact one of the main features of representative democracy. In this system citizens elect their representatives on the basis of party identification, or because they approve the programme presented by parties and/or individual candidates during the electoral campaign, or because they are moved by the personalities of the candidates. Policy options are debated by citizens' representatives within the parliamentary arena (most of the time on the basis of governmental proposals), and finally policies are adopted by the parliament and implemented by the public administration.

This system can only work if the political elites are transparent and honest; that is, if they act according to what they have promised during the electoral campaign, otherwise the door is open to all sorts of manipulations that can lead to policies that favour parochial or private interests and may lead to an inequitable distribution of rights and wealth. But indeed, does it happen? For several decades Western countries have been implementing basically the same policies, no matter who wins the elections, thus proving that factors other than those linked to electoral and parliamentary politics are at work, despite whatever differences may be present in campaign rhetoric. These cannot but come from the embedded unacknowledged systemic deciders: the military-industrial and financial elites et al.

When one knows that controller and controlled often share the same university and professional training and values, and often have previously worked in the organization they are supposed to supervise, it is not surprising that cases of capture of the controller by the controlled have been frequently discovered. For example, during the 2008 financial crisis, see: *Los Angeles Times,* October 6, 2008 ('Regulator takes heat over IndyMac Bank failure'); *The Washington Post,* November 23, 2008 ('Banking regulator played advocate over enforcer'); *Dollar&Sense Real World Economics,* available online at: www.dollarsense.org (accessed 12 March 2009) '(Mis)understanding a banking industry in transition.'
90 This principle corresponds to the practice of the incremental implementation of liberal democracy in Western countries. For a very long time only people considered as sufficiently knowledgeable were granted the right to vote, by using different criteria such as:1. a sufficient amount of economic wealth measured by the level of taxation, 2. the role played in the economy, according to which only men would qualify, as women were not active in the economy, 3. literacy competence, as it has been used in the U.S. with the main consequence of excluding Afro-Americans.

These embedded elites succeed because they possess more competencies, and they are well organized. And this is why oligarchies are

the core of the most durable regimes, especially if they are open, and capable of co-opting social elements that are becoming important within other classes. If selection and co-optation are based upon common interests (as is most of the time the case in the West) and not upon an ideological basis (as was the case in the Soviet Union) then this process is more efficient and stable.[91]

This way of seeing the role of elites allows accounting for the functioning of systems that may differ in many respects from one another. A big mistake of the Soviet leaders was to believe that it was sufficient to expose the oligarchic character of Western democracies. They did not understand that 'the strength of the Western model was to combine the substance of the oligarchy with the construction of a consensus about the dominations of the oligarchy, even if this entailed the passing from "democracy" to fascism, and from fascism to democracy. This is the foundation of the vitality of Western "oligarchies."'[92]

There are therefore some good reasons for concluding that 'freedom' as often used in the rhetoric of both private and public defenders of the free market and of liberal democracy has been reduced in practice to the 'freedom to shop,' as an American economist said a few years ago.[93] Finally, neoliberal globalization, one of the main goals of the U.S. foreign policy supported by the European Union, is in fact an attack on the State, the only organization in which democracy can be implemented today.[94] The conclusion is that Western countries do not possess the ma-

---

91 Canfora, *L'imposture démocratique*, p. 80. It is interesting to note that this is exactly the aim of Jiang Zemin's Theory of the Three Represents, as I explain below in Chapter 2 (pp. 195-198).

92 Canfora 2002b, pp. 80–81. Canfora is in line with the well-established research tradition that points to the development of oligarchies within organizations, no matter their ideology, democratic or authoritarian: Robert Michels, *Political Parties: A Sociological Study of The Oligarchical Tendencies Of Modern Democracy*, New York, Collier, 1962; Gaetano Mosca, *Ruling Class*, London, McGraw-Hill, 1960; C. Wright Mills, *The Power Elite*, Oxford Press (USA), 1956.

93 Galbraith 2008, pp. 15–24.

94 It is well-known that functioning of international organizations that pretend to regulate the world, such as the World Bank, the International Monetary

jor features of a true democracy (liberal or illiberal). Their polities and policies are dominated by big money and by those who possess and use it in power relations. In short, they are, to different degrees, plutocracies. No wonder then if the Western model has lost its attractiveness for the rest of the world. For example, one of the most influential Chinese intellectuals, Wang Hui, already in 2009 considered that China should not find the solution to its problems by imitating the Western model of democracy, as there is 'a universal democratic crisis, one closely connected to the conditions of marketization and globalization.'[95] Further, he notes that:

> In China and in the West, there has been an 'intense permeation' of State apparatuses by special interests. In the face of this loss of neutrality, what can be done? The answers to these questions must be based on China's increased self-reliance, not in the sense of nationalistic and ethnocentric tendencies, but rather the re-establishment of values and politics along different lines—if anything, it is a new internationalism. The global significance of this exploration should be obvious, given the universal crisis of democracy and market.[96]

Let us now briefly examine some myths related specifically to the U.S.: the myth of the invincibility of the U.S. military, the myth of U.S. power based upon its exceptional superiority, and the myth that U.S. behaves in all circumstances according to international laws and with respect for and with a view to advancing human rights.

Fund and the World Trade Organization, do not possess the features of genuine democratic entities.
95 Wang Hui 2009, p. xxx.
96 Wang Hui 2009, p. xxxii.

SPECIFICALLY AMERICAN MYTHS

THE MYTH OF THE SUPERIORITY AND INVINCIBILITY OF THE U.S. MILITARY

American military superiority is a recurrent myth in the speeches of U.S. politicians, think tanks researchers, mainstream media, and even university professors.[97] Clearly, the U.S. spends much more on its military than any other country, and is continuously increasing its expenditures in this domain.[98]

In the face of this formidable armada, what has been the actual performance of the U.S. military? Since the beginning of the 20th Century the U.S. has not won a single great war on its own. When they entered WW1 quite late (in 1917), their contribution was decisive, but for four years, the burden of fighting against the imperial policy of Germany had rested upon the shoulders of the other European allies. For WW2 the U.S. entered the war only when it had been attacked by Japan in December 1941, more than 2 years after its beginning,[99] and in fact it opened the European front only in 1943–44. While it is true that they financed their allies, especially the UK and Soviet Russia,[100] it is clear

---

97 We have already mentioned above a speech by President Obama on the importance of military resources as the foundation of U.S. power.

98 For example: U.S.A 2016a, U.S.A 2016b; Trump 2017, U.S. 2018a, U.S.A 2018b, U.S.A 2018c, as well as documents by influential think tanks, e.g. for the Brookings Institution, Chollet et al. (2017).

99 It is worth noting that in fact the U.S. military air campaign waged against Japan began in earnest in mid-1944 and intensified during the war's last months of 1944. While plans for attacks on Japan had been prepared prior to the Pacific War, these could not begin until the long-range B-29 Superfortress bomber was ready for combat. Wikipedia, Air Raids on Japan, https://en.wikipedia.org/wiki/Air_raids_on_Japan, accessed 5 January 2021.

100 'Roosevelt's Lend-Lease program was a major factor in Russia's salvation. The list of goods that Roosevelt committed to send to the Soviet Union was astounding. It included shipments every month of 400 planes, 500 tanks, 5,000 cars, 10,000 trucks and huge quantities of anti-tank guns, anti-aircraft guns, diesel generators, field telephones, radios, motorcycles, wheat, flour, sugar, 200,000 pairs of boots, 500,000 pairs of surgical gloves and 15,000 amputation saws. By the end of October 1941, ships were carrying 100 bombers, 100 fighter planes, 166 tanks all with spare parts and ammunition, plus 5,500 trucks.' Chung 2020a. See also the second part of this article: Chung 2020b. For a total calculation, see 'Equipping the Red Army,' *ShareAmerica* (U.S. Department of State's platform for communicating American foreign policy worldwide) , https://share.america. gov/america-sent-equipment-to-soviet-union-in-world-war-ii/, accessed 5 January 2021.

that Soviet Russia bore the burden of fighting the formidable Nazi army in the Eastern front. And at what cost![101] Moreover, during the inter-war period, which was in fact the prelude to WW2, when Italy became fascist in 1922, and when Germany became Nazi in 1932, the U.S. economy considerably increased its investment in these two countries, which were clearly not democratic in fact dictatorships.[102]

The same can be said regarding Japan. The U.S. did not move when Japan aggressed China in 1932, nor when from 1937 on it extended its invasion to the South of China and to other Asian countries. As already mentioned, it is only in December 1941 that the U.S. entered WW2 against Japan after it was attacked at Pearl Harbor. Even the U.S. victory over Japan merits further consideration when it comes to an evaluation of the U.S. military's role and its demonstration of actual fighting capacity. The U.S. began by dropping thousands of incendiary bombs (later called Napalm bombs) on more than 60 Japanese cities, killing more than 200.000 people, mainly civilians[103] with a view to curbing the morale of the population and thus convincing the Japanese leadership to surrender. Despite Japanese willingness to surrender, the U.S. deployed nuclear weapons against Hiroshima and Nagasaki, which according to former Secretary of State McNamara would have ended by the condemnation of the U.S. for war crimes, should the U.S. have been defeated in World War II.[104]

In fact, one can say, with no offence, that the only significant conflict that the U.S. won on its own was against a domestic effort at secession: the American Civil War. In other wars primarily against under-developed countries, the U.S. has not realized a single significant victory, if by victory we mean winning the war and the peace that should follow, whether against, inter alia, North Korea, Vietnam, Iraq (twice),

101 Soviet Russia lost between 20 to 26 million people of whom several million were civilians, while the U.S. lost 419.000 people (of which only 12.100 were civilians). According to Wikipedia, *World War II casualties.*
102 Lacroix-Riz 2014, pp. 31–46; Migone 2015, pp. 141–149, 165–170.
103 From January 1944 to August 1945, the U.S. dropped 157,000 tons of bombs on Japanese cities, according to the U.S. Strategic Bombing Survey. It estimated that 333,000 people were killed, including the 80,000 killed in the Aug. 6 Hiroshima atomic bomb attack and 40,000 at Nagasaki three days later. Other estimates are significantly higher. Fifteen million of the 72 million Japanese were left homeless, according to Associated Press, Mar. 9, 2015, https://www.tampabay.com/author/associated-press/, accessed 2 December 2020.
104 McNamara, R. (2009). McNamara attributes this statement to General Curtis Lee May, and he approves it.

Afghanistan, Syria, or Libya. It seems that the formidable U.S. infantry is not as efficient as it is in the speeches of the U.S. politicians. The U.S. laughs about the Chinese army saying that it has not actually fought in a real war for a very long time. But could we not say the same for the U.S. infantry which has been unable to quell resistance in Afghanistan, leaving most U.S. military successes to its air power?

The Russian-American military expert, Andrei Martyanov, points out the U.S. has never fought a war waged against it on its own territory, if we do not count the Indian Wars (from the time of the 13 English colonies to 1890), the Independence war against England (1775–1786) and the civil war (1860–1965). But this was a long time ago and since then military warfare has changed considerably. The consequence is that today the U.S. does not know, from experience, what a war fought on one's own territory really is.[105] Moreover, having gone to war far away from home has given the U.S. establishment the feeling that their sacred land is not vulnerable to a foreign army. This should be worrying for Europeans, as the U.S. leadership gives the impression of envisaging a war in Europe (of course against a Russian invasion) with an unbelievable nonchalance. Not least, because such a war would be fought on their territories. Confronted with this situation, European countries seem nevertheless to remain faithful to the notion of their sheltering under the U.S.-dominated military NATO alliance.

On the other hand, the U.S. confidence in its ability to fight overseas has persuaded other countries that they cannot avoid being attacked by the U.S., should they not comply with the U.S. demands pursuing its national interests, unless they have an effective military deterrent. North Korea, a rogue state in the U.S. view, having been reduced to colonial status by Japan at the beginning of the 20th century (under the benevolent eye of the U.S.) and attacked by a United Nations U.S.-led coalition that reduced the country to a mass of rubble during the Korean war (1950–53), has succeeded in avoiding being attacked again by building a nuclear deterrence and by forming a *de facto* alliance with China. The same cannot be said of other countries that have tried to resist U.S. dictates such as Iran, Chile, Syria, Libya, Afghanistan, Iraq, etc. No U.S. president can afford to run the risk of a nuclear missile launched on an American populated area.

It remains the case that on paper, considering the size of the Pentagon budget, the U.S. military looks like a formidable asset for

---

105 Martyanov 2018, 2019, 2021, Ch. 7.

realizing American national interests. Should this asset be used only for deterrence, there would be no reason for concern. No state would be so foolish as to risk a nuclear conflict with the U.S., which would be devastating not only for the state concerned but very likely also for the rest of the world. Unfortunately, this has left the U.S. free to use its military force either for bullying or attacking countries that have not complied with its dictates. Instances include those countries which have tried to sell their oil in other currencies, such as Syria, Iran, Iraq, Libya and Venezuela. We know what happened next: regime change and overt or covert warfare against these countries.

Paradoxically, in spite of the criticism addressed to the 'very aggressive' President Trump, he has in fact continued to follow the Obama strategy. First, President Obama, while keeping several hundreds of military bases scattered all over the world, has been no less assertive in using military resources:

> As Commander-in-Chief, I have not shied from using force when necessary. I have ordered tens of thousands of young Americans into combat. I have sat by their bedside sometimes when they came home. I've ordered military action in seven countries. There are times when force is necessary, and if Iran does not abide by this deal, it's possible that we don't have an alternative.[106]

Second, the 'new Obama doctrine' was quite different from the policy of his predecessor, George W. Bush (2000–2008), who privileged the launching of full-scale regional overt wars. Obama changed the U.S. strategy by increasing covert warfare, while keeping a foot in Iraq and Afghanistan, thereby keeping the ultimate goal of maintaining U.S. military domination, exchanging Bush's policy of full-scale overt regional wars for a strategy of covert warfare. Both cases, covert or overt warfare, are based upon the necessity to maintain the appearance of the invincibility of the U.S. army. As explained by Nick Turse, the 'new Obama doctrine' consisted of six dimensions: special operations forces, drones, spies, civilian partners, cyberwarfare and proxy fighters. In 2016 the U.S. elite special operations forces (such as the Navy SEALs and Army Green Berets) conducted operations in 138 countries, 70 per cent

---

106 Obama 2015. Obama refers to the nuclear deal with Iran. 'Remarks by President Obama on the Iran Nuclear Deal.'

of the world total, under the responsibility of SOCOM (U.S. Special Operations Command), an increase of 130 per cent since the end of the Bush administration. Under Trump they were operating in '149 countries, about 75% of the nations on the planet, more than double those of the final days of George W. Bush's White House.' In 2019, Special Operations forces operated in 141 countries, according to figures provided to TomDispatch by U.S. Special Operations Command (SOCOM). In other words, they still deployed to roughly 72% of the nations on this planet. While down from a 2017 high of 149 countries, this still represents a 135% rise from the late 2000s when America's commandos were reportedly operating in only 60 nations. In 2019 Special Operation Forces deployed to 82 countries weekly.[107]

Moreover, since the U.S. has become worried about China's increasing economic activities in Africa, it has increased the operations of its commandos on that continent. Operations cover a wide range of activities: training of military and security local forces, civil military support, military information support, unconventional warfare, counterterrorism and drills.

Overall, the goal is to develop and sustain military relationships across the continent:

> the 2012 SOCAFRICA strategic planning document obtained by *TomDispatch*, reveals that Special Operation Command Africa's primary aim is not fostering African development governance, or military professionalization. 'SOCAFRICA's foremost objective is the prevention of an attack against America or American interests,' according to a declassified secret report.[108]

The analysis of the special commandos' operations in Africa allows Turse to establish a clear link between the development of military bases and special operations, a kind of vicious circle: the development of an efficient network of military bases facilitates the location and deployment of special operations forces, and the development of operations requires

---

107 Turse 2012a, 2012b on new Obama doctrine; Turse 2017a, 2018 and 2020 on Special Operation Forces. The articles give several maps on which you can locate the sites of the operations. See as well Turse's regular updates published online by *TomDispatch:* www.tomdispatch.com. Nick Turse is a journalist and historian, managing director of *TomDispatch* and a fellow at the Nation Institute.
108 Turse 2017b.

a consequent development of military bases.[109] The development of these activities may lead to tensions and conflict with China, especially if the U.S. is going to use military bases and special forces to prevent China from developing its commercial activities in Africa. President Trump did not initiate a new war, as Obama did in Syria and Libya. Nevertheless, he basically followed the new Obama strategy of using preferably covert warfare (as we have seen above) and maintained military forces in the U.S. operation fields (i.e., Afghanistan and Syria). Moreover, President Trump continued the long U.S. tradition of not respecting international rules and human rights. This leads us to the following myth.

THE MYTH THAT THE U.S. ALWAYS BEHAVES ACCORDING TO INTERNATIONAL LAW AND RESPECTS HUMAN RIGHTS

War seems to be the 'natural living condition' of the American Republic: U.S. has been at war 93% of its history. i.e., for 222 out of 239 years between 1776, the year of the Declaration of Independence, and 2015.[110] A report by the Senior Research Librarian of the U.S. Congress that covers 1798–2020, provides a list of "hundreds of instances in which the United States has used its Armed Forces abroad in situations of military conflict or potential conflict or for other than normal peacetime purposes."[111] The U.S. long history of illegal aggression started during the Indian Wars, as attested by the historian of the State Department.[112] More recently, it set up several secret armies in European countries

---

109 Turse 2016 and 2017b.
110 *Washington Blog* 2015.
111 Salazar Torreon 2020.
112 The website of the Historian of the State Department subdivides the history of U.S. foreign policy into several 'Milestones.' In the milestone entitled 'Indian Treaties and the Removal Act of 1830' it is written: 'The U.S. Government used treaties as one means to displace Indians from their tribal lands, a mechanism that was strengthened with the Removal Act of 1830. In cases where this failed, the government sometimes violated both treaties and Supreme Court rulings to facilitate the spread of European Americans westward across the continent. As the 19th century began, land-hungry Americans poured into the backcountry of the coastal South and began moving toward and into what would later become the states of Alabama and Mississippi. Since Indian tribes living there appeared to be the main obstacle to westward expansion, white settlers petitioned the federal government to remove them. Although Presidents Thomas Jefferson and James Monroe argued that the Indian tribes in the Southeast should exchange their land for lands west of the Mississippi River, they did not take steps to make this happen. Indeed, the first major transfer of land occurred only as the result of war.'

during the Cold War, launched 13 illegal wars of aggression during and after the Cold War, and undertook at least 59 attempts at regime change during and after the Cold War.[113]

During its irrational 'war on terror' initiated after September 11 attacks on the Twin Towers in New York, the U.S. has displaced at least 37 million people, though 'ultimately no number can convey the immensity of displacements' damage. For individuals, families, towns, cities, regions, and entire countries, displacement has caused incalculable harm physically, socially, emotionally, and economically.'[114] The U.S. invasion of Iraq in 2003 was explicitly deemed illegal by former UN Secretary General Kofi Annan, albeit after the fact. The NATO attack on Libya, primarily a U.S. effort, far exceeded its UN R2P mandate in order to illegally achieve regime change (and not incidentally, country destruction).

If it is true that Trump did not initiate new overt wars, he has nevertheless followed his predecessors by pursuing the illegal U.S. covert war against Syria and attempting to achieve regime change in Venezuela and Iran—though. Unlike the Obama orchestrated regime change in Ukraine (2014), he failed.

In addition to increasing the use of covert warfare, Trump also increased the use of illegal extraterritorial sanctions, that were already being used by his predecessors. This is part of the general U.S. policy of opting to make decisions or even to adopt laws that it claims give the U.S. the right to exercise extraterritorial interventions all over the world each time it considers that its national interests are at stake but that have no merit in international law. The U.S. is presently using economic embargos and economic sanctions against a number of countries without regard to their passage by the UN Security Council, which alone has the international legal right to impose sanctions. As of June 2021:

---

113 On NATO's secret armies: Ganser 2005; on NATO's illegal wars: Ganser 2016 and Jones 2017; on meddling in other countries elections: Shane 2018 and Levin 2016; on regime changes: Blum 2013–2014, 2014a, b, 2018, and Valentine 2017; on secret prisons: Marty 2018, pp. 153–193.
114 5.3 million Afghans (representing 26% of the pre-war population) 3.7 million Pakistanis (3% of the pre-war population), 4.4 million Yemenis (24% of the pre-war population),4.2 million Somalis (46% of the pre-war population), 1.7million Filipinos (2% of the pre-war population), 9.2 million Iraqis (37% of the pre-war population), 1.2 million Libyans (19% of the pre-war population), 7.1 million Syrians (37% of the pre-war population) (Vine et al 2020, p. 17).

countries or regions subject to U.S. sanctions (either uni-
laterally or in part) include the Balkans, Belarus, Burma,
Burundi, Central African Republic, Cuba, Democratic
Republic of Congo, Hong Kong, Iran, Iraq, Lebanon, Libya,
Mali, Nicaragua, North Korea, Somalia, Sudan, South Sudan,
Syria, Ukraine/Russia, Venezuela, Yemen, and Zimbabwe.[115]

Even if sanctions seem less damaging than direct military destruction and killing, it remains the case that sanctions have an inordinate
impact on the living conditions of civilians, as is today the case in Syria,
Iran, Venezuela and Cuba, in a clear violation of human rights of the citizens in these countries.[116] It should not be forgotten that the U.S. use of
sanctions against Iraq led to the U.S.-acknowledged death of more than
500,000 Iraqi children, a statistic then U.S. Secretary of State Madeline
Albright described as 'worth it.'

Moreover, Trump has also imposed illegal sanctions on U.S. allies,
for example to dissuade European countries and enterprises to complete
the construction of Nord Stream 2, that will bring gas from Russia to
Europe.[117] The reason given: Europe would jeopardize its security by
importing from Russia instead of from the U.S. The problem: importing
from the U.S. will be 30–40% more expensive. On July 2021 President
Biden waived U.S. sanctions on the pipeline. A clear victory for Germany
and Russia, as explained above.

More startlingly, the U.S. has also threatened to sanction members
of the International Criminal Court who dared to investigate or prosecute
U.S. personnel for war crimes. Not a very coherent policy for a country
that systematically accuses other countries of violating human rights.

While the U.S. does not behave in all circumstances according to
international law and to the promises it has made either in international
treaties or otherwise,[118] it nonetheless claims to be promoting a 'rules-

---

115 U.S. Department of the Treasury. "Sanctions Programs and Country
Information." Accessed June 16, 2021.
116 See for example Vohra 2020.
117 It is enough here to mention the earlier U.S. administration gains of billions
of dollars gained from penalties against Banque Paribas, Deutsche Bank, UK's
HSCB, inter alia and the French company Alstom, among others.
118 For example, the promise made to Gorbachev not to expand NATO and the
EU eastwards in exchange for Soviet Russia's agreement to the reunification of
Germany. This promise has been the source of a controversy for a long time.
Nevertheless, newly-declassified documents show that the promise was made:
Smith Yves (Smith, Y. (2017) Newly-Declassified Documents Show Western

based' international order, a claim which remains in ongoing use as part of its representation of itself to the world, including by the new Biden administration, as the new Secretary of State, Anthony Blinken, has announced in his 2021 speech of on foreign policy:

> President Biden has pledged to lead with diplomacy because it's the best way to deal with today's challenges. For the U.S. the most important challenge is the attack on democracy by countries such as Russia and China. So, the U.S. will do whatever is in their power to defend and promote democracy (…) We will use the power of our example. We will encourage others to make key reforms, overturn bad laws, fight corruption, and stop unjust practices. We will incentivize democratic behaviour. (…) But we will not promote democracy through costly military interventions or by attempting to overthrow authoritarian regimes by force.[119]

As for other U.S. relations to international law and treaties, we might cite
- the withdrawal from the Paris climate agreement
- at least 81 instances of meddling in other countries' elections during and after the Cold War,
- setting up numerous illegal prisons where torture of U.S. enemies could be secretly practiced
- the withdrawal from the internationally negotiated Nuclear (JCPOA) Agreement with Iran

This behaviour contradicts the theory according to which the U.S. has been getting its way by the use of soft power. While hard power is implemented by using economic (e.g., sanctions) and military resources, 'soft power rests on the ability to shape the preferences of others. […] The ability to establish preferences tends to be associated with intangible

---

Leaders Promised Gorbachev that NATO Would Not Move "One Inch Closer" to Russia. *Naked Capitalism,* 15 December. Retrieved January 3, 2018, fromwww.nakedcapitalism.com/2017/12/newly-declassified-documents-showwestern-leaders-promised-gorbachev-nato-notmove-one-inch-closer-russia.html.2017). See also Richard 2018, significantly entitled: 'Lonely Russia. No room for Moscow in 'common European home.'
119 Blinken 2021. We will see in Chapters 2 and 3 that this statement is not implemented in U.S. foreign policy in actuality.

assets such as attractive personality, culture, political values and institutions, and policies that are seen as legitimate or having moral authority.
[…] It is also the ability to attract, and attraction often leads to acquiescence.'[120] But do countries accept to behave as the U.S. wants, thereby
realizing American national interests, because they admire the way the
U.S. behaves at home as a liberal democracy, and behaves abroad according to liberal values, the respect of human rights and international
laws?[121] Clearly this belief contradicts the information provided above
about U.S. behaviour.

Moreover, even when the U.S. does not resort to economic and/
or military means, it has the habit of sending 'clear messages' to its enemies, such as 'all the options are on the table,' implementing military
drills, alone or with allies and/or partners, and frequently reminding the
world about its military superiority, in order to obtain compliance.[122]
Nevertheless, the success of this behaviour has considerably decreased
since at least the beginning of the 2000s. Threats do not always obtain
the expected result. It seems that a number of countries have not understood the message and are not complying with U.S. dictates. Or, maybe
more likely, they have very well understood that they are going to be
attacked by economic means and/or militarily, but are willing to stand
up to it. Accordingly, several countries have implemented a strategy to
avoid being dependent upon the U.S. dollar (to protect against some
parts of the sanctions) and to build military resources in order to send
back a 'clear message' to the U.S.: if you attack us, we can strike back
and we are even capable of hitting you on your homeland (e.g. Russia,
North Korea). Many countries are progressively decoupling from the
U.S. dollar in order to avoid economic sanctions (e.g., China, Russia,
Iran), by establishing formal or informal alliances and partnerships (e.g.,
China and Russia), and by developing their military means (e.g., again
China and Russia, but also Iran and North Korea).

North Korea is a good example of a country that has very well
understood the U.S. 'clear messages.' North Korea, still today a developing country, has been able to develop nuclear weapons and a variety
of missiles, from medium to long range (i.e., inter-continental). It has a

---

120 Nye 2004, pp. 5–6, see also 2012, pp. xiii-xviii, 3–4, 81–109.
121 I have provided elsewhere a critique of this typology in Urio 2018, pp.
36–43.
122 For some examples of 'clear U.S. messages' see Bandow (2020b) 'When
Washington Sends a Message by Threatening War. Other Countries Hear "Build
Nukes!"' *AntiWar.com,* 30 December.

long history of being at war with the U.S., since the middle of the 20th century.[123] History has taught North Korea that it is not wise to blindly trust the U.S. North Korea has not been blind to the U.S. behaviours towards medium and small countries when it has not obtained compliance by diplomatic (i.e., 'soft') means. Countries that have not developed sufficient military forces have been attacked, either directly or by military proxies, when they were an obstacle to the U.S. interest, such as Libya (even after having cancelled its nuclear programme under U.S. pressure) Syria, Iraq, Afghanistan, Vietnam, Laos and North Korea in 1950.

These cases show that the U.S. does not hesitate to use 'hard power' (economic and/or military means) when soft power does not work.[124] Power cannot be theorized as soft or hard. This typology is an intellectual fraud. Power is always hard, either as an actual use of economic and/or military actions or as a threat, i.e., in the form of the very frequent 'clear messages' the U.S. has the habit of sending to its enemies, the clearest message being 'all the options are on the table.'[125] This American behaviour had, and still has today, the negative consequences of further damaging the U.S. reputation as a liberal democracy at home and a responsible actor in the international system.

During the Trump administration the U.S. witnessed several instances of 'blowback.' To begin with, North Korea has resisted the explicit menace in the form of the bombastic language that it will be '*obliterated*' from the earth by the U.S. military power, should it not comply with the U.S. demand to de-nuclearize. Clearly, this language is typical of President Trump, but it is indeed consistent with the traditional

---

123 Cumings 2005 and 2011, Stone, Isidor, 1952, Bovard 2020, Leebaert 2011, Conway-Lanz 2006. For an excellent short history of U.S. policy towards North Korea and the Korean war, see: Cumings, 2017. In his 2011 book Cumings writes: 'Americans sought to grab hold of this war and win it, only to see victory slip from their hands and the war sink into oblivion. A primary reason is that they never knew their enemy—and they still don't. So, this is also a book seeking to uncover truths that most Americans do not know and perhaps don't want to know, truths sometimes as shocking as they are unpalatable to American self-esteem,' p. xv. Also see Abrams, *Immovable Object: North Korea's 70 Years at War with American Power,* 2020.
124 See the quotations of Barack Obama, Robert Kagan and Joe Biden above.
125 I will not develop here the important theme of the 'bad behaviour' of both the U.S. army and of some of its soldiers. It suffices to recall the use of the atomic bomb to win the WW2 against Japan, and the massacres of the Native Indians (in particular the last one known as the Massacre of Wounded Knee—1890), the No Gun Ri massacre (1950, Korea), the My Lai Massacre (1968, Vietnam), and the numerous massacres during the Iraq and the Afghanistan wars.

U.S. behaviour in similar circumstances. Hillary Clinton earlier threatened to obliterate Iran.[126] Here, in another blowback, by the time of the U.S. assassination of General Soleimani, Iran had developed its capacity to the extent that it had the temerity to strike back at U.S. forces after which the U.S., even though suffering a surprising hit, decided to decline further escalation. A third: the Chinese digital yuan may soon open for cross-border trade.

China has stepped up its efforts to internationalize the yuan, partly to limit any fallout to its own economy from increasing tensions with Washington. In addition, China is responding to concerns that Washington is weaponizing the dollar to impose sanctions on China. Already Washington has sanctioned Chinese companies like Huawei Technologies as well as Chinese officials dealing with Hong Kong and Xinjiang. A cross-border digital payments system means China is setting the stage for fuller yuan convertibility, which would accelerate the use of the currency in foreign exchange settlements.[127]

And yet another, from Chris Hedges:

> The American empire would, years later, find itself desperately trying to destroy its own creation. In April 2017, in a classic example of this kind of absurd blowback, the United States dropped the "mother of all bombs" — the most powerful conventional bomb in the American arsenal — on an Islamic State cave complex in Afghanistan that the CIA had invested millions in building and fortifying.[128]

There are a number of indications that the world seems less intimidated by U.S. power than before. One came on 15 November 2020, when 15 countries, led by China, signed, after 8 years of negotiations, the Regional Comprehensive Economic Partnership (RCEP). This is the world's largest trade bloc; it will cover 30% of global trade and of global input, comprising 2.3 billion people. India did not join, but it is interesting to note that this is also China's first multilateral trade agreement and

---

126 https://www.reuters.com/article/us-usa-politics-iran-idUSN2224332720080422
127 Narayanan Soma Sundaram "Will China's Digital Yuan Vanquish the Dollar?" *Nikkei,* August 11, 2021. https://asia.nikkei.com/Spotlight/The-Big-Story/Will-China-s-digital-yuan-vanquish-the-dollar
128 Chris Hedges, "The Collective Suicide Machine," *Scheerpost,* https://scheerpost.com/2021/07/26/hedges-the-collective-suicide-machine/

the first trade agreement including China, Japan and South Korea. The influential International Institute of Strategic Studies did not hesitate to qualify this agreement as 'a geopolitical win for China.'[129] Another is the clear message given to the U.S. by the European Union which on 30 December 2020 signed, after seven years of negotiations, an important deal with China: the China-EU Comprehensive Agreement on Investment (CAI). This has taken the U.S. establishment by total surprise, as if such a deal was unthinkable. Bloomberg has without hesitation qualified this deal as a big mistake: "For the sake of an agreement with Beijing, the EU has snubbed the incoming Biden administration and damaged the transatlantic cause."[130] A few days later, the American Economic Institute published an article significantly entitled "Biden's first defeat: The China-EU trade agreement."[131] Clearly, the Empire and its media do not like international deals of which it is not the initiator or at least one of the contracting parties and, more worrying, the U.S. establishment does not seems to be able to understand the meaning of these 'clear messages.' It is true that after the beginning of the Biden administration the EU Parliament has blocked the ratification of the China-EU agreement, in the hysterical anti-China (and also anti-Russia) climate fomented by the U.S. establishment. But the economic interests of several European countries that have already important trade exchanges with China will not fade away. Moreover, can the U.S. provide a viable alternative?

THE MYTH THAT U.S. POWER IS BASED UPON ITS EXCEPTIONAL SUPERIORITY

This myth is based upon an evaluation of America's excellence on a number of counts: intellectual skills, willpower, entrepreneurship in all domains, and organizational capacity to take advantage of its power resources. This has certainly been true in many domains starting with science and technology, university training, and the economy. Nevertheless, it is necessary to recall that the U.S. dominance in the world economy was achieved thanks to the Allied victory in WW2, even if, as mentioned above, it was the Soviet ally that enabled the U.S. victory on the European front—and subsequent projection of itself as the primary if not sole victor. The U.S. economy was already very powerful at the beginning of the 20th century and ready to project the country

---

129 Ward 2020; see also the *Financial Times:* Brunsden 2020 et al.
130 Kluth 2020.
131 Barfield 2021.

into the touted 'American Century.'[132] Notwithstanding, it has profited from a number of exceptional geo-political advantages from the very beginning, with the Declaration of Independence of 1776 and the creation of the American republic: a territory protected by two wide oceans which spared the country from wars of invasion, the inability of native inhabitants to resist Western colonizers, a declining colonial power at the southern border (Spain) not prepared to sustain war with the U.S., and in the North an ideologically compatible neighbour (Canada). These were ideal pre-conditions for developing a strong economy shielded by strong protectionist laws that remained in force until the end of WW2. It was only then that the U.S. became a defender of free international trade. Moreover, the U.S. benefited from the suicidal foreign policies of the European powers, that not only devastated the rest of the world during two world wars, but also put an end to their military and economic might, as well as to their cultural reputation.

The belief in the 'natural' superiority of the U.S. and in the invincibility of its army encountered no major problems until the end of WW2, when the U.S. superiority was not only a belief but also a reality. That superiority was so great, it gave the U.S. the privilege of making mistakes with little negative consequences. But when the gap between belief and reality becomes so great that what is believed has now become a myth, making a mistake, especially a strategic one, can have some devastating consequences in the long run. History shows that empires fold, that it is not possible to remain the only super-power for ever. The consequence of over-estimating present power can be even more devastating if a competitor is on an ascending trajectory as far as its power resources are concerned. To counter this trend, it is necessary to acquire a profound knowledge of the competitor, its culture, its history, and its fundamental objectives in foreign policy. Can one really say that such a process is underway with regard to the U.S. and China?

---

132 This meme was created by the American media magnate Henry Luce in a famous article published in his *Life* magazine editorial, February 17, 1941, where he urged the United States to forsake isolationism for a missionary's role, acting as the world's Good Samaritan and spreading democracy. He called upon the U.S. to enter World War 2 to defend democratic values. Notably, Luce was borne in China in a missionary family, and at 15 left China to pursue his education. He developed a media empire and became one of the most influential opinion leaders of his time. As was typical of American leaders since the beginning of the 20th Century his goal was to educate China into modernity ... with an American flavour. See for example the classic winner of the 1973 Pulitzer Prize *Luce and His Empire* by Swanberg, 1972.

Having an ideological faith in the U.S.'s exceptional superiority does not encourage it to invest in acquiring knowledge about any potential competitor. This is what happened toward the end of WW2 in the Pacific. The explosion of the first atomic bomb in the American desert gave the U.S. (and more particularly President Harry Truman) the certitude that the U.S. could do anything in warfare, without running the risk of losing the game. No other country could match U.S. military power, then the sole atomic power. The full transcription of the radio broadcast made by President Truman informing *urbi et orbi* of the use of the first atomic bomb on Hiroshima is a clear warning to all the countries, first to Japan, but also to other enemies that may rise in the future (especially the Soviet Union): the U.S. is the sole global superpower; so be very careful and behave.[133] Here are some passages of President Truman's broadcast (emphasis added):

> What we are doing to Japan now—even with the new atomic bomb—is only a small fraction of *what would happen to the world in a third World War*. (…) The British, Chinese, and United States Governments have given the Japanese people adequate warning of what is in store for them. We have laid down the general terms on which they can surrender. Our warning went unheeded; our terms were rejected. Since then, the *Japanese have seen what our atomic bomb can do*. They can foresee what it will do in the future. *The world will note* that the first atomic bomb was dropped on Hiroshima, a military base [*sic*]. That was because *we wished in this first attack to avoid, insofar as possible, the killing of civilians [sic]*. But that attack is only a warning of things to come. *If Japan does not surrender*, bombs will have to be dropped on her war industries and, *unfortunately, thousands of civilian lives will be lost*. I urge Japanese civilians to leave industrial cities immediately and save themselves from destruction. I realize the tragic significance of the atomic bomb. (…) *The Japs [sic] will soon learn some more of the other military secrets agreed upon at

---

133 This speech may be considered as a premonition of what President George H.W. Bush famously declared when the Soviet Union collapsed, and America remained the only superpower: "What we say goes."

Berlin. They will learn them first-hand—and they will not like them.[134]

This belief in the overwhelming superiority of the U.S. military at that time due to its possession of the atomic bomb was one of the major motives that led the President to use it to defeat Japan, the other being to avoid the occupation of Japan (and its surrender to Russia), as the Russians entered the war against Japan (fulfilling a promise made to the U.S. and the UK) and were rapidly occupying the Korean peninsula and moving in the direction of Japan. If this was the basis for the belief in American military superiority, it should have driven the U.S. leadership to moderate its confidence in the superiority of its conventional military. The fact is that the U.S. refrained from attempting to occupy Japan by conventional military means, after it was attacked on Pearl Harbor in December 1941. Only on August 1945 the U.S. decided to launch a criminal attack on Japanese civilians using the atomic bomb, with the intent to force Japan to an immediate unconditional surrender.[135] Clearly, this was because the U.S. feared that the Russians may be able to arrive in Japan before it, after having defeated the formidable Nazi army. Then Japan would surrender to Soviet Russia instead to the U.S. This was an unacceptable consequence for the U.S., given the already mounting rivalry between the two major allies in WW2. The sequence of these events means that the confidence the U.S. had in its conventional military superiority was not as strong as it publicly advertised.

But there is more. Defeating Japan 'in the air and on the sea' meant that the U.S. did not place enough military power (i.e., infantry) on the continent where Japan had an army of at least half a million soldiers. A clear military victory called for the transfer of infantry troops. But maybe that was the problem? Conducting warfare by sea and the air with sailors and pilots demanded much fewer military personnel than by using the infantry. While another goal of the U.S. military command was to limit the death of the U.S. soldiers, the U.S. would have been in a much better position to support Chiang Kai-shek in his fight against

---

134 August 9 1945 Radio Report to the American People on the Potsdam Conference: https://millercenter.org/the-presidency/presidential-speeches/august-9-1945-radio-report-american-people-potsdam-conference, accessed 10 October 2020.
135 On the criminal character of the use of the atomic bomb on Japan see McNamara (2009). Robert McNamara attributes this statement to General Curtis Lee May, and he approves it.

the Communists of Mao by having placed the infantry on the continent when the civil war started again after the defeat of Japan. Whatever the reason, it remains that the U.S. failed to provide a sufficient support to the Nationalist government, which led effectively to the U.S.' first defeat, so soon after having proclaimed its military invincibility. The U.S. command had forecasted it would demobilize in three years after the victory over Japan. In fact, demobilization took only six months, very likely under pressure from the U.S. people, eager to welcome their heroes back home as soon as possible. The result is that Mao won the civil war in China. And this was certainly a strategic mistake of considerable consequences for the shaping of the power balance for a very long time. As a Chinese proverb says: 'an incorrect step (decision) leads to unending regrets ('Yī shī zú chéng qiāngǔ hèn'). Indeed, the U.S. understood its mistake and started to build a strategy to contain China, the first move being allowing Chiang to stay (as a dictator) on one part of the Chinese territory, Taiwan,[136] clearly contrary to what generally happens at the end of a civil war, including the American one: the victor acquires sovereignty over the whole of the national territory.

By helping Chiang Kai-shek to win the war against Mao by bringing the war on Japan to the continent, the U.S. might have been in the same position in Asia as it had been in Europe: as the liberator from Imperial Japan (the ally of the Nazi-Fascists) and liberator of a large portion of Asia from Communism. The U.S. might then have been able to create a military alliance similar to NATO, with a similarly formidable territorial basis comprising Japan, Korea (North and South), China and the Philippines.[137] Soviet Russia would have been totally encircled. True, but then the U.S. made its second, and very likely fatal, strategic mistake.

Despite its effective failure to win in the Korean War, its humiliating departure ending the Vietnam war, its wobbling lack of achievement

---

136 It is interesting to note that the Republicans, who won the presidential election in 1952 after twenty years of Democratic Presidents (Roosevelt and Truman, 1932–1952) very bitterly accused the Democratic Party of having 'lost China.' We will see in Chapter 3 that since the beginning of the Republic there were signs that the U.S. was attracted by China mainly for trade and enrichment. This attraction became evident after the conquest of the Philippines and the fall of the Chinese Empire: the economic attraction was supported by the development of an imperial power posture that was to last until today.
137 The U.S. gave the latter independence in 1946, but pressured the former colony into a 99-year rent-free lease on 23 military installations. See the article published in the *Washington Post* by David Vine, significantly entitled: 'Most countries have given up their colonies. Why hasn't America? (Vine 2017).

in Iraq and Syria, and conclusive loss in Afghanistan, the U.S. persists in overestimating its military strength in dealing with Russia. Instead of drawing Russia into partnership with the West (recall Putin's much reiterated, wishful reference to 'our American partners'), it has considered Russia as a territory to be conquered. With an unbelievable arrogance, it has dismissed all attempts made by the Russian authorities (already by Yeltsin and then by Putin) to include Russia in the managing of security in Europe. But an empire does not share its dominant position. It dominates. Full stop! So, the U.S. expanded the territories under its power in Europe as far as it could toward the Russian borders, not respecting the verbal promise made to Gorbachev. Another strategic mistake. Russia reacted to the U.S. aggressions in Georgia in 2008 and then in Ukraine in 2014 and finally, having been unable to integrate with the West, it turned its foreign policy to the East, and became, with China, a formidable economic, technological and military pole able to attract other countries and to contest thereby the supremacy of the U.S. This became clear when China launched the Belt and Road Initiative in 2013 (see 'The Decline of the American Empire' in Chapter 3). Another mistake that is leading today, as the Chinese proverb mentioned above would say, 'to some additional unending regrets,' leaving the U.S. now struggling with the question of how to counter the China-Russia 'dangerous emerging partnership.'[138]

---

138 See for example the article published by *Foreign Affairs* by two Senior Fellows of the Center for a New American Security: Kendall-Taylor and Shullman 2021. It is interesting to quote the authors' suggestion to the new Biden administration: 'Creative thinking about how to limit cooperation between Beijing and Moscow—while avoiding actions that reinforce their entente—will be critical to promoting U.S. interests and liberal democracies in the decades to come.' Vast programme! The Center for a New American Security (CNAS) is a Washington, D.C.-based think tank established in 2007 by co-founders Michèle Flournoy and Kurt M. Campbell. It specializes in the United States' national security issues. Michèle Flournoy was Deputy Assistant Secretary of Defense for Strategy under President Bill Clinton and Under Secretary of Defense for Policy under President Barack Obama. Flournoy crafted the Obama administration's counter-insurgency policy in Afghanistan and helped persuade President Obama to intervene militarily in Libya. In 2007, Flournoy co-founded the Center for a New American Security. In 2020 she was a possible candidate to lead the Pentagon, however Biden appointed a former commander of the American military effort in Iraq, retired Gen. Lloyd J. Austin III. CNAS is led by CEO Victoria Nuland, who served as the Assistant Secretary of State for European and Eurasian Affairs under Secretary of State John Kerry and organized the regime change in Ukraine in 2014. CNAS top donors include Northrop Grumman

The Myth that America's Original Sins Against Blacks and Indians Have Been Overcome

The Black Lives Matter protest movement that broke out in Spring 2020 has forced America to return, painfully, to the beginning of the U.S. Republic. Most of the time comments about this movement refer to the American original sin, i.e., the legal institutionalization of slavery in the plantations of the South.[139] No doubt slavery has been a sin that has obsessed America for a long time.[140] While not its primary objective, the civil war (1861–1865) is purported to have freed, at least in principle, the descendants of enslaved Africans working in the plantations after more than two centuries of slavery. But the sin did not stop there, it continued until the mid-1960s when the Civil Rights Act of 1964 freed Afro-Americans of the discriminatory laws that had kept them for another century as second-class citizens in an apartheid state in the American south. Now, in the 21st century, has the sin been cured? The answer is clear: no, it has not been cured.[141]

Nor have the Native Indians recovered from the European and American onslaught. Is this not also an original sin? Not only because of the ferocious treatment to which they were subjected, but also because their place in the American society was worse than that of those then termed Negroes. The latter had at least some economic value. The owner of the plantation invested his money for buying them, as a kind of

Aerospace Systems, Open Society Foundation, Airbus Group, The Boeing Company, Chevron Corporation, Lockheed Martin Corporation, Raytheon Company, the Taipei Economic and Cultural Representative Office, the United States government, BAE Systems, BP America and Exxon Mobil Corporation.

139 See the article by the Afro-American professor in history and law at Dartmouth College (Harvard Law School): Gordon-Reed Annette (2018), 'America's original Sin,' *Foreign Affairs,* January/February. It is interesting to note that the article refers to the legal practice of slavery in the U.S., but does not mention the Indian Wars. The enslavement of Africans began well before the Declaration of independence (1776): a significant starting point to slavery in America is 1619, when the privateer *The White Lion* brought 20 African slaves ashore into the British colony of Jamestown, Virginia, from *Slavery in America,* by History.com Editors, https://www.history.com/topics/black-history/slavery#section_2, accessed 27 December 2020.

140 Let us remark that the sin was not limited to the South, as many investors of the North made a fortune by financing the slave trade. See Anne Farrow, Joel Lang and Jenifer Frank, *How the North Promoted, Prolonged and Profited from Slavery,* New York, Ballantine Books, 2006.

141 See for example Worland 2020, with the significant title: 'America's Long Overdue Awakening to Systemic Racism.'

cheap labour. They were a factor of production to be taken care of, to be provided with adequate food and shelter, to ensure they would work efficiently, and not result in an economic loss for the owner. The American Indians had no economic value at all; on the contrary they were a cost, the cost of the Indian Wars. The Afro-Americans obtained their rights in 1964, so did the Native Indians already in 1924 (the Indian Citizenship Act). Nevertheless, as happened to the Afro-Americans, even after 1924, some Native Americans weren't allowed to vote. And today, the theft of their land is still going on as a de facto expropriation to make room for economic activities.

In the Declaration of Independence, the Negros were not even mentioned in the text, many of whose signatories, were slave owners, including Thomas Jefferson, while the Indians are described as "the merciless Indian Savages whose known rule of warfare, is an undistinguished destruction of all ages, sexes and conditions."

After Independence, the presidents of the U.S. evaluated American Indians in no less merciless a manner.[142] The most ferocious judgement on the Native Indians is certainly the one by President Andrew Jackson:

> My original convictions upon this subject have been confirmed by the course of events for several years, and experience is every day adding to their strength. That those tribes cannot exist surrounded by our settlements and in continual contact with our citizens is certain. They have neither the intelligence, the industry, the moral habits, nor the desire of improvement which are essential to any favourable change in their condition. Established in the midst of another and a superior race, and without appreciating the causes of their inferiority or seeking to control them, they must necessarily yield to the force of circumstances and ere long disappear.'

To find some compassionate feelings one must wait for President Lyndon Johnson:

---

142 *Native News Online.net,* 20 February 2017: http://nativenewsonline.net/currents/us-presidents-words-concerning-american-indians (accessed 6 March 2017). See for example the opinions of George Washington, Thomas Jefferson, and Theodore Roosevelt.

The American Indian, once proud and free, is torn now between White and tribal values; between the politics and language of the White man and his own historic culture. His problems, sharpened by years of defeat and exploitation, neglect and inadequate effort, will take many years to overcome.

While compassionate, the quotation conceals something more profound. The Indians, 'once proud and free,' deserved compassion only when they ceased to be 'the enemy' [143] and indeed were in such a condition that they could no longer pose a threat.

This has been a constant attitude of the American establishment towards other people no matter the colour of their skin: black, red, or yellow, and even white; no matter the nature of their political system: democratic, authoritarian, or dictatorial. They are not the enemy, or cease to be the enemy, only so long as their behaviour conforms to the interest of the American establishment. Many dictatorships have been and are still today the friends of the U.S. (Saudi Arabia, Chile's Pinochet, Iran's' Shah, the list could be completed with numerous cases). The Japanese became an official enemy only after the attack on Pearl Harbor and until they were defeated in WW2; then they became one of the most obedient allies of the U.S., starting with the engagement of Japanese officials against North Korea during the Korean War (1950–53).[144] The Germans were the enemy during two world wars, until they were defeated and

---

143 This is not to say that there were not some voices criticizing the slaughter of the Native Indians. For example, *Harper's Weekly* published, on 16 September 1786, an illustration showing a wagon train attacked by Indians with the comment: 'It is undeniable that all our Indian wars have been provoked by the whites. Every treaty made with the Indians has been violated as soon as it was for the interests of the whites to break it. Despoiled of their lands, demoralized by whiskey, taught treachery and fraud by the "superior race," it is but natural that they should fight for the possession of their lands.' *Harper's Weekly* was a popular American political magazine based in New York City. Published by Harper & Brothers from 1857 until 1916; it featured foreign and domestic news, fiction, essays on many subjects, and humour, alongside illustrations. Nevertheless, such comments were very rare at that time.
144 When we know that Korea suffered from the Japanese colonization, established at the beginning of the 20th century, under the benevolent eye of the U.S., we can understand the feeling of the North Korean leadership towards the U.S., and why they are so keen in developing all the power resources they can to avoid another aggression. See A.B. Abrams, *Immovable Object: North Korea's 70 Years at War With American Power,* Atlanta, Clarity Press, 2020.

became one of the best allies of the U.S.[145] The case of the Russians is particularly revealing: ideological and political enemies after the Bolshevik Revolution that threatened to destroy the capitalist economy by putting an end to the private ownership of capital, they turned into allies during WW2 when needed to defeat Nazi Germany, then became enemies again during the Cold War. Once again they were friends during the marvellous Boris Yeltsin' years (1990s) when the U.S. praised Russia for introducing democracy and capitalism, and especially for opening the country to American (and more generally to Western) investors, speculators, multinationals, economic advisers, and NGOs that rushed to Russia as a territory to be conquered. The result was the seizure of a significant portion of the wealth of Russia, often with the support of new local oligarchs, and the accession to NATO of several Eastern European countries representing the culminating point of the strategy of encirclement of Russia. When Putin put an end to this process, Russia returned to its role of the U.S.'s mortal enemy which it had acquired after the Bolshevik Revolution, Russian democracy and capitalist system notwithstanding

Finally, there is the case of the U.S. relationship with China which I will analyse in greater detail in chapter 3. For the moment it suffices to point out the changing attitude of the U.S. towards China: first between the founding of the U.S. Republic and the beginning of the 20th century as a country to be civilized and conquered, then as an informal ally to be protected from the Communists of Mao and then from the Japanese, and finally, after the victory of Mao in the Civil War, as an enemy to be contained. To implement this policy the U.S. started by allowing the loser, Chiang Kai-shek, to retain under his authority in a part of China, Taiwan.[146] It was the first move to encircle China.

In fact, we are here at the heart of 'the American original sin.' It is not so much the 'Negros' slavery' and the 'Native Indian ethnic cleansing' that are the essence of the sin. They are certainly part of it, but

---

145 Look at the way U.S. propaganda during WW1 that presented the Germans as a nation of savages. See Creel (2012) with the significant title: *How We Advertised America: The First Telling of the Amazing Story of the Committee on Public Information That Carried the Gospel of Americanism to Every Corner of the Globe Corner,* Forgotten Books (Classic Reprint). Retrieved from https://www.forgottenbooks.com/en (first edition 1920); see also Ponsonby 1928.
146 It is interesting to note that this is not what happened at the end of the American Civil War, when the victorious North acquired sovereignty over the whole of the territory of the U.S. Republic.

they are both founded upon the primary partition between 'We' and the 'Others,' we the 'good people' and they, the 'rogue people and states,' the 'Good' and the 'Evil,' that is at the heart of the American ideology, as I will explain in chapter 2 below.

WESTERN MYTHS ABOUT CHINA

Several myths are often used in the West to describe China, its ideology, the nature of its political system, and its behaviour in international affairs. I will start with the myth that is used by both the West and China. On the one hand, the West believes that the Chinese consider their civilization and culture as superior to any other cultures, and on the other, the Chinese themselves think that their own civilization is superior to any other cultures, whose peoples are, moreover, considered as 'barbarians.' Afterwards, we will analyse the following myths:

- the myth that China today is a dictatorship,
- the myth that China has developed a state-capitalist economy,
- the myth that China is only able to imitate the West, especially in science and technology,
- the myth that China's middle class will one day demand a democratic political system,
- the myth that China wants today to impose its political and economic model on the rest of the world, and finally the most fearful of them all,
- the myth that China is implementing an imperial foreign policy aimed at replacing the U.S. as a world hegemon.

Let us examine to what extent these myths correspond to the Chinese reality.

THE MYTH OF THE SUPERIORITY OF CHINESE CIVILIZATION AND CULTURE

This myth, when put forward by American pundits, is based upon an analogy with American exceptionalism that, as we will see in Chapter 2, is an important feature of the American ideology. The consequence is that the U.S. feels called upon to project a sense of its own superiority, as well as the will, and even the right, to diffuse American values all over the world. The same faith in the exceptional character of one's own culture is attributed to China. It is a typical case, very frequent in the West, to attribute to other countries the same behaviour the West has manifested in similar circumstances: that when China will have developed enough power resources, it will act as the West has done since the discovery of the Americas, and even more so since the U.S. emerged from WW2 as the primary world power. Today, this time has come for China! So, the myth says, Chinese exceptionalism will drive the Chinese leadership to manifest, *mutatis mutandi*, the same kind of behaviour typical of the West during the last 5 centuries.

Of course, the Chinese are indeed proud of their country, and 'believe in China's exceptionalism, based on its different history and culture that is perhaps seen as superior to the West.'[147] But this is not a significant position. I do not know of any people who do not think that their own country is exceptional: the French, the British, the Germans, the Italians, even the citizens of small Switzerland share the same feeling. Where the difference lies between the U.S. and China in that regard is that China has never, so far, tried to conquer militarily the rest of the world, or to change it in its own image. Exceptionalism, yes, but no 'manifest destiny' giving the right and the duty to 'expand' and to impose its values and its rules on the rest of the world.[148] China's Imperial leadership was quite satisfied with its culture and felt no need to change it. It did not want to militarily conquer other countries, nor to mix its economy and polity with other countries, especially distant ones such as England.

Two examples to illustrate this posture. In 1662 Emperor Kangxi authorized Christian missionaries to preach in China. Unfortunately, on 19 May 1715 Pope Clement XI published a bull that condemned the Chinese rites, thus making them incompatible with the Catholic faith. Reading a Chinese translation of the bull, Emperor Kangxi is reported to have added a note saying:

> After reading this decision, I wonder how these uncivilized Western people can talk about the great philosophical and moral principles of China [...] Most of their words and arguments are ridiculous. In light of this decision, I finally found

---

147 For example Harris 2014, p. 5.
148 'To expand' is taken from a statement made by President Jefferson in 1801 in a letter to the governor of Virginia, James Monroe, I will deal with in Chapter 2.

that their doctrine is of the same kind as the petty heresies of the Buddhist and Taoist monks. We have never seen such a nonsense. From now on I forbid Westerners to spread their doctrine in China. This will avoid much hassle.[149]

The second example concerns the mission sent to China in 1792 by King George III of Great Britain to Emperor Qianlong with the aim of further opening up trade between the two countries, which at that time was limited to the port of Canton. The interaction between the British ambassador, Lord Macartney, and the Chinese Emperor, is an interesting case that shows with what arrogance the two empires saw each other, both based upon an unshakable sense of superiority. The Emperor arrogantly looked down on the British 'barbarians' as representatives of a secondary power, not understanding that the Chinese Empire was already on the decline. The British behaved no less arrogantly, proud of their modern technology (including their military), but not daring (yet) to frontally impose their will.[150] According to Platt, mountains of gifts were exchanged. The British came with the products of their finest technology with the intent to impress the Chinese. Their representative, Macartney, made it clear that unfortunately the goal of the mission was to negotiate for more advantageous trade policies in the future and to establish a permanent British minister in Beijing. The Emperor reciprocated with a quantity of gifts, silks, porcelain and tea, considering that, according to a well-established custom with other countries, the meeting was limited to the exchange of gifts, and that the British would simply take theirs home and sell them.

Macartney learned that he was not the only ambassador in attendance, but he did not understand that these countries had not come to impress the Emperor, but rather to seek the Emperor's approval, which would give them political clout back home. He had no idea how deeply he had offended the Emperor with his 'negotiations.' No surprise then that the Emperor, while not revoking Britain's existing privileges, rejected all of the British requests: 'When foreigners who come seeking

---

149 Gernet 1991, pp. 252–53.
150 Platt 2018, pp. 15–44. The following quotations are from pp. 38, 41 and 40. Stephen Platt gives a detailed account of the 2-year British mission. The whole book is a must for those who want to understand the origins of the first Opium War and find an answer to the question: was it inevitable? More generally, the book is a brilliant analysis of the transition from the decline of the Chinese Empire and the rise of Imperial Britain.

audience with me are sincere and submissive, then I always treat them with kindness (...) but if they come in arrogance, they get nothing.' Macartney had to return to England without daring to further offend the Emperor, fearing that this might have had the consequence of damaging the already existing trade with China. But on his way back home he could not help writing in his journal, with no less arrogance: 'Can they be ignorant that a couple of British frigates would be an overmatch for the whole naval force of their empire, that in half a summer they could totally destroy the navigation of their coasts and reduce the inhabitants of the maritime provinces, who subsist chiefly on fish, to absolute famine?' This would in fact occur in less than half a century with the first Opium War (1839–1842).

Nevertheless, it would be wrong to say that China was not interested in some aspects of Western culture, such as paintings, architectures, mobile objects, and musical instruments. The Museum adjacent to the Forbidden City exhibits a large number of these objects collected by the Chinese Emperors, including several grand pianos. Moreover, Emperor Qianlong entrusted the Italian painter, Giuseppe Castiglione, with the task of conceiving the impressive Western-style palaces in the Eastern part of the Summer Palace Park. But it is true that Imperial China was quite satisfied with its culture and did not want to militarily conquer a territory 'over which the sun never sets,' which is a proclaimed feature of the British and the French colonial empires. At the end of this chapter, I will further develop this point when dealing with the myth that China's strategy goal is to dominate the world, as a consequence of its sense of cultural superiority. Moreover, I will deal with this myth in Chapter 3 in relation to the Belt and Road Initiative, that many in the West interpret as the means used by China to dominate the world.[151]

The Myth of China Being Today a Dictatorship

It is easy, and trivial, to confirm that the Communist Party of China (CPC) has constituted the dominant group within Chinese society throughout the life of the People's Republic of China (PRC) from Mao to the present. In short, the Party controls, still today, large spans of the Chinese system: its socio-biological, economic, legal, cultural and communication structures.[152] This is true in spite of the numerous changes

151 Hancock 2017, writing for the *Financial Times,* used the significant title: 'Silk Road: China encircles the world with One Belt, One Road strategy.'
152 Urio 2019, pp. 43–82.

that have been introduced within Chinese society and its power structure. Many Western and especially American scholars point to the non-democratic, authoritarian or even totalitarian power of the CPC to explain its present difficulties and, even more, the coming of the inevitable collapse of the PRC.[153] Even today this attitude persists in spite of the astonishing improvements in the social and economic living conditions of the Chinese people, and the quality of the decision-making process that has oriented the public policies implemented in China since Deng's reforms.

As we have seen dealing with the reality of democracy in the West and more particularly the U.S., the U.S. has the habit of interpreting events in China based on the evaluation system and the parameters of its own world instead of evaluating China on the basis of China's principles.

There is little point in evaluating China's power by using the standards of Western liberal democracy. This has been done by numerous Western scholars. Certainly, their analyses contribute to the understanding of China, but only in part. Indeed, these analyses point out China's weaknesses that they contend will inevitably cause it to collapse, unless it changes according to Western values. But they fail to explain why and how China, notwithstanding, has managed to keep to the road it has chosen by constantly adapting the management of its economy, polity and society to changing domestic and international conditions. Contrary to China critics' forecasts, the collapse of China is not coming soon ... doubtfully ever to occur in the foreseeable future.

It's more interesting and pertinent to analyse how the Party has managed to bring about reforms and the related changes in China's society, while safeguarding the Chinese fundamental values of harmony, unity, stability—and to find out whether this has improved the living conditions of the Chinese people. By doing so, we will see how China's power is exercised in a very different manner from that of dictatorship, as often contended by Western scholars and mainstream media. It is true that the control the Party has over the system of power constitutes an obstacle to the introduction of liberal democracy in China. But does China need a liberal democracy for improving the living conditions of its population and for sustaining the market mechanisms it has in fact introduced into its economy?[154] Would it not be sufficient to take advantage of

153 For example: Chang 2001 and 2006, Wolton 2007, Sorman 2008.
154 Joseph Stiglitz's book on the crisis also uses 'market mechanisms' when referring to the reform introduced in East Asian countries, including China: Stiglitz 2010, p. 245.

the economic and social efficiency the market mechanisms provide—but regulated by the State so that it produces what society needs instead of allowing a small minority to enrich itself while large parts of society suffer from poverty, underemployment, and lack of affordable public services? Is this not an important step towards a society where people would be freed from fear and want, as stated in paragraph 2 of the Preamble of the Universal Declaration? The answer is, so far, clearly yes, if we examine China's experience after 1949, and even more so since 1978, as we will do, below.

In the process of introducing the market mechanisms, the Party has taken, implemented, and monitored all the decisions. But, as is the case with Western liberal democracies, the relationship between the Party-State and the people is by no means a one-way one, in which the Party-State gives orders, and the citizens obey. Ever since the Mao era, the goal of the Party-State has been to restore China's power and to provide the Chinese People with better living conditions, the two objectives being strictly linked to each other in a two-way causal relationship. This is the source of legitimacy for the Party-State that had already been obtained during the Mao era, although its limited economic results were overshadowed by the mistakes of the Great Leap Forward and of the Cultural Revolution. In this perspective, Deng's choice in favour of market mechanisms is strictly in line with the objectives of Mao's strategy: restore a strong China, able to avoid the aggressions against it of the 19th century.[155] Only the means differ.

Of course, by introducing market mechanisms within its economy, China has automatically given more freedom to the people in this domain. One of the consequences have been the emergence of professional associations, which are not really a novelty for China as similar organizations already existed under the Imperial regime and during the first half of the twentieth century.[156] Moreover, mass organizations such as the Trade Unions and the All-China Women's Federation have developed many activities all over China that are linked to the changes in Chinese society after the introduction of market mechanisms, even if these are Party organizations. For example, following the increasing number of divorces that are, at least financially, more harmful to women, and following the emergence of unemployment (that touches more women than

---

155 'Ours will no longer be a nation subject to insult and humiliation. We have stood up,' Mao Zedong (1949).
156 Bergère 1986, 2007.

men) the Women's Federation has implemented a variety of activities aimed at helping women who suffer from their consequences. Similarly, the partial retreat of the State from the social domain has given way to an increasing number of Non-Governmental and Non-profit organizations. Changes have also been introduced into the socio-biological and legal structures. By relaxing and then repealing the one-child policy, China has given

> couples the freedom to decide how they want to manage the size of their families.[157] Moreover, the legal structure has progressively introduced important changes such as the right to private property, linked to the introduction of market mechanisms in the economic structure.[158]

The changes that have occurred within the cultural and the communication structures are even more interesting. As happens in the West, the dominant group (the Party) seeks control over the production of ideas, values, and the intellectual means for understanding and eventually supporting the way society is organized. On the one hand, the Party seeks to ensure that representations of reality produced and diffused by publications, film, broadcasting, think tanks, mass media, internet, NGOs and teaching institutions at all levels are not contradictory to the power structure and the public policies of the state. But this is due to Chinese awareness that these channels may used to diffuse ideas with subversive potential, or even to promote regime change, practices the West has unfortunately deployed against targeted states for a long time.[159] Precedents in China including the U.S. interventions in Tibet in the 1950s and in Hong Kong since the 1980s have not been forgotten, while the more recent Western (especially U.S.) interventions in Hong Kong and in Xinjiang have made it increasingly difficult for China to accept interferences within its national territory that have the clear intention of supporting Hong Kong and Xinjiang political secessionist groups, which eventually would also drive a regime change in China. Additional control means have been introduced by Xi Jinping, such as by security cameras

---

157 The one-child policy had only been implemented in the urban areas and not in countryside, where a second child was allowed under certain conditions. Notably, ethnic minorities such as the Uighurs were not subjected to this policy.
158 Peerenboom 2002, 2006, 2007.
159 Urio and Ying 2014.

and surveillance systems, means not dissimilar to those used in the West, and more particularly by the U.S.[160] After facing months of social and political unrest, in 2020 Beijing passed a security law for Hong Kong. The West and the U.S. reacted violently, oblivious to the natural interest that China has in preserving the integrity of its national territory. Indeed, the U.S. would react similarly if China were to interfere in U.S. internal affairs by supporting the protest movements that have been erupting in the U.S. over the years, and in particular during the last months of the Trump administration and the months afterward. Ever since 1949 China has been surrounded by an increasing number of U.S. military bases, and has been the target of numerous U.S. economic sanctions and several attempted cases of subversion, still going on today. Add to this the West's support for subversive movements on the Chinese mainland, you will understand why China is forced to enact security measures in order to safeguard its sovereignty. History shows that most powers, even the more democratic, use all the means (legal and illegal) at their disposal to fight against real or perceived existential threats to their sovereignty.[161]

The reason the West puts forward to justify its criticisms and interferences within China is that the Western political system is not only better (whatever the criteria used) than the Chinese one, but also, per Fukuyama's notion of "the end of history," the Western system is also inevitable, insofar as all countries are inexorably and ultimately driven to adopt a liberal democracy and market economy. Furthermore, as Western pundits acknowledge, China is presently at a difficult stage of its economic and social development, insofar as Chinese society is

---

160 Two articles published by the *Monde Diplomatique* on these practices show very clearly the similarity between the West and China: Zuboff (2019a), Raphaël and Ling Xi (2019).

161 During the Cold War, Switzerland, a neutral country but de facto aligned with the NATO military strategy, feared a Soviet invasion, mirroring the mood that prevailed in the West at that time. In order to be ready to face this possibility the Swiss government took two illegal measures of great importance, considering the Swiss liberal democratic system based upon the rule of law: it set up an illegal army (as other European countries had done during the Cold War) and illegally spied on thousands of its own left-wing citizens. This last measure was clearly based upon historical precedents reflecting the reality that an invading country always finds within the country it invades a significant part of the local elite ready to cooperate. It was therefore predicted that the Soviet Marxist invader would find some support from that part of the Swiss elite who would share basically the same leftist profile. When these illegal measures were discovered, they were met by a general outrage: democracy does not tolerate illegality, nevertheless ...

more open than when Deng started its reforms at the end of the 1970s. Therefore, a further relaxation of societal control will open the door to internal and external forces critical of the present power structure. It is significant that the Party has cracked down on both neo-Maoist and neo-liberal movements. Western media has only condemned the crackdown on neoliberal movements, while remaining silent on the curtailment of neo-Maoist elements. Needless to say, China still bears in mind the negative consequences Russia experienced in the 1990s at the time of its opening up, thanks to the shock therapy promoted by self-proclaimed Western experts, that dramatically decreased its GDP and skyrocketed the rate of poverty.

While it was easy to master the introduction of market mechanisms at the beginning of the reform process, today, Western experts warn, the Chinese economy has become so complex (as has the Western one) that it needs additional and more in-depth reforms, or the system will collapse. Clearly, the implication is that this necessitates a freer market economy, with further opening to the global economy, especially to the financial system, as strongly recommended by the World Bank, and all this sustained by liberal democracy.[162]

Here the important considerations are: first, what are the benefits for the Chinese people of the reforms introduced since 1978, and second, does the Party enjoy the approval and support of the majority of the Chinese people? It's a well recognized fact that remarkable improvements in the standard of living of the Chinese people have been realized, especially after the reform started in the 1980s, and accelerated after the 1997 Party Congress. What, then, has been the reaction of the Chinese population? While official records show an increasing number of protest movements throughout the country, these are mainly due to the difficulties the Chinese leadership had, at least until the Xi Jinping era, to combat illegal and immoral behaviour on the part of those, especially but not only at the local level, who were ruthlessly profiting from the opportunities (i.e., from more freedom) offered by the reforms of the economy, as reflected in increased corruption, the illegal sale of land to real estate promoters and consequent destruction of old habitations and the displacement of the tenants, non-payment of wages to migrant workers, etc.

In spite of these problems, which the Party-State has been taking very seriously under the leadership of Xi Jinping, the majority of the

___
162 World Bank 2012.

Chinese people seem to support the development strategy set up by the Party-State. The support that the Party-State enjoys from the Chinese citizen cannot be denied. It seems that the rebalancing policies have achieved the intended goal.[163] Clearly, there are not throughout the country the vast protest movements against the regime that many naïve Western observers have ceaselessly predicted throughout the history of the PRC, basing their forecasts mainly on the conception of the freedom that is dominant in the West.[164] But it seems that the Chinese people prioritize economic development as a means of achieving freedom and human rights: seeing these in terms of freedom from poverty and hunger, and the human right to health care and education. This orientation has consistently been followed by the Chinese leadership.

The Myth that China Has Developed a State-Capitalist Economy

To deal with this myth I return to the analysis of Fernand Braudel, whose views were earlier addressed concerning the myth of the free market. Again, in his historical analysis of the production and consumption processes Braudel noted the coexistence of three layers of economic activity: material life, market and capitalism, and that there is a substantial difference between a market economy and capitalism. According to Braudel, only when one of the three layers acquires a dominant role can we use its name to describe the whole economic system: material economy before the advent of market economy, market economy before the advent of capitalism, capitalism when the upper layer succeeds in dominating the two subordinate layers. The difficulty arises when we have to decide at what point in time the characteristics of one layer have become so widespread and important that it has become the dominating layer.

Many Western pundits addressing China's economic development consider that a market economy is equivalent to capitalism, and therefore conclude that China's economy has become capitalist, even if they are compelled to qualify this statement by terming it 'state capitalism.' It

---

163 Cunningham, Saich and Turiel 2020, Saich 2016; Forsythe 2015. More on this point below: The myth that China middle class will demand one day a liberal democratic political system.

164 The *South China Morning Post* has published several articles about this type of social protest movements, as well as on the more invasive control the Party is today exerting on social dissent.

seems that this conclusion is quite superficial. According to Braudel, during the historical process that modifies the organization of the relation between production and consumption, the scope of market economy may be limited by three phenomena: by the persistence of importance sectors of material life; by the state, which can take part in the production process to fulfil its own needs or to address needs it regards as of benefit to the people whether directly or through economic policy; or even more so by the role of money that can artificially intervene in price formation in thousands of different ways, which is one of the main features of capitalism. So, we can say that a market economy can be limited from below by the extent of material life within the society, as well as from above by those holding the reins of capitalism and/or by state intervention.[165] In the West the limitations on the market economy have been imposed from above by the neoliberal capitalistic New Public Management, with the help of the state, that has in fact been privatized by the economic actors. In China the limitations on the market have been introduced from the beginning of the 1980s by the Party-State, that has reserved for itself the task of controlling, orienting and limiting the role of demand and supply in the economy. This is why I consider that China has not (yet) developed a true market economy but has simply introduced into its economy some market mechanisms.

Indeed, following Braudel's approach, it would be only partially correct to talk about the 'Chinese market economy.' It is true that China has introduced some market characteristics (i.e., competition and transparency) into parts of its economy. It is for this reason that the Chinese government has for a long time been asking the Western governments to recognize its economy as a market economy. Nevertheless, the market economy covers only part of China's economic system. Indeed, it is also true that markets do not exist in other parts of China's economy, as they are in fact owned by, or under the monopolistic control of the Party-State. On the other hand, it is also true that in some parts of China's economy some new capitalists are quite active and control pricing to a certain extent by using monopolistic or quasi-monopolistic strategies.[166] So again, while some Western authors use this situation to describe the Chinese economy as a 'state capitalism' this is certainly not the case, as I will explain hereafter.

---

165 Braudel 1979a, vol. 2, p. 262.
166 Dickson 2003, 2008.

Using 'market economy' to describe the Chinese system risks implying that China's economy is similar to the Western one, or that it is at least moving in that direction. Indeed, when referring to the partial abandonment of the planned economy of the Mao era, and to the opening up of economic activities to private entrepreneurship and capital (both domestic and foreign) it conforms more to the reality of China's economy to qualify these innovations as 'market mechanisms' instead of a true adoption of a 'market economy.'[167] The form of economic organization that has emerged in China after 1978 is by no means a capitalist market economy, but rather should be viewed as a 'socialist market economy,' which is very different from the 'capitalist market economy' of the West. Many features of the new China system point in this direction:

- The freedom of the new Chinese capitalists mentioned above is limited by the Party-State: nothing can be done in the economic sphere without the explicit or implicit approval of the Party-State.[168] Contrary to what happened in the transition from the Soviet Union to today's Russia, in China, economic reforms introducing market mechanisms have been decided, implemented, developed and controlled by the Communist Party-State for a period of more than 70 years with demonstrated success. There is evidence that the majority of Chinese capitalists have no reasons for opposing the Party, as it seems that the policies of the Party-State underpin their economic and social success (Jie Chen and Dickson 2008).[169]

- Land is still collective property held by the state in China, and this constitutes a powerful instrument in the hands of the Party-State for orienting and controlling economic and social development.

- Since the mid-1990s and even more so since the 2000s, the Party-State has reoriented its public policies away from a strategy of 'economic development first' towards a strategy of

---

167 Stiglitz 2010, p. 245. I was pleased to see, on reading Joseph Stiglitz's book on the crisis, that he also uses 'market mechanisms' when referring to the reform introduced in East Asian countries, including China: Joseph E. Stiglitz, *Freefall*, p. 245.

168 See for example: Longling Wei, 'China Eyes Shrinking Jack Ma's Business Empire,' *Wall Street Journal*, 29 December 2020. https://www.wsj.com/articles/china-eyes-shrinking-jack-mas-business-empire-11609260092?mod=djemalertNEWS, accessed 29 December 2020.

169 Jie Chen and Dickson 2008.

'putting people first,' marking a clear departure from the neoliberal policies in strategic domains such as health and education that were carried out between the beginning of reforms until the mid-1990s. Moreover, the Party has started to replace the social functions of the state-owned enterprises of the Mao era with a modern safety net.[170]

- The banking system is still under the political control of the Party-State, despite several measures taken for improving its economic efficiency that have given to Western observers the impression that it was progressively being reformed in order to make it compatible with capitalist criteria.

This predominance of the Party-State is a very clear indicator that the Chinese economy is by no means a capitalist economy. It is important to bear in mind that while some important but not dominant capitalist economic agents are present in elements of material life (i.e., in large sectors of the informal economy), these market mechanisms have been introduced by a dominant Party-State that occupies a large sector of the economy and orients and controls the development of China's economic activities. This clearly indicates several differences from what happens in the West, where the economic agents of capitalism dictate the essential items of the political agenda and content of public policies, as the ways the West has managed the 2008 financial crisis and the 2020 Covid-19 crisis clearly demonstrate.[171] The features of the present-day Chinese economic and political systems mentioned above are clear indicators of the progressive implementation of a 'socialist market economy,' in which the economic side enables the development of market mechanisms under the control of the Party-State (and not of a neoliberal elite), and the socialist side intervenes by policies that 'put people first.'

Of course, this does not mean that there are no problems in the management and control of the interface between material life, the informal economy, market mechanisms and capitalist elements of the Chinese economic system. However so far, the capitalist elements are not yet sufficiently widespread and important to qualify China's economic system as a capitalist economy, whatever the further qualifying adjective. For the time being, the difference between China and the West is therefore one of nature. The two systems cannot be considered as

---

170 Urio 2010 pp. 119–52, Urio 2019, pp. 119–51.
171 Prins 2011 and 2018. See note 68 above and Takian et al. 2021.

simple variations within the type of 'capitalist economy.' This does not mean either that the Chinese system may not evolve towards a capitalist economy in the future; but for the time being many indicators point to the opposite direction.

THE MYTH THAT CHINA IS ONLY ABLE TO IMITATE THE WEST

This is a statement that Western pundits have asserted for a long time. It is true that China started the development of its economy by investing in intensive labour activities requiring a relative low level of skills. Inevitably imitation occurred in sectors where it facilitated speedier development, given the context then existing. Nevertheless, since the Mao era, China has invested in its population, which has proved a decisive factor for its development of a modern economy. Health and education have shown a spectacular improvement.[172] Moreover, by 1963, Zhou Enlai had already defined the Four Modernizations: in agriculture, industry, science and technology, and defence.[173] The West did not take this statement very seriously, considering it a manifestation of Communist propaganda. But the decades that followed demonstrated that the Four Modernizations were fundamental objectives in order to avoid the 100 years of humiliation that began with the first Opium War (1839–42). They oriented China's leadership towards developing the most important power resources.

In 2006, five decades after the announcement of the Four Modernizations, the State Assets Supervision and Administration Commission (SASAC) published a list of seven sectors critical to the national economy and in which public ownership was considered essential: armaments, electrical power and distribution, oil and chemicals, telecommunications, coal, aviation, and shipping.[174]

---

172 During the Mao era life expectancy increased from 35 to 61 years, and adult literacy increased from as low as 20 per cent to about 70 per cent. These are approximate figures, as data of this period are not totally reliable according to most scholars. But the scope of the improvement is not debated.

173 At the Conference on Scientific and Technological Work held in Shanghai in January 1963, Zhou Enlai called for professionals in the sciences to realize "the Four Modernizations." In February 1963, at the National Conference on Agricultural Science and Technology Work, Nie Rongzhen specifically referred to the Four Modernizations as comprising agriculture, industry, national defense, and science and technology. The Cultural Revolution prevented and delayed implementation of the Four Modernizations for years. In 1975, in one of his last public acts, Zhou Enlai made another pitch for the Four Modernizations at the 4th National People's Congress (from Wikipedia under 'Four Modernizations').

174 In 2011 the SASAC announced 7 strategic industries that would receive

In his speech at the 2007 Party Congress, President Hu Jintao insisted upon the necessity for China to improve its economy by developing innovations independently from the West in many crucial domains, such as: re-balancing between regions, general management, banks, enterprises and their modernization, the army, science and technology, Chinese investments abroad, and use of Foreign Direct Investments (FDI) in China.

In 2008 China launched the Thousand Talents Programme, with the declared purpose of strengthening innovation and international competitiveness, by attracting to China scientists, academics and entrepreneurs, both foreigners and Chinese nationals living abroad—a clear sign that China would not continue to imitate the West. This ambitious programme targeted top level academics with a well-established international reputation.

In 2017, less than a decade after the launching of the Thousand Talents Programme *Forbes* considered that China was becoming attractive to global talent on an unprecedented level because of the nation's economic size and vibrancy,[175] predicting that the country would become a major exchange hub for global talent flow by 2022:

> By that time, China will be not only the largest export country of students studying abroad, but also a major destination for global talent to settle down. China's role as a hub in global talent mobility will further consolidate, and it will help the country to integrate its educational resources globally. Meanwhile, it will provide more competitive job opportunities for overseas talent,' said Russell Flannery, Shanghai bureau chief of *Forbes China*.[176]

---

new support from the government: energy saving and environmental protection (clean energy technology); next generation IT (modernization of the country's telecommunications infrastructure); bio-technology (pharma and vaccine manufacturers); high-tech equipment (airplanes, satellites, manufacturing technology); new energy (nuclear, wind, solar); new materials (rare earths); and new energy cars, i.e. electric and hybrid cars, and batteries. *Xinhua*, updated: 18 December 2006.

175 *Forbes, The 2018 Global Talent Mobility and Wealth Management Report.*
176 According to the *Straits Times* (Singapore), 24 October 2017 (https://www.straitstimes.com/asia/east-asia/china-a-strong-magnet-for-global-talent-forbes-report), accessed 20 December 2018.

By 2015, the recruitment of scholars and scientists trained in the U.S., and employed in China in sensitive high-tech domains, was raising some serious concerns in the U.S., to the point that the FBI devoted special attention to the Chinese 'talent programmes' within its Counterintelligence Division.[177] It is interesting to note that in September 2015, only 5 months after China's announcement of its 'Made in China 2015' programme (to be dealt with hereunder), the FBI issued a note entitled 'Chinese Talent Programs.' This was a sign that, at last, competent people in the West were aware of the threat that China was posing to the U.S. dominant role in science and technology.

In this note the FBI considered that recruiting scholars and scientists in the U.S. allowed China to: (1) gain access to research and expertise for cutting edge technology; (2) benefit from years of scientific research conducted in the United States supported by U.S. Government grants and private funding; and (3) severely impact the U.S. economy. The FBI note providing an overview of the reason why this programme poses a variety of potential threats to the U.S. is even more interesting. While the FBI concedes that it is important to conduct collaborative research, its note points out that it is vital for the survival of U.S. businesses and universities that they protect their information and mitigate lost or stolen information. In the last part of its note, the FBI explains how businesses and universities can protect themselves. The consequence of this situation, worsened by the U.S.-China trade war, is that it has become more difficult for Chinese scholars to obtain a visa, and 'fewer U.S. Universities are willing to accept Chinese visiting scholars, and U.S. professors are reluctant to invite Chinese since it may trigger an investigation.'[178]

The U.S. worries were further confirmed in May 2015 when China published a strategy for transforming China into a modern economy, based upon technological innovation. This was defined in a document called "Made in China 2015."[179] This project, made public only 19 months after the announcement of the Belt and Road Initiative (BRI) (to be dealt with in Chapter 3), is a ten-year comprehensive blueprint

---

177 FBI 2015.
178 Huang and Lo 2019.
179 Information on this project can be found in the *Financial Times;* the American Enterprise Institute; the Council of Foreign Affairs (its journal *Foreign Affairs*); Mercator Institute for China Studies (MERICS), the *South China Morning Post,* the *Caixin* magazine, and the official Chinese websites such as the official news agency, *Xinhua.*

aimed at transforming China into an advanced manufacturing leader.[180] This plan defines several key domains in which China has decided to develop first-class technologies. It consists of eight broad domains, subdivided into 22 sectors: (1) Biotechnology; (2) Information Technology (3) Advanced Materials Technology; (4) Advanced Manufacturing Technology; (5) Advanced Energy Technology; (6) Marine Technology; (7) Lasers Technology; and (8) Aerospace technology.

Reading this list, one can well understand the importance the Chinese government attributes to this vast programme, and the challenge it constitutes to the West, especially to the U.S., should it wish to maintain its dominant role in the world, as is indeed the case. The impact that this project has made on the West, on governments, think tanks, media, and scholars is attested to by the numerous reactions, statements, analyses, and even bombastic declarations, as this project is much more than one simply limited to technology improvements.

In fact, if and when fully realized, this project will have an impact on practically all the dimensions that determine the power of a country and therefore its relations with other countries. This is especially true for the U.S. which for a long time has considered itself as the 'indispensable' dominating power and which tries to perpetuate the character of the world it made.[181] Even if many pundits in the West have put forward doubts about the capacity of China to realize this project, especially after the U.S. declared a trade war on China, and more particularly in sectors mentioned in Made in China 2015, the worries that were already evident in the 2015 FBI note have not vanished, as the speech given by Vice-President Mike Pence 4 October 2018 at the Hudson Institute very well demonstrates.[182] This speech shows that, if necessary, the trade war between the U.S. and China could become much more than a trade war.

180 PRC 2015c.
181 European Chamber 2017, U.S. Chamber of Commerce 2017, Wübbeke 2016, PRC 2015c, Hu Angang and Ren Hao 2016.
182 Pence 2018. The Hudson Institute is a politically conservative, nonprofit American think tank based in Washington, D.C. It was founded in 1961 in Croton-on-Hudson, New York, by futurist, military strategist, and systems theorist Herman Kahn and his colleagues at the RAND Corporation. According to its website, the Institute is committed to innovative research and analysis that promotes 'global security, prosperity and freedom.' It promotes public policy change in accordance with its stated belief that "America's unique and central role in the global system offers the best foundation for security, the defence of liberty, and assuring economic growth.,' https://en.wikipedia.org/wiki/Hudson_Institute, accessed 15 January 2019.

In fact, this speech is a foreign policy statement addressed to the Chinese leadership with a view to forcing it to comply with U.S. demands. This speech can be considered as a neoconservative document confirming the imperial policy the U.S. has been implementing for a very long time. It has subsequently been confirmed by other speeches and by foreign policy statements by President Biden, as mentioned above.

In fact, what worries the West is that today there is sufficient information to demonstrate that China has already made several improvements in the mastering of high technology in several sectors mentioned in the project. Two specialists of strategic innovation had already warned that 'today every senior executive of a Western corporation needs to understand the tidal wave of innovation flowing from China that is about to engulf Western markets (…) We believe this challenge is unprecedented in the global economy and more substantial and longer lasting than the Japanese challenge of the 1970s.'[183] The advance of China's high-tech technology was recognized by the 2018 Annual Report to Congress on *U.S.-China Economic and Security Review Commission,*[184] that introduced for the first time a new chapter entitled *China High-Tech Development*. This Report made clear that there is a direct link between 'Made in China 2015' not only to trade, but also to the capacity of China to develop high-tech military resources. Moreover, this Report has recognized that China's high-tech project is meant to strengthen the BRI, the global Chinese strategy that will connect China with the rest of the world, enabling China to sustain competition from any country, including from the U.S.[185] Here are a few examples that show the domains in which China has made and is still making significant improvements.

Transportation: 'Beijing has spent an estimated $58.8 bn subsidizing its electric car industry over the past decades (…) creating the world's largest market for electric cars as well as a dominant position in batteries, surpassing Japan and South Korea. Subsidies also helped propel Chinese solar makers into the ranks of the world's largest producer,

---

183 Yip and Mickern 2016, p. 3.
184 U.S. 2018b.
185 I will not deal with the question as to know whether China has already surpassed the U.S. in all the domains which constitute a country's Comprehensive National Power, as what is certain is that China is likely to develop an economy as powerful as that of the U.S., unless China makes some serious mistakes. Considering how China has, so far, avoided to make such mistakes, it is more interesting to evaluate how it is organizing the development of its power resources. This is exactly what I will do in Chapter 3.

overtaking competitors in the U.S. and Europe.'[186] At the beginning of 2021 China presented its prototype maglev train based upon magnetic levitation technology which is forecasted to attain 800 km/h.[187] Great! But did you know that China started to work on this technology in the early 2000s? This project is part of Beijing's ambitious plan to create faster links between cities. Japan is also developing maglev trains, but Chinese scientists who are developing this technology in China said that theirs is less expensive.

Vaccine production: As a consequence of the Covid-19 pandemic, China has accelerated its production of vaccine. In December 2020, Sinopharm announced that it would have the capacity to produce 1 billion doses in 2021. China, contrary to the U.S., which is mainly concerned with the provision of their vaccine to the American population, 'has promised developing countries in Africa, Asia and Latin America priority access to its successful vaccine.'[188] Whereas at the moment of writing it is still too early to ascertain if this promise is likely to be maintained, the volume of production that the Chinese Pharma are apparently able to produce makes this promise potentially plausible, especially as there are at least five vaccines presently developed by Chinese Pharma.

Quantum technology: "Beijing is striving to become a world leader (…) through large-scale state-guided investments, which may total tens of billions of dollars in the years to come. (…) which aims to achieve major breakthroughs in these technologies by 2030. (…) China is also building the *National Laboratory for Quantum Information Sciences*, which, with over $1 billion in initial funding, could emerge as a key centre of gravity for future research and development."[189]

Space exploration: China is also developing its ambitious space exploration programme. China's robotic Chang'e 4 mission touched down on the floor of the 115-mile-wide (186 kilometres) Von Kármán Crater on the moon on 2 January 2019, pulling off the first-ever soft landing on the mysterious lunar far side. To realize this performance, China launched a relay satellite called the Chang'e 1 and Chang'e 2 orbiters in 2007 and 2010, respectively, and pulled off a near-side landing with the Chang'e 3 mission in December 2013. China also launched a return capsule on an eight-day trip around the moon in October 2014,

---

186 Sanderson 2019.
187 Ho Matt 2021.
188 Reuters Staff 2020, Flounders 2020.
189 Kania 2018.

a mission known as Chang'e 5T. That was a test run for the Chang'e 5 sample-return effort, which was successfully launched in December 2020. The landing site contains rocks and soil that fill an important gap for scientists to better understand the Moon's volcanic activities. The mission will verify the viability of manned lunar landing missions, and even the building of a lunar research base.[190]

Energy: here there are three achievements. First, China successfully powered up its "artificial Sun" nuclear fusion reactor for the first time, marking a great advance in the country's nuclear power research capabilities. The HL-2M Tokamak reactor is China's largest and most advanced nuclear fusion experimental research device, and scientists hope that the device can potentially unlock a powerful clean energy source. It uses a powerful magnetic field to fuse hot plasma and can reach temperatures of over 150 million degrees Celsius, according to the *People's Daily*— approximately 10 times hotter than the core of the Sun.[191] *Science Alert* quotes the official *People Daily* saying that 'the development of nuclear fusion energy is not only a way to solve China's strategic energy needs, but also has great significance for the future sustainable development of China's energy and national economy.' Even if the cost of fusion is difficult and prohibitively expensive, as *Science Alert* reminds us, fusion emits no greenhouse gases and carries less risks of accidents or the theft of atomic material. Here again, Chinese scientists have been working on a nuclear fusion reactor since 2006.

Second, since its foundation, China's Renewable Energy Institute has worked to establish the Asia Super Grid across Eurasia and beyond, to support investments, thanks to the exchange of abundant natural renewable energy resources, such as wind, solar and hydropower. This project must be seen in the framework of the Belt and Road Initiative.

Third, the Chinese Institute for High Energy Physics[192] announced in November 2018 plans to build its own particle accelerator, the CEPC (Circular Electron Positron Collider), which will be five times more powerful than the CERN Large Hydron Collider in Switzerland. Two documents describing the project were published in December 2018, after six years of preliminary research.[193] Construction is to be preceded by a five-year 'research and development' phase (2018–2022) during which

---

190 Wall 2019, Deng and Fan 2020, Planetary 2020.
191 *Science Alert* 2020.
192 IHEP 2018, within the Chinese Academy of Sciences.
193 IHEP 2018.

prototypes of key technical components would be built. Construction was expected to start in 2022 and be completed in 2030. The last two projects show that China is ready to cooperate with the World Bank, the Asian Development Bank and international scientists all over the world, indicating that China is on its way to becoming a world leader in high-tech.

Artificial Intelligence (AI): This is the domain that is certainly the most promising sector for China, because it may lead to potential applications in many sectors, including the military. One of the most renowned experts in this domain, Kai-Fu Lee,[194] commented upon China's decision to develop an ambitious plan to build artificial intelligence (AI) capabilities, that. 'when Chinese investors, entrepreneurs, and government officials all focus on one industry, they can truly shake the world. Indeed, China is ramping up AI investments, research, and entrepreneurship on a historic scale. Money for AI start-ups pouring from venture capitalists, tech juggernauts, and Chinese government.' Referring to the decades needed to arrive at today's stage of development, and linking AI with deep learning and big data, Lee considers 'that revolution has finally arrived. It will usher an era of massive productivity increases but also widespread disruptions in labour markets, and profound sociopsychological effects on people, as AI takes over human jobs across all sorts of industries.' Moreover, 'the Chinese government's sweeping plan for becoming an AI superpower pledged widespread support for AI research, but most of all it acted as a beacon to local governments throughout the country to follow suit.' In summary: 'putting all these pieces together (…) China's world-class entrepreneurs and proactive government, I believe that China will soon match or even overtake the U.S. in developing and deploying artificial intelligence. This new AI world order will be particularly jolting to Americans who have grown accustomed to a near-total dominance of the technological sphere.' Rebecca Fannin, a leading expert on global innovation confirmed Lee's analysis and forecast.[195]

---

194 Lee 2018. The quotations are from pp. 5, 17–18. Kai-Fu Lee is chairman and CEO of Sinovation Ventures, a leading technology-savvy investment firm focusing on developing the next generation of Chinese high-tech companies. Before founding Sinovation in 2009, Lee was the president of Google China. Previously he held executive positions at Microsoft, SGI, and Apple.

195 Fannin 2019. In particular, Rebecca Fannin writes: 'Chinese tech entrepreneurs are already charged up enough—crazy work schedules, fire in their bellies, ambition with no boundaries, passion with no end. They make Silicon

THE MYTH THAT CHINA'S MIDDLE CLASS WILL ONE DAY DEMAND A DEMOCRATIC POLITICAL SYSTEM

This Western forecast is based, once again, upon the Western experience, a special instance of the convergence thesis. China's middle class has experienced an impressive increase in its income. Western pundits predict that, as has happened in the West, in the not too distant future it will ask for freedom in the political arena, thus eventually leading to the collapse of the regime. Although this hypothesis cannot be discarded in theory, it is by no means plausible, if we take into consideration the different systems of fundamental values that emerged out of the very different paths along which the Western and the Chinese societies have developed through the centuries. In short, peoples' behaviours tend to be formed by the political culture (or ideology) that transmits to the people the dominant values of the society in which they live, a process governed by those exercising power in any given society.

It is difficult to have a precise idea of the size of the Chinese middle class, as this depends on the definition of the level of income necessary for manifesting purchasing habits similar to those of the middle classes of developed countries. McKinsey has studied the development of China's middle class since the 2000s. Their 2006 study is based upon 2005 data from the National Bureau of Statistics of China on urban households (number of households and their disposable income) for the year 2005.[196] On this basis, this study forecasted that by 2025 the middle class would comprise a staggering 520 million people, more than half of the expected urban population of China.

In a 2013 study, McKinsey used more than 70,000 interviews with Chinese consumers in 60 cities, representing 74% of China's GDP and 47% of its total population.[197] Here, the middle class is defined as having an income between 60,000 and 229,000 RMB a year, with the upper middle class earning between 106,000 and 229,000 RMB. It is forecasted that whereas the total middle class in 2012 numbered 256 million, it will increase to 357 million in 2022. This is less than the 520 million forecasted in the 2006 study for 2025. Nevertheless, based on these premises, McKinsey forecasted that the upper middle class would change its purchasing habits by buying more expensive goods such as

Valley entrepreneur look sleepy.' (p. 223).
196 Farrel et al. 2008.
197 Barton et al. 2013.

laptops, digital cameras, specialized household goods such as laundry softeners, and luxury goods. Within the middle class, the authors forecast the behaviour of what they call 'Generation 2,' i.e., typically teenagers and people in their early 20s, born after the mid-1980s and brought up in a period of relative abundance. In 2012 they represented only 15% of the urban consumers but it is forecasted that their numbers will surge to 35% in 2022. For the McKinsey researchers this is the most Westernized generation to date:

> prone to regard expensive products as intrinsically better than less expensive ones, they are happy to try new things (…) seek emotional satisfaction through better taste or higher status (…), [however they] share with their grandparents a bias for savings, an aversion to borrowing, a determination to work hard, and a definition of success in terms of money, power, and social status. In spite of the continuity with traditional behaviour (i.e., savings) the research forecasts that when they age, and eventually retire, they will have a 'younger' consumption mind-set than today's elderly do.[198]

The China Power Report of the CSIS, a more recent research using a slightly different methodology, confirms McKinsey's findings, especially the spending habits of the middle class.[199] Finally, a paper by China Briefing using McKinsey data, subdivides the Chinese consumers into 4 layers with different purchasing power.[200] The authors estimate that in 2022 the size of these layers, as a percent of urban households, will be: 9% for the affluent households (with income above $34,000), 54% for the upper middle class (income between $16,000 and $34,000), 22% for the mass middle class (income between $9.000 and $16,000), and 16% for poor people (income less than $9,000). Given that the urban population in 2022 will be approximately 60% (810 million) of the total population (equal to 1350 million), the middle class in the urban areas (upper middle plus mass middle) will be 76% of 810 million, i.e. 615

---

198 On the development of the Chinese consumer spending as the main driver of economic growth see The Economist Intelligence Unit, The Chinese consumer in 2030, *The Economist.* London, 2016.
199 China Power Report 2018.
200 China Briefing 2019.

million. This is quite impressive as it is considerably larger than the total population of the European Union before Brexit.[201]

These results seem to suggest that this new middle class will be an asset for the new development strategy redirecting the development drivers away from investment and export towards domestic consumption. This is certainly good news as it concerns the development of a market economy. Nevertheless, as the China Power Report quite rightly points out, this new trend may also exacerbate the tendency towards consumerism and individualism (especially in the forms of selfishness) that may further deteriorate (given its impact on consumption and production) the already heavy burden on the environment, as well as on the traditional collectively cooperative attitude of Chinese people, not to speak of a further increase of income inequalities. This is what the neoliberal revolution of the West may teach China.

In spite of the interest of these analyses for understanding the development of China's middle class and its consumer habits, nothing is said about its political preferences that may eventually be in favor of a regime change.[202] We are left with the forecast that the Chinese middle class as it becomes more affluent, will necessarily demand political reforms, as the Western middle classes have done in the West. Research done at Harvard University since 2003 by the American sinologists Tony Saich and Edward Cunningham shows that for the time being the Chinese people are overall satisfied with the way the Party-State has managed the transition from a rural country society to a relatively well-off urbanized one where its middle class is the most emblematic dimension.[203] In its

201 Given the relatively low income of the mass middle class, we may be tempted to exclude it and replace it with the affluent households, thereby having the total urban population with a U.S.D income between $16,000 to more than $34,000 (Affluent plus Upper middle class). These households will be the real driver of consumption. They will correspond to 63% of the urban population, i.e. 510 million, equal to the European Union population before Brexit. Less than 615 million, but still very impressive!

202 The 2019 McKinsey report is also limited to the analysis of consumers' general attitudes and purchasing behaviour, key trends regarding their consumption patterns and leisure habits, and attitudes toward life, success, money, and health, Ho and al. 2019. On the difficult task of evaluating the impact of the growing Chinese middle class on the political system, i.e. on the possible change towards democratization 'Western style,' see Jie Chen and Chunglong Lu (2006), and Jie Chen (2013).

203 This is the longest-running independent effort to track Chinese citizen satisfaction of government performance. China has expressed its satisfaction with Harvard findings: 'Harvard survey finds Chinese satisfaction with govt

latest 2020 report, this research team finds that Chinese citizen satisfaction with the government has increased virtually across the board, and that they rate the government as more capable and effective than ever before.[204]

Even more interesting, this research finds that the more marginalized groups in poorer inland regions are actually comparatively more likely to report increases in satisfaction. This contradicts the opinion we can find quite often in mainstream U.S. media that seems to take pleasure in pointing out the dissatisfaction of Chinese people at the lowest level of the income distribution, especially in the less developed areas. The present satisfaction is certainly the consequence of the extraordinary endeavours of the Party-State, since at least the mid-1990s, that heavily invested in the infrastructure of the inner provinces and in the rural areas, as well as in the development of social benefits, such as unemployment, health and old age (addressed more extensively in chapter 3).

Finally, the Harvard research shows that, irrespective of the Party-State's propaganda and censorship, the attitudes of the Chinese citizen appear to respond (both positively and negatively) to real changes in their material well-being. Consequently, quite rightly the authors point to the fact that the citizens' support of the government cannot be taken for granted, as it may be undermined, should the Party be unable to meet the challenges of a declining economic growth and a deteriorating natural environment. Nevertheless, for the time being, the Harvard research seems to support the narrative of the resilience of the Communist Party, also considering the efficient way with which it has reacted to the Covid-19 pandemic. Moreover, as the satisfaction with the government is shared by the different components of Chinese society, and even by the less well-to-do, it is not likely that the class that has most benefited from the economic development, the middle class, would suddenly demand that the Party change its policies, in the absence of a major crisis. The Chinese middle class is even less likely to rise up against the Party and call for a regime change. It seems therefore that any demand for regime change from within China's society reflects rather the wishful thinking of Western pundits not well-acquainted with the internal dynamics of Chinese society.

---

rises,' *China Daily,* 17 July 2020; see also William Zheng (2020).
204 Cunningham, Saich and Turiel 2020.

THE MYTH THAT CHINA IS TODAY IMPLEMENTING AN IMPERIAL FOREIGN POLICY

This myth has two interrelated dimensions: (1) China wants today to impose its political and economic model on the rest of the world, (2) the goal of China's foreign policy is to replace the U.S. empire and therefore to dominate the world. This returns us to the myth put forward in the introduction: the Chinese are coming! They invest in our countries and in our former colonies, they steal our technologies, they meddle in our democracies, they do not play honestly in the global economy, they over-spend on their military, they menace their neighbours, they aggressively develop their footprint on the China Seas,—and so on. They even had the nerve to establish a military basis in Djibouti! Imagine! An unbearable challenge to the U.S. over 800 military bases. Clearly, fear of the Chinese has replaced fear of the Native Indians. I cannot help paraphrasing the Lyndon Johnson quotation mentioned above about the 'Native Indians, once proud and free.' It goes like this:

> The Chinese, once proud and free, are torn now between White and Chinese values; between the politics and language of the White man and their own historic culture. Their problems, sharpened by years of defeat and exploitation, neglect and inadequate effort, have taken many years to overcome. But now, they are proud and free again. How frightening!

Let us then see if the U.S. has better reasons to fear the Chinese than it had to fear the Native peoples.

The first dimension of this myth can be easily dismissed. It is true that quite often Chinese authorities present the astonishing development of China's economy as the consequence of the way its economy and polity has been organized since 1949, and especially after the beginning of the 1980s. Moreover, it is true that the Chinese are very proud of their own success. But they are also well aware that China's success is not exportable without it being adapted to the local situation, and indeed, that there will never be one similar to China's, at least in particular considering the size of the Chinese population. What China means to developing countries is that development is better organized when the state contributes significantly to the development endeavour. Contrary to what the West has done for a long time, and is still doing today, China does not seek to impose the adoption of its model on the countries with which it establishes economic and cultural exchanges. There are no requirements for changing their political, economic and cultural systems, such as the West has done, demanding privatizations of public sector activities, and the introduction of liberal democracy.

China advertises its international cooperation with the formula 'win-win,' proposing the establishment of cooperation that is simultaneously to the advantage of all the parties concerned, no matter the exact share of these advantages. What is important is that the receiving country regards its advantage overall as positive. To date it appears that countries are pleased with this way of organizing cooperation, not only because it does not apply political pressure, but also because thereby it gives a range of choices between Chinese, European, American and Japanese investors. Moreover, China contributes to investments in the infrastructures, reflecting the success of its own development experience. Thereby, China indicates that economic development is impossible without first improving a country's infrastructure with the support and guidance of the state. The West should remember that the state has played a decisive role in the development of England, the U.S. and Western Europe. Only when the economy of these countries became strong enough to compete, did they support the limitation of the State's role and the liberalization of the global economy.[205]

Today Western pundits criticize China's investments in developing countries on two counts. First, China's investments often come in the form of long-term loans, which may plunge the recipient countries into the so-called 'debt trap.' Of course, Western critics, who know the history of the relations between the West and these countries, are rather hypocritical in formulating these fears, insofar as the West has implemented exactly this policy by investing in these countries to its own advantage, most of the time in the form of long-term loans under the cover of the so-called 'Washington Consensus.'[206] When these countries were not able

---

205 Bairoch 1993. Paul Bairoch gives many examples of the strategy followed by the U.S. and UK in the early stages of their economic development. For example, in 1875 the average levels of duties on manufactured goods in the U.S. was between 40 and 50 per cent (p. 24). The idea that industrialization is not possible without tariff protection was put forward for the first time by Alexander Hamilton, the first Secretary of the Treasury (1789–1795) in the first U.S. government. It was later theoretically developed by Friedrich List, whose book, *The National System of Political Economy,* was published only in 1841.
206 Let me remind the reader that the policies imposed upon the developing countries by the 'Washington Consensus' were based upon the neoliberal ideology, according to which the state cannot be considered as one of the main

to pay the interest on the loans so obtained, Western countries imposed radical changes in the political and economy systems of the beneficiary countries, including privatizations of whole pieces of state sectors (especially social policies, education and health) should these countries be wanting to obtain additional loans. This policy has devastated the countries in question.[207] However, this does not mean that the receiving countries should not be careful in managing their own public finances. Therefore, they should remember what happened during the Washington Consensus years. Much will depend upon the impact of Chinese investments on the development of these countries. A positive outcome will strengthen their economy and will make them able to pay the interest and repay the capital. Also, much will depend upon the willingness of China to restructure the loans, should the recipient countries experience difficulties. In this respect, China should not forget that it is the ruthless behaviour of the West towards the countries in question that explains their resentment towards the West.

Second, the West criticizes Chinese companies because they bring to the recipient countries their own manpower, thus not transferring their know-how to the local workers, employees, managers and engineers. But this was exactly the practice of the West at the time of the colonial empires, as well as after these countries had recovered their political independence after WW2, at least in theory. A research conducted by McKinsey shows exactly the reverse for the Chinese behaviour of companies investing in Africa.[208] The report considers that although there are

means to solve the problems of development. On the contrary it is itself an obstacle to development. The dysfunctions of the governments of the developing countries are due to the corruption of civil servants, militarism, and the protection of non-competitive national industries. Consequently, liberalization (in fact deregulation) of the market, as well as privatization and decentralization. The market is the main means to sustain economic development, thanks to its driving force, as competition assures the optimal allocation of resources as well as the optimization of their use, and should imbalances occur, the market will resolve them thanks to its capacity to regulate itself without state intervention. For a critique of this ideology: Stiglitz (1998), Urio (1999).
207 Notably, this happened with the support of the U.S. treasury, and the international organizations such as the World Bank and the International Monetary Fund, dominated by the U.S.
208 Sun, Jayaram and Kassiri 2017. The study is based upon 8 African countries: Angola, Côte d'Ivoire, Ethiopia, Kenya, Nigeria, South Africa, Tanzania, and Zambia.

areas for significant improvement, the high percentage of local employees contradicts the Western media's contentions: 81% for SOEs and 92% for private enterprises. Moreover, Chinese enterprises run apprentice or professional programmes to develop local capacity (62% for SOEs and 64% for private).

The second dimension, i.e. the myth that China is implementing an imperial foreign policy with the aim of replacing the U.S., is also related to the hypothesis that China will follow the same trajectory of the West (and especially the U.S.) once it has developed sufficient power resources to allow it to project its ambitions abroad. In fact, here again, Western pundits transfer to China the way of thinking and behaving the West has developed since at least the conquest of the Americas. Another manifestation of the myth of Western universalism, we have already seen above dealing with 'Western universal values.'

History in fact shows that, contrary to what the West has done, China has never invaded or colonized America, Africa, the Middle East, and large parts of Asia. It could have done so well before the discovery of the Americas by the West. Already during the XIV and the first half of the XV centuries China had the economy, the military, and the technological resources to project its power all over the world as the West would later do. It is a fact that China could have behaved as the West has done, when its power resources were far superior to Western countries. It is a fact that it has not conquered the world as the West has done. Moreover, China limited its military external interventions to its immediate neighbourhood (what the Russian call their 'near abroad'). This is quite understandable as no major power can accept to have hostile countries at its border that moreover may benefit from the support or incitement of a great power.[209] China's excursions outside its borders have never gone beyond Asia, Eastern Africa and the Middle East, and in any case, they were not motivated by the will to conquer foreign countries.[210] Not so the U.S., which has done so ever since the publication of the Monroe doctrine in 1823 (only a half century after the Declaration of Independence) prohibiting European powers to intervene in the Western hemisphere. More recently, in 1962, quite understandably the U.S. very

---

209 Temple 1998, Needham 1954–2004 and 1969. It is interesting to note that this is the case of Taiwan (even if China considers it as a Chinese province) that the U.S. has used since 1949 as a menace to mainland China.
210 Nevertheless, for excursion to Europe and America, see the analysis of the expedition of the eunuch admiral Zheng He by Levathes 1994, Menzies 2003 and 2008.

strongly opposed the installation of Soviet missiles in Cuba, a few miles from its southern coasts.[211]

The Chinese leadership insists every time it has the opportunity to do so, that its foreign policy reflects its 'peaceful rise.' Since ancient times, China has established relationships with other countries. Most of the time these contacts have been motivated by the interest in other cultures and in hope of developing commercial exchanges without territorial conquest. The famous Chinese historian Sima Qian has reported the exploration of Central Asia (and beyond) by the imperial envoy Zhang Qian between the second and first centuries B.C. After translating Sima Qian, the French sinologist Jacques Pimpaneau synthesizes Zhang's life as follows: 'He lived and took wife amongst these people of the West [of Asia] […] and defended the idea, not of armed conquest but of cultural and commercial exchanges on an equal footing.'[212] Notably in 2013, President Xi Jinping, announcing the launch of the new 'One Belt One Road,' came back to Zhang Qian's travels:

> Over 2100 years ago during China's Han Dynasty, a Chinese envoy, Zhang Qian, was sent to Central Asia with a mission of peace and friendship. His journey opened contacts between China and Central Asian countries, as well as the Silk Road linking East and West, Asia and Europe.[213]

Nevertheless, Western scholars and journalists try to cite events in the history of China that contradict the official history accepted by Chinese authorities and scholars, according to which China is a peaceful country. In fact, China has developed through the centuries a whole set of weaponry, most of the time well before the West[214] and has used it both internally in several civil wars and externally, as there have been events in which China has attacked foreign countries. Western authors generally refer to the Qing (Manchu) dynasty expansion in the 17th and 18th centuries during which the Qing fought wars in Burma and Vietnam.[215]

---

211 It is true that at the same time the U.S. had installed military bases and missiles not far from the Russian border. Another example of double standards.
212 Pimpaneau 2011.
213 Xi Jinping 2013a. See also 2013b.
214 Temple 1998.
215 Kyle Crossley at al. 2017.

Moreover, some scholars mention the Qing interventions in Tibet in 1718 and 1720, and in the region of today's Xinjiang in the 1750s. Nevertheless, Buckley Ebrey informs the reader tha the Qing intervened there not to conquer but to repel several invasions by the Dzungar Mongols in what were already two of their provinces. Indeed, Tibet and Xinjiang were incorporated into the Chinese Empire by the Yuan dynasty at the end of the 13th century, practically in the same way as Europe built its nation-states by submitting large parts of its territory to the domination of powerful regional absolute monarchies. Such has been the fate, inter alia, of Catalonia, Ireland, Wales, Auvergne, Languedoc, Sicily, and Sardinia. Moreover, Buckley Ebrey reminds us that

> the Qing interfered relatively little in Tibet and in Xinjiang affairs, allowing local leaders to do most of the actual governing. The local populations were allowed to keep their own religious leaders, follow their own dietary rules, and not wear the queue [which was required for the Han majority in sign of submission to the ruling Manchu dynasty].[216]

This situation, similar to that of other empires, lasted until the fall of the Chinese Empire in 1912, when it was replaced by a European invention, the Republican state. As we shall see in chapter 3, the republican state does not allow its regional subdivisions such as the provinces, to keep forms of local organizations that contradict the constitutional rules of the centre: no regional monarchy in a republic.

Now the question is: why did China start to develop its power resources towards the end of the last decades of the Empire, and even more so after the proclamation of the People's Republic of China? Why did it start to project its power abroad towards the end of the 20th Century? When the West aggressed China in the 19th century, China was sure of the superiority of its culture, whose fundamental values were based on an interpretation of Confucius: harmony (meaning absence of contradictions and conflicts, i.e., peace), stability and unity, to be developed in Chapter 2. Its quasi-isolation from the rest of the world, in terms of military and political power relations, allowed China to avoid being entangled in major international conflicts and to preserve its fundamental traditional values. But when China was forced to open to the West and

---

216 Buckley Ebrey. See also Ch. 9: 'Manchus and imperialism: the Qing Dynasty 1644–1900,' pp. 227, 220–258.

to integrate, *volens nolens*, in the conflictual Western-made international order, the harmonious and peaceful international environment China had enjoyed until then was torn to pieces. The only way to reconstruct a peaceful international environment where each country's values are preserved and respected was, first, to reconquer the status of a great power able to resist foreign aggression, and second, to work for the establishment of a peaceful international environment. As we will see in the following chapters, China has done so by integrating within its traditional culture ideas and ways of doing imported from the West. But by keeping the features of her traditional culture she has succeeded, so far, to remain faithful to herself.

How can we understand China's foreign policy? Clearly this is not an easy task. Still today the West persists in believing that it remains the reference for ways of thinking and doing. This has two consequences: first, the West has difficulties in opening its mind to other ways of thinking and doing that are outside those with which it is familiar, those that for it are self-evident. Second, it has difficulties in integrating China's cultural dimension with its other dimensions, i.e. economy, polity and society, both internally and internationally. This is an important point for those who want to understand China's behaviour in the international system and how it has implemented the strategy for realizing its fundamental goal: to reclaim world power status and therefore to be respected again.[217] Remember Mao's statement at the beginning of the People's Republic: 'Ours will no longer be a nation subject to insult and humiliation. We have stood up.'[218] In order to understand China's strategy, it is important to recognize that its civilization developed outside Western languages, outside Western history, independently from the West and indifferent to it. Moreover, China's strategy, directed to the realization of the dream to escape from poverty and to reclaim world power status, needed to develop within the international world the West has made, first by European powers in the nineteenth, then by the U.S. in the twentieth centuries. By building upon its pluri-secular long history, its fundamental values, and by integrating into its thinking the Western values that were compatible with its culture, China has succeeded in realizing that dream, little by little, by following its traditional way of conceiving and implementing the strategy.

---

217 Jullien 2006, pp. 302–303, Jullien 2005a, pp. 8–10.
218 Mao 1949.

If the West is to succeed in understanding China from inside, as we will do in the following chapters, it will discover that China is not projecting any plan for the future, and in particular that it has no imperial project. Instead, China exploits at its best, day after day, the potential of the environment, both national and international (what Jullien calls the 'situation potential'), by making the best out of the favourable factors in all domains: economy, polity and technology, both nationally and internationally. Its goal was to build a set of power resources necessary for dissuading the type of aggressions it suffered in the past for such a long time. It is only towards the beginning of the 20th century that the West has started, with some astonishment, to take stock of the results China has realized. Is it possible for the West to recognize that China has realized this goal by integrating its economy and polity in a rational system based upon a set of values, of ways of thinking and doing that combines Chinese and Western features? As Jullien says: 'Today China walks on its two legs, the Chinese and the Western.' And this explains its success.

Of course, history shows that myths may be abandoned and ways of organizing the polity, the economy and society may evolve in time, as do ideologies and foreign policies. This means that the conclusions at which I will arrive by the end of the book should be presented with several caveats, meaning that in spite of facts strongly pointing to the permanency of some of the country's features in the short and medium term (e.g., ideology), we cannot exclude that (as I have mentioned in my previous books) things may evolve in the opposite direction. This is for example the case for the hypothesis of the inevitable convergence of China toward the Western political and economic model. This hypothesis cannot be dismissed without careful examination. Facts show that the hypothesis is not plausible in the short and medium terms, but some other facts advise us not to exclude that the convergence may happen in the long term. As somebody said jokingly: it is difficult to make forecasts, especially in regard to the future.

CHAPTER 2

The Ideological Divide[1]

Ideology, one of the dimensions of a country's culture, can be defined as the set of fundamental values, beliefs and rules that orient the behaviour of individuals, groups, organizations and governments, both nationally and internationally.[2] Today's American ideology is easier to analyse and to understand than China's ideology. This is because it possesses a remarkable coherence, and moreover, it has not fundamentally changed since the first decades of the U.S. republic. On the contrary, China's ideology has gone through several important changes since at least the last decades of the 19th century. This makes it difficult to understand today's Chinese ideology by simply referring to the traditional imperial ideology that dominated China's society for at least two millennia.

Moreover, this difficulty is even more challenging, as there is a huge difference between the American and Chinese cultures. Some Western pundits have come to consider that as China has adopted some of the features of the Western ideology (e.g., the idea of the market), it will inevitably converge towards the Western model, or else it will collapse. In fact, China has retained several features of its traditional ideology, has not become a copy of the Western model and, notwithstanding, it has not collapsed. Western pundits have difficulties in understanding this, and most of the time they explain China's failure to adopt the Western model by referring to what they regard as the dictatorial character of the Communist Party, that keeps the Chinese mind under its grip, forbidding it to fully adopt the Western ideology.[3]

---

1 I have developed the analysis of ideology in more detail in Urio 2010, 2018 and 2019.
2 I would like to be very clear that I will not develop a culturalist approach. Taking culture as one of the keys for understanding American and Chinese foreign policies is not to say that culture can explain everything. Nevertheless, it would be a mistake to leave aside this source of information and of understanding.
3 I have pointed out in the first chapter that some Chinese liberal intellectuals consider that China should adopt (Western) liberalism as it is the only viable road 'to become civilized.' According to the Singaporean professor Zhang Yongnian, who has established the philosophical basis of Chinese neoliberalism: 'individual freedoms resulting from market-oriented economic reforms and capitalist development cannot be regarded as a process of "westernization." If

116

François Jullien offers a more plausible explanation: Westerners still today persist in believing that the West remains the reference for ways of thinking and doing. The consequence is that we have difficulty in opening our minds to other ways of thinking and doing that are outside those with which we are familiar, those that for us are self-evident. We cannot understand how it is possible that China managed to develop such a powerful economy without adopting our fundamental values, beliefs and rules, i.e., our ideology. For the West, China's ideology is irrational, a non-sense. This makes it difficult to articulate China's cultural dimension with its other dimensions, i.e., economy, polity and society, as they appear both nationally and internationally.[4] So, I will have to explain why China has not collapsed. My answer is that China has succeeded in integrating several Western values into its traditional ideology to build a new ideology whose coherence explains its remarkable resilience to internal problems and external threats.[5] In this chapter I will discuss the first part of my answer, i.e., the development of China's ideology, which the Chinese leadership has constantly changed and enriched by importing other elements from the West, while keeping its remarkable coherence. In Chapter 3 I will develop the second part of my answer, i.e., the economic, social and power achievements, obtained by orienting behaviour according to the evolution of the environment and the necessary adaptation and modification of the ideology.

China wants to be "civilized," it has to accept liberalism,' quoted by Zheng and Liu (2004) pp. 167 and 169.

4 (Jullien 2006, pp. 302–3, Jullien 2005, pp. 8–10.

5 Moreover, it is also possible that some elements that we consider typically Western (e.g., the idea of the market) existed already during the centuries of the Chinese Empire (Bergère, Braudel). For the emergence of a market in China see *Civilisation matérielle, économie et Capitalisme*, vol. 2, and especially pp. 116, 120–125, 139–140, 146 and 255–256. On the emergence of capitalism see ibid., pp. 268–287 for the use of 'capital, capitalist, and capitalism,' and for the emergence of capitalism in China see ibid., and more especially pp. 354–356 and 708–23. Also, the interested reader may consult the remarkable works of the French sinologist Marie-Claire Bérengère 1986, and 2007.

AMERICAN IDEOLOGY,
PAST & PRESENT

Let me start with a quote from a letter President Thomas Jefferson sent on 24 November 1801 to the Governor of Virginia, James Monroe, who was to become President of the U.S. in 1817:

> However our present interests may restrain us within our limits, it is impossible not to look forward to distant times when our multiplication will expand it beyond those limits, and cover the whole northern, if not the southern continent, with people speaking the same language, governed in similar forms, and by similar laws.[6]

Jefferson hereby summarizes the foundational goal of U.S. foreign policy. It was formulated only 25 years after the Declaration of Independence and, *mutatis mutandi*, was to persist until today. It certainly did set a grandiose endeavour for the young Republic, which clearly could not have been achieved without the support of such a formidable and unshakable ideology, to be reconstructed hereafter. But let us examine the elements of the quote. First, Jefferson is aware of the limits of the U.S. interests at that time. But immediately thereafter he acknowledges the 'multiplication' of the U.S., i.e., the increase of its population and the socio-economic activities that go with it. He then states that the multiplication will need an additional 'space,' hence the 'expansion.' And finally, in spite of the limits existing at that time, he envisages the grandiose

---

6 The complete text of the letter can be found at: https://founders.archives.gov/documents/Jefferson/01-35-02-0550, with several footnotes that briefly explain the circumstances: 'In the aftermath of the discovery of the slave conspiracy of 1800, the Virginia General Assembly passed legislation allowing for the eviction from the state, rather than the execution, of condemned slaves. By a resolution of 31 Dec. 1800, which Monroe enclosed to Thomas Jefferson on 15 June 1801, the legislature requested the governor to correspond with the president to find a place to send such transported criminals.' Jefferson's letter is his answer to Monroe. Amongst the several possibilities examined by the President, it is the first that triggered the quote mentioned above: Virginia could buy a piece of land in one of the U.S. territories wherein to place the 'criminals.' But as at that time the U.S. planned already to 'expand' Westwards, and transform the territories into States of the Union with people, institutions, churches, schools, etc., inevitably Jefferson raised the question: 'should we be willing to have such a colony in contact with us? Clearly not!'

development of the endeavour: why not look forward, with the goal of expanding beyond those limits, and cover the whole northern, if not the southern continent? With what kind of people and institutions? Quite naturally, with people speaking the same language, i.e. English. No matter the languages of the Native Indians, nor those of the other Europeans who were present in the Americas: Spanish, Portuguese and French.

But then comes the more important part of the quote, i.e. the institutions, which it is reasonable to interpret as twofold in nature: first, the form of the state of the members of that community should be similar to that of the U.S. Republic; second, the rules governing the relations between those countries should be defined, implemented and monitored by the U.S. This is in fact what has happened since the beginning. First, the Native Indians were integrated, *volens nolens,* within the U.S. Republic with the obligation to conform to its laws. Second the Latin American countries had to conform to the rules (national and international) set by the U.S. It is interesting to recall that the recipient of Jefferson's letter, James Monroe, when elected President, then proclaimed the doctrine that bears his name, forbidding European states to interfere in the Western Hemisphere. Already, it was proposed that the U.S. had the exclusive right to set the rules in that part of the world.[7] As we shall see in the first part of Chapter 3, after WW2, and especially after the collapse of the Soviet Union, the U.S. went on to elaborate a U.S.-led rules-based, liberal international system, which the U.S. tries today to preserve with all the means in its power, against the revisionist countries, especially Russia and China, which seek modifications of it. The Monroe doctrine has now gone global.

Let us see upon what ideological grounds the U.S. foreign policy has justified its 'expansion' since the beginning of the U.S. Republic. As ideology and practice, i.e. foreign policies, are inextricably connected,

---

7 The doctrine's greatest extension came with Theodore Roosevelt's Corollary (December 2004) that formally announced the intention to use military force to defend the Western Hemisphere against European incursions and justified unilateral U.S. intervention in Latin America. National Security Advisor John Bolton reminded the international community of this doctrine on 16 April 2019 when he announced new sanctions against Venezuela, Cuba and Nicaragua: 'today, we proudly proclaim for all to hear: the Monroe Doctrine is alive and well.' One could say that this is merely a statement by a well-known neoliberal coup-monger at that point still linked to the Trump administration. But at the time of writing, it seems that Bolton's statement reflects, on the contrary a permanent posture of U.S. foreign policy, as the Biden administration continues to work towards a regime change in Venezuela and elsewhere.

it is not possible to deal with ideology without at least mentioning the major elements of the strategy the U.S. has implemented since the last decades of the 18th century. This will give greater meaning to the dimensions of the ideology. A more systematic and in-depth analysis of the U.S. foreign policy will be discussed in Chapter 3.

In spite of the cultural similarities between Europe and America, the U.S. has developed an ideology that is quite different from the European one. Among the several dimensions explaining this peculiarity, one is worth mentioning right from the beginning: the very special geo-political situation of the U.S.[8] The U.S. has had the advantage of being protected by two wide oceans which has spared the country from wars of invasion by foreign countries. Its native inhabitants were badly equipped for resisting Western colonizers, while a declining colonial power at the southern border (Spain) was unprepared to sustain war with the U.S., and in the North, Canada has proved an ideologically compatible neighbour.[9] These were the ideal pre-conditions for developing and consolidating a peculiar ideology for the country, which was separated geographically and also culturally from the original homeland of the Pilgrim Fathers.

GOD, 'CHOSENNESS,' 'EXCEPTIONALISM' AND UNIVERSALISM

The ideology that took form in the 13 British colonies and then in the United States of America since the 18th century is rather complex, but if one has to identify one feature upon which all its other dimensions depend, I approve the one that Stephanson has called 'chosenness,' i.e. the profound belief shared by the Founding Fathers that the American people had been *chosen by God.* This belief is the ideological foundation of the two dimensions of U.S. foreign policy. The first dimension is *exceptionalism,* meaning that having been chosen by God (whereas the

---

8 The U.S. geo-political situation will also explain part of the way the U.S. has implemented its foreign policy from the beginning to the 21st century (See Chapter 3).

9 It is interesting to note that one of the most influential neo-conservatives, Robert Kagan (2021), in an article significantly entitled 'A superpower, like it or not,' seems to believe that the U.S. is still today protected by the two vast oceans, and thus is still capable of projecting its power all over the world. Does Kagan ignore the dramatic changes in warfare that occurred since the last decades of the XX century? Several countries, including North Korea, can hit the 'sacred land' with their nuclear heads. As I will show hereafter, the majority of American pundits still analyse international relations in the framework of and with the mentality of the XX century.

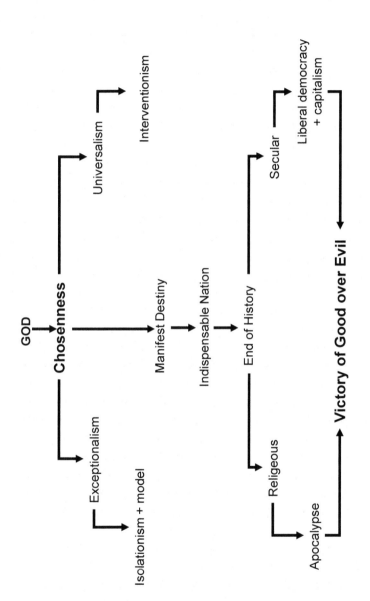

FIGURE 1. FUNDAMENTALS OF AMERICAN IDEOLOGY/TELEOLOGY

other countries have not) America is, thanks to this choice, exceptional, i.e., different from the corrupt European countries that the English Pilgrims had left behind. The goal of the 'exceptional people chosen by God' is to create a new republic, distanced from 'corrupt Europe,' free from the European wars, persecutions, absolute monarchy. etc., and to organize it as a 'pure' and exceptional example that the rest of the world should imitate.[10] This dimension has been translated into the most important passage of the Declaration of Independence which is often quoted as the quintessential feature of the U.S. Republic:

> We hold these truths to be self-evident, that all men are created equal, that they are endowed by their Creator with certain unalienable Rights, that among these are Life, Liberty and the pursuit of Happiness. That to secure these rights, Governments are instituted among Men, deriving their just powers from the consent of the governed. That whenever any Form of Government becomes destructive of these ends, it is the Right of the People to alter or to abolish it, and to institute new Government, laying its foundation on such principles and organizing its powers in such form, as to them shall seem most likely to effect their Safety and Happiness.[11]

Of course, it would be too easy to criticize the wording of this passage, as it is evident that at the time of the Declaration not all men were regarded as having been created equal and endowed by their Creator with certain unalienable Rights. In fact, at that time, U.S. was keeping several hundreds of thousands of Africans in slavery (later to become millions) and had already started the process to dispossess the Native Indians of their territories and their cultures. Clearly, these were peoples that the Declaration did not consider equal to the white master race, the *Herrenvolk*. Nevertheless, this statement could be interpreted in the normative mode, i.e. the purpose of the U.S. Republic is to organize itself in order to transform this ideological equality into reality. The revolutionary meaning of the Declaration would thus be preserved. In the

---

10 Stephanson 1996. See also, Griffin 2018:'Since its formation, U.S. politicians have referred to America in divine terms,' and 'America as Divinely Founded and Guided,' p. 9, with quotations of Presidents George Washington, Andrew Jackson, Ronald Reagan and George W. Bush, pp. 9–18.
11 U.S. Congress 1776.

first part of Chapter 3 we will evaluate whether the organization of the U.S. Republic has realized this goal.

In practice, most of the time, **exceptionalism** has been interpreted as the necessity for America to distance itself from Europe in order to avoid being contaminated by European despotism and barbarism, or the dream of establishing a pure republic will vanish for ever. So, **isolationism** has been the consequence of exceptionalism and constitutes the first dimension of U.S. foreign policy. That said, isolationism does not mean that the U.S. should be completely isolated from Europe. Rather, the exceptional U.S. Republic provides **a beacon, a model** that European countries should imitate. In 1816 Thomas Jefferson put this very clearly:

> We are destined to be a barrier against the return of ignorance and barbarism. Old Europe will have to lean on our shoulders, and to hobble along by our side.[12]

It is important to understand the profound meaning of **this first element of U.S. ideology**: it **establishes a partition** between the U.S. and the rest of the world, between 'WE' and 'THEY.' The U.S. is already viewing itself as exceptional, meaning that, having been chosen by God (whereas the other people have not), America is, thanks to this choice, exceptional, i.e., different from the corrupt European countries that the English Pilgrims had left behind. This American vision of itself and the world has persisted until the present day, where the clearest recent formulation was that of President George W. Bush in his 2002 State of the Nation speech where he labelled North Korea, Iraq and Iran as constituting an 'axis of evil,' thereby establishing a clear partition between 'WE, being equated with the Good, and THEY, being qualified as the Evil.'

The U.S.'s attitude towards Europe was later strengthened by President James Monroe, whose 1823 Doctrine forbade European states to interfere within the Americas. Moreover, U.S. **isolationism** towards Europe persisted until WW2. True, the U.S. entered WW1 in 1917 and President Wilson imagined and promoted a new organisation of the world (the League of Nations) that may have rendered impossible the resurgence of European wars, inter alia by calling for the right of self-determination of peoples, a right then focused on Europe but seized

---

12 Jefferson 1816. It is interesting to note that 'old Europe' has been used on 22 January 2003 by Secretary of Defence Donald Rumsfeld, two centuries after Jefferson used it.

upon later by developing nations. But the American Senate refused to ratify the treaty of the League of Nations, thereby forbidding the U.S. to become part of that organization. Notably, during the interwar period that followed WW1, the U.S. did not interfere with the establishment of Fascism in Italy in the 1920s, of Nazism in the 1930s (though indeed leading American industrialists had been embroiled in same), nor did they interfere when Imperial Japan attacked China in 1932, nor when Germany attacked Poland in 1939 and the Soviet Union in 1941. Only when the U.S. was attacked by Japan at Pearl Harbor, did it enter WW2 at the end of 1941,[13] and it delayed attacking Italy starting from Sicily until July 1943, and Germany, starting from Normandy, in June 1944.

The second dimension of U.S. foreign policy, **universalism**, is also based upon 'chosenness.' Having been chosen by God, as God is universal, God's chosen people were entrusted with universal values. But as these can only be universal in reality when they are implemented all over the world, hence the right, and even the duty, for the chosen people to intervene abroad to make it happen.[14] So, the other face of universalism is **interventionism** for the purpose of diffusing the universal values all over the world. We will see in the first part of Chapter 3 how the U.S. has implemented this dimension of its ideology.

It is clear that these two dimensions of U.S. foreign policy—isolationism and interventionism—are contradictory. Nevertheless, they have in fact coexisted and are at the origin of numerous debates within the U.S. elite when confronted with international events that they may or may not see as requiring the U.S. to intervene abroad.[15] Indeed, right from the beginning of the U.S. republic, interventionism has been a dominant dimension of U.S. foreign policy. Putting aside the war of independence with England, which might be regarded as a civil war, the first important act of U.S. foreign policy were the wars against the native peoples (the so-called Indian Wars) that lasted until the end of the 19th century, and officially ended with the Wounded Knee massacre in 1890. Then followed the wars against Spain, Mexico, etc. Moreover, ever since the Monroe Doctrine of 1823 mentioned above, the U.S. has kept its grip over Latin America, continued its expansion in the Caribbean and the Pacific, and in the interwar period maintained economic relations

---

13 Indeed, as frequently argued by revisionist historians, FDR was well aware of the forthcoming attack and allowed it to proceed, as the only way it would be possible to drag Americans into a European war.
14 Stephanson 1995, p. xii.
15 Kinzer 2017, p. 3.

with Europe, including Fascist Italy and especially Nazi Germany. These relationships became useful after WW II for sustaining the U.S. policy of Europe's reconstruction, especially that of Germany.[16] Needless to mention the numerous and persistent U.S. interventions abroad since 1945 (to be addressed in Chapter 3).

THE MANIFEST DESTINY OF THE INDISPENSABLE NATION

In 1845, the ideology described above was encompassed in the newly invented notion of 'Manifest Destiny,' a label that itself accords formidable strength to the exemplary status of a People chosen by God and to its right of intervention. Clearly, having been chosen by God, the American people are evidently blessed by a manifest destiny. In the words of John O'Sullivan, an advocate of Andrew Jackson who invented this expression: 'the right of our manifest destiny to overspread and possess the whole continent that providence has given us for great experiment of liberty and federated self-government.'[17] Moreover, as Europeans had already asserted, 'land not occupied by recognized members of Christendom was theoretically land free to be taken.' So, manifest destiny 'became a catchword for the idea of a providentially or historically sanctioned right to continental expansionism.'[18] Surely, at the beginning this mission was limited to the conquest of the American West, but in fact, the only long-term limit to the 'expansion' of this model to the rest of the world was the capacity to do so. That capacity then manifested itself first in the Americas, then in the Asia-Pacific, and then in the rest of the world after World War II. It culminated with the apotheosis of American domination that followed the collapse of the Soviet Union.[19] The manifest destiny appeared to have reached its logical conclusion. And here in the 1980s another belief of the U.S. ideology emerges that further strengthens all the others: the idea that the chosen people, entrusted with a divine manifest destiny to serve as a model for humanity and having the right and the duty to intervene abroad to diffuse

---

16 Lacroix-Riz 2014, pp. 31–46; Migone 2015, pp. 141–49, 165–70.
17 (Anderson 2015, p. 4, see also Stephanson 1995, pp. 38–48)
18 Stephanson 1995, p. xii. Stephanson further comments that this attitude 'was anything but new. Already in 1616, an agent of colonization had ended a prospectus of fabulous green vistas in North America to an English audience with this rhetorical flourish: "What need wee then feare, but to *goes up at once as peculiar people* marked and chosen by the finger of God to possess it?"' [Emphasis in original.]
19 Todd 1979.

the universal values that it is the only one to possess, is now indisputably the '**Indispensable Nation.**'

THE MERGER OF THE SACRED AND THE SECULAR

Also, it is necessary to insist upon the religious sources and foundation of this ideology. In fact, the British immigrants who first colonized New England were a 'particularly fierce and uncompromising phalanx within the Reformation— the Puritans. (…) English Protestantism, early on, had developed a notion of England as not only spatially but also spiritually separate from the European continent, as the bastion of true religion and chief source of its expansion: a place divinely singled out for higher missions.' It is upon this religious basis that the idea of exceptionalism and separateness took form. Moreover, this religious way of conceiving of manifest destiny is clearly tainted with a kind of messianic belief, enabling the messianic activism necessary for the realization of this project within the second dimension of U.S. foreign policy, interventionism.

Within this religious vision, manifest destiny is not only a possible outcome of separation (exceptionalism) or intervention (universalism) but it also defines the duty of the Puritan Christian:

> to be a Protestant and especially a Puritan was to master the Bible as an epistemic code of revelation, to understand the always causally effective providential hand in the world. Current events were fulfilments or re-enactments of the Scriptures. By mastering prophecy, one would be able to understand the course of history and "cooperate" with it. To be free was precisely to *understand this destiny* and conform to the direction of divine will, to "make our destiny our choice" (…) Once destiny was known with reasonable certainty, there remained the personal responsibility of choosing to follow it or to turn away. [20]

The missionary aspect of this endeavour was therefore well-established from the beginning. And Stephanson further comments: 'obscure but enormously suggestive [this thinking] offered the fullest vision of the end of history and the aftermath. It is a story of deadly struggle between

---

20 Stephanson 1995, pp. 5–9, emphasis in the original.

the forces of good and evil, ending after many phases in final victory for the good and the Messiah's reappearance.'

It must be noted that the Puritans' way of interpreting Christianity is based upon the belief that there is a division of mankind between the believers and the others: WE are not just apart from THEM (isolationism), but even possibly against THEM (interventionism). This interpretation clearly goes contrary to the real message of Christ: a practice of communion which is the contradiction of separation, and even more so of intervention. This is shown by Christ's 'welcome of the sinners, the prostitutes, the tax collectors, the adulterous woman, i.e. of people considered [at that time] as morally impure or contaminated because of their contact with the pagans.' As Marguerat and Junod put it the Puritans had in fact a defensive conception of purity, quite the opposite of Christ's teaching: there is nothing exterior to man that can make him impure, but only what comes out of man. This conception displaces the origin of impurity: the words and deeds of man are the origins of purity or impurity, not what exists in his environment. The relation to the other is thus no longer a danger, but an opportunity—not a potential risk of contamination and impurity, but a domain where the believer is invited to put into concrete action his purity.[21] What is even more significant is that this orientation of Puritanism still persists in a variety of American churches that trace their origins to Protestantism and consider the Book as an epistemic code of revelations.[22]

This posture of this variant of Protestantism is even more surprising as it contradicts one of the main features of Christianity, maybe the most important and the most revolutionary: contrary to the Old Testament where the believers are clearly the People chosen by God, with the New Testament all the people on earth are chosen by God. There cannot be a partition between WE (chosen by God) and the OTHERS. There can be a fight between the Good and the Evil within each man's heart, but

---

21 Marguerat and Junod, pp. 32–33, my free translation from the French. Not being an expert in religion, I base this comment on the work of a world-famous specialist of the New Testament, Marguerat, author of the first part of the book.
22 It is beyond the scope of this book to deal with the spread all over the world, e.g. in Latin America, Eastern Europe, Russia, and Africa, of a variety of Protestant Churches that still today share this posture with the Puritans. Needless to say that, insofar as these Churches tend to cooperate with conservative political forces, it should be necessary to take into consideration their activities and influence in the perspective of an overall analysis of the restructuring of the power within both the national and the international systems.

not between one part of humanity against the other. It would be a total contradiction with the preaching of Christ, as the preceding paragraph very well shows.

One of the most notable features of this ideology is the mix of religious and secular values. The duty to behave in such a way as to fulfil the prophecies of the Book is clearly a religious imperative. But the English colonists who came to the New World, took with them not only Puritanism, but also the ideas that had emerged in Europe at that time about new ways of managing the State (republicanism, later translated into liberal democracy) and managing the economy, (market economy/ capitalism). Similar to the religious values, these secular values were also considered as universal. So unsurprisingly, their consequence is similar: the belief that other countries should imitate U.S.'s liberal democracy and capitalism and the *American* believers in democracy and capitalism have the duty (and the right) to do whatever is in their power to diffuse these values all over the world. What is remarkable about American ideology is how this mix of religious and secular values has been combined and perpetuated throughout America's history.[23]

THE RIGHT AND THE DUTY TO LEAD THE WORLD TO THE END OF HISTORY

Although the belief that the U.S. was destined to lead the rest of the world was not explicitly affirmed until the messianic activism of President Wilson[24] and systematically asserted since the time of World War II, it was certainly imbedded in the American ideology since the beginning. Indeed, we have seen above the references to the duty of Europe 'to hobble along by the U.S. side,' which would allow the U.S. to limit its foreign policy to its first dimension (i.e. isolationism), but failing this, the messianic activism takes over: the believer has the right and the duty to understand the course of history, 'cooperate' with it and diffuse the content of the ideology to the rest of the world, and lead it towards the end of history.

The ideology I have reconstructed above, constitutes a formidable and coherent set of interrelated beliefs. It has become a way of thinking that, when it is embedded into the human mind, it is practically im-possible not to follow when analysing the world and giving meaning to one's position and action inside that world. This ideology has been

---

23 Stephanson 1995, p. 16, Anderson 2015, p.5.
24 Karp 1979, Part I, Stephanson 1995, pp. 112–121.

used throughout its history as the guide and a permanent justification of
U.S. foreign policy. It has in fact operated since the foundation of the
American republic, and still operates today. If one looks at the implementation of this ideology since the foundation of the U.S. republic, one
cannot but help considering that this ideology has become a formidable
weapon of mass destruction.

Most significantly, it has destroyed the capacity of the American
elite to conceive of a world in which the U.S. could play any other role.[25]
Such a capacity would have been necessary for taking into consideration the formidable changes that continue to occur in the distribution
of power resources within the international system, ones that no longer
correspond to those existing at the end of World War II. On the contrary,
the American elite still today tries desperately to maintain the international order America made after 1945, especially after the fall of the
Soviet Union.

Second, by implementing this ideology, the U.S. has thought it to
be its duty and its right (in practice of God's imperative) to embark on a
long series of mass destructions all over the world, many of which could
hardly be justified by any existential threat posed by an enemy ready
to defeat and destroy the 'people chosen by God' and with it the values
they claimed to defend.[26] On the contrary, the U.S. has invariably ended
up justifying its own operations of mass destruction (and those of its
allies) that combine economic and military resources while condemning
the same type of mass destructions being perpetrated by its enemies.[27]
Hence, the well-known use of double standards by both the U.S. and the
EU.

Here's a recent example. On the one hand, in March 2021 the U.S.
imposed sanctions upon Russia for the alleged poisoning of the Russian

---

25 Porter 2018a, 2018b
26 Ganser 2016 and 2020, Blum 2013–14. For example, the napalm bombing
of 67 Japanese towns (spring of 1945), followed by the atomic bombing of
Hiroshima and Nagasaki (August 1945), which according to former Secretary
of State McNamara would have ended in the condemnation of the U.S. for
war crimes, should the U.S. have been defeated in World War II (McNamara
2009). Then followed a long series of attempted and very often successful mass
destructions: in Korea, Vietnam, Iraq, Afghanistan, Syria, Libya, Iran, to quote
just a few.
27 These resources are equated by Joseph Nye (2004 and 2011) with 'hard
power' (comprising economic and military resources) and 'soft power'
(comprising cultural resources). I have criticized elsewhere this absurd typology,
that in fact constitutes an intellectual fraud (Urio, 2018, pp. 36–43).

opposition leader Alexei Navalny, who had been found guilty of embezzlement by a Russian court and given a five-year suspended prison sentence in 2013. Navalny was arrested in January 2021 after returning home from Germany, where he had been recovering from the poisoning that he and Western governments have blamed on the Kremlin without providing any proof. Russia denied the accusation, but on another matter, Navalny was sentenced to 32 months in prison on the grounds that he had broken the terms of the probation agreement tied to his 2013 embezzlement conviction. The U.S. swiftly reiterated its call for the Russian government to immediately and unconditionally release Mr. Navalny, sharing the EU's concerns regarding Russia's purported deepening authoritarianism and welcoming the EU's determination to impose sanctions on Russia. On the other hand, since 2012 the U.S. has organized, with the complicity of the UK government, what must be viewed as an unbelievably lengthy persecution of Julian Assange for publishing U.S. documents revealing war crimes committed by U.S. armies abroad. This has led to his imprisonment in solitary confinement in a UK prison, awaiting the decision of a British court to extradite him to the U.S. under the Espionage Act of 1917, which may lead to a sentence of more than 170 years in prison. It is also well-known that the U.S. practices similar prosecutions against all the whistle-blowers who bring into the open crimes committed by U.S. armies. At the time of writing, it seems that the Biden administration will continue to seek the extradition of Julian Assange to the U.S.[28]

Finally, its frequent use of economic, and especially military means against targeted countries contradicts another fundamental belief of the American elite: that in general the U.S. has been able to exercise its power mainly thanks to the attraction of all dimensions of its culture, conceived of as human rights, freedom and democracy.[29] By so perceiving its relations with the rest of the world, the American elite appears to have been unable to understand that it is mainly thanks to the exercise of its economic and military power that this has been possible. Nevertheless, several members of the U.S. establishment, indeed those likeliest to have influenced the decision to implement such policies, have very clearly understood that military means are the most important element of U.S. power, when the other means have failed to obtain compliance with the U.S. national interests.[30]

---

28 For more detail see Wikipedia under 'Assange.'
29 Nye 2004 and 2011.
30 For example, Kagan 2003, 2017a.

This is not to say that this ideology has not been contested within America right from the beginning. Many American 'voices denounced the megalomania of Manifest Destiny, the plunder of Mexico, the seizure of Hawaii, the slaughter of the Philippines, attacking every kind of racisms and imperialism as a betrayal of the anti-colonial birth right of the republic.'[31] Indeed, even today there are voices that denounce the same megalomania and the devastating consequences of its implementation in many parts of the world, especially since the end of World War II.[32]

Nevertheless, history shows that in spite of these voices, the U.S. tendency has remained, constantly and consistently, to intervene everywhere, whenever possible, by any means, to diffuse the good news of the new world order.

TODAY'S AMERICAN IDEOLOGY AND ITS IMPACT ON FOREIGN POLICY

After the defeat of Donald Trump in the 2020 presidential election, one might have had some confidence in the capacity of the U.S. establishment to change at least some elements of the ideology de-constructed above, and consequently to re-orient the U.S. foreign policy away from its traditional imperial posture towards a more cooperative behaviour made necessary by changes in the distribution of power resources in the international system. The new President and some of the members of his team have on many occasions declared that the new administration would be very different from the Trump's presidency. Nevertheless, the first declarations and decisions taken by Biden and his team soon made it very clear that the new administration would not be that new, as in fact it looked more like an almost perfect carbon copy of the Obama administration policies, concerning both ideology and actual behaviour. So, back to normal. In fact, the announcement by the Biden administration that it would be different from Trump's implied that the Trump administration's foreign policy had been fundamentally different from Obama's. In spite of some differences nothing is more wrong.[33]

---

31 Anderson 2015, p. 5.
32 See amongst many others: Stephanson 1995, to be completed with Anderson 2015, Stephanson 2010, and Vidal 2003; La Feber 1994, 1998, and his magisterial article 2012; Griffin 2018; Scott 2007; Pfaff 2010; Bacevich 2008, 2012; Bradley 2009, 2015; Andersen 2017.
33 Urio 2018, pp. 129–43, and 2019, pp. 230–45.

There has been a remarkable continuity at least from the presidency of George H.W. Bush to Biden's, which I will elaborate on in Chapter 3. Trump's foreign policy has been fundamentally in line with that of his predecessors. It could have been very different if his major foreign policy proposals had not endangered the interests of large sectors of the establishment. One thing the Trump administration should have made clear to those who until then had not yet understood it: it is not the President who has the power, the establishment holds it. The President may well announce some decisions, but the establishment has the power to nullify them, should they endanger its vital interests. It can do so by all sorts of tactics that support its overall strategy of maintaining the implementation of foreign policy options that have so well served its interests to date. Not only there has been opposition to specific Trump policies but also there was a strategy, already in action well before the election day, to destitute the president. This strategy accompanied the four years of the Trump presidency, and has been, to my knowledge, the only example in the history of the U.S.[34]

To appreciate the validity of this contention, one might carefully analyse how Biden has built his team. In Chapter 1 I have already mentioned that the Biden Administration has manifested a clear propensity to appoint people who have built their career by using 'revolving doors' between positions in the public sector and jobs in private investment companies and think tanks, many of them with clear links with military procurement companies and with the military-industrial complex. Politico has been following the build up of President Biden's team since the beginning of the new administration.[35] In its issue of 23 March 2021, Politico described the Biden team as a 'Team of Rival Consulting Firms. Around 20 Biden administration officials have ties to the same three firms, including some of the highest-ranking national security and

---

34 I would like to make it clear: I am not a supporter of Donald Trump. I am not a moralist, nor an ideologue. I am just a political scientist working, as far as possible, on the basis of facts. I leave to those who are directly concerned with the U.S. presidency, i.e. the American people, organizations and institutions, to evaluate the Trump years from the point of view of American values and interests.
35 *Politico*, known originally as *The Politico*, is an American political journalism company based in Arlington County, Virginia, that covers politics and policy in the United States and internationally. It distributes content primarily through its website but also via television, printed newspapers, radio, and podcasts. Its coverage in Washington, D.C. includes the U.S. Congress, lobbying, the media, and the presidency (Wikipedia, 'Politico,' where you can find information about the controversies concerning its political and ideological line).

foreign policy officials and nominees. Six of them are former colleagues of Secretary of State Tony Blinken at WestExec Advisors, the consulting firm he co-founded.' It seems that President Biden is quite at ease with these conflicts of interest.[36]

To lead the world following the neo-conservative ideology

I will discuss the U.S. foreign policy in Chapter 3. For the moment I will show that the new Biden Administration is faithful to the traditional ideology of America I have de-constructed above. In fact, it has based its very first declarations and decisions of foreign policy upon this ideology. Not very promising for the four years to come: in summary, the new administration will be faithful to its major traditional slogans: 'we will lead the liberal-rule-based-international order America made to realize peace, stability, prosperity, democracy and human rights.' But do

---

36 'But even more—10 and counting—are veterans of Albright Stonebridge Group, a bigger and older Washington consulting firm co-founded by former Secretary of State MADELEINE ALBRIGHT (…). The firm boasts of its "long-term relationships with decision-makers around the world," allowing it to advise clients on international policy and global markets; its alumni in the Biden administration advised clients such as Merck, Pfizer, Amazon, Lyft, Microsoft, the Bill & Melinda Gates Foundation, Hilton, the Mayo Clinic and the Israeli airline El Al, according to their financial disclosures. (…) Albright Stonebridge alumni in the administration include LINDA THOMAS-GREENFIELD, Biden's ambassador to the United Nations; JEFFREY De LAURENTIS, Thomas-Greenfield's acting deputy; WENDY SHERMAN, his deputy secretary of State nominee; VICTORIA NULAND, his nominee for under-secretary of State for political affairs; UZRA ZEYA , his nominee for under- secretary of State for civilian security, democracy and human rights; MOLLY MONTGOMERY, the deputy assistant secretary of State for European and Eurasian affairs; PHILIP GORDON, Vice President KAMALA HARRIS' deputy national security adviser; and JULIE MASON, Second Gentleman DOUG EMHOFF's chief of staff. In addition to Blinken, Biden's Director of National Intelligence AVRIL HAINES; White House press secretary JEN PSAKI; DAVID COHEN, the deputy CIA director; ELY RATNER, who's leading the Pentagon's China task force; and LISA MONACO, Biden's deputy attorney general nominee all hail from WestExec Advisors. And National Security Adviser JAKE SULLIVAN and Veterans Affairs Secretary DENIS McDONOUGH were partners at Macro Advisory Partners, which describes itself as "a strategic advisory firm that interprets global developments for its clients and analyses their impact on business strategies." BILL BURNS, who was confirmed last week as CIA director, was paid $150,000 a year to sit on the firm's advisory board.' (Politico's 2021 Transition Playbook, 23 March 2021, received by e-mail subscription).

not forget that this statement has always been based upon the assumption that these policies should satisfy 'our American values and interests.'

To reiterate: the major characteristics of the American ideology presented above are these: the American people chosen by God have built an exceptional pure Republic the rest of the world should imitate and, being the depository of universal values, have the right and the duty to diffuse them all over the world, wherein they are acting as the indispensable nation entrusted with the manifest destiny to lead the world to the end of history and the victory of the GOOD over the EVIL. To lead the world: this is the mission of the U.S. in the world. It is the consequence of all the components of the U.S. ideology. In the first chapter I have already pointed out Biden's *Foreign Affairs* article where he very heavily insisted upon the leading role of the U.S., mentioned no less than 20 times.[37] Then there's his most frequently used slogan: 'America is back'—presumably referring to a rebound from the Trump interlude. This is not to be mistaken for cooperating with allies and competitors on equal footing, but to lead them once again.[38] It is the American superiority (moral, economic and military) that gives it this right and this duty: WE are going, again, to lead YOU. It is the traditional American partition between WE and the OTHERS.

This should not come as a surprise as the Biden administration's policies are an almost perfect carbon copy of those of the Obama Administration, which implemented an impressive range of sanctions, regime changes, overt and covert military interventions, the exponential development of drones and other military weapons (including nuclear), the global evolution of Jefferson's 'expansion' (especially in Eastern Europe), and the strategy of containment towards Russia and China. Could someone well acquainted with the Clinton-Bush-Obama foreign policy honestly think that its 'Biden carbon copy' would change in any meaningful way the foreign policy of the sole superpower?[39] So Robert

37 Biden 2020a, his inaugural speech.
38 Urio 2018, pp. 108–195 and 2019, pp. 195–245). In his foreign policy speech of 3 March 2021 Blinken said: 'Yes, many of us serving in the Biden administration also proudly served President Obama—including President Biden. And we did a great deal of good work to restore America's leadership in the world.' (Blinken 2021).
39 According to an Associated Press news: 'President-elect Joe Biden on Saturday filled out his State Department team with a group of former career diplomats and veterans of the Obama administration, signalling his desire to return to a more traditional foreign policy after four years of uncertainty and unpredictability under President Donald Trump. Biden will nominate Wendy

Kagan, one of the most influential neo-conservatives, has brutally put it in a very clear message: 'A superpower, like it or not. Why Americans Must Accept Their Global Role.'[40] The formula ('must accept') is quite revealing, as it puts emphasis not on the right of the U.S. to lead (that clearly remains) but on the fact that the U.S. is asked to do so. By whom or by what? Very likely by the whole 'international community' due to the fact that the U.S. is the sole country able to avoid chaos in the international system—as opposed to cause it, as we will see below.

It is interesting to note that Anthony Blinken, chosen by Biden to act as his Secretary of State, had joined Robert Kagan in 2019 to write an article published by the influential Brookings Institution that announced: China and Russia are considered to be the major obstacles to U.S. supremacy. They very clearly consider that diplomacy alone is not enough:

> Yet force can be a necessary adjunct to effective diplomacy. In Syria, we rightly sought to avoid another Iraq by not doing too much, but we made the opposite error of doing too little. Without bringing appropriate power to bear, no peace could be negotiated, much less imposed [*sic*]. Today we see the consequences, in hundreds of thousands of civilian dead, in millions of refugees who have destabilized Europe and in the growing influence of Russia, Iran and Hezbollah. If the retreat from Syria announced by Trump proceeds, we will likely see the return of the Islamic State as well.[41]

Reflect on how irrational this statement is! It is because the U.S. did not use *enough* force that there have been hundreds of thousands of civilian dead and millions of refugees who have destabilized Europe. As we know that the refugee crisis was the consequence of the U.S. using military force throughout the Middle East (both 'too much' and 'too little') this statement is at the same time tragic and ridiculous. Even more so, as several American pundits have criticized European countries for not having been able to manage the refugee crisis America made, though quite often, it is fair to say, with the support of its European allies.

Sherman as deputy secretary of state and Victoria Nuland as undersecretary of state for political affairs — the second- and third-highest ranking posts, respectively. They were among the 11 officials announced to serve under the incoming secretary of state, Antony Blinken.' (Matthew Lee 2021).

40 Kagan 2021.
41 Blinken and Kagan 2019.

For Kagan and Blinken, the reason why the U.S. must accept to lead the world is clear:

> If the United States abdicates its leading role in shaping international rules and institutions—and mobilizing others to defend them—then one of two things will happen: some other power or powers will step in and move the world in ways that advance their interests and values, not ours. Or, more likely, the world will descend into chaos and conflict, and the jungle will overtake us, as it did in the 1930s.[42]

The dilemma between diplomacy and the use of military force and economic sanctions

The 2019 Kagan-Blinken statement on the indispensable leading role of the U.S. was confirmed in March 2021 by the Biden administration. In his 2021 speech of on foreign policy, Secretary of State Anthony Blinken confirms: 'President Biden has pledged to lead with diplomacy because it's the best way to deal with today's challenges.'[43] For the U.S. the most important challenge is the attack on democracy by countries such as Russia and China. So, the U.S. will do whatever is in its power to defend and promote democracy. But how, asks Blinken rhetorically? His answer: 'We will use the power of our example. We will encourage others to make key reforms, overturn bad laws, fight corruption, and stop unjust practices. We will incentivize democratic behaviour. (…) But we will not promote democracy through costly military interventions or by attempting to overthrow authoritarian regimes by force.' How commendable! Using the example of the virtuous American Republic as a means to make other countries adopt the virtues of the exceptional Republic is probably well meant, and moreover is in tune with one of the dimensions of the U.S. foreign policy, isolationism, as discussed above. But that Blinken could express a vision of the features underpinning America's role in the world to a world that increasingly knows otherwise, one that is so contradictory to America's actual role, should be a great cause for alarm. Has he, has America, truly lost its grip on reality? In fact, immediately after mentioning the 'use of the power of our example,' which is based upon isolationism, and excluding the use of 'military interventions or by attempting to overthrow authoritarian regimes by force,' Blinken

---

42 Blinken, Kagan 2019.
43 Blinken 2021.

turns to an apparently mild form of interventionism saying that the U.S. will 'encourage' and 'incentivize democratic behaviour.' OK, but why keep the military budget at least the same level as the Trump's budget?[44] Now the question is: how will the U.S. act to promote all the changes mentioned by Blinken so that democracy will be adopted by countries all over the world, without military intervention or the use of force, in an updated version of the 'end of history'—particularly in view of the resounding failure in Afghanistan? History in fact shows that the U.S. has quite often used other means than military force to promote democracy, even if the use of force has been always there as a last resort.[45] Examples abound. Would it be by investing in the economy of the targeted country, as it was done in Russia in the 1990s and in Ukraine in the 2000s? Or by using proxies as in Afghanistan and in Syria—with Afghanistan's 20–year bungled occupation cloaked by military and administration lies freshly and iconically embedded in the global public mind (to be further addressed below)?[46] Or by imposing economic sanctions with the purpose to starve the population so that it overthrows the non-democratic government, that hopefully will be replaced by a client government of the U.S. and its national interests, as it is still doing today to Iran and Venezuela? Or by using organizations funded by the U.S. government and labelled 'Non-governmental Organisations' such as the National Endowment for Democracy (NED) or Freedom House? These organizations have been very active in financing and training 'pro-democracy' movements all over the world, even when this has produced violent behaviour on the part of the 'pacific' demonstrators, as has been the case in Hong Kong and more recently in Thailand?[47] Blinken does

---

44 The President's budget proposal for fiscal year 2022: 753 billion for national defence programs, a 1.7 percent increase, the highest in U.S. history (source: The White House, accessed 18 April 2021)
45 This was for example included in the 'clear message' used by the Trump administration: 'all the options are on the table.'
46 Daniel Davis, 'Failed Policymakers Have No Shame on Afghanistan,' *Washington Examiner*, August 20, 2021. https://www.washingtonexaminer.com/opinion/failed-policymakers-have-no-shame-on-afghanistan
47 It is interesting, and worrying, to see Blinken quoting Freedom House: 'A new report from the independent watchdog group Freedom House is sobering. Authoritarianism and nationalism are on the rise around the world. Governments are becoming less transparent and have lost the trust of the people. Elections are increasingly flashpoints for violence. Corruption is growing. And the pandemic has accelerated many of these trends' (Blinken 2021). But Freedom house is not as independent as Blinken says. According to Wikipedia 'Freedom

not say. The exclusion of 'force' and of 'military means' clearly leaves the door wide open to any kind of non-military means that can be no less devastating for the populations concerned. This is the case for sanctions, which the U.S. currently imposes upon a raft of countries. A correspondence posted by the *Lancet* (one of the world-leading medicine journals) quite rightly considers that

> although sanctions do not seem to be physical warfare weapons, they are just as deadly, if not more so. Jeopardising the health of populations for political ends is not only illegal but also barbaric. We should not let history repeat itself; more than half a million Iraqi children and nearly 40 000 Venezuelans were killed as a result of UN Security Council and U.S. sanctions in 1994 and 2017–18, respectively. The global health community should regard these sanctions as war crimes and seek accountability for those who impose them.[48]

Moreover, should an unacceptable resistance arise from countries so foolish as to prefer to stick to another type of political organization, the option to use force will always be there, Blinken reassures us: 'At the same time, we'll make sure that we continue to have the world's most powerful armed forces. Our ability to be effective diplomats depends in no small measure on the strength of our military.'[49] Good to know! More precisely, in the last part of his speech, after referring to the President's promise that diplomacy will always come first, not military, Blinken reminds us that the U.S., 'will never hesitate to use force when American lives and vital interests are at stake. That's why President Biden authorized an airstrike last week against Iranian-backed militia groups targeting U.S. and coalition forces in Iraq.' Or course, Blinken did not feel compelled to explain that it would be the U.S. which will define unilaterally what U.S. national interests are at stake. We know from experience that the U.S. has the habit of finding that its national interests of one kind or another are at stake anywhere and anytime, even in remote parts of the world by countries that do not possess the slightest

---

House is a U.S.-based, U.S. government-funded non-profit non-governmental organization (NGO) that conducts research and advocacy on democracy, political freedom, and human rights.' Wikipedia and Blinken should explain how an organization that is funded by the U.S. government (such as many others including the NED) can be qualified as independent.
48 Takian, Raoofi and Kazempour-Ardebili 2020.
49 Blinken 2021.

capacity to constitute a vital threat to the U.S. In short, there will be a continuation of the traditional interventionist U.S. imperial foreign policy for the years to come. Indeed, the U.S. remains addicted to interventionism even today, after having botched it in some many places. But as sustained above the U.S. attraction to isolationism, strong as it might be, has been offset by its even stronger attachment to intervention. Right from the beginning of the U.S. Republic the temptation to go abroad and expand there, whenever possible, has been the main driving force of U.S. foreign policy.

At this point, it is interesting to see how Blinken in his 2021 speech explains why the leadership of the U.S. is necessary, be it through diplomacy and/or the use of force: 'When the U.S. pulls back, one of two things is likely to happen: either another country tries to take our place, but not in a way that advances our interests and values; or, maybe just as bad, no one steps up, and then we get chaos and all the dangers it creates. Either way, that's not good for America.'[50] In fact, Blinken reaffirms what he had already written with the neoconservative Robert Kagan in the 2019 article mentioned above.

This idea is not new. It is exactly what Robert Kagan had already written in 2012 in the *Wall Street Journal*:

If and when American power declines, the institutions and norms that American power has supported will decline, too. Or more likely, if history is a guide, they may collapse altogether as we make a transition to another kind of world order, or to disorder. We may discover then that the U.S. was essential to keeping the present world order together and that the alternative to American power was not peace and harmony but chaos and catastrophe—which is what the world looked like right before the American order came into being.[51]

---

50 Blinken 2021.
51 See also Robert Kagan, 'Why the World Needs America' (Kagan 2012c). Even Hillary Clinton, who could have been U.S. President had she won the elections in 2008 or in 2016, expressed the same opinion: 'when America fails to lead, we leave a vacuum that either causes chaos or other countries or networks rush into fill the void. So, no matter we lead. What kind of ideas, strategies, and tactics we bring to our leadership. American leadership means standing with our allies because our network of allies is part of what makes us exceptional.' Speech given at the American Legion's national convention, *Time*, 31 August 2016, full transcription available at, http://time.com/4474619/readhillary-clinton-american-legion-speech/, retrieved March 5, 2017.

This message has been consistent over time and despite the chaotic results of actual American use of force. While it might be argued that Kagan's 2012 article only reflects the point of view of an influential representative of the neoconservative movement and did not reflect the policy of the Obama administration, here again we have Blinken, who had been an official in the Obama administration, repeating in 2021 what President Obama said in 2015, speaking as the commander in chief at the American University in Washington, DC, about the Iran Nuclear Deal: 'As Commander-in-Chief, I have not shied from using force when necessary. I have ordered tens of thousands of young Americans into combat. I have sat by their bedside sometimes when they come home. I've ordered military action in seven countries. There are times when force is necessary, and if Iran does not abide by this deal, it's possible that we don't have an alternative.'[52] OK, message received!

Given the permanence of American ideology, it is easy to forecast that the policies of the new President would be fundamentally the same as those of its predecessors, especially in foreign policy. In fact, addressing the 100 or so guests at a fundraiser at the Carlyle Hotel in New York City in June 2019, Biden said that nothing would fundamentally change if he would be elected. He was right.[53]

What changes has the Biden administration introduced into U.S. foreign policy?

To be fair, it is necessary to start by mentioning some positive changes.[54] First, with only two days remaining until its expiration, the United States and Russia officially extended the 2010 New Strategic Arms Reduction Treaty (New START) for five years, keeping in place

---

52 Obama 2015.
53 Mosbergen 2019.
54 As I focus my analysis on foreign policy, I will not deal with the changes in domestic policies such as taxation, Covid-19 strategy, investment in infrastructure, gun control, etc. To be fair to Biden, it is probably in these domains that his administration will seek and may indeed be able to reverse some of Trump's domestic policies. Nevertheless, at the time of writing, several of these new policies have not yet been transformed into laws and have not yet obtained the approval of the Congress. And the history of the U.S. shows good intentions are often shredded during the legislative process, where political opposition and lobbyists' interventions abound. Moreover, it is not at all certain that such policies are apt to improve the health of U.S. economy as they are based upon printing money and increasing the public debt, another addiction of the U.S. administrations since 1971.

the treaty's verifiable limits on the deployed strategic nuclear arsenals of the world's two largest nuclear powers.

We cannot afford to lose New START's intrusive inspection and notification tools,' Pentagon press secretary John Kirby said in a Jan. 21 statement (...) Failing to swiftly extend New START would weaken America's understanding of Russia's long-range nuclear forces.' And the Russian Foreign Ministry emphasized the importance of New START's extension for maintaining strategic stability. In a statement, the ministry said, 'Considering the special responsibilities that Russia and the U.S. carry as the world's largest nuclear nations, the decision taken is important as it guarantees a necessary level of predictability and transparency in this area, while strictly maintaining a balance of interests.'[55]

Of course, this is good news not only for the U.S. and Russia, but also for the rest of the world. Nevertheless, this much needed agreement did not diminish the extraordinary U.S. aggressivity towards Russia, as it manifested itself in the *Brussels Summit Communiqué* issued at the end of the NATO summit of June 2021.[56]

Second, Biden announced that the U.S. would re-join the Paris agreement on the environment signed in 2016. To support this decision Biden cancelled the Keystone XL pipeline between the U.S. and Canada, and his Interior Department mandated that only top agency leaders could approve new drilling permits over the next two months. Moreover, in January 2021, 'according to people familiar with the plans, Biden will go even further: suspending the sale of oil and gas leases on federal land, where the U.S. gets 10% of its supplies.'[57] Nevertheless, this is only 10% of the total supply. Moreover, we have to wait and see whether these decisions will outlast their public announcements, as the businesses active in these sectors have already indicated their opposition, reminding that jobs will be lost. It will be a difficult task for the President. Nevertheless, after this decision has been confirmed, it seems that Keystone XL

---

55 Kingstone and Bugos 2021.
56 NATO 2021.
57 Dlouhy 2021a, 2021b.

protestors want Biden to revoke more pipeline permits, which shows that the problems posed by the pipeline is far from been settled.[58]

As for the Paris agreement, nothing is really binding for the signatories, as the behaviour of the majority of them very well demonstrates. A good test for Biden's environmental policy will be the case of the Line 3 Pipeline between Canada and the U.S. Line 3 is an oil sands pipeline owned and operated since 1968 by Enbridge, a Canadian energy transportation company. It runs from Alberta to Wisconsin. In 2014, Enbridge proposed the construction of a new route for the Line 3 pipeline which would increase the volume of oil they could transport daily. While that project has been approved in Canada, Wisconsin, and North Dakota, it has sparked continued resistance from climate justice groups and Native American communities in Minnesota.[59] The promoters of Line 3 mention the three positive impacts usually put forward in such circumstances: job creation, tax revenue and needs of the oil industry.

Third, Biden has also announced his willingness to re-join the Nuclear deal with Iran signed in 2015. Here we have a good example of a declaration that seems to change one of the most damaging decisions of the Trump administration, but in reality, nothing fundamentally is changing. In fact, the Biden administration does not want simply to re-join the deal Trump left unilaterally without any discussion with the signatories (among them two of the U.S. Western allies in the NATO alliance, France and the UK). Trump's sanctions are still in force, including the threat to impose sanctions upon countries (including U.S. Western allies) and their enterprises, should they violate the interdiction to trade with Iran.[60] Moreover, the Biden administration wants to re-negotiate the

58 Dlouhy and Tuttle 2021.
59 Wikipedia, 'Line 3 Pipeline,' Houska 2021. Tara Houska is a tribal attorney, founder of Giniw Collective, and a former advisor on Native American affairs to Bernie Sanders. She spent six months on the frontlines fighting the Dakota Access Pipeline and is currently engaged in the movement to defund fossil fuels and a years-long struggle against Enbridge's Line 3 pipeline. She is a co-founder of Not Your Mascots, a group committed to positive representation of Native peoples.
60 We know that this had the counter-productive consequence of enabling Russia and China to increase their trade with Iran. China even passed a trade and military partnership with Iran in June 2020 (Fassihi and Le Myers 2020). The axis Beijing-Moscow-Teheran is certainly more damaging to the U.S. leadership than the situation existing at the moment of the signing of the Nuclear Deal ... and one could even say at the time when the U.S. orchestrated the regime change in Iran in 1953 overthrowing the democratically elected Mossadegh and replacing him with a dictatorship has poisoned the relations between the U.S.

deal by adding something new, i.e. the development of medium range missiles by Iran, and the Iran policy in the Middle East that according to the U.S. is threatening stability and peace there. But this is exactly what Trump wanted: to force Iran to renegotiate the deal, by putting on the Iranian people an increasing number of cruel and illegal sanctions.

Fourth, regarding the appalling situation in Yemen, for which the U.S. bears an indisputable responsibility, the extent of Biden's good news was the reversal of the Trump administration's designation of the Houthis as a terrorist organization and the appointment of a special envoy for Yemen. Nevertheless, in a very ambiguous statement Biden said the massive U.S. sale of weapons to Saudi Arabia would be suspended, except for *defensive weapons*. 'This war has to end (…) We are ending all American support for offensive operations in the war in Yemen including relevant arms sales' which perhaps included Saudi Arabia. But this does not mean that the U.S. will cease to support Saudi Arabia, insofar as: 'at the same time, Saudi Arabia faces missile attacks, UAV strikes, and other threats from Iranian-supplied forces in multiple countries. We're going to continue to support and help Saudi Arabia defend its sovereignty and its territorial integrity.'[61] Biden did not say by what means, but the history of the support given by the U.S. to Saudi Arabia for a long time suggests that the support would take the forms of 'defensive arms sales,' training and intelligence. Overall, Biden's statement is not very encouraging as we know how skilful the military-industrial complex is in lobbying the White House. Clearly, the President confirms the intention of the U.S. to continue to meddle in the Middle East.

The traditional U.S. ideology and the persistence of the U.S. imperial foreign policy[62]

As the ideological goal to lead the world remains the major goal of U.S. foreign policy, China and Russia are inevitably targeted as the

---

and Iran that has endured until this very day.!

61 Biden 2021b, February 4.

62 In Chapter 3 I will deal with Biden's decisions (or non-decisions) that clearly confirm the traditional U.S. foreign policy. Here I will simply give a non-exhaustive list of statements and decisions taken (or announced) by the Biden administration in tune with the American ideology and the foreign policy of the previous administrations. I will not address Joe Biden's earlier career, especially his year as Obama's Vice-President. You will find the summary of his career in the mainstream media, that I advise you to complete with information given by the alternative media.

major threat to U.S. national interests as they are the sole countries that have the power to nullify the U.S. dream of continuing to lead the world. This has taken on increased urgency since they have established a *de facto* partnership, arguably another instance of blowback resulting from the U.S.'s own policies. Accordingly, sanctions on Russia are maintained, and the expansion of NATO and EU eastward is still on the agenda. The U.S. Defence Department announced at the end of February 2021 a $125 million allocation for the Ukraine Security Assistance Initiative that includes the traditional panoply of supports that go under this type of 'assistance': training, equipment and advisory effort to help Ukraine's forces to preserve the country's territorial integrity, secure its borders, and improve interoperability with NATO. This is in addition to the already impressive U.S. support for the build up of the Ukrainian army. On February 26, 2021 Biden affirmed the U.S. view that Crimea is part of Ukraine.[63] On March 24, 2021 the President of Ukraine, V. Zelensky, published his presidential decree of March 11, 2021 saying that Ukraine seeks the reintegration of the temporarily occupied territory of the Autonomous Republic of Crimea and the city of Sevastopol.'[64] Moreover, the admission of Ukraine into NATO has been discussed at the highest level for several years. Little wonder that Russia has started to place military forces not far from the Ukrainian border, as these moves from the U.S., NATO and Ukraine can be interpreted as the will of the U.S. to finalize the Maidan coup d'état of 2014 it orchestrated to replace the democratically elected Ukrainian president with a non-elected one chosen by the U.S. The mainstream U.S. and European media have interpreted Russia's response as proof of Putin's aggressive posture.[65]

---

63 'We reaffirm a simple truth: Crimea is Ukraine.' The White House, Statement by President Biden on the Anniversary of Russia's Illegal Invasion of Ukraine, February 26, 2021, https://www.whitehouse.gov/briefing-room/statements-releases/2021/02/26/statement-by-president-biden-on-the-anniversary-of-russias-illegal-invasion-of-ukraine/, accessed 18 April 2021

64 President of Ukraine Volodymyr Zelensky Official online representation, https://www.president.gov.ua/documents/1172021-37533, accessed 18 April 2021.

65 The above-mentioned Brussels Summit Communiqué announced that Georgia is preparing for its NATO membership, and that Ukraine will become a member of the Alliance with the Membership Action Plan. The Communiqué further warns that these countries should decide their own future 'free from outside interference'—discounting its own, and pointing where one might expect?

The U.S. also maintains sanctions based on the alleged poisoning of Russian dissident Navalny by the Kremlin, accompanied by the traditional flow of anti-Russian propaganda orchestrated by the U.S. government with the contribution of the mainstream American media. Finally, while Biden reiterated the U.S. opposition and sanctions to the almost completed Nord Stream 2 pipeline, that would double the furnishing of Russian gas to Germany, he was ultimately forced to cave on this longstanding and key U.S. foreign policy effort to prevent increased and positive German-Russian relations. The official reason given by the U.S. was that the pipeline is not in the interests of Europe, as it ran the risk of depending upon the good will of one of the two major foes of the U.S., Russia. There was also the fact that Europe's buying the Russian gas will be at the expense of American gas (30% more expensive) that the Obama administration had counted on being able to sell to Europe. This is another example of how the U.S. plans to lead the world and tell its allies what their interests are.[66]

I have already commented upon the U.S.'s will to re-negotiate the nuclear deal with Iran, by limiting the Iranian policy in the region, thus further supporting the U.S. policy favouring U.S. allies such as Saudi Arabia and Israel. The murder of the journalist, Adnan Khashoggi, responsibility for which U.S. intelligence has clearly laid at the door of the Saudi Prince, has only been followed, so far, by a mild and ambiguous reaction by the Biden administration.

President Biden also confirmed the U.S. addiction to the use of military means by bombing Syria, and by maintaining the military U.S. presence in that country, in Iraq and even in Europe, where the withdrawal of U.S. troops from Germany has been frozen, consequently leaving U.S. forces at their current level of about 36,000. Even the agreement with Afghanistan to withdraw U.S. forces from the country by end of May 2021, was postponed to September 11, 2021. But then, to the amazement of all concerned, the date had to be moved swiftly forward as the Taliban took Kabul in a feat of national liberation that has seen no parallel within the past century. Biden has indeed withdrawn the U.S. forces from Afghanistan in a manner which has been met with shock and dismay around the world at its lack of foresight and planning, overriding the iconic memory of the disastrous U.S. evacuation of Saigon with the scorching new image of Afghans clinging to the closed

---

66 More details about the U.S. opposition to the Nord Stream 2 below and in Ch 1.

doors of an American flight from Kabul, then dropping to their deaths, much as Americans had dropped to their deaths from the Twin Towers two decades ago. It's fair to say all sectors of the American establishment and population are in shock, to say nothing of America's friends and foes in the international community. It is hard to predict how this will impact the American military's budget, presently per President's budget proposal already standing at 753 billion for national defence programs, a 1.7 percent increase, the highest in U.S. history.[67]

How will this impact the future of foreign intervention elsewhere? At this writing, regime change, a U.S. foreign policy addiction, is nonetheless still on the agenda in Syria, and also in Latin America (Venezuela, Cuba) and even Russia and China (to be dealt with below). To this we can add another example that is rarely dealt with in the mainstream media: Thailand, where an intensive subversive activity is being developed by U.S. NGOs such as the National Endowment for Democracy, though here, to make sense of it, the target must be seen as China. The 1823 Monroe doctrine is certainly still alive and now even extended to countries far away from the Western hemisphere where it was originally implemented since the beginning of the 19th century.

U.S. foreign policy a matter of 'style'?

Two episodes reported by the U.S. media add some light to the style with which the new presidency will manage foreign relations and the reactions of its major competitors.

On 16 March 2021, in answer to a loaded question put to him by ABC News, Biden publicly assented to qualify President Putin as 'a killer.'[68] And so to the inevitable follow-up question: 'So, what price must he pay?' the President answered: 'The price he's gonna pay, we'll, you'll see shortly.'[69] Not a very good start for a President who has ostensibly put diplomacy first, nor an ideal declaration for developing a positive relation with the world's other nuclear super-power, especially after the

---

67 Source: The White House, Office of the President, accessed 18 April 2021. https://www.whitehouse.gov/wp-content/uploads/2021/04/FY2022-Discretionary-Request.pdf

68 The journalist introduced the question referring to a declassified report from the U.S. national intelligence director's office that, without provident evidence, found Putin authorized influence operations to try to help Donald Trump win re-election in the November U.S. presidential election. A frequent *modus operandi* of the U.S. intelligence community.

69 ABC News, March 16, 2021.

U.S. had just extended the New START nuclear arms control treaty with Russia for 5 years. It is difficult, without any detailed comments from the White House or the State Department, to give a definite meaning to this exchange, or where the responsibility lies. The White House Press Secretary simply said that the journalist asked a question, and the President gave an answer. What is clear is that Russia and the Russians will not be pleased with the new American president qualifying their president a killer. Let us recall that Putin is the president who lifted his country out of the mess into which the West had put it after the fall of the Soviet Union: a dramatic increase of poverty and substantial decrease of the GDP, thanks to the shock therapy promoted by Western pundits and speculators. Some may be willing to de-dramatize the event; after all, as some American media have written, this is the first time a U.S. president has qualified one of his colleagues as a killer. Nevertheless, this kind of crude behaviour of top U.S. officials is not new. Do you remember Hillary Clinton qualifying Putin as the 'new Hitler' or threatening to 'obliterate' Iran? Or Victoria Nuland encouraging a U.S. diplomat to 'fuck the EU' in case the Europeans would dare object to the regime change she was organizing in Ukraine? Or when she encouraged the U.S. to 'get the Russians to eat their spinach' as described thus by Tony Wood: 'Already on Washington's agenda even before the fall of the USSR, the expansion of NATO was treated as a given from 1994 onward, the only question being how to make the Kremlin swallow it—to get the Russians to eat their spinach.'[70]

A lot could be said about this 'killer' episode. But here's how Putin reacted to Biden's childish performance, on the official Russian television channels: with a sense of humour, a knowledge of history and of individual psychology. Putin wished good health to Biden, commenting that he said so without any irony or joking. Recalling his own childhood, Putin said: 'I remember in my childhood, when we argued in the courtyard with each other we used to say: he who said it, did it. And that's not a coincidence, not just a children's saying or joke. The psychological meaning here is very deep. We always see our own traits in other people and think they are like how we really are.' A clear instance of Freudian projection, to put it in terms Americans might understand. Indeed, Putin's

---

70 Wood 2017. Victoria Nuland was finally appointed for the position of number 3 in the State Department, after Secretary Anthony Blinken, and National Security Advisor, Jake Sullivan. This trio had already held top positions within the Obama administration's State Department. Can there be much doubt about the direction in which they will orient U.S. foreign policy?

response was then mistranslated and widely circulated as 'It takes one to know one…' Then, however, Putin went on to talk about U.S. history: the genocide of Native Americans, enslavement and the ill treatment of Black people, and the U.S. dropping atomic bombs on Japan at the end of World War 2.[71] It is clear that U.S. mainstream media did not appreciate Putin's performance and chalked up the unaccustomed lack of servility as yet another instance of Putin's aggressiveness.[72]

Second, U.S. mainstream media were more cheerful the day after Biden's performance, when the U.S. State Secretary announced additional U.S. sanctions on Russia and on the Nord Stream 2. According to British-Canadian agency Reuters: 'Any entity involved in the Nord Stream 2 pipeline risks U.S. sanctions and should *immediately* abandon work on the pipeline, Blinken said in a statement, adding the Biden administration is committed to complying with 2019 and 2020 legislation with regards to the pipeline and sanctions.'[73] The official reason: this Pipeline will make Europe dependant on Russia for its energy resources, and this is against Europe's own strategic interests. Moreover, the U.S. wants to sell to Europe American gas, which is 30–40% more expensive and obtained by fracking, which has devastated the environment of several American regions. Do Biden and Blinken consider that the U.S. has the right to tell the EU what is its interest in the economic domain?

Nevertheless, according to the CNN website, on 5 May 2021, President Biden had publicly declared that 'to go ahead and impose sanctions now would I think be counterproductive in terms of our European relations and I hope we can work on how they handle it from this point on.' And in July we learned that Biden had just concluded a deal with Angela Merkel.[74] Under the four-point deal, which will see America drop

---

71 According to ABC News Putin also told a Russian state television reporter: 'I've just thought of this now. I want to propose to President Biden to continue our discussion, but on the condition that we do it basically live, as it's called. Without any delays and directly in an open, direct discussion. It seems to me that would be interesting for the people of Russia and for the people of the United States.' (Reevell 2021).

72 Among many reactions from mainstream media see the reaction by CNN (Chernova, et al. 2021).

73 Osborn and Balmforth for *Reuters* 2021, emphasis added.

74 *Washington Post:* 'Why the world Worries About Russia's Nord Stream 2 Pipeline,' 22 July 2021; BBC: 'Nord Stream 2: Biden Waives U.S. Sanctions on Russian Pipeline,' 21 July 2021. The *Washington Post* article is interesting not only for its usual hostile tone towards Russia, but also for how it describes the relations between Russia and Ukraine (and incidentally also with the US):

sanctions against Nord Stream 2, Germany and the U.S. will seek to promote investments of at least $1 billion in a so-called Green Fund to help Ukraine's transition to cleaner sources of energy. Germany has committed to an initial $175 million investment in the fund. Germany would also appoint a special envoy—with $70 million in funding—to support bilateral energy projects with Ukraine. It will also pledge to push Russia into extending the current gas pipeline arrangement with Ukraine, which provides Kiev with $3 billion in annual transit fees. Moreover, if Russia attempted to use energy as an economic weapon or commit aggression against Ukraine, Germany would take action itself while also pressing for measures at the European level, including sanctions to limit Russia's energy exports.

As already mentioned in Chapter 1, reactions to the deal, as one could have easily forecasted, have been mixed, to say the least. But the dominant opinion has been that Germany and Russia were the clear winners of the deal. Does this mean that the capacity of the empire to impose its will is fading away?

The China threat: The New Cold War is here to stay

The Biden administration is even more assertive towards China than was Trump's. Sanctions will remain in force, waiting for their evaluation by the U.S.–China relations task force instituted by the president. China affords particular opportunities for another U.S. addiction mentioned above, i.e., the use of internal problems (that are real) to destabilize the country and, at their limit, to produce a regime change. The U.S. targets China by interfering in three very sensitive regions: Hong Kong, Xinjiang and Tibet.[75] The Biden administration has not announced its intention to reduce the pressure on China in these three regions. Moreover, in the region that the PRC still considers as one of its provinces, Taiwan, the U.S. is further increasing its support to the island, by increasing its

---

the relations 'between Russia and Ukraine have worsened, culminating in the Ukrainian popular revolt that kicked out the country's pro-Russian president and led to Russia seizing the Crimean Peninsula.' A distortion that is hardly surprising, when one knows how the U.S. mainstream media are keen on writing the history *ad usum delphini*, as if they have never heard about the 2014 coup d'état, the regime change orchestrated by the U.S.

75 Several U.S. federal laws have been approved by the U.S. Senate with an overwhelming majority concerning these three areas: The Hong Kong Human Rights and Democracy Act, The Uyghur Human Rights Policy Act, The Uyghur Forced Labour Prevention Act, The Tibet Policy and Support Act.

sales of military equipment and announcing its intention to further develop diplomatic relations, in violation of agreements between the U.S. and Taiwan. Note, the island is only 180 km from mainland China's coast. All the main U.S. components of the establishment (including the media and think tanks) agree that China is the most important existential threat to the U.S. imperial policy. Here it suffices to quote the new Secretary of State, Anthony Blinken, doubtless reflecting the position of President Biden:

> Several countries present us with serious challenges, including Russia, Iran, North Korea. And there are serious crises we have to deal with, including in Yemen, Ethiopia, and Burma. But the challenge posed by China is different. China is the only country with the economic, diplomatic, military, and technological power to seriously challenge the stable and open international system—all the rules, values, and relationships that make the world work the way we want it to, because it ultimately serves the interests and reflects the values of the American people. Our relationship with China will be competitive when it should be, collaborative when it can be, and adversarial when it must be. The common denominator is the need to engage China from a position of strength.[76]

So, here again, back to normal. If you behave as we say, we will collaborate with you, otherwise we will be competitive or even adversarial. And in any case, we will act 'from a position of strength.'

Even more worrying, this surge of anti-China propaganda, sanctions, military build-up in the China Seas, support to subversive activities in Hong Kong, Xinjiang and Tibet, is embedded in the U.S. Cold-War mentality, demonstrating that the U.S. strategy towards China today is still based upon its traditional ideology as described above. It would be easy to quote a great number of official documents, speeches by politicians and top civil servants, members of mainstream think tanks and media, and even university professors and researchers to confirm this orientation. Investigative American journalists have done an excellent job in this respect. Unfortunately, they are systematically marginalized

---

76 Blinken 2021.

by mainstream media and even censored by platforms such as You Tube, Twitter and Google.[77]

Here's one highly significant example, published by the influential *Foreign Affairs*, published by the Council on Foreign Relations.[78] *Foreign Affairs* gives the affiliations of the two authors:

> Hal Brands is Henry A. Kissinger Distinguished Professor of Global Affairs at the Johns Hopkins School of Advanced International Studies, a Resident Scholar at the American Enterprise Institute, and a Bloomberg Opinion columnist; Zack Cooper is a Research Fellow at the American Enterprise Institute and Co-Director of the Alliance for Securing Democracy. He previously served on the staff at the U.S. National Security Council and at the Department of Defence.

---

77 At the moment of writing, 15 July 2021, here are other proofs that the Biden administration will follow the traditional imperial policy of the U.S.: (1) nothing is said about Guantanamo prison, that the Obama administration (of which Biden was the Vice-President) promised to close down; (2) the U.S. supports French intervention in Mali, despite Macron's announced intention to withdraw; (3) Biden confirmed that his administration will seek extradition of Julian Assange to the U.S.

78 Brands and Cooper 2021. The Council on Foreign relations is certainly the most influential American think tank on U.S. foreign policy. 'The Council on Foreign Relations (CFR), founded in 1921, is a United States non-profit think tank specializing in U.S. foreign policy and international affairs. It is headquartered in New York City, with an additional office in Washington, D.C. Its membership, which numbers 5,103, has included senior politicians, more than a dozen secretaries of state, CIA directors, bankers, lawyers, professors, and senior media figures.' (Wikipedia) A more useful and extensive description of CFR's membership and clout was provided back in 1993 by *Washington Post* writer David Harwood, in his article, 'Ruling Class Journalists,' naming, inter alia, 'The president is a member. So is his secretary of state, the deputy secretary of state, all five of the undersecretaries, several of the assistant secretaries and the department's legal adviser. The president's national security adviser and his deputy are members. The director of Central Intelligence (like all previous directors) and the chairman of the Foreign Intelligence Advisory Board are members. The secretary of defense, three undersecretaries and at least four assistant secretaries are members. The secretaries of the departments of housing and urban development, interior, health and human services and the chief White House public relations man, David Gergen, are members, along with the speaker of the House and the majority leader of the Senate.' https://www.washingtonpost.com/archive/opinions/1993/10/30/ruling-class-journalists/761e7bf8-025d-474e-81cb-92dcf271571e/

Notably, both are active in the American Enterprise Institute (AEI), a strong neo-conservative think tank.[79] The article is significantly entitled 'U.S.-Chinese Rivalry Is a Battle Over Values. Great-Power Competition Can't Be Won on Interests Alone.' The authors inform the reader that 'although the competition with China is not a replay of the Cold War, the history of that struggle may still hold useful lessons for present-day policymakers.' Indeed, competition with China is not a replay of the Cold War. But why, in spite of the considerable differences between the Cold War years and the situation of the 21st century, to which the authors seem to refer, do they continue to consider that the policies the U.S. has implemented during the Cold War 'still hold useful lessons for today'? In fact, the whole article is based upon no less than 13 references to what the U.S. did to win the Cold War, and above all, asserts the paramount importance of the democratic values that the authors consider to be the 'asymmetric advantage' of the U.S. foreign policy, with the clear suggestion that these should forge the U.S. foreign policy today. No wonder then that the authors are pleased to quote Biden's interim *National Security Strategic Guidance* that labels democracy 'our most fundamental advantage' and insists 'our model isn't a relic of history; it's the single best way to realize the promise of our future.' This, despite the ongoing media and Congressional fixation on what they term the January 6, 2021 'insurrection'...

It is impossible to reproduce here all 13 references to the Cold War, but the descriptors of the new existential threat, China, are significant: (1) The Chinese Communist Party's aversion to the United States runs deep. (2) The Chinese leaders appear to believe that efforts to increase China's power and influence cannot fully succeed unless the global order becomes one in which an autocratic superpower can flourish. (3) China is providing surveillance equipment to illiberal rulers around the globe while also working to change the norms and operations of international organizations so that they favour autocratic models such as Beijing's. (4) China's leaders are promoting authoritarianism beyond their borders. (5) China commits horrifying abuses at home and is seeking to strengthen authoritarianism abroad, which offends ordinary Americans on a visceral

---

79 Mind you, I am not suggesting that the AEI is not a reliable source of information. As a matter of fact, it is, and I have extensively used their articles and reports in my books, when they are based upon robust empirical data. I just want to show how serious neo-conservative researchers are still today embedded into the ideology and strategy that oriented the U.S. foreign policy during the Cold War towards its existential foe: Soviet Russia.

level. (6) The COVID-19 crisis showed the world some of Chinese authoritarianism's most dangerous tendencies; (7) There are reports about Beijing's genocide in Xinjiang and repression in Hong Kong, with polls showing that 86 percent of Americans support sanctioning Chinese officials engaged in these abuses. (8) Although non-democratic rulers in frontline countries such as Vietnam may be put off by an agenda that values democracy, it is hard to imagine them rejecting Washington's help in managing an increasingly aggressive China.[80]

The events discussed in the preceding paragraphs constitute a blatant contradiction to Blinken's statement about the nature of U.S. foreign policy, to wit: 'We will balance humility with confidence. (...) Humility because we aren't perfect, we don't have all the answers (...) But confidence because America at its best has a greater ability than any country on Earth to mobilize others for the common good and for the good of our people.'[81] It is good to know that the U.S. leaders think that they are not perfect, nor that they have all the answers. But clearly, in practice, confidence relegates humility to oblivion, as confirmed by the declarations of President Biden and several members of his team, as well as by an impressive number of sanctions (old and new) against foes and allies, the build-up of the military resources (including nuclear) and the organization of massive military drills at the periphery of China, Russia and Iran.

But it is the latter, according to U.S. propaganda, who are undertaking a number of aggressive moves. It appears that just as the U.S., per its historical tendency, continues to confuse the chronological order of events, it is equally blind to the truths that geopolitical factors impose. None of these countries are in the vicinity of the U.S.; it is the U.S./NATO which seeks to encircle them and draw the noose ever tighter. David Vine, the best specialist of U.S. military bases scattered around the world, in his last book has posted two maps. The first, entitled 'Encircling Enemies,' shows the actual U.S. military bases around

---

80 I have already debunked some of the myths upon which several of these statements are based and will debunk some others in Chapter 3. It is also interesting to note that the article tries to give more weight to its argument by quoting the American politicians and high officials who were very active at the origins of the Cold War and during the years that followed (George Kennan, President Harry Truman and Robert Zoellick) praising the policies they supported and/or implemented, and indeed, thereby further demonstrating the entrenchment of such orientations.
81 Blinken 2021.

China, Russia, Iran and North Korea. In the second, entitled 'How would we feel?' A hypothetical Map,' Vine has placed the military bases China, Russia, Iran, and North Korea may build, but have not built, around the U.S.[82] Vine explains: 'this map is designed to encourage U.S. Americans in particular to consider how it would feel—and how we might react—if we were surrounded by foreign bases near our borders.' But does the U.S. establishment have the wisdom to understand? Or does it indeed understand, and is simply, willfully and continually, lying? Do either of these portend a happy prospect for the world?

The U.S. foreign policy orientation became evident at the Alaska meeting of March 2021, a meeting whose aim was apparently intended to re-establish dialogue between the U.S. and China after the Trump years. And yet, the introductory statements by Secretary of State Anthony Blinken and National Security Adviser Jake Sullivan were a remarkable litany of the arrogant U.S. imperial foreign policies, updated to Biden-era 'diplomacy': lecturing China on its internal affairs related to violations of democracy and human rights, aggressively bragging that the U.S. shared the same values as its allies (reminding the Chinese delegation that the U.S. had met several of them just before the Alaska meeting), warning China about its policy that damages the rules-based international order the U.S. promotes in favour of peace and stability. Not a very diplomatic welcome. The Chinese delegation replied in kind. It was a clear message that China will no longer accept unilateral criticism from a country that has waged wars and regime changes for decades, that has serious human rights problems at home, and should have understood that in today's multipolar world this is not acceptable. This is the first time that Chinese officials have warned the U.S. in such an unequivocal way. Clearly, this meeting constitutes the beginning of a new era in the relationships between China and the U.S.[83]

We may conclude that the decisions already taken by the Biden administration clearly confirm that its foreign policy is based upon the traditional ideology I have discussed at the beginning of this chapter. The Jefferson idea of expansion with the purpose of creating a space 'with people speaking the same language, governed in similar forms, and by similar laws' remains the guiding strategic goal. Jefferson referred to a space covering 'the whole northern, if not the southern [American] continent' at the beginning of the 19th century; but today's expansion

---

82 Vine 2020, pp. 310–11.
83 I will come back to this event in Chapter 3.

clearly refers to the whole planet. At the moment of the fall of the Soviet Union, the U.S. was convinced that the rest of the world would embrace liberal democracy and capitalism. Today, nothing is more uncertain. Nevertheless, the U.S. establishment still thinks and acts today as though this dream remains possible, inter alia by giving extraterritorial strength to the U.S. laws (e.g., sanctions on foreign countries and enterprises) and universal character to the U.S. values.

We have seen above how American politicians, scholars and think tanks insist upon 'values.' It is 'values' that give the U.S. the right and the duty to intervene wherever and whenever it considers that its projected values are at stake. Hence the implementation of all sorts of strategies to orchestrate regime change in countries that do not comply with these values. But is it generally a question of values? History shows that whenever the U.S. has acted with the declared purpose to free a country from dictatorship in the name of 'its universal values,' it has installed itself in the liberated country, one way or the other, with '*armes et bagages*' as the French say (with weapons and baggage): Latin America, Europe, the Middle East, and the Far East. Quite often, values have been put aside in favour of state power and economic interests. The policy of U.S. policy towards the Nord Stream 2 mentioned above is a good example.

It is possible, even likely, that the American mainstream thinkers actually do not understand or recognize the dictatorial, imperial character of the foreign policy of their country. But while Putin has rightly pointed out that Americans project their own way of doing and thinking on their major foes, especially China, who is explicitly accused of trying to export its economic and political model with the final objective to dominate the world—paradoxically, it may be that they do not recognize this as something they are doing, themselves. Perhaps they think that they are doing is simply what is right. Which, by the way, reflects the U.S. historical orientation over time and what it still holds to, today. I have already dealt with these topics in Chapter 1. In The second part of this chapter, I will show that China's ideology is quite different, and in Chapter 3 I will further develop the factual behaviour of the U.S. and China foreign policies.

For the moment it suffices to insist upon the main values of U.S. ideology that have oriented its foreign policy. Right from the time of the Declaration of Independence U.S. ideology was not only based on the idea of setting up a virtuous Republic away from corrupted Europe, but also that the values of that Republic had a universal character: other countries should adopt them by imitation, or they would be forced to implement them.[84] Then, very rapidly, these values have been defined more precisely, as those of liberal democracy and capitalism. Now, aside from their purported universality, the question arises: have these original values always been respected during the history of the U.S. Republic, and does it actually respect them today? The Declaration of Independence says: 'all men are created equal, they are endowed by their Creator with certain unalienable Rights, that among these are Life, Liberty and the pursuit of Happiness.' Great! But what about the lives, the liberty, and the happiness of the millions of people who have been bombed, killed, wounded, displaced, and tortured in the name of the values of the Virtuous Exemplary, Exceptional Republic? And also, what remains today of Jefferson's prophecy concerning the role of the U.S. in the world: 'We are destined to be a barrier against the return of ignorance and barbarism.'[85]

What kind of other values have been implemented years after years, decades after decades between 1619 (the arrival in the British American colonies of the first African slaves) and today's bombings and sanctions that hit above all the most vulnerable people in the 'ignorant and barbarian' countries? What is the reason? Would it be because when there is a contradiction between U.S. values and U.S. interests, quite often interests prevail? But what kind of interests? Or is it because the professed values of democracy and human rights are too often set aside to give precedence over non-democratic values? Or would it be for the apparently noble purpose of punishing the culprits, i.e., those who oppress or even kill their own citizens, as it is often put forward by the U.S. for justifying the use of force? In such cases, the members of the U.S. establishment would be well advised to meditate upon the terrible sentence of Bartolomé De Las Casas about the slaughter of the Indians by the Spanish *conquistadores*: 'it is a sin meriting eternal damnation to harm and kill innocents in order to punish the guilty, for it is contrary to justice.'[86] It is interesting to note that Confucius, Mencius and Xunzi

---

84 According to one or the other dimensions of U.S. foreign policy: exceptionalism/isolationism or universalism/interventionism (see above).
85 Jefferson 1816. The whole sentence already mentioned above is: 'We are destined to be a barrier against the return of ignorance and barbarism. Old Europe will have to lean on our shoulders, and to hobble along by our side.' Today the sentence clearly refers not only to Europe but to the whole world.
86 Las Casas 1974, quoted by Wallerstein 2006. See also Bartolomé de Las Casas 1992. In chapters 31, 32 and 33, Las Casas develops several arguments to

statements are even more severe than Las Casas's. The first goes like this: 'Lord Ji Kang asked Confucius about government, saying: "Suppose I were to kill the bad to help the good; how about that?" Confucius replied: "You are here to govern; what need is there to kill? If you desire what is good, the people will be good. The moral power of the gentleman is wind, the moral power of the common man is grass. Under the wind, the grass must bend"'[87] And Mencius and Xunzi go even farther: 'Mencius says that it is wrong to "kill one innocent man" or "take what one is not entitled to" in order to gain the empire, for doing so is contrary to rightness [or justice] (*yì*) and benevolence (*rén*)' (Mencius 2A.2, 7A.33; also 4B.4). Xunzi is of the same view, namely, that a gentleman 'would not commit a single act contrary to the requirements of justice nor execute a single blameless man, even though he might thereby obtain the empire. Such a lord acts with justice (*yì*) and faithfulness (*xìn*) toward the people' (Xunzi 8.2; also 11.1a, 4.8). For Mencius and Xunzi, then, justice is a moral constraint on people's pursuit of goals and benefits.[88] I will come back to these Confucian values in the second part of this chapter.

Having conceived the virtuous Republic as a model other countries should imitate and, moreover, as the depositary of universal values, the exceptional and indispensable country would inevitably project itself outside its original borders. Expansion would become the irresistible imperative of U.S. foreign policy. Consequently, the U.S. would consider countries who dare oppose this expansion as existential threats to the values and interests of the virtuous Republic and to the world it made. These countries, no matter their size, the forms of their government (democratic or despotic) would be fought by all means, overt and covert military actions, economic sanctions, provocations, as well as actions aimed at regime changes ... until the dream of the end of history would become true. But is this possible?

---

sustain his analysis (pp. 204–20).

87 *The Analects* XII:19, from Simon Leys, trans., *The Analects of Confucius*, New York, Norton, 1997, quoted by Joseph Chan (1999), p. 233.

88 Chan 2014, p. 164. Chan further comments that justice is understood as a non-consequentialist, non-utilitarian idea, meaning that justice has an intrinsic value, not to be evaluated by the goals pursued or by the consequences of action.

CHINESE IDEOLOGY, PAST AND PRESENT

In addressing the situation of China, this question cannot be avoided: how is it possible that China has been able to develop into such a powerful country in all its dimensions, modern science, economy, polity and even military, without adopting the Western model of liberal democracy, claimed by the West as the necessary precondition for development, well-being, moral virtue, and more? In answering this question, it seems reasonable to hypothesize that the way China has developed its power resources must have been supported, indeed underpinned, at minimum by a coherent ideology. Otherwise, as the Western dominant opinion affirms, it would have collapsed. China's ideology provided it with the intellectual resources necessary to succeed, without adopting the Western model. Again, per François Jullien, already mentioned in Chapter 1, I consider that culture is not a static phenomenon. The essential characteristic of culture is that it changes and transforms itself. A culture that does not transform itself is a dead culture.[89] And as culture changes, so do its values and its ideology. This transformation can be the result of an internal (endogenous) process or of a cross-cultural fertilization.[90] Moreover, values are not something that any particular culture owns, but rather should be considered as resources accessible by everyone. But this process should not be regarded as one country possessing cultural resources that other countries then borrow and import into their culture. Resources do not advertise themselves as slogans, do not impose themselves, they are not ideological and therefore they are not imbedded into a system, i.e. in an ideology. Contrary to values that possess intrinsic validity, resources are evaluated only by taking into consideration their effects.[91]

In order to understand the changes the Chinese culture has gone through since the last decades of the Empire, it is more fruitful to see the 'resource' dimension of values rather than values *per se*. The non-ideological characteristic of resources gives the decision-maker a greater flexibility to integrate them into the existing culture than values. And

---

89 Jullien, 2017, pp. 43–44.
90 Jullien 2015a and 2015b.
91 Jullien 2017, pp. 50–65. Consequently, Jullien goes even further sustaining that there is a substantial difference between values and resources. I will not go that far. I will use the expression 'value-resource,' and when, for the sake of simplicity, I use 'values,' I will always mean 'value-resource.'

it gives the decision-maker a better capacity to adapt to the changes of the environment. Because of their ideological characteristic, values are difficult to change, and even more difficult to abandon. This distinction will help us to better understand why the import of Western values has not transformed China into a liberal democracy. In actuality, China has not imported Western values, but simply Western intellectual resources useful for the realization of China's goal to become again a world power.

CHINA'S CULTURE AND THE COHERENCE OF ITS IDEOLOGY

Two dimensions of ideological coherence have sustained China's development strategy. The first is internal coherence, i.e. the absence of contradictions between the elements that constitute the ideology. The external coherence of the ideology should orient the behaviour of the government so that it realizes its objectives in the national and international environments. While environments are constantly changing, their fundamental features change quite slowly.[92] This means that the ideology should help the decision-maker to identify as soon as possible the changes that will inevitably occur in the environments. China's traditional culture is very well equipped to understand the importance of fundamental changes, and the need to discover them as soon as possible. This is one of the major tasks of the efficient decision-maker. This precept is taken from Wang Hui's definition of fundamental long-term changes: they are silent and invisible, therefore difficult to discover. This is based upon one of the fundamental ways the Chinese conceive the world where they live: that it is constantly changing and does not (as in the Western way) pass from one stage to the next (e.g. from weak to strong; from young to old). Nothing is static, even for a short moment, everything is constantly moving.[93] Chapter 3 addresses how China has been skilful in adapting to the changes of the environment and thereby in succeeding in its strategy to become again a world power; and *a contrario* we will see the difficulty the U.S. has in changing its strategy and adapting to the 'invisible and silent changes' that have been going on in the international environment since at least the end of WW2.[94]

---

92 (Braudel 1972, 1979, 1992, Jullien 1989, 1999, 2004, 2011, and Wang Hui 2003, 2011, 2014, 2016.
93 According to François Jullien this is why the Chinese are better armed for understanding change.
94 The Chinese wording is the following: qián yí mò huà, i.e. qián (latent, invisible) yí (movement, change, transformation) mò (silent) huà (transformation, change). Let us note that Jullien has taken only the 'silent' part of the definition

China has been able to change its ideology so that it has reached a high degree of external coherence. This has been done by introducing within the traditional ideology inherited from the Empire new values-resources imported from the West, without abandoning the essence of its traditional values-resources. By doing this, China has been able to adapt its public policies to the changes of the environment, and to realize its objectives without adopting the Western model, and, even more important, without collapsing. I will also show that China has been able to change some elements of the environment to its advantage, especially when dealing with China's conception of strategy.

Another feature of Chinese thinking that has certainly helped China to build such a coherent ideology, both internally and externally, is that Chinese thinkers have never established a clear demarcation between theory and ideology on one side, and practice on the other. This is in fact based upon the traditional way the Chinese have conceived the world in which they live. It is therefore interesting, before we go any further, to place our analysis in the general framework of Chinese philosophy.[95] The Swiss sinologist Nicolas Zufferey has analysed the major characteristics of the Chinese culture that help us to understand China's domestic and foreign policies.[96] First of all, Chinese thinkers have a wholistic approach to analysing the world, the relations between humanity and nature, the relations between society and the individual, as it is practiced for example in Chinese medicine. Second, Chinese philosophy has not based morality upon the revelation of a transcendent God, and the religion built upon it, as the West has done. We have seen above, when analysing American ideology, the importance of the reference to God, and how it has driven American thinkers and politicians to establish a partition between WE the believers and the OTHERS, between GOOD and EVIL, and how what was applicable for religion, then was applied to

---

and speaks of 'silent transformations.' Wang Hui has accepted this definition when correcting the proofs of the English translation of his books.

95 I will not attempt to determine what exactly were the teachings of Confucius; neither will I deal with the development of Confucianism. On the interpretation of the origins of Confucian thought and the transformations it has undergone throughout history, see François Billeter (2006), and especially Zufferey (2008). Chinese Imperial power, is in fact an interpretation of Confucius that is not totally faithful to Confucius' teaching. In this sense, see Zufferey 2008, pp. 19–32 and 60–61. For a Neo-confucian interpretation of Confucianism for modern times see Chan 2014. I will come back to Chan's interpretation below.

96 Zufferey 2008. The introduction to the book is significantly entitled: 'Understanding today's China thanks to yesterday's China,' pp. 13–18.

the economy and the polity. Third, Zufferey draws our attention to the revival of the ancient Chinese philosophy, namely Confucianism, through which China seems to be looking for a substitute or a complement to Marxism, in spite of the constant reference to the latter made in official political discourse, as we will see below.[97]

The fourth, utility, is an essential criterion for assessing the validity of philosophical postures in ancient China. Chinese philosophers do not like to be too abstract. Rather, they refer to circumstances or to examples drawn from the real world, both in the past and the present. Knowledge is always viewed in relation to action, to know *how to act* morally or politically. What is important is not 'what to know,' but 'to know how to do it.' This attitude is still operational today among Chinese high officials. When I was the director of a training program for senior Chinese officials, I had to discuss the content of the training with the leaders of the groups of trainees before they came to Europe to attend seminars at public and private institutions. They always wanted to have presentations showing how to do things, how to manage human resources, how to privatize state-owned enterprises (SOEs), how to improve the environment, how to protect natural and cultural monuments, and so on. When I suggested that our experts could also present the theoretical basis of the management tools related to those policies, they always, very politely, made me understand that this was not what they expected from the training, as they already had the theoretical knowledge. In other words, they were saying: give us the practical tools, and we will possibly use them in the framework of our theory. So, for them, the question was: we already know what to do (the theory) and at the same time we have our way of doing it (our practice); we just want to see how you do it (your practice), and if it is useful to us, we will introduce it into our 'what to do—how to do it.'[98] It is little wonder that the Chinese participants were also very interested in 'action learning,' as developed by some Western

---

97 The constitution of the CPC enumerates the main elements of the Party ideology, known as the Four Cardinal Principles, defined in March 1979 by Deng Xiao Ping, that are still valid today: every public policy is to be in conformity (1) with the Marxist, Leninist and Maoist thought, (2) with the Socialist way, (3) with the continuation of the democratic dictatorship of the people and (4) with the leadership of the CPC. The four principles have been completed with (5) the important thought of Three Represents (Jiang Zemin), (6) the Scientific Outlook on Development (Hu Jintao), and (7) Xi Jinping's Thought on Socialism with Chinese Characteristics for a New Era.
98 Urio 2012, pp. 20–21.

scholars and practitioners, which seemed to be in tune with the Chinese merging of theory and practice.[99]

Fifth, if practice is more important than theory, it follows that traditional Chinese thinkers are prone to give more importance to practice than to a pre-established plan (or model) contrary to the choice of their Western colleagues who consider that the plan should orient the practice. Plans are static, whereas the environment is constantly moving, even if slowly and silently. As the Chinese proverb says: the plan cannot catch up with the changes (*Jìhuà gǎnbushàng biànhuà*). So, again, it is important to evaluate the environment, to discover how it is changing, and adapt the ideology (the value-resources) and the strategy accordingly. Taking stock of the economic and social development realized by China since the 1980s and its emergence as a world power at the beginning of the 20th century, one has to concede that China must have achieved these remarkable results by adopting the methodology best suited for the different characteristics of the physical and the human environments they confronted. For analysing nature China has adopted the Western methodology based upon mathematical modelling; whereas for analysing human relations (e.g., in business and in political relations) China has relied more on its traditional way of thinking, especially in regard to strategy, as we will see below in this chapter and in Chapter 3.

This point is very important because it contradicts an opinion frequently put forward by Western pundits: that the Chinese have difficulty in criticizing their predecessors, especially the rulers, and a consequent difficulty to innovate in all domains. However, the preference in favour of practice seems to give the Chinese thinkers more flexibility than enjoyed by their Western colleagues, who most of the time are prisoners of a model, a plan or even an ideology, as is today the case for the majority of U.S. mainstream thinkers. For the Chinese thinkers, insofar as theory and practice are inextricably merged, a change in the environment necessitates a revision and eventually a change in both theory and practice.

This has been the case for China since the last decades of the empire, then even during the Mao era, and finally, even more dramatically, since the end of the 1970s. Already during the Empire, some Chinese thinkers had been open to changes. Zufferey quotes the case of Wang Chong, whom he considered a pioneer of the post-Maoist era, insofar

---

99 See, for example, Ian McGill and Liz Beaty, *Action Learning. A Guide for Professional, Management and Educational Development*, London, Kogan Page, 1995.

as he considers innovation and creativity to be the major qualities of the intellectuals.[100] Wang Chong's ideas were severely criticized during the Imperial era, very likely because they constituted a threat to the ideology upon which rested the Imperial power, but then were rediscovered in China during the twentieth century, and they may constitute today an interesting support to the new trends of the development strategy. Already at the Party Congress of October 2007, Hu Jintao (who was President of the CPC from 2002 to 2012) put a lot of emphasis on the necessity to introduce innovations autonomously (i.e. different from the West) into several important domains of Chinese society, as we shall see below.

How China Defines and Implements Strategy

We are now ready to discuss how the Chinese define and implement strategy. In other words, what should be the attitude of the skilful strategist? The traditional Chinese strategy is based not upon the prior definition of a model that is subsequently used to orient action (as in the West), but on the analysis of the situation aimed at discovering the 'situation potential,' i.e. the favourable and unfavourable elements that may have an impact upon the realization of the strategist's objectives.[101] Starting from this analysis, the Chinese strategist adopts a mix of inaction and action. On the one hand, this entails not acting when the analysis of the situation shows that the means to intervene with success are not available, and therefore necessitates waiting until the 'silent transformations' inevitably change ('transform') the situation, eventually in a way favourable to the realization of desired objectives. But on the other hand, action is in order when the situation offers the possibility to intervene with success upon some elements so that, in the long run, the situation becomes overall favourable to the realization of the intended objectives.

This contradicts the Western dominant opinion critiquing the propensity of Chinese strategist to inaction and slowness and the idea of 'an eternal China' incapable of change, innovation and progress. On the contrary, Chinese strategist acts very quickly when the situation is favourable, and when it is not he waits for the 'silent transformations'

---

100 Zufferey 2008, pp. 178–187.
101 Jullien, 2011, p. 70: the Chinese way looks like an 'unmodelled model of becoming.' In other words, there is no China model; or more precisely, and maybe also paradoxically, the China model is that there is no model, but a continuous transformation of the ways of thinking and managing the modernization process of this great country.

to materialize.[102] In the meantime, he acts upon the elements of the environment when he has a chance to change them to his advantage.[103] Finally, the essence of strategy is, on the one hand, to gradually trap the competitor into a fixed position upon which the strategist can act, and, on the other hand, to constantly change the strategist's position in order to make his own strategy incomprehensible for the competitor. By doing so, the best Chinese strategist wins the war without fighting, his opponent being inevitably led to lose when he understands, too late, that the 'potential of the situation' has become helplessly negative for him, following the 'silent transformations' and the changes introduced by the actions of the Chinese strategist.

Moreover, for the Chinese strategist it is very important to be able to manage time, understood not in the Western sense of chance, or destiny, but as 'time-opportunity' (Chieng 2006).[104] It is by leaving the course of 'things,' the occurrence of events, to develop without interfering that one can be most efficient; more precisely, by combining 'the acting' upon the elements of the situation that one can change to one's advantage, with 'the non-acting' when one does not have a reasonable possibility to change the elements to one's advantage. In order to act efficiently, one must wait for the favourable occasion, the favourable moment; and it is here that it is possible and necessary to act. But this does not mean that the strategist must wait passively for the opportunity to occur. On the contrary, by manipulating reality 'upstream of the silent transformations,' the Chinese strategist induces the opportunity, by a variety of covert actions. And this is the most efficient strategy. This is clearly linked to the concept of manipulation, in the sense of transforming the environment with the purpose of facilitating the advent of the

---

102 For example, China has negotiated for several years two trade and investment agreements with the EU and with 15 Asian countries, an evident move to escape the containment policy of the U.S. It seems that these agreements had reached a deadlock, especially thanks to the U.S. pressures on China's potential partners. Suddenly, during the troubled transition from the Trump to the Biden administrations, China managed to finalize these two agreements. It is very likely that China took advantage of the discontent of several of the countries concerned with the bullying posture of Trump's foreign policy and the weak signals that the Biden administration would substantially reverse Trump's foreign policy 'style.' This is what happened, as we saw above.

103 For example, Mao's investing in education and health after 1949.

104 André Chieng is a Sino-French economist born in Marseille, who applied Jullien's analysis to a variety of contemporary situations in both business and public policymaking in China and in the West.

favourable and intended outcome. The Chinese strategist does not wait for the 'chance' (in the Western sense) to appear; he induces it rather than force it, by working as far as possible 'upstream.'[105]

These references to manipulation and covert actions necessary for the implementation of an efficient strategy have been vehemently criticized by Western, and especially by American pundits. For example, in the view of Michael Pillsbury,[106] the U.S. helped China with the hope that China would become like it, i.e. a liberal democracy imbedded into global capitalism where China would play according to the rules America made. However, the Chinese leadership

> has misled and manipulated American policy makers to obtain intelligence and military, technological, and economic assistance. [...] The goal is to avenge or "wipe clean" (*xi xue*) past foreign humiliations. Then China will set up a world order that will be fair to China, a world without American global supremacy, and revise the U.S.-dominated economic and political world order founded (...) at the end of World War II. The [Chinese] hawks assess that China can only succeed in this project through deception, or at least by denial of any frightening plans.[107]

While it is clear that for Pillsbury China's deceptive and secret policies constitute a threat to the global supremacy of the U.S., he nevertheless admits (evidently with some regrets and fears) that Chinese leaders

---

105 Chieng 2006, pp. 181–182, 196, 210, 214, 218–223, 225.

106 Michael Pillsbury is the director of the Center on Chinese Strategy at the Hudson Institute (a neo-conservative think tank) a former analyst at the RAND Corporation and a member of the Council on Foreign Relations and the International Institute for Strategic Studies. During the Reagan administration, Pillsbury, who is fluent in Chinese, was Assistant Under-Secretary of Defense for Policy Planning and responsible for implementation of the covert aid program known as the Reagan Doctrine. In 1975–1976, while an analyst at the RAND Corporation, Pillsbury published articles in *Foreign Policy* and *International Security* recommending that the U.S. establish intelligence and military ties with China.

107 Pillsbury 2015, p. 12. See also the article by Campbell and Ratner (2028) significantly entitled 'How Beijing Defied American Expectations.' Campbell was Assistant Secretary of State for East Asian and Pacific Affairs from 2009 to 2013. Ratner was Deputy National Security Adviser to U.S. Vice-President Joe Biden from 2015 t0 2017.

are now beginning to talk about the goal of their strategy 'more openly, perhaps because they realize it may already be too late for America to keep pace'; a clear acknowledgement of the efficacy of China's strategy.[108] Pillsbury's analysis may be correct. It is true that, compared to China's, the U.S. strategy is more open. But he forgets that the 'openness' of U.S. policy has been possible until recently, due to the U.S.'s extraordinary advantages on almost every count, especially its military, technological, economic and even cultural resources. Moreover, some of the U.S.'s policies are not as open as one may think. Consider the official number of military bases, an astonishing total of about 900, that very likely hides some more.[109] Nor is the budget of the Pentagon an example of transparency and clarity. Furthermore, the U.S. has conducted military or quasi-military covert operations all over the world, to say nothing of its destabilization campaigns and use of proxies. Finally, several operations aimed at inducing 'regime change' with the purpose of setting up governments more favourable to American interests have been conducted covertly under the pretext of establishing democracy, human rights and free market economy, or more precisely capitalism.

In Chapter 3 I will show that the U.S. foreign policy remains deeply stuck in the 19th century original ideology analysed at the beginning of this chapter. Even the 'unusual' President Trump has not succeeded in escaping from the dictatorship of the dominant ideology.[110] At the same time, it seems that China has been successful in changing the 'situation potential' to its advantage, trapping the U.S. into a fixed position from which it seems unable to escape, i.e. continuing to implement a foreign policy based upon the threat, and eventually the actual use of economic and military forces. During the same period of time, Chinese strategy has given the impression of being constantly on the move, evolving from one approach to the other: from the economy to the military, to technology, to investments abroad, to the attraction of talent, to the diffusion of

108 Pillsbury, p. 16.
109 Vine 2020, 2015, and Nick Turse's articles published by *TomDispacth*. Vine has spent years on studying the development of military bases by the U.S. since the beginning of the U.S. Republic, i.e. from the last quarter of the XVIII century. In his 2020 book he summarizes his findings, with recent reliable data, comments and several tables that show the development of military bases as a formidable support for the U.S. wars, many of which have been aggression wars.
110 I have analysed Trump's foreign policy in Urio 2028 (pp. 129–143) and 2019 (pp. 230–243). Above, I have qualified this ideology as a 'weapon of mass destruction,' as it has destroyed the capacity of the American elite to conceive any other world in which the U.S. could play another role.

Chinese culture. It has changed from copying the West to innovating autonomously; from opening up its economy to the world to protecting its national market from predatory capitalists; from bilateral agreements to new multilateral organizations; from asserting local interests (the China Seas, Hong Kong, Xinjiang, Tibet, Taiwan) to developing global interests in Eurasia, Africa, Latin America, and the Arctic; from criticizing traditional enemies (e.g. Japan and India) to negotiating with them, etc. Thereby, China confirms that 'the essence of strategy is on the one hand to gradually trap the competitor into a fixed position [i.e. from which it cannot escape] upon which the strategist can act, and on the other hand to constantly change its position in order to make its own strategy incomprehensible to the competitor' … and when he starts to understand it, it is too late.[111]

Before I describe China's ideology as it exists today, we have to understand what the ultimate goal of the Chinese Party-State is, which then needs to be supported by such a coherent ideology. The central value-resource of the Chinese ideology is the Harmony, understood as the absence of conflicts. Harmony is sustained by unity and stability, and at the same time it strengthens them (see Figure 2 below). Of course, the Chinese know very well that conflicts are an inevitable aspect of life. But the architecture of society should be built in order to make the probability of conflicts as low as possible.[112] Now, the ultimate goal of the Communist Party (CPC) is to realize harmony both internally and internationally and to avoid the repetition of the foreign aggressions of the 19th century that are still underway today, as the aggressive foreign policy of the U.S. very well shows. But before we analyse the ideology of the CPC, we have to understand how China tried to safeguard harmony during the Empire and during the immediate predecessor of the People's Republic of China, i.e. the Nationalist Republic of China.

---

111 Chieng 2006, p. 210; Jullien 1995, Chap. 1.
112 Let us note that traditionally harmony must be realized not only amongst humans but also between humans and nature.

CONFUCIANISM: THE TRADITIONAL IDEOLOGY OF THE CHINESE EMPIRE

I have shown above that Chinese theory and practice (or ideology and strategy) are inextricably connected. Therefore, ideology and strategy are changed almost simultaneously, as it is necessary to adapt them to the transformations of both the national and the international environments. It is not possible to deal with Chinese ideology without at least mentioning the major elements of the strategy China has implemented since the last decades of the Empire. Towards the end of the 19th century, while being dominated by Western powers and Japan, China's ideology began to change. But how? How did China manage to become again not only a great civilization, but also a great power, capable of dissuading potential enemies from repeating the aggression of the 19th century? Through what strategies did China manage to realize this goal? Let us start with the Chinese Empire.

China is generally recognized as one of the greatest civilizations, not only for the arts, but also, more particularly, for its organization of its government. China was, together with ancient Egypt, the first country to develop a quasi-modern public administration, i.e. a public bureaucracy.[113] This great civilization suffered its most devastating humiliation between the 19th and the 20th centuries when Western powers reduced it to semi-colonial status. Of course, this was not the first time China had been defeated. The Mongols and the Manchus defeated China and ruled over it for several centuries. But they were then almost completely assimilated into Chinese culture and governed it according to the traditional Confucian way, so that there is no discontinuity in China's history, which is structured according to the sequence of the Chinese dynasties until the fall of the last dynasty in 1912.

But Western countries did not even dream of being assimilated into the Chinese culture. The reason why is very simple: they only wanted to do business in China, and quite naturally on their own terms. Chinese humiliation was rendered even more deep when China was defeated by its 'small cousin of the rising sun,' Japan, in 1894–1895, and that humiliation lasted until 1949 when Mao proclaimed the founding of the People's Republic of China. That said, it was during that period that Western ideas about the way of organizing economy and polity arrived in China, even if in a rather violent way.

---

113 Weber 1978, for Egypt, pp. 964, 971–973 and 1401–1402; for China, pp. 431, 477, 964 and 1401.

Chinese society did not remain unchanged from the beginning to the end of the Empire (i.e. from the second century B.C. to the beginning of the twentieth century A.D.). These changes have been very well summarized by the French sinologist Marie-Claire Bergère as follows:

> before the nineteenth century China was not a stagnant society as is too often described by Western observers. The remarkable dynamism between the sixth and the eleventh centuries was followed by an era of darkness, the Mongol conquest (1205–1279) and an isolation that came to an end only at the beginning of the sixteenth century under the Ming dynasty. A new economic development would then take place that would continue under the Qing dynasty until the beginning of the nineteenth century.'[114]

China has been a pioneer in the development of science and technology since the tenth century.[115] At the moment when Europe started its own scientific development (fifteenth-sixteenth century) China already possessed a considerable advance in science and technology over it. The Chinese scientific innovations exerted a remarkable impact on the organization of economic production, as well as on social structures, including the appearance of forms of market economy that are still partially present today.[116]

After its defeat in the Opium Wars (1839–1860), China had already begun to import value-resources (i.e. constitutional ideas and technology) from the West and set up factories and dockyards to manufacture Western-style weapons and war-ships. Needless to say, a country cannot build warships capable of confronting a technologically more advanced foreign navy overnight. The Sino-French war over Vietnam (1883–1885) ended in 1885 when it took only one hour for the French to destroy the

---

114 Bergère 2007, p. 23, my translation.
115 For an account of the Chinese contribution to science and technology (well before the European contributions since the Renaissance—fifteenth century) see Temple 1998, and Hobson 2004 (chapters 3 and 9 on Chinese influence on the West), Needham (1954–2004). For a comparative analysis of the rise of the natural sciences: Toby 2003.
116 Bergère 1986 and 2007. For the emergence of a market in China see Braudel 1979a, *Civilisation matérielle,* vol. 2, and especially pp. 116, 120–125, 139–140, 146 and 255–256. On the emergence of capitalism see ibid., pp. 268–287 for the use of 'capital, capitalist, and capitalism,' and for the emergence of capitalism in China see ibid., and more especially pp. 354–356 and 708–23.

new Chinese fleet of 11 steamers. The irony is that China had built its fleet in Fuzhou with the help of the French, but the war ended with the demolition of the Fuzhou shipyard. A decade later (1894–1895) China lost the first Sino-Japanese War that was decided at sea.[117]

In spite of these defeats, it is interesting to note that China was already trying to adapt to the new circumstances, and realized the importance at that time of building a modern navy capable of confronting potential enemies. Moreover, at the beginning of the twentieth century, the Western ideas of constitutionalism and parliamentary government were discussed at the Imperial court, and in 1909 consultative provincial assemblies met in each province. But these initiatives came too late: the empire of the Qing Dynasty, which had been weakened for decades by foreign interventions and internal contradictions, collapsed at the beginning of 1912.

During the Empire, harmony was sought through the application of authoritarian measures both within the family and the polity, following an interpretation of Confucianism. This ideology, which deeply modelled the Imperial bureaucracy, is a unique example of a system of thought that constituted the ideological support of Imperial power for two millennia, in spite of many periods of instability. This is not to say that during the Imperial era this was the only political philosophy discussed in China. As Zufferey explains, this ideology became in fact, during the Han dynasty (from 206 B.C. to 220 A.D.), a synthesis which combines with the Confucian values the yin/yang, legalism, Taoism, as well as other streams of the pre-imperial era.[118]

The main idea at the beginning of the development of official Confucianism was to manage the country by moral rules in order to master the political disorder of the end of the Zhou dynasty (second century B.C.). The ideal society for Confucius is the Dao where harmony reigns.[119] To attain this goal, each member of society must act in conformity with principles or rites (*li*), i.e. at the same time a set of moral principles which govern social relations, and of rites which ensure the order of society and the functioning of the state's apparatus. It is necessary to cultivate the virtue of avoiding to seek the satisfaction of personal

117 Buckley 1999, pp. 245 and 252–54. See also Britannica, https://www.britannica.com/event/Sino-French-War).
118 Zufferey 2008, pp. 73–90.
119 Dao is used in several meanings: way, method, doctrine, speech; and it takes three forms: philosophical, religious and political. For more details see Zufferey 2008, pp. 105–138.

interests. The honest man *(junzi)*, who seeks the general interest, must direct the vulgar man *(xiaoren)* who seeks personal advantage. Human relations are conceived on the basis of family relations. The civil servant (the Mandarins), thanks to the years-long study of traditional Confucian canons, must stand as the example of xiao (filial piety) in the family. This virtue is then transposed to extra-family relations. Filial piety is transformed into political fidelity towards the emperor. This society is hierarchical, and its management is paternalistic: the ministers must submit themselves to the emperor, the son to his father, the wife to her husband, the junior to the elder. Governing people are regarded as 'fumuguan' (parent-civil servant) and the governed ones as 'zimin' (child-people). This conception provides a solid base for the monopolistic power exerted by the emperor. The latter reigns like a supreme head of a household since, according to the doctrine, he is the representative of Heaven on Earth to manage 'Tianxia,' i.e. all that is under the Sky-Heaven, i.e. China. But this absolutist power is not without limits. The sovereign must improve himself to become a moral example, and govern in the interest of the people, otherwise Heaven will give him warnings by causing natural disasters, and eventually, if he persists in error, it will withdraw its mandate from him by means of popular revolts.

This way of organizing society may be shocking for Westerners whose behaviour is oriented by what they regard as universally accepted virtues-values of freedom, electoral democracy and human rights (regarded largely as civil and political rights). Some Western pundits consider that the persistence of Confucianism is an obstacle to the development of democracy. Nevertheless, Zufferey has sustained that Confucius' ideas are not necessarily an impediment for developing a political system based upon the ideas of democracy and human rights.[120] Quoting the recent development of neo-Confucianism, Zufferey mentions three points favorable to the development of democracy in China. First, in spite of the authoritarian character of Confucianism in the public domain, the emperor is entrusted with the responsibility for the wellbeing of his people. Failure in this regard accords citizens the right to overthrow the emperor.[121] In particular, the emperor has the duty to listen to

120 Zufferey 2008, especially pp. 242–243.
121 Let me remind the reader that the Emperor outlawed the commerce and consumption of opium in the 1830s that the British as other Western traders (including Americans) were importing in vast quantities into China (statistics are given in tons!). According to the Chinese law the administration could seize and destroy the cargoes of opium arriving at the Chinese ports. When this

the advice and criticisms of his subordinates. In fact, Chinese Emperors have seldom decided alone. Second, the importance given to education, already during the Mao era, will at term produce a class of educated young people, who, according to Zuffery, will eventually contribute to the development of democracy.

Third, Confucius' method of teaching encourages dialogue between the master and the students, thus developing their capacity to criticize, and this will also favor the development of democratic engagement. Moreover, Confucius shows a keen sense of humanity, especially towards the weakest members of a society. And this goes in the direction of the safeguard of human rights. These ideas are shared by several Chinese scholars, such as Joseph Chan of the University of Hong Kong.[122] I will revert to Chan's modernization of Confucianism when discussing the way China has implemented, especially after the Mao era, a strategy combining value-resources imported from the West with Confucian value-resources to build new ideology coherent enough to preserve some traditional values, especially the authoritarian character of the state.

Nevertheless, for the time being, one is forced to admit that a development of China's polity in the direction of liberal democracy is not very likely in a foreseeable future. In fact, Western ideas about the way of organizing the economy and the political system arrived in China in a not too friendly manner in the 19th century. After a period of 'polite encounters' between the end of the 18th century and the 1830s, China endured extensive Western aggression, suffering a long period of semi-colonial status and humiliations, starting in 1839 with the first Opium War. Such an introduction to Western values to a country proud of its pluri-millennial culture was far from an auspicious beginning for their embrace by the Chinese population. Nonetheless, when the Empire collapsed in 1912, it seemed that the ideas of constitutional government already discussed during the last decades of the Empire had a reasonable chance to be tested and implemented by the Nationalist Republic of China.

---

decision was finally implemented, the traders, outraged, referred to the British government, which, being similarly outraged, decided to teach the Chinese a lesson. This marked the beginning of the first Opium War and led to the reduction of China to a semicolonial status.
122 Chan 1999 and 2015.

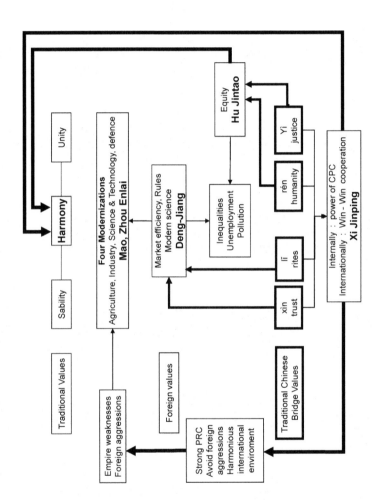

FIGURE 2: FUNDAMENTALS OF THE CHINESE IDEOLOGY

THE IDEOLOGY OF THE NATIONALIST REPUBLIC OF CHINA (2012–1949)

The fall of the Empire and the establishment of the Republic of China led by Sun Yat-sen in 1912 could have led to the adoption of the constitutional ideas which were already being discussed at the end of Empire and to the abandonment of the way the Empire had safeguarded harmony, unity and stability. Sun Yat-sen knew that it was not possible to rapidly implement the new ideas imported from the West. Therefore, he designed a long-term strategy comprising three phases: nationalistic revolution, democratic reconstruction, and social reform. Nevertheless, even this very careful strategy showed its limits. In fact, despite some remarkable innovations imported from the West, the revolutionary theory of Sun Yat-sen retains some continuity with the way the Empire had managed the country. True, in Sun's design, state power was divided into political power and governmental power. Political power is allocated to the people, who exert four political rights: right to elect, of revocation, of elaborating laws, and of re-examining the laws.[123] Moreover, at the local level Sun Yat-sen recommended the autonomy of the local authorities as a means of enabling the masses to take part in state affairs, as the foundation of a democratic republic. Nevertheless, traditional values led to a very swift reversion to an authoritarian form of the government, not only during the nationalistic revolution itself, but in the period thereafter, and were even strengthened after the death of Sun Yat-Sen in 1925.

The role of the Party was defined in the tradition of the unity principle, i.e. unlike a system where different parties compete for popular approval and thereby the right to exercise power. Indeed, it was specified that the government must be directed by a party, which must be revolutionary in nature.[124] The party was to govern through its organizations at the various administrative levels. The control of the government by the Nationalist Party (Kuomintang) can be summarized as follows: (a) all the fundamental laws are elaborated by the Party, (b) the principles, programmes, policies of the government are initially adopted by the latter before being implemented by the government, (c) the most important persons in charge of governmental affairs are appointed from amongst the members of the Central Executive Committee of the Nationalist Party.[125] In summary, some bodies of the Nationalist Party do implement

---

123 Wang Yanan 1949, p. 17.
124 Wang Yanan, p 21.
125 Wang Zhaogang, p. 71.

actual governmental duties in place of the national government. The latter is only the executive body of the Kuomintang. The political ideal of Sun was soon abandoned and used only as pretext by the leaders of the Nationalist Party to preserve their power. As Immanuel Hsü put it:

> Of the three goals it set to achieve in 1928—nationalistic revolution, democratic reconstruction, and social reform—the government by 1937 had made considerable progress toward the first, modest advance toward the second, but failed miserably in the third. Moreover, its extension of the Tutelage period [i.e. the six years dominance period of the Nationalist Party envisaged by Sun Yat-sen's incremental model] beyond the original six years from 1929, under the pretext of foreign invasions and domestic insurrections, disenchanted the liberals, who came to regard the delay as an artful device of the Nationalists to prolong their monopoly of power at the expense of constitutionalism.[126]

Even worse, the death of Sun Yat-sen in 1925 paved the way for Chiang Kai-shek, who instituted a dictatorial political system where the Nationalist Party was the real centre of power, with the political institutions and the public administration being subordinated to the Party, and Chiang, with the title of 'Generalissimo,' as the supreme leader. This introduced the idea and practice of a Party-State into Chinese ideology and practice. Even more interestingly, it was to remain a fundamental feature of the way Chinese organize the state, even during the People's Republic of China. That said, the values of harmony, stability and unity remained at the core of the nationalist ideology, and the way to safeguard them was through an authoritarian government, similar to that of the Empire: the Emperor is replaced by the President, the mandarins by the civil servants, and the citizens are subordinated to the Party-State with little means for interfering in the political process. Unfortunately, harmony was made impossible by the permanence of foreign interferences (especially by the Soviet Union and the U.S.), the Japanese aggression and by the creation of the Communist Party in 1921.[127] Moreover, the

---

126 Hsü 1995, p. 573.
127 Western powers were still present in their Concessions (with extraterritorial status) with increasing interferences by the Soviet Union and the U.S. Moreover,

new form of the state abandoned those Confucian values aimed at limiting the freedom of the Emperor and the President, such as the mandate from heaven that imposed upon the Imperial power the duty to govern in the interests of the people. Were the Confucian values abandoned for ever or would they re-emerge one day?

The inevitable civil war that burst out between the Nationalists and the Communists in the 1920s was put to a halt during the Japanese aggression of the 1930s, but restarted after the defeat of Japan by the U.S. in 1945, a defeat to which both Nationalists and Communists contributed. It ended with the Communists' victory in 1949. The door was then open for another type of political system that, as we shall see, despite many novelties, retained several features of the ideology through which the Chinese Emperors had governed China for two millennia.

THE IDEOLOGY OF THE COMMUNIST PARTY OF CHINA DURING THE MAO ERA

The Communist Party of China (CPC) was established in 1921 in Shanghai with the support of the Soviet Union, during the period of the Nationalist Republic of China (1912–1949). It took 28 years before it could take the helm of China following its victory over the Nationalist party, the Kuomintang, in 1949. During this period the Party assimilated Marxism-Leninism and, under the leadership of Mao, it adapted it to the local Chinese situation, by giving more importance to the peasants than the USSR's Communist Party had done in Russia. By the time the CPC established the People's Republic of China in 1949, it was ready to actually implement Marxism. So, this is the first important value-resource China imported from the West and practically implemented in China. If one were to wonder how this radical novelty could have been implemented without discarding the traditional values of harmony, unity and stability, the answer is simply that Marxism was more in tune with the Imperial (and even the nationalist) way of managing the state than liberalism. The latter, as we have seen in Chapter 1 is based upon the values of freedom, liberal democracy, a pluri-partisan system, etc. that clearly are not compatible with the Imperial governance to which the Chinese had been accustomed for millennia. In fact, we can say that the Party replaced both the 'party of the mandarins' of the Empire and the Nationalist Party.

---

in 1932 Japan further developed its own aggression by occupying large parts of China, that had already started in 1894–5 when it defeated China and occupied Taiwan.

Moreover, Marxism, especially in its Leninist form, the one chosen by the CPC, is even more in tune with the traditional Chinese governance as it attributes a special leading role to the Party, under whose leadership the country would be led to socialism. Accordingly, the new ideology could easily integrate Marxism and the traditional values of harmony, unity, and stability, safeguarded, as in the past, by an authoritarian government dominated by the Communist Party. This is not to say that the CPC has not introduced some radical reforms, whose essence was the deconstruction of the old class system.

The ideological rift between the Nationalists and the Communists inevitably transformed into a power struggle for the control of the country. While the Nationalists were able to keep the control of the State, two massacres happened in Shanghai that were at the origin of the civil war.[128] The 1925 Shanghai massacre began when the Shanghai Municipal Police opened fire on Chinese protesters in Shanghai's International Settlement on May 30. The order was given by Inspector Edward Everson, commanding Shik and Chinese police officers. Protesters were organized by the May Thirtieth Movement, a major labour and anti-imperialist movement, which significantly demanded the end of extra-territoriality and the closure of the Shanghai International Settlement.[129] The Municipal Council answered by declaring a state of martial law on June 1, calling up the Shanghai Volunteer Corps militia and requesting foreign military assistance to carry out raids and protect Chinese and foreign vested interests. The estimated numbers of Chinese killed and injured varies: figures normally vary between 30 and 200 dead, with hundreds injured. Policemen, firemen and foreigners were also injured, some seriously, and one Chinese police constable was killed. The second massacre was more murderous. The Shanghai massacre of April 12, 1927, entailed the violent suppression of the Communist Party's organizations in Shanghai by the military forces of Chiang Kai-shek and conservative factions in the Nationalist Party (KMT). Following the incident, the KMT carried out a full-scale violent purge of Communists in all areas under its control. Casualties are estimated to range between 5,000 to 10,000 deaths. It marked the beginning of the Chinese civil war.[130] We can say that this

---

128 In fact, the Nationalist Party never controlled the whole territory of China, because the War Lords (1916–1928) and the Communist Party (1927–1949) controlled parts of the national territory.
129 According to Wikipedia. For more details see Wikipedia, 'May Thirtieth Movement.'
130 According to Wikipedia. For more details see Wikipedia, 'Shanghai

is when the Mao era started during the 1920s within the Nationalist Republic.

During the Civil war, the CPC organized itself in ways that were to persist after the creation of the People's Republic in 1949. The choice of Marxism-Leninism inevitably led to the establishment of single-party rule, in spite of the existence of factions and personal rivalries, from which Mao emerged as the unchallenged leader. The persistence of the traditional value of unity, stability and harmony was further strengthened by the armed conflict not only with the Nationalists but also with the Japanese aggressor.[131] This is not to say that there were not elements of democracy. It is true that in the 1930s the CPC did institute a Soviet, but in fact it is the organizations of the CPC that replaced the Soviet and managed the Party exactly in the same way as the Nationalist Party was governing, at the same time, the Republic of China. Fundamentally, even if supported by opposing ideologies, the Nationalists and the Communists organized their power technically in the same way. Moreover, it is significant to see that during the time of the Republic of China, the CPC governed the territory under its control in ways that prefigure the government of the People's Republic of China.

When Mao proclaimed the People's Republic of China on 1 October 1949, the form of the state was ready to be implemented: one-party rule, predominance of the party's hierarchy over the state hierarchy. For example, at the provincial level, the Secretary General of the CPC has precedence over the Governor of the province. The principles of harmony, stability and unity are still at the core of the Chinese political culture after 1949 in spite of (or maybe because of) the adoption of Marxism–Leninism, although Mao has adapted this ideology to the Chinese situation.[132] Harmony, stability and unity were basically safeguarded through

---

Massacre.' The estimated deaths are considerably greater than the estimated casualties in Tiananmen square in June 1989. Nevertheless, the 1927 Shanghai massacre is rarely, and to my knowledge never, commemorated by Western mainstream media.

131 This is not typical of a war led by a communist party; *mutatis mutandis,* it is also the case of liberal democracies: when at war, the rights of the elected bodies are at least limited.

132 It is not necessary in the context of this book to evaluate to what extent Mao was able to effectively adapt Marxism–Leninism to the Chinese situation. For an evaluation of the positive and negative aspects of Mao's policies between 1949 and 1976 one can rely upon the vast literature available in the West by both Chinese and Western scholars. An interesting evaluation made officially by the historians of the CPC can be found in Hu Sheng (Chief editor), *A Concise History*

the same form of state that for two millennia organized the Empire, despite the Cultural Revolution, to be addressed below. Moreover, as has been the case since the first Opium War, the pressure on China by the West continued, especially from the U.S. which, having 'lost China,' allowed the loser of the civil war, Chiang Kai-shek, to set up a rival Republic in Taiwan, and would not recognize the PRC until 1 January 1979.[133] This too did not create a favourable international environment for facilitating the introduction of Western ideals into China such as constitutional government and multi-party system.

Mao proclaimed the People's Republic of China on the first of October 1949. But an equally significant event took place slightly ahead of it, on September 21, when at the First Plenary Session of the Chinese People's Political Consultative Conference, Mao proudly declared: 'Ours will no longer be a nation subject to insult and humiliation; we have stood up.'[134] Of course, at that time China was still an underdeveloped country. To make it strong enough to avoid further humiliation, China had to reconstruct its power resources while taking into consideration the national and the international environment. In order to realize this objective, it was necessary to simultaneously realize three interrelated goals: (1) reclaim world power status by developing the economy and the military as quickly as possible because foreign aggression may occur at any time, (2) provide a reasonable amount of goods and services to the Chinese people, (3) preserve harmony, unity and stability.

This has not been an easy task. But it is here that the Chinese way of implementing strategy has revealed its remarkable efficacy. China's leadership understood from the beginning that this was to be a very long process. Mistakes could slow the movements, or even lead to further humiliations. It was necessary, as above mentioned, to evaluate the 'situation potential,' act on the elements of the environment where you

of the Communist Party of China, Beijing, Party History Research Centre of the CPC Central Committee, Foreign Language Press, 1994. It is interesting to note that in spite of considerable differences (due mainly to different ideological and theoretical perspectives) both Western and Chinese analyses deal with both the positive and the negative aspects of the Mao era.

133 The expression 'lost China' comes from the Republicans who accused the Democrats, who held the U.S. presidency between 1932 and 1952, of having 'lost China' between the end of WW2 in 1945 and the defeat of U.S.'s protégé Chiang Kai-shek in 1949. This very clearly shows that the main objective of the U.S. in the Far East was the conquest of China, one way or the other. It does not refer to the Nixon/Kissinger recognition of China.

134 Mao 1949.

have a reasonable chance to succeed, for the rest, wait until the silent transformations will have changed the environment (or at least some of its elements) to your advantage, i.e. which now enable you to act. Mistakes should have been detected in time and corrected. It is only during the first decades of the 21st Century that the process has become successful: nobody ever again dared attack China as had happened in the 19th century.

What have been the positive and the negative outcomes of the Mao era? First, by defeating the Nationalists supported by the U.S., Mao was successful in reclaiming sovereignty for his country after a century of foreign aggressions that had reduced China to a semicolonial status. This was certainly a fundamental achievement. Second, it is reasonable to conclude that Mao chose to close the country to foreign influence in order to autonomously intervene in those elements of the internal situation that it was reasonably possible to improve: first of all, education and health, then industrialization of the economy in the framework of a command economy. Mortality rates dropped significantly both for young and adult people; life expectancy at birth increased from about 37 in 1950 to almost 66 by 1980. Moreover, this system assured a fair access to health care to all Chinese people. Literacy improved in this period from as low as 25.5% to more than 65%.

Third, Mao and Zhou Enlai defined the Four Modernizations that was to become the guiding strategy for recovering world power status, targeting these key sectors: agriculture, industry, science and technology, and defence.[135] The process of industrialization was accelerated, and the real GDP growth was quite impressive. In spite of Mao's mistakes it increased every year at an annual average of 4.5%, except in 1961 (–27.3) and 1962 (–5.6%) as a consequence of the Great Leap Forward, and in 1968 (–4.1) and 1976 (–1.6%) as a consequence of the Cultural Revolution.[136] Taking stock of what China has realized since then, we can

---

135 'The Four Modernizations were introduced as early as January 1963. At the Conference on Scientific and Technological Work held in Shanghai that month, Zhou Enlai called for professionals in the sciences to realize "the Four Modernizations." In February 1963, at the National Conference on Agricultural Science and Technology Work, Nie Rongzhen specifically referred to the Four Modernizations as comprising agriculture, industry, national defence, and science and technology. (…). In 1975, in one of his last public acts, Zhou Enlai made another pitch for the Four Modernizations at the 4th National People's Congress.' From Wikipedia, https://en.wikipedia.org/wiki/Four_Modernizations, accessed 20 September 2018.

136 IMF World Economic Outlook, April 2018

better appreciate the paramount meaning of the building blocks of Mao's era. Today China has a strong agriculture, a booming industrial sector, modern science and technology that can compete with the U.S., and a sufficiently strong military that is able to dissuade potential aggressors. Certainly, Mao's strategy had its negative consequences: poor economic performance, strong limitation of personal freedom, few incentives for innovations, environmental damages, as well as the catastrophic impact of the Great Leap Forward and the Cultural Revolution. Both tragic events show that in his will to develop the economy (especially industry) by transferring millions of peasants from agriculture to industry (Great Leap Forward) and more generally by governing in a quasi-permanent state of revolution, Mao did not see that economic development necessitates some new value-resources such as technical expertise. Moreover, Mao's strategy to govern in a permanent state of Revolution clearly contradicted his aim of restoring China's power by developing its economy. Certainly, as mentioned above, GDP increased at an average annual rate of 4.5%. Nevertheless, it is clear that it could have been much higher (as would be the case during Deng's era) should Mao have not made the tragic mistakes just mentioned. Mao's revolutionary management required politicians and civil servants to be 'red,' i.e. to share his ideology. As Max Weber has demonstrated, the development of the economy (be it in the form of a market economy or a command economy) will inevitably entail the development of technological competences in all parts of society, that are enabled to develop within a special type of organization, bureaucracies, based, among other characteristics, upon technical competencies. Bureaucrats accomplish tasks necessary for the realization of the goals of public policies and thus they will inevitably acquire power. By launching the Cultural Revolution, Mao sought to fight against three technocracies-bureaucracies that were in the process of gaining power and stealing power from him and deviating the governing of China from his ideological line: the Party, the Government and the intellectual bureaucracies.

It is fair to say that harmony could have been preserved, had Mao not committed the mistakes of the Leap Forward and the Cultural Revolution. Despite the well-known dramatic consequences of these mistakes for the Chinese people, it is fair to recognize that Mao nonetheless realized several goals, which then enabled his successors to launch the spectacular social and economic development of China starting in the 1980s only a few years after Mao's death (1976). It is certain that Mao set the bases that allowed Deng Xiaoping to further develop the Chinese economy, society and power resources. Moreover, Deng took stock of the negative consequences of Mao's personal leadership, and changed the economy by progressively introducing market mechanisms, opening China to the global economy, and reinstitute collective leadership, which Mao had abandoned after 1958.[137]

BRIDGE VALUES AND THE IDEOLOGY OF TODAY'S PRC

We have seen above that the process of reclaiming world power status had already started during the last decades of the Empire. The Nationalist Republic of Sun Yat-sen, too, had started with great expectations, though transforming China into a constitutional republic did not succeed due to the civil war, the persistence of foreign interferences and the Japanese aggression. We have also seen that Mao succeeded in realizing some major advances in the process of rebuilding China's power resources. Nevertheless, the forms of the state elaborated by the Nationalist Republic and the PCR during the Mao era, were not, at least technically, very different from the governance system of the Empire: a one-party system with the Party dominating the political process. The impact of the introduction of values-resources imported from the West was marginal, as these did not challenge China's traditional authoritarian form of the state. It is true that the adoption of Marxism-Leninism deconstructed the class structure of Chinese society, but it did not change the authoritarian form of the state. On the contrary, it required the authoritarian domination of the Communist Party and the adoption of a centralized command economy.

Deng Xiaoping's contribution to the CPC's ideology: Economic efficiency, market mechanisms and bridge values

With Deng Xiaoping, things were going to change. Deng had the formidable task of rescuing China from the damages of Mao's Cultural Revolution (1966–1976). He had to re-establish the reputation and leadership of the CPC, to give to the Chinese people some reasons to hope again for a bright future, and further, to build China's power resources. He chose to realize these goals simultaneously by introducing into China a form of market economy, or more exactly, some market mechanisms. We have seen above that some forms of market were present in ancient

---

137 Hu Angang 2014.

China as they were in fact all over the world.[138] But the market Deng imported from the West had some special features that were considered an improvement from what had existed before the advent of market economy, more precisely capitalism, and its first spectacular manifestation, the industrial revolution. Economic efficiency is the fundamental value of this new form of economy, i.e. to produce a unit of a product with the minimum resources possible (i.e. labour and capital). Competition and transparency are the means to realize this objective—not something to which the Chinese managers and employees were accustomed. Moreover, the dominant Western opinion is that the market economy and liberal democracy go hand in hand and reinforce each other. Otherwise, the whole system will collapse, or at least the economy will be unable to compete with countries in which competition and transparency are implemented. And this is even more true as, under the impulse of the West (especially the U.S.), the process of globalization of the economy that had already started at the end of WW2 accelerated at the beginning of the 1980s under pressure from the neoliberal ideology. Moreover, Deng was ready to open China's economy (even if progressively) to the world. The problem is that China was not at all ready to abandon the authoritarian form of the state, as deemed necessary by Western pundits. If not, then, how could China succeed?

Under Deng's leadership China started to introduce some market mechanisms without simultaneously adopting liberal democracy, which is in blatant contradiction to some fundamental elements of the ideology of the Communist Party as enumerated in the Cardinal Principles, namely Marxism-Leninism and its corollary, the exclusive leadership of the Party. We will see that after a phase of relative success, serious problems appeared at the end of the first decade of reforms, that produced the protests on Tiananmen Square in June 1989. But after a few years, the Chinese economy started to boom and facilitated China's entry to the World Trade Organization (WTO) at the end of 2001. Since then, China's economy and its power resources have continued to grow until it was able to reclaim world power status during the first decades of the 21st century.[139]

How did China succeed in developing its economy starting from the 1980s, and more significantly, to restart development after the

---

138 Braudel 1979a, vol. 2, for the emergence of capitalism in China see pp. 354–56 and 708–23.
139 Urio 2018.

appearance of negative consequences in economy and society (especially in the 1990s), such as unemployment, and various other disparities between households, between urban and rural areas, between coastal and the inner provinces, and the negative impact on the environment? I suggest that China found in its traditional Confucian ideology some value-resources similar to those Western ones that it used for supporting the market mechanisms and to correct the negative consequences of economic development. I term these values 'bridge values' as they helped to integrate Western values with the traditional authoritarian Chinese way of managing the country, to form a new Chinese ideology compatible with the new values imported from the West.

I started to explore this approach in several conferences given in Switzerland, France and China between 2016 and 2018. Discussions with my Chinese teacher and my Chinese assistant working on her Master's dissertation on the compatibility between Confucianism and liberal democracy encouraged me to further explore this approach.[140] I presented a tentative use of this approach in my 2019 book.[141] When I was organizing the framework of this Chapter, I came across Joseph Chan's book, a stimulating endeavour that integrates Confucian and Western values into a Confucian philosophy for modern times.[142] This encouraged and helped me to further develop the approach I will explain hereafter. I have to warn the reader that Chan's project is much more ambitious than mine, which is simply to explore a possible explanation of the resilience of China's Party-State, based upon a mixture of Western values (especially those linked to the market) and an authoritarian state at odds with the values of liberal democracy. Quite interestingly, Chan evaluates the colonial era of Hong Kong, especially in the 1970s, as follows: 'many Hong Kong people's experience of Chinese Confucian culture was positive, and that of British culture not negative, despite its domination through colonial rule. What they experienced was not so much a clash of cultures as their mutuality.'[143] This confirms the statement of François Jullien about the cross-fertilization of cultures.[144] It is therefore possible, as I have contended many times, to envisage a transformation of China towards a new form of state more open both

---

140 Chen Yali, *Confucianisme et Démocratie Libérale : une étude comparative*, Master dissertation in Political Science, University of Geneva, 2016.
141 Urio 2019, pp. 249–250.
142 Chan 2014.
143 Chan 2014, p. ix.
144 See above, and also chapter 1.

internally and internationally. Will it combine Confucian and Western values in the framework of a Confucian philosophy for the modern times (as in Chan's approach) or in the framework of a Western philosophy integrating Confucian values? Or neither? Difficult questions! For the moment I will deal with the question of China's resilience despite its lack of liberal democracy. I will show that the answer can be found in the mix of Confucian and Western value-resources implemented within an authoritarian political system.

In the West the resilience of the People's Republic of China is most of the time explained by its authoritarian, or even its totalitarian character. There is certainly some truth in this, as I wrote in Chapter 1 dealing with the nature of China's political system. More difficult to admit is the claim by the majority of Western pundits that China oppresses its people. Really? All the people? If not, what part of the people? Clearly, this radical Western negative opinion of the relationship between the Chinese people and the Party-State is contradicted by the satisfaction of Chinese citizens with the Communist Party, as attested by reliable surveys.[145] After all, even during the Chinese Empire, Confucian ideology admitted that the people could revolt and destitute the emperor, should he not govern by making the 'good life' for its people—and indeed, as subsequent events were prove, that is exactly what they did in the 20th century. As Chan explains, for the masses of people, having a 'good life' means having sufficient material goods.[146] As I have shown elsewhere,[147] and I will summarize and update in Chapter 3, material conditions have considerably improved since the beginning of the reforms since 1980s, and are still improving today. Certainly, there are serious problems in China but one cannot honestly contest the reality of the improvement of material life in China for the great majority of the Chinese people. Or maybe for some Western pundits this is the problem: how is it possible that a country that is not organized according to our image has been able

---

145 Cunningham, Saich and Turiel 2020; Saich 2016; Forsythe 2015. The title of the Cunningham et al. article is quite revealing: 'Understanding CCP (Chinese Communist Party) Resilience: Surveying Chinese Public Opinion Through Time.' The authors proudly qualify their endeavour as follows: 'This policy brief reviews the findings of the longest-running independent effort to track Chinese citizen satisfaction of government performance.'
146 Chan 2014, pp. 165–67. The paragraph is significantly entitled 'The centrality of material goods to people's lives,' within Chapter 7 entitled: 'Social Justice as Sufficiency for All.'
147 Urio 2019 and 2019.

to achieve such outstanding results? Moreover, a vibrant middle class is constantly increasing in size and in wealth. The Chinese people are not going to revolt or destitute the Party so long as its governance continues to provide them with a 'good life.'

Now the question is: are the Confucian values still present in China today? Whereas for a long time since the creation of the CPC Confucian values as such have been practically banned from the official ideology as they have been made responsible for the backwardness of China during the last century of Imperial power, this is no longer the case as is witnessed by the increasing interest of both Chinese intellectuals and political leaders in the values of Confucianism, especially for (re)affirming the originality of Chinese political culture and creating a barrier to the westernization of Chinese society.[148]

This revival of Confucian values in China must be placed and interpreted within the context of today's situation.[149] During the Imperial era the values of harmony, stability and unity were instrumental in maintaining the structure of Chinese society as it had been for centuries. My suggestion is that in the post Mao era, these same values are today used in the framework of a new ideology that orient the economic and social development of China. It integrates Western values in a new framework that is still today shaped by some Confucian values. It is likely that this renewed orientation took form progressively, confirming the statement of François Jullien that ideology, as part of a country's culture, is not static, but changes in time to adapt to the silent transformations of the environment that occur as time goes by. Moreover, in doing so, here again, I follow the findings of David Chan, which have demonstrated that there are many similarities and overlapping between several elements of Confucianism and the Western political thought, despite some remarkable differences.[150] In this way, Western values could be accepted in China, as the Party could not consider them as 'totally foreign.'

148 Zufferey 2008, pp. 221–250; Bell and Chaibong Hahn 2003; Bell 2008, Chan 2014.
149 Chan 2014.
150 Chan 2014. In a way, Joseph Chan follows the same approach as François Jullien, by suggesting a cross-fertilization between cultures (above, chapter 1). In fact, Chan built a political philosophy that he qualifies in his book by that title, as *Confucian Perfectionism: A Political Philosophy for Modern Times*, analysing and comparing Western and Confucian political philosophies. In particular he criticizes statements by Western scholars who see a fundamental contradiction between Confucianism and liberal democracy and human rights. But he is very clear in saying in the title of the book that his is a Confucian political philosophy.

For Chan the grand ideal of modern Confucianism is social harmony, as it was in traditional Confucianism. Social harmony comprises the development of human virtues, of social relationships based on mutual trust and care. The means to realize this goal include: 'government by people who are virtuous and competent; moral edification by example and persuasion; rites as a method of socialization and governance; and benevolent rule to ensure material sufficiency for all people.'[151] Chan says that the Confucian conception of the ideal ruler-ruled relationship is one of mutual commitment, entailing the ruler's commitment to take care of the people and the people's willing submission to or acceptance of the ruler's control. The benevolent ruler protects and promotes the people's good life (especially material well-being) through a set of social and economic policies, that must be oriented by justice. This is a political duty, an imperative laid down by Heaven, and an objective requirement for legitimate authority. Moreover, Mencius understood benevolent rule as a set of social and economic policies that all legitimate rulers must implement.[152] Chan summarises the main principles of a rudimentary Confucian perspective of social justice as follows: (1) sufficiency for all: each household should have an amount of resources sufficient to live a materially secured and ethical life; (2) Priority should be given to the badly off—people who fall below the threshold of sufficiency or have special needs; (3) Merit and contribution: offices and emolument should be distributed according to an individual's merits and contributions to society; any subsequent inequality of income is not illegitimate.[153]

As Daniel Bell comments in his Foreword: 'Chan aims to defend liberal democratic political institutions, but he asserts that traditional liberal arguments for those institutions need to be modified and enriched by integrating modernized Confucian values.' (Bell Forward to Chan 2014, p. x)

151 Chan 2014, p. 2. It is not possible to develop here all the dimensions so brilliantly discussed in Chan's book; moreover, this is not the purpose of my present book. I have taken from Chan the suggestions, analyses, and comparisons between Western a Chinese values that allow me to better understand the integration of these values within today's Chinese ideology.

152 Chan 2014, pp. 160–6. The similarity with Max Weber's theory of legitimate power is evident (Weber 1978), vol. I, pp. 212 227 for the socio-psychological processes that legitimate power, and vol. II, pp. 941–955 for the provision of goods and services to the people also necessary for legitimizing power.

153 Chan 2014, pp. 175–77. Chan notes: needless to say, much more work needs to be done to develop this perspective into a full-fledge theory for modern times and to provide a philosophical defence of this perspective against competing theories of justice.

Even if summarized as I have done above, the modernity of Chan's Confucianism for the modern time will allow us to better understand the rationale and the sequence of the public policies implemented by China since the beginning of reforms in the 1980s. Following the general framework presented by Chan, here are the major Confucian values that, according to me, have permitted the CCP's Party-State to improve the living conditions of the Chinese people, to correct the negative consequences of these policies when they have arisen, to preserve the authoritarian character of the state, and to avoid its collapse.

I suggest to take into consideration the following Confucian values that have their corresponding values of the West. They will be useful to show how they contributed to the implementation of Western values into the Chinese governance. First, *rén* is probably the most important value because, together with *yì*, it is the condition that confers legitimacy to the ruler. *Rén* can be translated as humanity, love of humanity, or benevolence to humanity as a whole and the people. It corresponds to the Christian 'love thy neighbour,' and to the motto: 'do not to others what you do not want them to do to you.' *Yì* is translated with justice or righteousness. Associated with *rén* it allows the ruler to implement public policies that satisfy the three conditions for governing with justice, mentioned above. Third, *lǐ*, which is translated often as 'good manners,' and includes rites or rituals that guide behaviour. However, Chan warns us that this value

> is a rich and elastic concept. Confucian masters believe that rites are not just a form of social etiquette but also perform important social functions—they help moral cultivation by regulating unhealthy desires and refining feelings and attitudes; they express the basic principles of human relationship and roles, and help regulate society according to these principles; these functions in turn help achieve a harmonious, ethical society, which is the goal of Confucian governance that cannot be achieved by the use of penal law.[154]

---

154 Chan 2014, p. 2. The last sentence corresponds to the Confucian idea that good behaviour cannot, most of the time, be obtained by punishment or litigation, but rather by illustrating and cultivating moral behaviour. It does not mean that Confucians would never agree to the use of force or punishment, but they treat punishment and litigation as a last resort. (Chan 2104, pp. 13, 124–26, and 148–49).

In this sense, this value strengthens *rén* and *yì* by contributing to orienting the ruler's behaviour towards benevolent governance. Furthermore, rites can perform a similar function as rules (i.e. laws and regulations), or at least can function as a bridge toward the introduction of legal norms implying punishment when norms are not respected. This has been the case when, under pressure from the internal and the international market, China had to introduce step by step a legal system similar to the Western one.[155] Finally, *xìn* is translated as trust, a value that is also important in Western ideology both between people and between the ruler and the ruled. *Xìn* (trust) too can strengthen the compliance with rites.

China has demonstrably been able to integrate into its ideology several Western values such as economic efficiency, market rules, social equity, justice and law, without abandoning the traditional authoritarian Chinese way of management as means to safeguard harmony, unity and stability.[156] Based upon this mix of Chinese and Western values, China has been very skilful in choosing the institutional arrangements that allowed it to build year after year, in the 'long time,' after a careful analysis of the 'situation potential,' the resources that constitute today its Comprehensive National Power.[157]

The dominant Western opinion is that today this integration is not entirely satisfactory and/or successful and will remain unfinished, and for some, will end with the collapse of the Party-State. To avoid this, they advise that China should abandon its authoritarian form of the state, within which it is difficult (or even impossible) to integrate traditional Chinese and Western values. Moreover, China should adopt liberal democracy and complete the transition from what remains of the command economy to free market economy. In short, China should 'become like us.' So far, the results obtained by China are impressive for the development of the economy and the standard of living of the great majority of its people by means of its policies adopted over time and as they currently stand. Moreover, significant improvements have been achieved for freedom and human rights, even if the Party-State maintains all the components of society under its control.[158]

---

155 Peerenboom 2002, 2006, 2007.
156 Chan 2014, pp. 148–149 and pp. 41–43 for a comparison of the references to values in the speeches of Jiang Zemin and Hu Jintao at the Party Congresses of October 2002 and November 2007, to be dealt with below.
157 Urio 2018, Chapter 3.
158 Urio 2010; Urio 2012; Urio and Yuan Ying 2014, and Urio 2016.

The market and Confucian values of *li* (rites) and *xin* (trust)

Deng introduced market mechanisms at the beginning of the 1980s in order to correct the negative consequences of the Mao era. This recourse to market mechanisms has been possible thanks to two traditional values, rites (*li*) and trust (*xin*) (Figure 2). We have seen that rites can have basically the same function as rules, even if in Confucianism they are not, most of the time, followed by punishment when they are violated. In the West good behaviour is obtained by market rules (competition and transparency) that are subject to punishment in case of violation. The fear of punishment is the most important means to dissuade violation. Its implementation needs a complex legal system, where recourse to the law to resolve disputes, and/or to correct violation, requires not only rules but also tribunals, procedural norms, judges, lawyers, appeal against decisions of first level courts and, maybe more important, the feeling that the recourse to tribunal is acceptable as a positive move, both for individuals and society, as it corrects misbehaviour. In Confucianism good behaviour is not pursued, most of the time, by threats of punishment but by cultivating moral behaviour. For Chan, Confucianism prefers mediation, reconciliation and compromise to punishment.[159] Now, the transition from rites to rules, a radical change from Confucian to Western ways of organizing interactions between people, cannot be achieved in months. In my 2010 book on China, I discussed the major difficulties on the road to the Chinese market economy.[160] In particular, I pointed out the belief of Chinese people that law and litigation have the consequence of exacerbating conflicts, which is contrary to harmony. For a long time, this attitude prevented the Chinese from recourse to litigation before courts, especially in case of conflicts between workers and owners. Nevertheless, the phenomenal increase in litigations before courts, and the increasing success for workers (attested by official statistics) show that trust (*xin*) in the judicial system has considerably increased, and that the transition from rites to rules, or as Chan would say, from traditional

---

159 Chan 2014, pp. 13 and 124–127.
160 Urio 2010, in particular point 1.4 (pp. 175–182), where amongst the major obstacles to market economy I mentioned the weaknesses of the legal system: the belief that law and litigation have the consequence of exacerbating conflicts, the respect and/or fear of authority, and weak attitudes favourable to written documents and the lack of precision of legal texts; the fact that the Chinese governmental system has no separation of powers, and is consequently vulnerable to interferences by the CPC in judicial, legislative and executive procedures.

Confucian rites to modernized Confucian rites is en route to being realized, greatly improving the functioning of the Chinese market.

Deng's reforms worked for a few years, but China's lack of knowledge of macro-economy devices necessary for the mastering of the smooth opening of the economy to market mechanisms resulted in several negative consequences that in 1989 exploded in serious protest movements. The Party-State put to an end to these movements violently in June 1989. Generally, the Western media reacted to this event with outrage and by imposing economic sanctions, as they considered that the protest was suppressed because of its demand for democracy, that could have led to the end of the dictatorship of the Communist Party. And since then, every year Western media has expressed its outrage when it commemorates this event. But in fact, the situation was more complex. At the 20th anniversary of those tragic events, the *Financial Time's* journalist James Kynge wrote an article significantly entitled 'The West miscasts Tiananmen protesters.'[161] Reminding us that he covered the 1989 events as part of a team of Reuters' reporters, Kynge now writes:

> I cannot help feeling troubled. (. . .) I'm concerned because I don't think we—the western media—got the narrative of those days quite right. (. . .) The powerful iconography of those days (. . .) supports *a clear dichotomy between good and evil, freedom and repression, democracy and dictatorship. In a world of moral fluidity, Tiananmen is an anchor, a gratifyingly fixed reference for our judgments of others.* But is it? I don't deny the atrocity of the event. (. . .) *I do question, however, the western media's basic assertion that the demonstrations had been 'pro-democracy.'*[162] Even now, a raft of editorials commemorating the event's 20th anniversary *repeats the mantra that the students were 'demanding democracy.'* The reality was less coherent (...), as shown in *Beijing Coma*, a recent novel by Ma Jian.[163] By interweaving

---

161 Kynge 2009.

162 This commentary appears frequently in mainstream Western media every time there are protest movements anywhere else, especially in countries that are in process of transition to modernity. New ideas inevitably clash with traditional ideas, quite often violently. The history of protest movements since Tiananmen in several countries shows that the situation is more complex than a simple call for democracy.

163 Kynge refers to Ma Jian, *Beijing Coma*, London, Vintage Books, 2008.

individual motives and broad themes, Ma shows that the movement never adhered to tidy definitions. It was, above all, the unburdening of the hopes of a generation easing itself free of the strictures left from Chairman Mao's rule. Almost everything fell within its scope: campaigns against corruption, nepotism, inflation, police brutality, bureaucracy, official privilege, media censorship, human rights abuses, cramped student dormitories and the smothering of democratic urges. *But to say the demonstrations were to 'demand democracy' is an oversimplification.* (. . .) [the protesters] *were motivated more by outrage at the betrayal of socialist ideals than by aspirations for a new system.* The mood in the square was at least as much conservative as it was activist. [Emphasis added.]

The situation in China at that time did not present the three conditions necessary for the break-out of a revolution. First, society should be already in the process of decomposition, undermined by chaos. Second, there should exist an organization, that is, a network affording the revolutionaries some solid support. Third, there should be a strategy aiming at reversing the power. The Chinese demonstrators were revolted, they said 'no,' they affirmed the existence of a limit that the power cannot cross, of a border separating the tolerable from the intolerable. But that was as far as it went—whereas the revolutionary also says 'yes,' affirms the will to replace the existing order by a new order, and is moved by a political project, i.e. 'the revolutionary sees beyond the riot.' The revolting students in Tiananmen were more 'against' than in favour' of something. The crisis of Tiananmen was the expression of disappointment, of discouragement, even of rage against corruption, inflation, inequalities, official privilege, against a power which refuses any freedom of expression (see the complete list in Kynge' quotation above). But there is no revolutionary situation. Moreover, Chinese civil society is not organized politically; it has been dominated by political power for too long, as we have seen discussing power and ideology during the Empire, the Nationalist Republic of Chiang Kai-shek and the Mao era. Lastly, there was no will, no true project aiming at reversing the existing power. The students of Tiananmen Square were revolted, but they were not revolutionaries advocating a new political project.

This lack of a revolutionary movement is certainly one factor that allowed the Party-State to re-start and even to accelerate the reforms process based upon market mechanisms and the opening of China's economy to the world. This happened during Deng's so-called Southern Tour between 18 January and 21 February 1992, only 20 months after the Tiananmen events.

This strategy put a priority on speeding up development, probably because of the evaluation the Party made of what had happened during and after the fall of the Soviet Union. During his Southern Tour Deng gave his interpretation of the reasons for the fall of Soviet Russia: above all, the failure of the USSR to improve its economy. It is thus necessary to fight the leftist opponents to the reforms, who are likely to slow down the reforms that would improve the economy, albeit while risking reviving the rightist opposition.[164] Moreover, China had good reason to suspect that foreign interferences were also responsible for the Russian collapse and decline after the fall of the Soviet Union, as it did concerning the outburst of the Tiananmen protests. It was therefore urgent to develop China's power resources, especially the economy, to make China strong again as soon as possible. Deng Xiaoping advocated an imbalanced development, allowing some regions and some people to get rich first, by concentrating on the development on coastal regions where resources were more apt to sustain a rapid economic development than the less developed inner provinces. This resulted in greater regional disparities, in enlarging gaps between urban and rural people, not only in terms of income, but also in consumption and access to public services such as education and health.

Inevitably, the same type of negative consequences that had just start to appear at the time of the Tiananmen protest burst out: disparities between regions and provinces, as well as between people within regions, provinces and municipalities. This trend, and especially the appearance of new forms of poverty, also led to an increase in crime, especially petty crimes.

The absence of regulations aimed at protecting the environment resulted in considerable deterioration of the already precarious condition of the Chinese environment. But this time, the Party had understood the lesson of the Tiananmen revolt and was ready to act to correct these imbalances.[165]

---

164 Zhang Wei Wei, p.163.
165 Urio 2010, pp. 54–101.

The rapid introduction of market mechanisms and competition led state organizations (especially state-owned enterprises, but also state bureaucracies) to drastically reduce their staff and to lay off millions of employees and workers. This resulted in a huge rate of unemployment, as well as the emergence of new forms of poverty, that ran the risk of counterbalancing the impressive decrease in poverty achieved thanks to the reforms. Moreover, the introduction of market mechanism led to the government freeing the SOEs from the obligation of providing their workers and employees with the social services they were used to enjoying under the former command economy. To be competitive in the market it is necessary to reduce the cost of production. One way of doing so is to reduce the cost of labour by reducing the number of employees and workers. Unfortunately, this was realized in the absence of a modern safety net covering the risks of life, i.e. health, unemployment and old age. This new way of organizing the production process, in conjunction with the one-child policy was destroying both the traditional State's and the intra-family solidarities of the Mao era.

The final and comprehensive result of the imbalances within society and the economy had a negative impact on the realization of the traditional values of harmony, stability and unity. As the Party was not ready to radically change the political system by importing the value-resource of Western democracy, it was nevertheless necessary to introduce several changes at different levels of the strategy, and first of all to introduce some new values-resources in the ideology of the Party that were imported from the West, such as social equity, law, ruling by law or according to law, and innovation. This has been possible by combining these values with some Confucian values that could be interpreted as presenting some overlapping with the Western ones. In fact, these Western and Confucian values strengthen each other. They are acceptable to the Chinese leadership not only because they are not totally foreign, but also because they produce results. We have seen above that in China, theory and practice are not strictly separated, and moreover the validity of the couple theory is evaluated by the practical results of its implementation.

The introduction of other Western and Confucian values accelerated under the leadership of Jiang Zemin. The negative consequences of the reforms clearly contradicted the idea of a benevolent ruler moved by *rén* (benevolence toward his people) implementing policies based upon the three conditions for justice (*yì*): (1) sufficiency for all; (2) priority to the badly off; (3) Merit and contribution: offices and emolument should be distributed according to an individual's merits and contributions. Clearly the results of the reform process were not in tune with any of these requirements: not sufficiency for all, as attested by the permanence of poverty for parts of the population; not respect of the priority for the less well off, as the development strategy privileged those who were allowed 'to get rich first'; corruption and privilege as a contradiction to the requirement of Merit and contribution. It was therefore necessary to resort to the values of *rén* (benevolence) and *yì* (justice). But as China had been studying the policies used in the West for overcoming some of these problems, it was natural for China to refer at least to such Western-style social policies as social insurance for unemployment, illness, and old age. Figure 2 shows the support that Confucian values *rén* and *yì* gave to the rebalancing and social policies the Party-State has started to develop since the mid-1990s. Needless to say, this change could not have been realized in a few months, nor in a few years.[166] The intent here is only to show how traditional Confucian values can support the introduction of Western values, especially if they are revised, as Chan has done, as Confucian values for the modern times. In fact, the ensuing ideology could even be qualified as neither typically Western nor typically Chinese. Following Jullien, it is the result of the ideological changes necessary to keep pace with the changes in the national and international environments.

Chinese Party Secretary Jiang Zemin, certainly more than any other Party secretaries, was a leader of this transition. In this sense he was at once a leader who remained faithful to Deng and the one who opened the way to the ideological changes and new policies that 'put people first.' For this reason, he is placed together with Deng in Figure 2. Jiang Zemin introduced three important changes in the ideology of the Party: the idea of centralization of fiscal policy; the 'open up the West' policy; and the Three Represents.

Jiang started to address some of the contradictions of the Deng era by implementing policies to re-balance the Chinese economy and society (that would become the central goal of his successor, Hu Jintao), especially via investments in social policies and infrastructure in the western provinces. For this purpose, it was necessary to transfer part of the fiscal capacity from the provinces to the central government, as the new policies needed to be coordinated in a rational way. This decision

---

166 I have dealt with these policies elsewhere. See Urio 2010, pp, 103–155, Urio 2019, pp. 119–152.

was suggested by a report written by two Chinese young scholars who were to become two influential supporters of the Party's development strategy. In 1993 Wang Shaoguang and Hu Angang published a report that circulated in China in favour of the centralization of Chinese fiscal policy and was at the origin of the centralization of fiscal policy decided by Jiang Zemin in 1995.[167] Thanks to these additional financial means, the Party was ready to depart from Deng's strategy that 'put rapid and unbalanced development first' to a new balanced development strategy that 'put people first.'[168]

The Chinese leadership started to move towards the new development approach by first defining the 'Campaign to open up the West' that became a top priority for the government in the next decade.[169] This new strategy clearly changed the focus of development from a purely economic perspective to a socio-economic one, whose declared objective was to narrow the gap between the costal and the inner regions.[170] This strategy was first defined by Jiang Zemin in the mid-1990s, and was later developed by Premier Zhu Rongji in his 'Report on National Economic and Social Development during the Tenth Five Year Plan' (2001–5) delivered to the People's Congress on 5 March 2001.[171]

At the 2002 Party Congress Jiang developed his 'Three Represents' theory that has become, along with Marxism-Leninism, Mao's thought and Deng's thought, the recognized ideological basis of the Party. This theory affirms that the Party represents the advanced social productive forces, the advanced culture, and the interests of the overwhelming majority of the Chinese people. This is quite a radical change compared

---

167 Wang Shaoguang and Hu Angang 1993.
168 Deng's strategy comprised three steps: the first step consisted of doubling GDP during the 1980s; then with the second step, the GDP should be doubled by the end of the twentieth century; finally, the third step should double again GDP twice during the first 30 to 50 years of the twenty-first century.
169 Chow 2002, p. 168.
170 See, for example: Holbig 2004.
171 The major dimensions of this strategy are: 1 infrastructure construction, such as land, air and water transportation facilities, power generation plants, and water conservation projects; 2 environmental protection; 3 adjustment of the industrial structure of the West, namely by putting more emphasis on the consumer goods industry and less on heavy industry and the defence industry, as had been done in the past; 4 the promotion of science, technology and education; 5 making the Chinese West benefit from the open-door policy. This strategy combines hard and soft infrastructure as two complementary components of the development strategy in favour of the West. I have developed elsewhere the reasons in favour of this strategy: Urio, ed., 2010, chapters 1,2 and conclusion.

to the previous ideology that considered that the Party represented the interests of the proletariat. The impressive increase in GDP that China realized thanks to the implementation of Deng's and Jiang's development strategy, has been achieved at the expense of a fair distribution of the new wealth so created. The consequence was that, although the living conditions of the Chinese people have been improved, the old egalitarian social structure has been replaced by an increasingly non-egalitarian one, with the emergence of new social strata, categories, or even social classes.

In this framework, and considering that the values of harmony, unity and stability are still at the core of the Party ideology, the 'Three Represents' can be appreciated as a rational decision whose goal is to reconstruct and reconcile within the Party the social fragmentation that has arisen within Chinese society, and to prevent the emergence of contradictions that may result from it which could jeopardize the trend of reforms under the Party's leadership. It is well known that Jiang Zemin, at the moment of making his theory public, had earlier addressed an appeal to the private Chinese entrepreneurs (the new 'red capitalists'), inviting them to join the Party. Informal evidence collected in China and interviews undertaken in China prove that many private entrepreneurs have in fact joined the Party, and some of them sit in several official bodies, like the national parliament.[172]

In spite of these important changes, Jiang starts his speech at the Party Congress of 2002 by reaffirming some fundamental principles, i.e. Marxism-Leninism, Mao thought, and above all the necessity of reinforcing the capacity of the Party to continue to exercise its leadership over Chinese society. And here again we have a clear reassessment of the concept of unity. Even when dealing with his theory of the Three Represents, Jiang is very careful to affirm that the goal of this fundamental change is to reinforce the Party. The theory of the Three Represents, says Jiang, is a powerful theoretical weapon for strengthening and improving Party building and promoting self-improvement and development of socialism in China.

Jiang further reaffirms that

> Party organizations in enterprises must carry out the Party's
> principles and policies and provide guidance to and supervise
> the enterprises in observing the laws and regulations of the

---

172 Jie Chen and Dickson 2008.

state. They should exercise leadership over trade unions, the Communist Youth League and other mass organizations, rally the workers around them, safeguard the legitimate rights and interests of all quarters and stimulate the healthy development of the enterprises. We should intensify our efforts to establish Party organizations in mass organizations and intermediaries. We should fully carry out Party building in Party and government organs, as well as schools, research institutions, cultural groups and other institutions.

Hu Jintao's contribution to the CPC's ideology: Equity, justice, innovation and scientific development

Jiang's successor, Hu Jintao, while introducing some important novelties which I will deal with hereafter, in his speech at the Party Congress of October 2007 remains nevertheless in line with some fundamental elements of the communist political culture: the Four Cardinal Principles[173] are confirmed as well as the necessity to further strengthen the Party. But there are some differences.

First, both Jiang and Hu make many references to science as a legitimizing value, but Hu is the only one to mention scientific development in relation to social harmony, and not just once, but 34 times. This difference will become even more striking when we consider the reference to Chinese characteristics as a source of legitimation. Although both mention the necessity to take into consideration Chinese characteristics in the process of implementing the development strategy, as well as the importance of safeguarding stability in the development process, the necessity to realize harmony and a harmonious society was mentioned only once by Jiang but 35 times by Hu.

Even more striking, Jiang only mentioned innovation twice, whereas in Hu's speech innovation is mentioned 47 times and appears to be one of the most central and important values. Hu develops a very complex discourse on innovation by first considering that it must be independent from other sources of inspiration. Very likely he refers here to the fact that in the recent past China has above all imitated foreign countries. For Hu, in the future innovation should be initiated by the Chinese people. Moreover, Hu stresses that independent innovations should be implemented in a large number of important domains: re-balancing between regions, general management, banks, enterprises and

---

173 See Note 95, above.

their modernization, the army, science and technology, Chinese investments abroad, and the use of Foreign Direct Investments in China. This is clearly a sign that opens a new era in the development of Chinese society.

This new trend is even more evident when we turn to the necessity of establishing a balance between economic efficiency and equity necessary for implementing the new policies so that they achieve the proclaimed objective of reducing all sorts of disparities, thereby re-establishing *rén* (benevolence) and *yì* (justice) and consequently harmony within Chinese society. Another striking difference appears: contrary to Hu, Jiang never mentioned 'equity' and only 3 times 'justice,' whereas Hu mentions equity 12 times and justice 9 times. Of course, this does not necessarily mean that Jiang was not sensitive to equity and justice. It simply shows that there has been a change in the priority that Hu is giving to the core values of the Chinese official ideology. This is a clear sign that the new Chinese leadership has taken very seriously the contradictions that have emerged in Chinese society in the process of modernization under Deng and Jiang. Moreover, at least at the ideological and political level, it also shows that the new Chinese leadership is ready to take several serious measures in order to re-balance Chinese society. Very clearly Hu says that it will be necessary to manage the relationship between efficiency and equity in the distribution of income by market mechanisms, and that the Party-State should pay an increasing attention to the redistribution of income.

Xi Jinping's contribution: Strengthening the Party and an assertive global foreign policy

It is clear that Xi Jinping has defined his strategy by building on the strategies of his predecessors. Nevertheless, with Xi Jinping we cross an important limit in the construction of CPC's ideology; the vision of China presented by Xi Jinping is clearly projected to address China's role outside its borders and, to be precise, at the global level. By the time Xi Jinping became Secretary General of the CPC, China had been able to develop a whole range of power resources that made it easy to now present China's idea of its role in the world in the open. The time has come for China to actually realize Mao's assertion that: 'Ours will no longer be a nation subject to insult and humiliation; we have stood up.'

The most spectacular sign of this change is, of course, the Belt and Road Initiative. Certainly, in his 2017 Party Congress speech Xi Jinping still referred to the traditional values of harmony (32 times), stability (19 times), and unity (16 times).[174] Moreover, he still referred, as did his predecessors, to Marxism and Marxism-Leninism (12 times). Even more interestingly, he only mentions Mao (twice) by name, among his predecessors, and not Jiang Zemin and Hu Jintao, who are referred to only through their 'Three Represents Theory' (Jiang) and the 'Scientific Outlook' (Hu). Finally, the clear sign that China will remain faithful to its culture is proved by the incredible number of times Xi Jinping mentions the 'Chinese characteristics' (sometimes in relation to the 'China Dream': 69, against 30 for Jiang Zemin (2002 Party Congress) and 57 for Hu Jintao (2007 Party Congress).

But while being faithful to these traditional values, Xi makes it very clear that China is ready to assume an important role in the modern, contemporary international system by offering to the world a whole set of international agreements and partnerships that will be beneficial to everybody, under the slogan of 'win-win.' Clearly, benevolence (*rén*) as implemented by the new benevolent China leader is directed not only towards China itself, but also toward the rest of the world. As we will see in Chapter 3, this is not how the West perceives Xi's foreign policy, which it rather qualifies as aggressively wanting to establish China as the new world hegemon. But for the moment let us hear what Xi said at the 2017 Party Congress In particular, Xi Jinping stated that:

> We have made all-round efforts in the pursuit of major country diplomacy with Chinese characteristics, thus advancing China's diplomatic agenda in a comprehensive, multilevel, multifaceted way and creating a favourable external environment for China's development. We have jointly pursued the Belt and Road Initiative, initiated the Asian Infrastructure Investment Bank, set up the Silk Road Fund, and hosted the First Belt and Road Forum for International Cooperation, the 22nd APEC Economic Leaders' Meeting, the G20 2016 Summit in Hangzhou, the BRICS Summit in Xiamen, and the Fourth Summit of the Conference on Interaction and Confidence Building Measures in Asia.'[175]

174 For example, Xi Jinping says: 'There is greater unity in thinking both within the Party and throughout society.' All the quotations are drawn from the official English translation published on the *China Daily*'s website.
175 See also the following significative statements by Xi Jinping about China's will to play an important international role: 'China's cultural soft power and

Moreover, Xi makes it clear that the major aims of Chinese diplomacy with Chinese characteristics are to foster a new type of international relations and to 'build a community with a shared future for mankind.' Also:

> The dream of the Chinese people is closely connected with the dreams of the peoples of other countries; the Chinese Dream can be realized only in a peaceful international environment and under a stable international order.

Finally, after having enumerated the results so far achieved (first phase), Xi Jinping projects his country's progress into the future (second phase):

> In the second stage from 2035 to the middle of the 21st century, we will, building on having basically achieved modernization, work hard for a further 15 years and develop China into a great modern socialist country that is prosperous, strong, democratic, culturally advanced, harmonious, and beautiful. By the end of this stage, the following goals will have been met: new heights are reached in every dimension of material, political, cultural and ethical, social, and ecological advancement; modernization of China's system and capacity for governance is achieved; China has become a global leader in terms of composite national strength and international influence; common prosperity for everyone is basically achieved; the Chinese people enjoy happier, safer, and healthier lives; the Chinese nation will become a proud and active member of the community of nations.

Clearly Xi Jinping's speech is based upon a version that is certainly modernized but remains basically faithful to traditional Confucian values. The appeal to 'build a community with a shared future for mankind,' the statement that 'The dream of the Chinese people is closely connected with the dreams of the peoples of other countries,' and the reference to a 'peaceful international environment and under a stable international

---

the international influence of Chinese culture have increased significantly. (…) Taking a driving seat in international cooperation to respond to climate change, China has become an important participant, contributor, and torchbearer in the global endeavour.'

order' clearly refers to the Confucian values of *rén*, *yì* and *xìn* applied to China's foreign policy. The goal is to establish a benevolent and just international order, i.e. aiming at realizing the three conditions of justice: (1) sufficiency for all; (2) priority to the badly off; (3) Merit and contribution: offices and emolument distributed according to an individual's merits and contributions. This is a clear call for a multilateral pluri-polar world, avoid of unilateral actions by countries that try to realize their national goals through the threat, or even the actual use of economic and military forces, intervening in the national affairs of other countries, and using all sorts of subverting measures to produce regime changes in countries that do not comply with their national interests.

CONCLUSION: COMPARING U.S. AND CHINA IDEOLOGIES

It is difficult to compare two ideologies embedded in such different cultures. One runs the risk of evaluating the U.S. ideology using the values of the Chinese ideology, and vice-versa. Without falling in the trap of ethnocentrism, let us just summarize the major objectives features of these ideologies as they are declared in official documents and speeches by the leadership of both countries.

The U.S. ideology presents a remarkable internal coherence as all its elements strengthen each other with not the slightest contradiction. It is based on the partition between 'us' and the 'others,' covering the contradiction between 'good' and 'evil.' This belief is based upon the conviction that the U.S. possesses universal values (democracy, human rights) that other countries do not possess (except some of the U.S. allies). This way of conceiving the world has several consequences. First, that these other countries should imitate the exceptional U.S. republic, and failing this, the U.S. has the right and the duty to impose these universal values on them. Second, the U.S. foreign policy is oriented by the necessity to build and safeguard an international order based upon these universal values, as well as upon the rules the U.S. establishes for this purpose; this international order is equated with the U.S. national interests, and in its view is the only means for achieving peace and prosperity for all the countries of the world. Third, to achieve this goal, it is necessary for the U.S. to lead the world, and therefore to expand the U.S. domination, ideally all over the world. Forth, the realization of these objectives must be achieved by using all the necessary means, including the threat and actual use of economic and military means, and the organization of 'regime changes' in countries that contest this international order, including the use of a wide range of subversive tactics. China's ideology also presents a remarkable internal coherence. But contrary to that of the U.S., which has achieved this coherence practically from the beginning (between 1776 and the mid-1850s) China has had to constantly revise its ideology in order to be able to master both internal and external challenges. China entered the global world with an ideology inherited from its Empire, that was not suited to facing these challenges, especially the transition from a feudal society to modernity. Moreover, insofar as it was not protected, as the U.S. had been, by two vast oceans, it was forced to undertake this transition from a position of weakness. The violent Western opening of China to the world was followed by a 'century of humiliations' that reduced China to a quasi-colonial status. China mastered the transition, step by step, by importing values from the West (such as market, justice, equity, rules, etc.) and by combining them with a modernized form of traditional Confucian values such as *rén* (benevolence, love for humanity), *yì* (justice), *xìn* (trust) and *lǐ* (rites, rules). The modernized Confucian values made it possible to build a new ideology integrating Western and Confucian values with Marxist-Leninist and Maoist ones, within which Confucian values not only strengthened the Western values but also made them look less foreign and thus more acceptable by the Chinese leadership: accordingly, the market and its rules are supported by *lǐ* (rites, rules) and *xìn* (trust); social policies are supported by *rén* (benevolence, love for humanity) and *yì* (justice) and thus they improve the *xìn* (trust) of the ruled towards the ruler. The result is a new ideology that aims at establishing harmony both within China and the international system, by implementing *rén* (benevolence) and *yì* (justice). In the international system this translates into a foreign policy not based upon military expansion and occupation, but offering partnerships based upon the idea of 'win-win,' meaning that all the parties concerned must gain something.

We will see in Chapter 3, by analysing the foreign policies of the U.S. and China, whether their coherence is not only internal but also external, i.e. apt to adapt to the changes of the international environment and to realize their national interests. In particular we will have to evaluate whether, by refusing to integrate liberal democracy into its ideology, the Communist Party runs the risk of leading China toward a final collapse of the system it has built since 1949. I anticipate that we will see, contrary to the forecast of many Western pundits, that China has avoided collapse and has become a powerful player in the international system, whereas the U.S. is experiencing increasing difficulties in maintaining its dominance over the 'world it made.'[176]

---

176 A reference to the title of a book by the influential neoconservative Robert Kagan: *The World America Made,* New York, Alfred A. Knopf, 2012b.

CHAPTER 3

The Policy and Power Divide

When dealing with the relationship between China and the U.S., this truism must be kept in mind: it is the U.S. that 'went' to China and not the reverse.[1] This information becomes meaningful when we take into consideration the manner and motives of the U.S.'s 'journey' to China, which unsurprisingly is similar to that of the Europeans to Africa and Asia. England's journey to India is a good example. The British Government did not start that journey, rather, a private organization, the East India Company, took the initiative of colonizing India with its own capital, organization, administration, and even police and army. It is only when this colonization derailed, that the British government stepped in by submitting the Company to governmental control, and finally taking over the task of colonizing India with the known historical consequences.[2]

THE AMERICAN CHINA DREAM AND THE LONG U.S. MARCH TO CHINA

So, it is the U.S. investors and traders that started the American journey to China. In February 1784, only 6 years after the Declaration of Independence, the *Empress of China* became the first commercial ship to sail from the United States to China. It marked the beginning of a long story of U.S. expansion towards the Pacific, not surprisingly, almost at the same time as the 'Jeffersonian expansion' into the American Northern and Southern continents.[3] Today, U.S. companies and investors are in

---

1 I have analysed in more depth the build-up of power resources and the foreign policies of the U.S. and China in my books, Urio 2018, pp. 108–95 for the U.S., pp. 196–232 for China, and Urio 2019, pp. 195–320 for the U.S. and China. Here I summarize with many up-dates and new comments.

2 Tharoor 2016.

3 Here is again the 1801 Jefferson's sentence already referred to in Chapter 2 (page 118): 'However our present interests may restrain us within our limits, it is impossible not to look forward to distant times when our multiplication will expand it beyond those limits, and cover the whole northern, if not the southern continent, with people speaking the same language, governed in similar forms,

China and the U.S. armada is in the China Sea with its navy. Moreover, in the vicinity of China's borders the U.S. has placed hundreds of military bases, and created military alliances and partnerships in a desperate endeavour to contain China, and thereby maintain the dominant position of the U.S. in the 'world America made.'[4] Although China has been investing in the Americas since at least the beginning of the 21st century, and has established win-win relations with several countries in Latin America, it does not have a single military base in the Gulf of Mexico, nor in the vicinity of the Californian coast.[5]

THE U.S. EXPANSION 1776–1900

The U.S. expansion towards China had already started between the end of the 18th and first half of the 19th centuries. At that time, the goal of the U.S. government was mainly to safeguard American economic interests by joining the European powers to sign an unequal treaty with China, whereby they obtained the same economic advantages, thanks to the application of the most favoured nation principle. The U.S. signed the treaty of Wangxia only 2 years after Britain had signed the first of a long list of such treaties after the end of the first Opium War (the Treaty of Nanjing). In fact, we have here the first manifestation of the 'China Mirage' or of the 'American China Dream' that would become the dominant driver of U.S. expansion into the Far East that is still advancing, today.[6]

The following is a short list of the major U.S. 'expansions' as analysed, explained and termed 'U.S. Foreign Relations' by the Historian of the U.S. State Department, with a few minor editorial changes (emphasis added).[7] I will insist more particularly on the Indian wars that started

---

and by similar laws.'
4 Reference to Robert Kagan's book with the significant title: *The World America Made,* New York, Alfred A. Knopf, 2012.
5 Vine 2020.
6 Bradley 2009, 2015. According to an article published by the influential American Enterprise Institute (AEI), since the last quarter of the 18th Century, 'from the American perspective, there was the potentially vast Chinese market to tap into, millions of Chinese to preach the Christian Gospel to, and cheap Chinese labour to help build the American West,' Schmitt (2019). Founded in 1938, AEI is closely associated with conservatism and neoconservatism, although it is officially non-partisan.
7 I encourage the reader to consult: U.S. Department of State, Office of the Historian, *A Short History of the Department of State, Milestones in the History of U.S. Foreign Relations, Key Milestones 1750–2000*: https://history.state.gov/

before the Declaration of Independence (1776) and lasted at least until 1890. During this long time, the U.S. experimented with the different types of expansionist tactics that it was going to implement later, starting with the Mexican-American war (1846–1848), tactics it has continued to employ, to this date, as I will explain hereafter.

- **1750–1890: the Indian Wars: The dispossession of Native Americans and the Road to Indian Territories[8]**
  Under the title 'Indian Treaties and the Removal Act of 1830' the Historian gives the following useful information on the Indian wars, in fact the first foreign war the U.S. fought.
  The U.S. Government used treaties as one means of displacing the native peoples from their tribal lands, a mechanism that was strengthened by the Removal Act of 1830. In cases where this failed, *the government sometimes violated both treaties and Supreme Court rulings* to facilitate the

---

milestones (accessed 18 April 2017). The introduction informs the reader that: '*Milestones in the History of U.S. Foreign Relations* provides a general overview of the history of U.S. engagement with the world through short essays on important moments, or milestones, in the diplomatic history of the United States. The basic objective of these essays is to provide a clear, accurate, narrative account of the events being discussed, with a brief discussion of each event's significance for U.S. foreign policy and diplomatic history. The publication is divided into 19 chapters covering time periods from 1750 until 2000, with brief introductions providing context for each period.' Unfortunately, on 9 May 2017 the Office has informed the readers that the 'Milestones in the History of U.S. Foreign Relations,' has been removed. The text remains online for reference purposes, but it is no longer being maintained or expanded. Why remove 'Milestones'? The Office of the Historian recently reviewed its online offerings and concluded that extensive resources would be needed to revise and expand this publication to meet the Office's standards for accuracy and comprehensiveness. At the same time, the events described in the 'Milestones' essays are amply covered by numerous respected secondary sources. Rather than duplicate these efforts, the Office of the Historian has decided to focus its resources on areas where it is uniquely suited to make a contribution, such as coverage of the Department of State's institutional history. In keeping with the publication's new status, it can now be found under 'More Resources' in the site-wide menu. Nevertheless, the 'Milestones' remain a useful information showing how the Historian of the State Department analysed international events from 1750 to 2000.
8 This subtitle is not from the Historian of the State Department, but from Claudio Saunt's book, *Unworthy Republic*, bears exactly this very informative subtitle: 'The dispossession of Native Americans and the Road to Indian Territory' (Saunt 2020)

spread of European American settlers westward across the continent.

As the 19th century began, land-hungry Americans poured into the backcountry of the coastal South and began moving toward and into what would later become the states of Alabama and Mississippi. Since the Indian tribes living there appeared to be the main obstacle to westward expansion, *white settlers petitioned the federal government to remove them.* Although Presidents Thomas Jefferson and James Monroe argued that the Indian tribes in the Southeast should exchange their land for lands west of the Mississippi River, they did not take steps to make this happen. *Indeed, the first major transfer of land occurred only as the result of war.*

In 1814, Major General Andrew Jackson led an expedition against the Creek Confederacy climaxing in the Battle of Horse Shoe Bend (in present day Alabama near the Georgia border), where *Jackson's force soundly defeated the Creeks and destroyed their military power. He then forced upon the Indians a treaty* whereby they surrendered to the United States over twenty-million acres of their traditional land—about one-half of present-day Alabama and one-fifth of Georgia. Over the next decade, Jackson led the way in the Indian removal campaign, helping to negotiate nine of the eleven major *treaties to remove Indians.*

From a legal standpoint, the United States Constitution empowered Congress to "regulate commerce with foreign nations, and among the several States, and with the Indian tribes." In early treaties negotiated between the federal government and the Indian tribes, the latter typically acknowledged themselves *"to be under the protection of the United States of America, and of no other sovereign whosoever."* When Andrew Jackson became president (1829–1837), he decided to build a systematic approach to Indian removal on the basis of these legal precedents.

To achieve his purpose, Jackson encouraged Congress to adopt the Removal Act of 1830. *The Act established a process whereby the President could grant land west of the Mississippi River to Indian tribes that agreed to give up their homelands.* As incentives, the law allowed the Indians

financial and material assistance to travel to their new lo-
cations and start new lives and guaranteed that the Indians
would live on their new property *under the protection of the
United States Government forever. With the Act in place,
Jackson and his followers were free to persuade, bribe, and
threaten tribes into signing removal treaties and leaving the
Southeast.*

Through a combination of *coerced treaties and the contravention
of treaties and judicial determination,* the United States Government
succeeded in paving the way for the westward expansion and the incor-
poration of new territories as part of the United States.

- **1839–1844 The Opening to China Part I: the First Opium
  War, the United States, and the Treaty of Wangxia**
  The Treaty of Wangxia was the first formal treaty signed
  between the United States and China in 1844. It served as
  an American counterpart to the Anglo-Chinese Treaty of
  Nanjing that ended the First Opium War in 1842.

- **1845–1848: The Annexation of Texas, and the Mexican-
  American War**
  During his tenure, U.S. President James K. Polk oversaw
  the greatest territorial expansion of the United States to date.
  These events brought within the control of the United States
  the future states of *Texas, California, Nevada, New Mexico,
  Arizona, Utah, Washington, and Oregon, as well as portions
  of what would later become Oklahoma, Colorado, Kansas,
  Wyoming, and Montana.*[9]

---

9 This information should be completed with some additional references as it
is during this war that the U.S. experimented expansionist tactics similar to the
ones used during the Indian Wars, that it was to implement after that war until
today. See for example Sjursen 2020 and 2021. Daniel Sjursen is a retired U.S.
Army officer, contributing editor at Antiwar.com, senior fellow at the Center for
International Policy, and director of the Eisenhower Media Network. He served
combat tours in Iraq and Afghanistan and later taught history at West Point.

- **1853–1854: The Gadsden Purchase, finalized in 1854**
  In which the U.S. agreed to pay Mexico $10 million for a 29,670 square mile portion of Mexico that later became *part of Arizona and New Mexico.*

- **1853: The United States and the Opening to Japan**
  The same combination of economic considerations and belief in '*Manifest Destiny*' that motivated U.S. expansion across the North American continent *also drove American merchants and missionaries to journey across the Pacific.* At the time, *many Americans believed that they had a special responsibility to modernize and civilize the Chinese and Japanese.*

- **1849–1861: Territorial Expansion, Filibustering, and U.S. interest *in Central America and Cuba***
  While U.S. Government officials attempted to acquire territorial possessions in that region, *private citizens (known as 'filibusters') also organized armed expeditions to various places in Mexico, Central America, and Cuba.*

- **1857–1859 The Opening to China Part II: the Second Opium War, the United States, and the Treaty of Tianjin**
  Following the First Opium War in the 1840s, the Western powers concluded a series of treaties with China in *an effort to open its lucrative markets to Western trade.* In the 1850s, the United States and the European powers grew increasingly dissatisfied with both the terms of their treaties with China and the Qing Government's failure to adhere to them. *The British forced the issue by attacking the Chinese port cities of Guangzhou and Tianjin* in the Second Opium War. As a result, France, Russia, and the United States all signed treaties with China at Tianjin in quick succession in 1858.

  These treaties granted the Western powers a number of rights and privileges. The number of treaty ports increased, with *new ports opened to Western trade along the Chinese coast, on the islands of Taiwan and Hainan, and along the Yangtze River in the interior.* With the opening of the Yangtze River, foreigners also gained full access to the interior, and were *free to travel and conduct business or missions any-where in China.* British (and therefore, French, American and Russian) diplomats were permitted to establish legations and live in Beijing. The agreements reached at Tianjin also set a new, low tariff for imported goods, *giving foreign traders an important advantage.* Frustrated by irregularities in Chinese customs services, *British and U.S. merchants finally established the Imperial Maritime Customs Service,* which regulated trade for the benefit of foreign merchants and provided a steady source of revenue to the Chinese Government.[10]

Although the Chinese signed the treaties in 1858, it took two more years of fighting before the Chinese Government was disposed to ratify them and accept the terms.

Under the most-favoured-nation clause, the U.S. ratification allowed the other powers to take advantage of the treaty provisions of the Treaty of Tianjin secured by American diplomacy.

For years, *the Chinese had conducted their foreign policy through the tribute system,* in which foreign powers wishing to trade with China were required first to bring a tribute to the emperor, acknowledging the superiority of Chinese culture and the ultimate authority of the Chinese ruler.[11] Unlike China's neighbours, the European powers ultimately refused to make these acknowledgements in order to trade, and they *demanded instead that China adhere to Western diplomatic practices, such as the creation of treaties.* Although the unequal treaties and the use of the most-favoured-nation clause were effective in creating and maintaining open trade with China, both were also *important factors in building animosity and resentment toward Western imperialism.*

---

10 Founded in 1854, the Service split in 1949 into services operating in the Republic of China in Taiwan, and in the People's Republic of China.

11 Chapter 1 (section: 'The Myth of the Superiority of Chinese Civilization and Culture') discussed the mission sent to China in 1792 by King George III of Great Britain to Emperor Qianlong with the aim of further opening up trade between the two countries and explained the mutual misunderstanding between the British delegation and the Chinese Emperor about the goal of such meetings, with the British wanting to negotiate a further opening of China to international trade, while the Emperor simply expected to receive a tribute from the British.

- **1867: The Purchase of Alaska,**
  An important step in the United States' rise as a great power in the Asia-Pacific region.

- **1866–1898: The Continued Expansion of United States Interests**
  Following two devastating economic recessions, U.S. foreign policy leaders focused on *finding foreign markets to absorb excess goods*. This renewed emphasis on exploring international business opportunities resulted in a *build-up of U.S. naval forces to protect commercial shipping and overseas interests.*

In the meantime, European powers were busy colonizing the rest of the world and fighting against each other, with their power struggle leading to the catastrophe of WW1. After its unification in 1871, Germany emerged as a new empire. Its first chancellor, Otto von Bismarck, organized an international conference in Berlin (the Berlin Conference, November 1884 – February 1885) with the goal of regulating European colonization and trade in Africa. Its outcome, the General Act of the Berlin Conference,

> can be seen as the formalisation of the scramble for Africa, but some scholars of history warn against an overemphasis of its role in the colonial partitioning of Africa and draw attention to bilateral agreements concluded before and after the conference. The conference contributed to ushering in a period of heightened colonial activity by European powers, which eliminated or overrode most existing forms of African autonomy and self-governance.[12]

Twelve European countries attended the Conference, as well as the Ottoman Empire and the United States. In fact, the latter did not ratify the General Act of the Conference signed in Berlin because the presidential candidate, Grover Cleveland, who had anti-imperialist tendencies, won the election and did not submit the treaty to the Senate.[13] Moreover, for John Kasson, one of the American delegates at the Conference, modern

---

12 Wikipedia, under 'Berlin Conference.'
13 Munene 1990, p. 77.

international law was leading to the recognition of the right of native tribes to dispose freely of themselves and of their hereditary territory, and that principle was to be 'extended' to require the 'voluntary consent of the natives whose country is taken possession of, in all cases where they had not provoked the aggression.'[14]

Notwithstanding, returning to the enumeration provided by the Historian of the Department of State, the U.S. continued its expansion without obtaining 'the voluntary consent of the natives whose country is taken possession':

- **1998: The Annexation of Hawaii and the Spanish-American War**
  This war *ended Spain's colonial empire* in the Western Hemisphere and secured the position of the United States as a Pacific power. *[Spain] relinquished claims on Cuba, and ceded sovereignty over Guam, Puerto Rico, and the Philippines to the U.S.* The U.S. also annexed the independent state of *Hawaii* during the conflict. Thus, the war enabled the United States to establish its predominance in the Caribbean region and to pursue its strategic and economic interests in Asia.

- **1898–1902: The Spanish-American War and The Philippine-American War**
  The process of U.S. maritime expansion in the Pacific eventually became a goal in and of itself, culminating in the acquisition of the Philippines from Spain in 1898. The Spanish-American War began with a dispute over Cuba, but *a rising tide of interest in overseas empire among U.S. leaders,* such as President William McKinley and future President Theodore Roosevelt, helped expand the conflict to Spanish possessions in Asia. After a swift victory over Spain, *the United States established full colonial rule over the Philippines in 1900* during the Philippine-American War.

To this remarkable 'expansion' we have to add that towards the end of the 19th century, the U.S. removal of Native Indians from their territories officially came to an end after the massacre of Wounded Knee in 1890, while the U.S. consolidated its grip over the Americas, and

---

14 Craven 2015, p. 47.

considerably developed its economy after the defeat of the South in the American Civil War (1860–1865). This war put an end to slavery and to the South's dream of free international trade, allowing the U.S. to institute a formidable protective tariffs policy with the aims of favouring the development of its Northern industry.[15] The U.S. was then able to leave behind the 19th century that saw the 'Birth of a Nation' (though the South then instituted an American form of apartheid termed 'segregation') and triumphantly entered the American Century with the brutal conquest of the Philippines.[16]

It would be tempting to provide a personal comment on the spirit in which the U.S. undertook its journey towards China. In order to avoid again any criticism accusing me of manifesting 'primary anti-Americanism,' let me quote once again the earlier cited Historian of the U.S. State Department. Under the title 'United States Maritime Expansion across the Pacific during the XIX Century' the Historian very well explains the motivation of the U.S. expansion in the Pacific and the importance of China (my emphases added):

> The westward expansion of the United States during the XIX century was not limited to North America, but rather included an ongoing push to establish a stronger U.S. presence in and across the Pacific Ocean. This maritime expansion, driven mostly by commerce, had important implications for U.S. foreign policy. The appeal of profits to be earned from the

---

15 This was the main cause of the Civil War. The agricultural economy of the South, based upon cheap slave labour, was exporting its cotton abroad, and importing manufactured products from Europe, as the U.S. industry in the North was not competitive. Hence the South needed free international trade. On the contrary, the North had just started its industrial revolution and was unable to compete with European manufactured good. It was, as the first U.S. Secretary of the Treasury, Alexander Hamilton, said, an economy in its 'infant industrial stage' and therefore needed a protectionist trade policy to give it time to catch up with Europe.

16 *The Birth of a Nation*, originally called *The Clansman*, is a 1915 American silent drama film directed by D. W. Griffith, adapted from Thomas Dixon Jr.'s 1905 novel and play *The Clansman*. Its plot, part fiction and part history, chronicles the assassination of Abraham Lincoln by John Wilkes Booth and the relationship of two families in the Civil War and Reconstruction eras over the course of several years: the pro-Union (Northern) Stonemans and the pro-Confederacy (Southern) Camerons. The film was controversial even before its release and has remained so ever since; it has been called "the most controversial film ever made in the United States" (Wikipedia, under 'The Birth of a Nation').

China trade served as the initial impetus to motivate U.S. citizens and officials to enter into the Pacific region.[17] China was the source of some of the world's most sought-after commodities—tea, porcelain, and silk—and Western merchants had sought access to this highly lucrative trade since at least the XVII century. Following U.S. independence, U.S.-based merchants continued to seek opportunity in China. In February 1784 the 'Empress of China' became the first [commercial] ship to sail from the United States to China, and in its wake came a steady flow of merchants in search of wealth. During the first decades of the XIX century, U.S. merchants amassed sizeable fortunes that they subsequently invested in the development of their homeland.[18]

As this trade grew, U.S. traders built a small outpost in China and their interactions with Chinese subjects became more complex and occasionally contentious. The U.S. Government realized that it had to establish formal diplomatic ties *in order to protect the interests of its citizens.* (...) Making the journey to China and maintaining the U.S. presence there also required *a network of ports* extending across the Pacific Ocean, and as such, the China trade soon drove the United States to expand its presence throughout the Pacific region. U.S. *expansion* across the Pacific fundamentally changed the global position of the United States (U.S. Department of State 2017).

The significance of this systematic and impressive expansion in the Pacific region became clear with the brutal conquest of the Philippines, revealing the U.S.'s ultimate goal in the Far East: China. No less an authority than Indiana Senator Albert J. Beveridge, in his speech to the

---

17 It is interesting to remark that the British expansion in Asia, especially in India, was also motivated by the will of private investors to enrich themselves, well before the government took over the policy from the British East India Company: Ferguson (2004). For the role of the British merchants in the making of America see Butman and Targett (2018).

18 This was the classical behaviour of the colonial powers. Many of these merchants enriched themselves by being very active in the opium trade (Bradley 2015, pp. 17–19, 47–49).

U.S. Congress, confirmed the idea that China was the final goal of t U.S. expansion in the Pacific:[19]

> Mr. President, the times call for candor. The *Philippines are ours forever,* "territory belonging to the United States," as the Constitution calls them. And just beyond the Philippines are *China's illimitable markets. We will not retreat from either.* We will not repudiate *our duty* in the archipelago. We *will not abandon our opportunity in the Orient.* We will not renounce our part in *the mission of our race,* trustee, under God, of *the civilization of the world.* And we will move forward to our work, not howling out regrets like slaves whipped to their burdens but with gratitude for a task worthy of our strength and *thanksgiving to Almighty God that He has marked us as His chosen people, henceforth to lead in the regeneration of the world.*'[20] [Emphasis added.]

---

19 'Beveridge is known as one of the most prominent American imperialists. He supported the annexation of the Philippines and, along with Republican leader Henry Cabot Lodge, campaigned for the construction of a new navy. In 1901, Beveridge became chair of the Senate Committee on Territories, which allowed him to support statehood for Oklahoma. However, he blocked statehood for New Mexico and Arizona because he deemed the territories too sparsely occupied by white people. In his opinion, they contained too many Hispanics and Native Americans, whom he described as intellectually incapable of understanding the concept of self-governance. He celebrated the "white man's burden" as a noble mission, part of God's plan to bring civilization to the entire world (Wikipedia under Albert J. Beveridge).

20 Beveridge 1900. In more popular mood, an Emil Flohri cartoon, published by *Judge* (a weekly satirical magazine published in the United States from 1881 to 1947) illustrates a scene where Uncle Sam is seen stepping across the ocean into the Philippines loaded down with symbols of modern civilization, including books labelled 'Education' and 'Religion,' bridges, railroad trains, sewing machines, farm machinery. A short distance beyond the Philippines a small figure representing China stands with a happy expression and open arms, surrounded by signs saying large quantities of modern goods are wanted, https://commons. wikimedia.org/wiki/File:Flohri_cartoon_about_the_Philippines_as_a_bridge_ to_China.jpg, accessed 15 December 2018.

How Its 19th Century Expansion Taught the U.S. How to Deal with Its 20th Century Expansions

During the expansion of the 19th century into the Americas, the U.S. had already started to implement tactics that, together, supported its imperial strategy. Many of these tactics are still used today.

The use of military bases

The U.S. used military bases for occupying, step by step, the Indian territories. According to Vine no less than 90 'Forts' (t corresponding to today's military bases) were used by the U.S. government to protect the white settlers from the 'aggressions' of the 'savage Indians,' thereby consolidating and developing the population of those territories so they could in future become member States of the Union.[21]

Encouraging U.S. citizens and businesses to settle abroad

The U.S. had openly encouraged private European settlers to set up their social and economic activities within the Indian and Mexican territories. These were clear provocations; the Indian and Mexican communities, like any others, might well have been expected to try to protect their lands from such sizeable incursions of foreign populations. In the 20th century, when the U.S. economy was ready to develop economic activities abroad, the U.S. government supported and encouraged American enterprises and investors to relocate their economic activities and investments abroad.[22] By doing so the U.S. created national interests abroad that it could then claim must be protected if endangered. China

---

21 As David Vine puts it: 'hundreds of frontier forts helped enable the westward expansion of the U.S., and they were built on land that was very much *abroad* [emphasis in the original] at the time. [...] By the middle of the nineteenth century, there were sixty major forts west of the Mississippi River and 138 army posts in the western territories (Vine, 2015, pp. 19–22). For an update, see Vine 2020, Chapter 3, significantly entitled: 'Why are so many places named forts?,' pp. 43–62. The 2020 Vine book is a development of his 2015 book (entitled *Base Nation. How U.S. Military Bases Abroad Harm America and the World*) covering more comprehensively 'America endless conflicts from Columbus to the Islamic State.'

22 In his historical history of the development of capitalism, Fernand Braudel has shown that 'capital and credit have always been the surest way of capturing and controlling a foreign market. Long before the twentieth century the exportation of capital was a fact of daily life, for Florence as early as the thirteenth century,' Braudel 1979, p. 113.

is but one instance; European countries had already been territories for American investments since at least the beginning of the 20th century: U.S. investments exploded even in Nazi Germany and Fascist Italy between the two World Wars.[23] Thereby, the U.S. can claim that the interests of its enterprises in these countries were in fact U.S. national interests. It is therefore not surprising that today the U.S. can therefore claim to have 'national interests' all over the world.

The use of provocations

Another type of provocation which was used against the Native Indians and the Mexicans, and which has become today a tactic frequently used by the U.S., is to provoke its adversaries to deploy actions that may be considered as aggressive or even illegal, which then justify U.S. military reactions or economic sanctions against them. The present crisis in Ukraine is a good example among many. For several years the U.S. has supported political forces (some of them clearly manifesting a neo-Nazi ideology) favourable to its interest in Ukraine. The U.S. started by investing several $ billion in the Ukrainian economy, then organizing a regime change when the democratically elected president manifested the will to prefer a financial agreement with Russia instead of with the U.S.-dominated IMF.[24] The U.S. move could be with some good reasons interpreted as a project, inter alia, to dislodge Russia from its military bases in Crimea.[25] This provoked a civil war in Ukraine, as its citizens of Russian language and culture were physically attacked by rightist neo-fascist Ukrainian militia and finally by the Ukrainian army itself. Faced with this blatant provocation (a remake of the Georgia crisis of 2008), Russia reacted and annexed Crimea after two favourable popular referendums in Crimea, whose predominantly Russian-speaking citizens

---

23 Lacroix-Riz 2014, pp. 31–46; Migone 2015, pp. 141–49, 165–70.
24 On the U.S. investments in Ukraine see YouTube video 'Victoria Nuland: U.S. has invested $5 billion in Ukraine,' 25 April 2014, https://www.youtube.com/watch?v=rPVs5VuI8XI. On the Ukrainian regime change listen to the record of the telephone call between Victoria Nuland and the U.S. ambassador in Kiev: 'F*** the EU: Alleged audio of U.S. diplomat Victoria Nuland swearing,' YouTube, 7 February 2014, https://www.youtube.com/watch?v=L2XNN0Yt6D8.
25 In 1954 Crimea had been transferred from the Russian Soviet Federative Socialist Republic to the Ukrainian SSR. At that time the transfer did not mean much, as Ukraine was part of the Soviet bloc. The situation changed dramatically when Soviet Russia collapsed in 1991 and Ukraine became an independent republic.

massively approved its return to Russia. The U.S. (and many European countries) accused Russia of not respecting international law.[26]

The use and manipulation of international treaties

The U.S. used dozens of treaties with the Native Indian Tribes to advance its occupation of what it regarded as its Promised Land, as earlier attested to by the Historian of the U.S. State Department, who admitted that

> the U.S. Government used treaties as one means to displace Indians from their tribal lands, a mechanism that was strengthened with the Removal Act of 1830. In cases where this failed, the government sometimes violated both treaties and Supreme Court rulings to facilitate the spread of European Americans westward across the continent.

Breaking treaties has become almost a U.S. habit when it considers that its national interests are no longer covered. This has occurred as well in the domains of international armaments control (notably with Russia), environment protection (Kyoto), and nuclear agreements (JCPOA). Then there are second-hand betrayals, such as that which occurred after Qaddafi agreed to abandon his nuclear program, following which the authorization given by the UN Security Council to intervene in Libya to establish a no-fly zone, was in fact illegally transformed into a regime change operation. Indeed, if written and signed treaties failed and continue to fail to ensure that the U.S. keeps to its agreements, what could truly have been expected from the verbal U.S. promise given to Gorbachev not to expand NATO and the EU onto the republics of the former Soviet

---

26 In fact, this is exactly what the U.S. did after it dismembered Yugoslavia and promoted the independence of Kosovo, yet another clear manifestation of the 'double standards' which have been a common occurrence during the U.S.'s imperial expansion. The 2008 Kosovo declaration of independence was adopted on 17 February 2008 by the Assembly of Kosovo. As a result, a 3-meter-high statue of President Clinton was unveiled on November 1, 2009 on the Bill Clinton boulevard in the Kosovo capital, Pristina, at a ceremony at which the former president spoke. Elsewhere in Pristina, another street was named after U.S. President George W. Bush. It was perhaps inevitable that the U.S. would build several military bases in Kosovo, the most important being Camp Bondsteel, that can host more than 7000 troops on site, and is currently the largest and widest base run by the United States of America in the Balkans. Clearly, liberation (from Serbia) has a price.

bloc? [27] Unfortunately, the trail of such behaviour over time gives the impression that the U.S. considers itself as not subject to international laws and regulations. This attitude is further damaged by its imposition of economic sanctions for which it has no international legal authority on countries whose behaviours do not comply with U.S. interests.

Putting liberated, invaded or defeated countries under U.S. protection

In the early treaties negotiated between the federal government and the Indian tribes, the latter typically acknowledged themselves "*to be under the protection of the United States of America, and of no other sovereign whosoever.*" This attitude still prevails today as the U.S. pursues its purported duty to explain to its allies that their U.S. protection against the wrongdoings of 'malign states' entails a purported right to interfere in their foreign policy relationships. The clearest example is the case of the Nord Stream 2 pipeline between Russia and Germany (and therefore Europe). The U.S. tried (but has failed) to forbid the completion of the pipeline by all means, including economic sanctions, explaining that 'the pipeline will jeopardize the interests and independence of Europe.' Clearly, for the U.S. it is much better for Europe to be dependent on America, to buy American gas obtained by fracking (polluting the environment), which is at least 30% more expensive, and to continue to happily comply with the dictates of the benevolent Empire. Such is 'the protection of the United States of America.'

The use of foreign markets to serve U.S. economic and/or power interests

The U.S. does not hesitate to recourse to foreign markets in case of national economic difficulties and to deploy military strength if necessary. As the Historian of the State Department writes:

[between 1866 and 1898] following two devastating economic recessions, U.S. foreign policy leaders focused on finding foreign markets to absorb excess goods. This renewed emphasis on exploring international business opportunities

---

27 Declassified documents show very clearly that the promise was given to Gorbachev that NATO and the EU would not move close to Russia, in exchange of Russia accepting the reunification of Germany, Smith 2017, Richard 2018 with many references.

resulted in a build-up of U.S. naval forces to protect commercial shipping and overseas interests.[28]

This has been a constant American practice since the end of WW2, and especially after the U.S. abandoned the Gold Standard, thereby transferring to other countries the burden of financing the U.S. deficit and its endless wars.[29] It had already started with the Marshall Plan that clearly helped Europe to recover from WW2, but whose main objectives nonetheless were to prepare Europe to face the purported Soviet threat, and especially to help the U.S. to sell the surplus of the goods that its economy, not damaged by the war, could not totally absorb by its domestic demand. Should it fail to sell to Europe, the consequence, feared by the U.S. leadership, might portend a return to the unemployment of the 1930s.[30] Later, the Obama administration, with the support of U.S. multinationals, tried to set up two mega-treaties for trade and investment, the Transatlantic Trade and Investment Partnership (TTIP) and the Trans-Pacific Partnership (TPP). These treaties would have given the U.S. two formidable means to further contain Russia and China, and to the American multinationals, two vast markets in which to develop their businesses, had not President Trump suspended the ratification of these treaties at the beginning of his presidency.[31]

When did the U.S. start to implement an imperial foreign policy?

The beginning and/or development of U.S. imperial foreign policy is a matter of debate: some pundits see it as occurring during the transition from the 19th to the 20th century[32] or after World War

---

28 U.S. Department of State 2017.

29 For an explanation see Hudson 2003, 2005, 2019a, 2019b.

30 Of course, the U.S. had a complex set of motives for supporting Western Europe, especially the policy of containment of Soviet Russia, and not only the unselfish generosity of financing the reconstruction of the devasted European continent. For a critical analysis of the establishment of the Marshall Plan see La Feber (1994), Chap. 14: 'The Cold War, or the Renewal of U.S.-Russian Rivalry (1945–1949)'; Griffin (2018), Chap. 8 'Creating the Cold War'; Green (2017), Part Three: The Rise of the Soviets; Lacroix-Riz (1985), Chap. 4 'La mise en place du plan Marshall: les mechanisms de la dépendance européenne (mai-décembre 1947)' and Chap. 5 'Le poids de Washington sur la politique française au début du plan Marshall'; Lacroix-Riz (2014).

31 See Chapter 1 section, 'Universal Values and the Myth of Liberalism.'

32 E.g. Karp 1979; McCormick 1995, Chap. 2.

II, or even after the collapse of the Soviet Union,[33] and are certainly interesting for understanding U.S. foreign policy after these dramatic events. However personally, I have been convinced by the writing of those who consider that the U.S. imperial posture appeared right at the very beginning of the U.S. Republic.[34] This preference was analysed in Chapter 2 addressing the origins of the U.S. ideology and its translation into U.S. foreign policy. The imperial character of a foreign policy does not depend upon the size of the territory upon which it develops, but on its intrinsic characteristics.[35] The events reported above addressing the U.S. expansion make sense when interpreted and understood through the ideology therein presented.

Only a nation whose ideology terms it to be the exceptional, virtuous, indispensable Republic chosen by God to lead the world towards the end of history can explain the vigour, determination and the sincere sense of justice (based upon its own values) with which the U.S. has pursued its expansion over vast territories occupied by other peoples. That ideology has been the unrelenting mainstay of U.S. foreign policy, whether it be amplified by economic interests, the quest for political power, or messianic or religious motives, all of which, over time, tended to reinforce each other.

Above, I have showed how this policy developed towards the Far East, and especially towards China from the end of the 18th century to the conquest of the Philippines in 1899 and thereafter to the Theodore Roosevelt Corollary to the Monroe Doctrine (1904) stating that the United States would intervene as a last resort to ensure that other nations in the Western Hemisphere fulfilled their obligations to international creditors, and did not violate the rights of the United States or invite 'foreign aggression to the detriment of the entire body of American nations. As the corollary worked out in practice, the United States increasingly used military force to restore internal stability to nations in the region.'[36]

During this period the U.S. developed its military resources (especially the Navy), and accelerated the development of its economy, under the screen of protectionist laws. It was then ready to make the new century the 'American century.'

---

33 E.g. Scott 2007; Bacevich 2008, 2012.
34 E.g. La Feber 1994; Zinn 1999; Griffin 2018; Green 2018; Losurdo 2007, 2011.
35 Even relatively small and medium sized countries have developed an imperial foreign policy, such as Belgium, The Netherlands, and Italy.
36 U.S. 2017.

THE AMERICAN CENTURY AND THE DEVELOPMENT OF U.S. POWER RESOURCES

While the U.S. entered World War I in 1917, the U.S. Senate went on to vote against the participation of the U.S. in the League of Nations, despite strong support for so doing from President Woodrow Wilson.[37] The U.S. then entered a period of relative isolation, but maintained its dominance over the Americas, followed the events of the interwar period in Europe,[38] maintained its presence in the Pacific (especially in the Philippines and China), and continued to develop its economy under the shield of a very strong protectionist trade policy.[39] After the Japanese aggression on Pearl Harbor (7 December 1941) the U.S. entered World War II, defeated Japan, installed its military forces there (later transformed into military bases) and promoted the development of a liberal democratic Japan favourable to U.S. national interests in the region. By intervening

---

37 On the foreign policy of Woodrow Wilson, see Stephanson 1995, Ch. 4, with the significant title: 'Falling into the world,' pp. 112–129.

38 In fact, political and economic relationships between Europe and the U.S. were quite intense during the inter-war period; for a short summary see Lacroix-Riz 2014, Ch. 2: Le facteur américain. De la reintegration 'européenne' du Reich, pp. 31–46.

39 For the protectionist U.S. policy see Bairoch 1993, pp. 16–43. For the U.S. presence in China after the fall of the Chinese empire in 2012, see Tuchman (2017) who provides a brilliant biography of one of the most knowledgeable American Generals in China, Joseph W. Stilwell. 'Between the wars, Stilwell served three tours in China, where he mastered spoken and written Chinese and was the military attaché at the U.S. legation in Beijing from 1935 to 1939. In 1939 and 1940 he was assistant commander of the 2nd Infantry Division and from 1940 to 1941 organized and trained the 7th Infantry Division at Fort Ord, California. It was there that his leadership style, which emphasized concern for the average soldier and minimized ceremonies and officious discipline, earned him the nickname of "Uncle Joe." Just prior to World War II, Stilwell had been recognized as the army's top corps commander in the Army, and he was initially selected to plan and command the Allied invasion of North Africa.[12] When it became necessary to send a senior officer to China to keep it in the war, Stilwell was selected, over his personal objections, by U.S. President Franklin Roosevelt and his old friend, Army Chief of Staff George Marshall. Stilwell became the chief of staff to Generalissimo Chiang Kai-shek, served as U.S. commander in the China Burma India Theater, was responsible for all Lend-Lease supplies going to China, and later became deputy commander of South East Asia Command. Despite his status and position in China, he became involved in conflicts with other senior Allied officers over the distribution of lend-lease materiel, Chinese political sectarianism and proposals to incorporate Chinese and U.S. forces in the 11th Army Group under British command.' (Wikipedia, under Joseph Stilwell).

in Europe, the U.S. put a term to its isolationist policy of the inter-war period. It came back to the original homeland of the Pilgrim Fathers as the liberator and established a massive military presence (also later transformed into numerous military bases) within the Western European countries with a view to containing Soviet Russia. By the end of the war, the U.S. was ready to reclaim a leading role in international affairs, by implementing a formidable mix of power resources. Moreover, the U.S. offered the Marshall Plan for the reconstruction of Europe to both Westerns and Eastern European countries (a clear violation of the Yalta Agreements)[40] and, after the inevitable refusal of the latter under pressure from Moscow, and after the Soviet Union set up communist regimes in Eastern Europe (also a clear violation of the Yalta agreements), in 1949 the U.S. concluded a military alliance (NATO) with Canada and Western European countries and favoured the integration of Europe.[41]

This is generally considered the beginning of the Cold War. Nevertheless, some authors consider, not without reasons, that the beginning must be found in the transition from the presidency of Franklin Delano Roosevelt (who died 12 April 1945) to his Vice-President, Harry Truman, i.e. between April 1945 and September 1947.[42] Let us limit ourselves to facts that pertain to understanding the beginning of what today is known as the American establishment. Truman dissolved the intelligence organization set up by Roosevelt in 1942 (the Office of Strategic Services—OSS) and purged it of the officials who had supported Roosevelt's anti-imperial policy. In 1947 he created the CIA, staffed with officials favourable to the new imperial policy of the U.S. To this we can add that during WW2 and the post war era, the U.S. developed what President Eisenhower labelled the military-industrial complex in his farewell speech of January 1961, a speech that should be read and pondered by all American citizens proud of their country, but ashamed of the destruction the U.S. establishment has wreaked so often after the end of WW2, and of the influence the military has acquired over the life of their Republic. Eisenhower warned:

---

40 'The Americans and the British generally agreed that future governments of the Eastern European nations bordering the Soviet Union should be "friendly" to the Soviet regime while the Soviets pledged to allow free elections in all territories liberated from Nazi Germany,' U.S. (2017), Department of State, Office of the Historian, The Yalta Conference, 1945, https://history.state.gov/milestones, last accessed 18 April 2017.
41 See note 30 above.
42 For example: Chung 2019, 2020a, 2020b, 2020c, 2021.

This conjunction of an immense military establishment and a large arms industry is new in the American experience. The total influence—economic, political, even spiritual—is felt in every city, every state house, every office of the Federal government. We recognize the imperative need for this development. Yet we must not fail to comprehend its grave implications. Our toil, resources and livelihood are all involved; so is the very structure of our society.

In the councils of government, we must guard against the acquisition of unwarranted influence, whether sought or unsought, by the military-industrial complex. The potential for the disastrous rise of misplaced power exists and will persist.

We must never let the weight of this combination endanger our liberties or democratic processes. We should take nothing for granted. Only an alert and knowledgeable citizenry can compel the proper meshing of the huge industrial and military machinery of defense with our peaceful methods and goals, so that security and liberty may prosper together.'[43]

A few years later, former President Harry Truman addressed an additional warning to the American People, this time referring to the activities of the CIA. In a letter published by the *Washington Post*, Truman wrote:

I decided to set up a special organization charged with the collection of all intelligence reports from every available source, and to have those reports reach me as President without department "treatment" or interpretations. (...) But the most important thing about this move was to guard against the chance of intelligence being used to influence or to lead the President into unwise decisions—and I thought it was necessary that the President do his own thinking and evaluating. (...) I never had any thought that when I set up the CIA that it would be injected into peacetime cloak and dagger operations. Some of the complications and embarrassment I think we have experienced are in part attributable to the fact that this quiet intelligence arm of the President has been so removed from its intended role that it is being

---

43 Eisenhower 1961.

interpreted as a symbol of sinister and mysterious foreign intrigue—and a subject for cold war enemy propaganda. (…) I, therefore, would like to see the CIA be restored to its original assignment as the intelligence arm of the President, and that whatever else it can properly perform in that special field—and that its operational duties be terminated or properly used elsewhere. (…) There is something about the way the CIA has been functioning that is casting a shadow over our historic position, and I feel that we need to correct it.'[44]

The military-industrial complex and the CIA were to become the core of what is today referred to as the American establishment. Right from the beginning another institution joined the establishment: the State Department. To this core, we have to add the mainstream media, think tanks and academics, as well as a large number of politicians of both parties, especially in matters of foreign policy where the differences between the two parties are very narrow.

Having become the most powerful state in the world, despite the competition with the Soviet Union (the other emergent superpower after World War II and the actual battlefield winner), the fundamental guiding principle of U.S. strategy since 1945 has certainly been the containment of potential competitors. Clearly, expansion since the end of World War II could not be envisaged as it had been in the 19th century when U.S. power had expanded into the Americas, as we have seen above. At the end of World War II, further expansion could only have been possible by implementing a different strategy combining a variety of different means. It is here that containment became a fundamental principle to orient U.S. foreign policy first toward the Soviet Union, then toward China.[45]

In order to understand today's China foreign policy, we have to evaluate the means at the disposal of its major competitor, the U.S. The U.S. foreign policy, as we have seen above, is a global policy whose aim is to establish and maintain the supremacy of the U.S. in the world. The impressive number and types of power resources implemented by U.S. foreign policy are well known and have been dealt with in a great number of publications by the U.S. government, think tanks, university researchers, and investigative journalists. The U.S. foreign policy combines

---

44 Truman 1963.
45 Kennan 1947, Menand 2011, Rojansky 2016.

1. military resources supported by a budget more than three times that of China, including both conventional and nuclear weapons that can be deployed all over the world thanks to hundreds of military bases with the support of the world's most powerful navy and air force, whereas China has only one military base;

2. the control of maritime routes;

3. over a dozen domestic intelligence agencies, in addition to the world infamous CIA, supplemented by the agencies of those countries included in the so-called 'Five Eyes' as well as by agencies from countries outside the Anglosphere;

4. the use of NGOs and think tanks such as the National Endowment for Democracy to diffuse American values of liberal democracy and human rights, often financed by the U.S. budget; most of the think tanks were introduced at the beginning of the 20th century and were intended at the outset to promote a global agenda. These organizations (mainly foundations such as Carnegie, Rockefeller, Ford, Soros, etc.) share 'a common Universalist project aiming at building a global system strongly based upon American values (…) that we can summarize in three words: peace, democracy and market economy.' Their strategy consists 'firstly "to rely on the elites of knowledge," seen as the main driving force of change and progress both in the United States and anywhere else in the world. This explains why "the research and higher education institutions or think tanks" are privileged vehicles';[46]

5. a network of political and military alliances and partnerships such as NATO, Japan, South Korea, Philippines, Australia, New Zealand;

6. the use of a variety of devices for diffusing American values: radio and TV broadcasting companies, mainstream media, governmental agencies, the 'American Cultural Centres,' and mainstream think tanks;

---

46 Tournès 2010, pp. 5, 9; also: Kelstrup 2016; Rastrick 2018.

7. investments of American companies abroad, including in China; [47]

8. the use of the national cinema industry to diffuse positive images of the U.S., especially of its army, engaged against the target du jour, portrayed negatively;[48]

9. and last but not least, the use of the U.S. dollar as the world's major reserve and trade currency and the control of the SWIFT system used for financial transfers, access to which can be blocked as part of the strategy to sanction foes and even friends.

U.S. power has implemented these resources throughout history to become the dominant state in the world, especially after the collapse of the Soviet Union at the beginning of the 1990s. Little by little, since at least the end of World War II, the U.S. has managed to set up the rules that govern the international system that in fact, if maintained, will assure the safeguard of its own national interests: the so-called 'liberal U.S.-led-rule-based international order,' based upon the World Bank, the International Monetary Fund and the General Agreement on Tariffs and Trade (the predecessor of the World Trade Organization) and the dominant role of the U.S. dollar.[49] This is why the U.S. establishment is doing whatever it can to maintain this order. Understandably, given this formidable set of power resources, the U.S. establishment both envisages and pursues the continuance of its dominant role in the world. Of course, the implementation of these resources is not a simple translation of power into action. On the individual as well as governmental level, it requires belief in the ultimate superiority of American values, even if quite often these values are put aside in favour of interests, and indeed, even if they lead to horrendous human costs.

---

47 Let us quote the historian of capitalism, Fernand Braudel: 'merchandise and capital have always circulated simultaneously, for capital and credit have always been the surest way of capturing and controlling a foreign market. Long before the twentieth century the exportation of capital was a fact of daily life, for Florence as early as the thirteenth century (Braudel 1979b), pp. 113–114.

48 Alford and Secker 2017.

49 To my knowledge, the best analyses of the U.S. strategy for establishing world domination since at least the Second World War, are developed by Michael Hudson's books, significantly entitled: *Super Imperialism. The Origins and Fundamentals of U.S. World Dominance* (Hudson 2003) and *Global Fracture. The New International Economic Order* (Hudson 2005).

Nevertheless, as we will see hereafter, this unshakeable belief in the right to act according to those values, is today jeopardized by changes in the distribution of power resources that has been going on for several decades. The problem is that the U.S. establishment has not taken stock of these changes. But before we examine the impact of their consequences upon the capacity of the U.S. to continue to play its leading role, it is fair to quote the best analysis presented to justify the persistence of that role.

The case for the leading role of the U.S.

In Chapter 2 we have already seen how the U.S. elites justify the leading role of their country in the world. My analysis of U.S. foreign policy led me to the conclusion that Robert Kagan's analysis of the international role of the U.S. is generally shared by all the components of the U.S. establishment. So, I think it is fair, before we examine today's weaknesses of the U.S. as it now confronts new powers such as Russia and China that contest its primacy, to summarize Kagan analysis, quoting his 2017 article, which in my opinion puts forward the best case in favour of the 'manifest destiny' that imposes upon the U.S. the duty to lead the world.[50] In February 2017, after Donald Trump's election, Robert Kagan summarized his views in a long article published simultaneously by the influential magazine *Foreign Policy* and the no less influential Brookings Institution think-tank's website.[51] The article can be considered as the most complete and coherent version of the 'New Manifest Destiny,' even if this term does not appear explicitly in the text.

---

50 One of the most influential neoconservatives, Robert Kagan is the co-founder of the neoconservative Project for the New American Century, a senior fellow at the influential think-tank Brookings Institution and a member of the no less influential Council on Foreign Relations. The Project for the New American Century (PNAC) was a neo-conservative think tank (1997 to 2006) that had strong ties to the American Enterprise Institute. PNAC's web site said it was 'established in the spring of 1997 as "a non-profit, educational organization whose goal is to promote American global leadership, and founded by William Kristol and Robert Kagan. (…) PNAC's stated goal was "to promote American global leadership." The organization stated that "American leadership is good both for America and for the world," and sought to build support for "a Reaganite policy of military strength and moral clarity." Of the twenty-five people who signed PNAC's founding statement of principles, ten went on to serve in the administration of U.S. President George W. Bush, including Dick Cheney, Donald Rumsfeld, and Paul Wolfowitz.' See Wikipedia: https://en.wiin 1996kipedia.org/wiki/Project for_the_New_American_Century, accessed 28 March 2017.

51 Kagan 2017b. See also Kagan 2008 and 2014.

Kagan starts out by asserting that it is absolutely necessary to maintain the 'dominant position that the U.S. has held in the international system since 1945,' referred to also as 'the U.S.-led post-war global order, the U.S. supported world order, or the world they [i.e., Americans] created after World War II,' a clear reference to his book *The World America Made*.[52] The reason is that otherwise 'the existing order collapses and the world descends into a phase of brutal anarchy.' The values that this event is likely to damage are the free market capitalism, democracy and political freedoms associated with American national interests. Moreover, 'the liberal enlightenment project elevated universal principles of individual rights and common humanity over ethnic, racial, religious, national, or tribal differences.'

The danger comes from the new enemies:

> two great revisionist powers, Russia and China (...) [who] are dissatisfied with the current global configuration of power. Both seek to restore the hegemonic dominance they once enjoyed in their respective regions. (...) Both Beijing and Moscow seek to redress what they regard as an unfair distribution of power, influence, and honour in the U.S.-led post-war global order. As autocracies, both feel threatened by the dominant democratic powers in the international system and by the democracies on their borders. Both regard the United States as the principal obstacle to their ambitions, and therefore both seek to weaken the American-led international security order that stands in the way of their achieving what they regard as their rightful destinies. (...) It is a myth, prevalent among liberal democracies, that revisionist powers can be pacified by acquiescence to their demands.

Consequently, and were his assertions true, quite logically, Kagan rejects the idea of the emergence of a multi-polar world that would be governed by a joint leadership shared between the U.S., Russia and China, because 'revisionist great powers are not easy to satisfy short of complete capitulation. Their sphere of influence is never quite large enough to satisfy their pride or their expanding need for security.' Moreover, 'revisionist great powers with growing military capabilities invariably make use of those capabilities when they believe the possible

---

52 Kagan 2012a.

gains outweigh the risks and costs.'[53] And this poses a threat not only to the U.S. but also to its allies and partners. The consequence is that the U.S. must remain the 'indispensable nation' and continue to lead the liberal world it made.

Very generously Kagan is willing to concede that

> within the liberal order, China can compete economically and successfully with the United States; Russia can thrive in the international economic order upheld by the democratic system, even if it is not itself democratic. But military and strategic competition is different. The security situation undergirds everything else. It remains true today as it has since World War II that only the United States has the capacity and the unique geographical advantages to provide global security and relative stability. There is no stable balance of power in Europe or Asia without the United States.'

And Kagan adds, not without reason, that 'soft power' and 'smart power' will always be of limited value when confronting raw military power.

To sustain his demonstration Kagan uses a few historical examples that, in his view, make it clear that these 'revisionist' powers are very aggressive towards the U.S.-led liberal order. On the one hand, Kagan considers that Russia has been far more aggressive, asserting that it invaded two neighbouring states, Georgia in 2008 and Ukraine in 2014, that Putin is implementing 'repressive policies toward his own people,' and sent 'substantial forces into Syria' where its role 'increased the refugee flow into Europe,' and furthermore 'funds right-wing populist parties across Europe,' and 'uses its media outlets to support favoured candidates and attack others.'

This exemplifies the tactic described by Diana Johnstone of creating the 'enemy' before attacking it, to be developed below.[54] We will not address the deception involved in Kagan's contentions regarding the Georgian and the Ukrainian conflicts (and as indeed maintained in the Western media bullhorn) but instead point out how it shows how neoconservatives (this could be said more generally of the U.S. establishment and the majority of Western governments) consider what constitutes the

---

53 The subtitles of the last section of the article is quite revealing: 'Give 'em an inch, they'll take a mile.'

54 Johnstone 2016, pp. 98–101.

'invasion' of one country by another. Clearly for them the only way to invade a country is to occupy it by military means, with all other intrusions such as those by NGOs, economic advisers and investors excluded from the category of 'invasion.' A rather restrictive way to define 'invasion.' Or should one explain this by reference to the U.S. will to simply 'expand' all over the world, anticipated by Jefferson since the beginning of the 19th century (see beginning of Chapter 2 section 'American Ideology, Past and Present') where 'expansion' very clearly is not considered as an 'invasion' but as a liberation of the ignorant and oppressed people, facilitated where needed by targeted use of force? While Kagan considers that 'Beijing, until recently has succeeded mostly in driving American allies closer to the U.S. out of concern for growing Chinese power' there is no reason not to ramp up the concern, since this 'could change quickly.'

One may think that these assertive policy analyses and proposals are merely products of independent think tanks and do not correspond to the official U.S. foreign policy choices. Nevertheless, these think tanks are among the most influential sources of policy proposals in the U.S., and many of their members are, or have been, high officials and/or advisers of the U.S. government. Moreover, if one looks at the speeches of an earlier U.S. president, we can see some remarkable similarities. President Obama often felt the need to reassure his fellow citizens as well as the U.S. military hierarchy and soldiers about the capacity of the U.S. to retain its leading role in the world.[55]

In fact, it appears that the main theme that summarizes American reactions to China's rise is the fear of losing the U.S. capacity to lead the world, to lose the status of sole world super-power that sets the rules of the international system, i.e. of the 'world America made,' according to Robert Kagan's famous meme.[56] Given these fundamental policy goals, shared by all the components of the U.S. establishment, it is understandable that the election of Donald Trump provoked an unbelievable hysteria which cannot be explained only by the domestic policies announced by candidate Trump. What appears to have worried the U.S. establishment

---

55 The reader is invited to check the following speeches by President Obama; quotations from some of the most important Obama speeches: State of the Union address, Obama 2016a; Remarks by the President Obama in Commencement Address to the United States Air Force Academy, Obama 2016b; Remarks by the President of the United States at the Military Academy Commencement Ceremony, U.S. Military Academy-West Point, Obama 2014.
56 Kagan 2012b: *The World America Made*.

more were the international policies changes announced by Trump, the re-appearance of some aspects of isolationism.[57] So, while Russia remains a serious competitor, China has emerged as an even more formidable one. These contentions advanced by Kagan are not new ideas. The experts in geopolitics have already been putting them forward for a long time. Zbigniew Brzezinski, one of the most influential American geopolitical experts, made it very clear: the future of U.S. leadership will be decided in Asia.[58] Moreover, he contended that Russia should be integrated into a larger network of European cooperation. As for China, he considered that much depended on its relationships with the U.S.:

> More specifically, the medium-term goal requires fostering genuine partnerships with a more united and politically defined Europe, a regionally preeminent China, a post-imperial and Europe-oriented Russia, and a democratic India. But it will be success or failure in forging broader strategic relationships with Europe and China that shapes Russia's future role and determines Eurasia's central power equation.[59]

But for Brzezinski, as for Kagan, the fundamental goal of U.S. foreign policy remains the same: to maintain U.S. dominance and, under the leadership of the U.S., integrate the other countries into the liberal and capitalistic global order 'that America made.'

The analyses presented above lead us to conclude that the fundamental goal of U.S. foreign policy is to maintain global dominance by implementing the fundamental principle guiding its foreign policy, i.e. a strategy of containment of potential competitors all over the world, wherein the only policy option for China and other potential competitors

---

57 Urio 2018, pp. 129–43, updated in Urio 2019, pp. 230–43.
58 Brzezinski 1997a, 1997b, 2016.
59 Brzekinski also encourages the enlargement of NATO and EU: 'Enlargement of NATO and the EU would also reinvigorate Europe's waning sense of a larger vocation while consolidating, to the benefit of both America and Europe, the democratic gains won through the successful end of the Cold War. At stake in this effort is nothing less than America's long-range relationship with Europe. A new Europe is still taking shape, and if that Europe is to remain part of the "Euro-Atlantic" space, the expansion of NATO is essential.' See also Brzekinski's timetable for realizing these objectives, that is in fact an accurate forecast of what really was going to happen in the following decade, especially in regard to Ukraine.

is to integrate into this world by adopting its major characteristics, i.e. liberal democracy and capitalism. Should they prefer to keep some of their non-liberal features at home, they will nonetheless have to integrate into the liberal international order and behave according to the rules America made.[60]

The election of Joseph Biden was welcomed by several pundits as a sign that the U.S. was ready to change its way of conceiving and conducting its foreign policy. A very hopeful but bad forecast, probably influenced by the extraordinary hostility the establishment (including the majority of its intellectuals) manifested against President Trump. Several clear demonstrations of the persistence of the traditional U.S. imperial posture occurred immediately, during the transition from Trump to Biden. In Chapter 2 (see 'Today's American Ideology and Its Impact on Foreign Policy'), I have already discussed some of these manifestations, in particular the choice of Biden's closest officials, many of whom came from the Obama administration and had taken part in practically all the U.S. military (overt and covert) and regime change endeavours. Here are two more events that are worth mentioning.

At his first press conference on 25 March 2021, Biden reported what he told President Xi Jinping, that:

> Mr. President, as I've told you before, Americans value the notion of freedom. America values human rights.[61] We don't always live up to our expectations, but it's a values system. We are founded on that principle. And as long as you and your country continue to so blatantly violate human rights, we're going to continue, in an unrelenting way, to call to the attention of the world and make it clear — make it clear what's happening.

Biden made it clear that the competition with China is above all a competition of values.[62] Although Biden did not say it clearly, the very firm

---

60 See for example the last book by one of the most renowned American sinologists, David Shambaugh, *China's Future*, Cambridge, UK, Polity Press, 2016. But be reassured China will not dominate the XXI Century, if you follow the demonstration by Jonathan Fenby, *Will China Dominate the XXI Century?*, op. cit.; the answer is given in the last chapter entitled : 'China will not dominate the XXI century,' pp. 117–131.

61 Biden 2021c.

62 See Chapter 2 under 'The China Threat: The New Cold War is Here to Stay,'

tone leaves little doubt that the U.S. is likely to promote those values by interfering in the internal affairs of China, as we shall see hereafter.

Biden went on to say:

> So I see stiff competition with China. China has an overall goal, and I don't criticize them for the goal, but they have an overall goal to become the leading country in the world, the wealthiest country in the world, and the most powerful country in the world. That's not going to happen on my watch because the United States is going to continue to *grow and expand.* [Emphasis added.]

Quite interesting! I cannot help recalling the quotation of Thomas Jefferson of 1801:

> However our present interests may restrain us within our limits, it is impossible not to look forward to distant times when our multiplication will expand it beyond those limits, and cover the whole northern, if not the southern continent, with people speaking the same language, governed in similar forms, and by similar laws.

With Biden the U.S. is on the same line it has followed since at least the end of WW2: expansion without borders! And it surfaced again at the opening of the Alaska meeting between the U.S. and Chinese foreign ministers.

Second, another clear demonstration of the persistence of this posture appeared in the open at the Alaska meeting, already dealt with in Chapter 2 under 'The China threat: The New Cold War is here to stay.' Even more clear has been the strategy implemented by the new president and his staff. In preparation of his meeting with President Putin in Geneva (16 June 2021) Biden met with his allies in the Far East (the newly-termed 'Quad'), in the UK (the G7), in Europe and in NATO.[63] It exemplified the American position that allies must come together under its leadership ('America is back') and fight against the existential threats

---

and the analysis of the article by Brands and Cooper (2021) significantly entitled 'U.S.-Chinese Rivalry Is a Battle Over Values.'

63 The Quad is an informal partnership initiated on 2007 comprising the U.S., Japan, Australia and India.

represented by China and Russia. The NATO document issued after the meeting is an unbelievable summary of provocations, to say the least, against other countries accused of intending the same thing the U.S. is doing, and has been doing, for a very long time. It contends that it is the Russian and the Chinese that aggresses against the U.S., as the Native Indian were claimed to have done in the 19th century. The document quotes Russia no less than 61 times compared to 10 times for China. It affirms, with a remarkable nonchalance, that NATO will continue the ongoing procedures for the admission of Georgia and Ukraine, last steps in its encirclement of Russia. Moreover, it informs that 'the allies stand ready for a mutually beneficial NATO-Belarus partnership' and confirms its interventions in the Middle East (Syria, Iran), and in the Far East (North Korea). In light of the aforementioned interventions, one hopes that indeed 'NATO maintains a constructive dialogue with China where possible…based on our interests.' Nevertheless, the document is quite clear about the conditions of the dialogue: 'Allies urge (sic) China to engage meaningfully in dialogue, confidence-building, and transparency measures regarding its nuclear capabilities and doctrine. Reciprocal transparency and understanding would benefit both NATO and China.' As usual, China has to change.

Problems with the U.S. strategy to lead the World

The first problem with the U.S. strategy is that the CIA (founded in 1947) has, from the beginning, been involved not only in intelligence gathering activities, but also in activities that have nothing to do with that,[64] activities which increased up to the end of the Cold War and remain, though fewer, still quite high after the end of the Cold War. These include: meddling in other countries' elections, attempts at regime change, setting up of secret armies in European countries, launching illegal wars and setting up illegal prisons where torture of U.S. enemies could be secretly practiced.[65] It should be noted that these interventions

---

64 On the transition from the CIA to the National Endowment for Democracy see Blum 2014a, Ch 19: Trojan Horse. The National Endowment for Democracy, pp. 238–43.
65 For meddling in other countries' elections (Shane 2018, Levin 2016); for attempts at regime change (Blum 2013–14, 2014a, 2014b, 2014c, Valentine 2017); for setting up secret armies in European countries (Ganser 2005); for launching illegal wars (Ganser 2016, Jones 2017) and for setting up illegal prisons where torture of U.S. enemies could be secretly practiced (Marty 2018, pp. 153–193). Levin (2016) has identified 81 cases of electoral meddling

have not only been against authoritarian countries, but also against democratic governments whose mistake was to be an obstacle to U.S. economic and geopolitical interests, such as the regime changes in Iran in 1953 and Chile in 1973, or meddling in the elections of countries favourable to U.S. interests but at risk of losing an election to leftist parties, such as the meddling in the Russian presidential election of 1996 for the purpose of ensuring the re-election of the U.S.-friendly Boris Yeltsin against his communist opponent, or in support of the non-democratic regime in Saudi Arabia.[66] These numerous interventions show very clearly that U.S. foreign policy is more determined by the U.S. national interest (especially that of the U.S. economy) than for a genuine defence of democracy and human rights.

In the forefront of these illegal activities, it is not possible to forget that the U.S. has actually been at war 222 out of 239 years between 1776, year of the Declaration of Independence, and 2015, i.e. 93% of the time.[67]

The second problem is linked to the limits of the use of military power and the consequences for U.S. strategy. Notwithstanding the massive contribution of the Soviet Union, of the United Kingdom and of the European national liberation movements, the U.S. emerged after World War II with a reputation as the major (or even the sole) defender of freedom and democracy. Nevertheless, despite its considerable accumulation of military resources, the Cold War and the diffusion of communism during the Cold War in Europe, Asia, Africa and Latin America inevitably led the U.S. to develop a more complex strategy to defend its interests and those of the West. So, the diffusion of American values

---

between 1945 and 2000, of which 19 occurred after the end of the Cold War, the most instructive classical example being the re-election of Boris Yeltsin in 1996 (Kramer 2001). Blum (2013–14) has identified 59 cases of attempted regime change (1949–2014), of which 14 after the end of the Cold War, 37 have been successful, of which 14 took place after the end of the Cold War; Ganser 2016 has identified and documented no less than 13 illegal wars between 1953 and 2015, of which in seven after the end of the Cold War; illegal armies had been set up during the Cold War (Ganser 2005).

66 Beinart 2018, Kramer 2001.

67 Washington Blog 2015, gives the complete list of wars during this period. For a comprehensive list of American armed interventions for the period 1798–2020, see the historian of the U.S. Congress (Salazar Torreon 2020). For an evaluation of the number of deaths and displaced people by U.S. military interventions see Vine (2020); a summary is given in the Preface, pp. xi-xxv. The whole book is a masterpiece of empirical research on American imperialism.

become a necessity for the U.S., should it choose or need to restrain from primarily using its economic and military resources to obtain compliance with its international policy. To this end, in addition to the statements by politicians, journalists and think tanks, the U.S. establishment has set up a whole set of instruments and platforms to diffuse its values of democracy, human rights and free trade: radio and TV broadcasting companies such as the Voice of America, Radio Free Asia and CNN; mainstream media, governmental agencies such as the U.S. Agency for International Development (USAID), the 'American Cultural Centres,' think tanks such as the Council on Foreign relations and the Brookings Institution; not-for-profit foundations dedicated to the growth and strengthening of democratic institutions around the world; and NGOs, some of them in fact government-funded organizations such as the National Endowment for Democracy and its subsidiaries.[68] To this we can add the financing of foreign students (including Chinese) to attend American Universities with the aim to open their minds to American values, such as liberal democracy and free market economy. Finally, in the military domain it is necessary to refer to the Western Hemisphere Institute for Security Cooperation (WHINSEC), formerly known as the School of the Americas, of the United States Department of Defense, whose mission is to develop and conduct instruction for the armed forces of Latin America. This has often been an asset for the CIA regime change activities. The U.S. has also implemented military training in other parts of the world, especially in Africa.

These means have been used all over the world, quite often to desta-bilize countries by supporting, financing and training opposition groups and organizations. Moreover, with the help of governmental agencies such as the CIA and the National Endowment for Democracy (NED) and its subsidiaries, there have been many cases where these activities have favoured regime changes with the aim of actually putting into power a new government more likely to support American interests. The most recent successful case is that of Ukraine in 2014. While the 20-year effort

---

68 For example, 'each year, NED makes more than 1,200 grants to support the projects of non-governmental groups abroad who are working for democratic goals in more than 90 countries. Since its founding in 1983, the Endowment has remained on the leading edge of democratic struggles everywhere, while evolving into a multifaceted institution that is a hub of activity, resources and intellectual exchange for activists, practitioners and scholars of democracy the world over.,' website of the NED, http://www.ned.org/about/, accessed 17 May 2017.

in Afghanistan has blown up completely and the attempt in Syria is at a semi-standstill, the attempt in Venezuela has foundered but is likely to continue, as with Cuba, while some others may also be proceeding more covertly in the Philippines, Myanmar and Thailand. These interventions are often prepared and/or accompanied by the training and financing of local police and armed forces, or even covert war interventions by special operation forces such as the Green Berets and the Navy SEALs. So, in these cases there is an overlapping between quasi-military and economic power resources on the one hand, and cultural resources on the other. If U.S. cultural power is so attractive, it remains to be explained why it has been so very often necessary to resort to military power (under the form of both overt and covert warfare) to obtain compliance with the U.S. interests.[69] This increasing disenchantment seems to be one of the important reasons that explains the loss of power of the U.S. since the end of the Cold War, irrespective of the emergence of new powers, such as China, and the re-emergence of old powers such as Russia, as well as the awakening of Europe that may develop a new defence and foreign policy more independent from the U.S.

The third problem is related to the collapse of the Soviet Union at the beginning of the 1990s.[70] The road was then wide open for the U.S. to the sole superpower, as it indeed proclaimed it had become. Then followed the years of 'great expectations' or of the '*folie des grandeurs*': the U.S. and its European allies started an aggressive policy towards Russia by expanding NATO to Eastern Europe and admitting several Eastern European countries into the European Union.[71] Moreover,

---

69 On the transition of American warfare from overt (Bush) to covert warfare (Obama) see Turse 2012a, 2012b, 2015, and 2018. For a short presentation Urio 2018, pp. 161, 165–66. According to Turse during the Bush administration the U.S. special operation forces intervened in 60 countries, under the Obama administration they operated in 133 countries and in 2017 under Trump they were operating in '149 countries—about 75% of the nations on the planet. At the halfway mark of this year [2018], according to figures provided to *TomDispatch* by U.S. Special Operations Command (USSOCOM or SOCOM), America's most elite troops have already carried out missions in 133 countries. That's nearly as many deployments as occurred during the last year of the Obama administration and more than double those of the final days of George W. Bush's White House' (Turse 2018).

70 Among the vast literature on the reasons explaining the collapse of the Soviet Union, see the interesting and unusual interpretation of the French historian and demographer, Emmanuel Todd 1979.

71 This is a reference to the title of an article by Andrew Bacevich: 'Bacevich, (2017). *The age of great expectations and the great void. History after "the*

military interventions in Yugoslavia allowed the U.S. to establish a huge military base in Kosovo (Camp Bondsteel), in addition to the many other military bases established by the U.S. after World War II in Europe and everywhere else.[72] This aggressive policy had the result (desired or undesired) of humiliating the defeated enemy, and rejecting its understandable need to assure security at its borders, despite the many moves by Russian leaders (and especially Vladimir Putin) to include Russia with the management of European security. Russia's only international policy choice was to have been to accept the dominance of the West and to integrate into the international world that the U.S. had made in its interest. This shortsighted U.S. policy was based upon the belief that the world that emerged after the collapse of the Soviet Union was there to stay forever, thus realizing Fukuyama's end of history.[73] For some observers of international politics this marked the beginning of Cold War II targeting Russia and later China with the aim of establishing a unipolar world dominated by the U.S. and its allies: the 'expansion' of U.S. power would then have realized Thomas Jefferson's dream above any optimistic expectations. But this type of behavior, as well as the two problems mentioned above, did not remain unnoticed by the Chinese leadership (or indeed, by Russia).

The strategy to use a mix of power resources to impose U.S. will: Regime change or war?

Although the threat of military power is always there as a backup, a great variety of means are implemented either before its use, or as a substitute to military power. Overall, these means nonetheless constitute a regime change strategy, which can be used in sequence and/or simultaneously.[74] First, it is a question of disqualifying the enemy by

---

End of History," *TomDispatch.com*, 8 January. Retrieved March 28, 2017, from http://www.tomdispatch.com/blog/176228/.
72 The illegal war against Serbia (1999), as well as the war on Iraq (2003) were started by the U.S. without the approval of the UN (Ganser 2016, Ch 11 and 13). Nonetheless, they have been justified by Robert Kagan in his 2003 book, on the basis of 'the humanitarian duty the civilized world has to intervene where and when the tyrant massacres his own people,' the presence of weapons of mass destruction and the support of terrorist organizations. This is a good example of the euphoria that oriented U.S. foreign policy after the collapse of the Soviet Union. See the statement by Las Casas about this type of justification, at the beginning of this chapter.
73 Fukuyama 1999 and 1992.
74 To my knowledge, the first attempt to analyse this sequence has been done

focusing on their leaders, by demonizing them as savages the Indians), dictators (Saddam Hussein), new 'Hitlers' or ' killers' (Vladimir Putin), or as non-human, an animal (Assad).[75] Moreover, whenever an election has taken place, or is about to be organized, a concomitant move consists in raising the issue of the government having rigged (or about to rig) the election. This necessitates 'a propaganda war,' waged by mainstream media and think tanks whose goal is to obtain the support of the majority of Western citizens and of the 'international community.' This propaganda, which is operating throughout the whole process, makes it clear that the dictator 'must go,' one way or the other.

The second measure concerns the implementation of economic sanctions that serve to destabilize the country by deteriorating its economy, with a view to making the enemy government lose the support of its people, i.e., by 'making the economy scream,' as happened in Chile in 1973 (currently in operation in today's ongoing sanctions against Iran, Venezuela, and Cuba).[76]

The third measure concerns the mobilization of local clients against the targeted government. These can either live in the countries concerned or, quite often, are hosted in the U.S. or in other Western countries with the support of American or Western NGOs and the U.S. Government. Numerous past examples might be quoted but let us mention only a few of the present-day instances of meddling—in Iran, Venezuela, Syria, ... and in China's territories such as Tibet, Hong Kong and Xinjiang, to be dealt with below.

The fourth stage, which can be concomitant with the third one, is the use of NGOs, especially those called Human Rights NGOs, but in fact any kind of NGO as well, especially those specialized in the diffusion of the ideal of market economy (i.e. capitalism), liberal democracy and

---

by Diana Johnstone analysing the U.S. (NATO) interventions in Kosovo and in Ukraine (Johnstone 2016, pp. 98–101). Hereafter I further develop the sequence based upon my research on U.S. Foreign policy.

75 The first three qualifications are well-known and do not need references. The last (Assad is an animal) concerns Donald Trump's comment on the alleged chemical attack by Syria of April 2018: 'Many dead, including women and children, in mindless chemical attack in Syria,' Trump tweeted. 'Area of atrocity is in lockdown and encircled by Syrian Army, making it completely inaccessible to outside world. President Putin, Russia and Iran are responsible for backing Animal Assad. Big price...,' reported by *CNN:* Watkins (2018).

76 This expression was used in 1970 when President Nixon ordered the CIA to 'make the economy scream' in Chile to 'prevent Allende from coming to power or to unseat him.' (Democracy Now, 2013).

human rights, such as those financed directly by the U.S. government, e.g. the National Endowment for Democracy and its subsidiaries. There are numerous examples in Eastern Europe and Russia after the collapse of the Soviet Union and of course since at least the beginning of the 1950s in China's territories such as Tibet, Hong Kong and Xinjiang. The goal is to create a climate of protest and disorder in the name of democracy that, should it become violent, will inevitably lead the local police and/or army to violently intervene. This may lead to a regime change, as in Ukraine in 2014, or it may force the enemy to negotiate, as happened with the first U.S. sanctions regime on Iran leading to the JCPOA, or, as just happened in Hong Kong, to force the central government in Beijing to take visibly repressive measures, such as the new security law and the revision of the electoral process. These measures restrict the use of civil and political rights as well as the activities of the NGOs mentioned above used to support the protest movements. The result is at least an additional pressure on China, under the form of an increase in Western criticism of 'China's dictatorial' intervention in Hong Kong that 'kills democracy.'

If the outcome of these actions is not satisfactory, the next move is to submit to the enemy a solution that it cannot accept. For example, in the case of Kosovo, Secretary of State Madeleine Albright inserted an unacceptable ultimatum (total military occupation of Serbia by NATO) in what were billed as 'negotiations' between the Yugoslav government and the Albanian Nationalists that obliged the Serbs to refuse, thus saddling them with the blame for refusing to negotiate. As said above, during these actions, it is possible (and necessary) to continue the criminalization of the enemy, especially if its intervention to control the protest is sufficiently violent to qualify it as 'genocide,' or at least support a claim that he is 'killing his own people.'

Finally, 'the sword of Damocles,' i.e., the threat to resort to military means, that is hanging over every dispute during the whole process may finally be implemented, should the 'evil enemy' fail to comply to the dictate of the 'good.'

The implementation of these power resources has allowed the U.S. to dominate the world (or at least, large parts of it) so long as the distribution of power means was biased in its favour. But what could happen should the distribution of power resources change?

THE DECLINE OF THE AMERICAN EMPIRE: INTERNAL AND INTERNATIONAL WEAKNESSES

The power of any country is based upon a mix of internal strengths and of power resources that can be implemented in the international arena. Internal features can include characteristics of the political system that can be admired abroad, such as a virtuous and reliable behaviour of political and economic elites both inside the country and internationally, the internal cohesion of its society, the strengths of its economy, the quality of its education system, its military resources. We will evaluate how the U.S. and China perform on these resources. The first step in this direction is to take stock of the decline of the U.S. and find out what its causes are.

Weaknesses of U.S. internal resources

The first, and probably the most important cause of the decline of the internal strengths of the U.S. is to be found in the traditional support the U.S. administration (both Democratic and Republican) has given to U.S. capitalism and to the elites that benefit most from it, to the detriment of the well-being of the United States overall as a nation and to its people. For a very long time America has been developing an ideological pro-business stance that constitutes a threat to democracy and promotes a massive imbalance between employers and workers.[77] One of the consequences has been the relocation of industrial activities in countries such as China, where the cost of manpower was considerably lower than in the U.S., and where the regulations concerning the management of owners-employees relations and the protection of the environment were much less stringent. The consequence is that the U.S. work force lost several millions of jobs in these sectors, as well as the related know-how. Of course, several pundits in the U.S. blame China for developing its industrial sectors thanks to these relocations, and for forcing Western companies to transfer their technology to their Chinese partners within joint ventures set up by China in the process of implementing market mechanisms. While no particular entity forced Western companies to

---

77 Stiglitz 2018a, 2018b. The example of anti-competitive work contracts is a good illustration of this imbalance: these contracts prohibit employees, not only managers, from leaving their job for a competitor. Starr, Prescot and Bishara (2018) have found that 'Nearly 1 in 5 labour force participants were bound by non-competes in 2014, and nearly 40% had signed at least one noncompete in the past.'

invest in China, it might be seen that the very capitalist system that the West wishes to promote, indeed did so, with inter-capitalist competition driving all to seek to comparatively lower their production costs. And while ostensibly their goal might be seen as being to considerably increase their return on investment—it was nice to be able to make a pair of sports shoes for a few dollars in China and to sell them for 100$ in the West. The Chinese simply took advantage of this greedy behavior and engaged in normal business practices by seeking their own interest in the negotiations, saying: OK, you can invest in our country, but these are our conditions; nobody forces you to accept them.

Add to this the U.S. pro-military ideological stance, and the expenditures by the military-industrial complex and the intelligence community required for its undertaking, which inevitably subtracted resources from other sectors, such as infrastructures, education, environment, social security and health, and again it becomes apparent that what is required to bolster the ideology has a contrary effect on the well-being of the nation and its people. As the composition of the Biden team shows, the establishment has further embedded these interests in its governing mechanisms.

The apparently increasing cooperation between the Pentagon and the Big Tech companies of Silicon Valley, in particular thanks to the practice of 'revolving doors' among the Pentagon, think tanks, high civil servants and politicians, lead to domestic and international concerns about the establishment's capacity to spy, censure and marginalize alternative opinion sources about the domestic and foreign policies of the U.S.[78]

Add further the 'kill list' that President Obama used from his first days as commander in chief, that led to the use of drones by the military and the CIA to hunt down and kill the people his administration deemed—through secretive processes, without indictment or trial—worthy of execution; a practice that has also been used by President Trump and seems to be in use still today under the Biden administration.[79]

---

78 Guyer 2021, and above beginning of Ch. 2.1.5.

79 According to Friedersorf (2021): 'These killings began under President George W. Bush, exploded under President Barack Obama, and continue today. They constitute the majority of federal executions. Just 50 people are on federal death row. (Add in the 50 states and America has approximately 2,553 total death-row inmates.) According to the Council on Foreign Relations, Obama authorized 542 drone strikes that killed an estimated 3,797 people, including 324 civilians. The Bureau of Investigative Journalism has higher death counts.

There is simply a vast range of additional policies and indicators that are running counter to national and general public well-being, and therefor counterproductive to ensuring the domestic peace and public support upon which sound government depends. The U.S. suffers from a fiscal policy that favours enterprises (especially multinationals) over employees; increasing inequalities, discriminations, racism, and unemployment (masked by inadequate statistics and exacerbated by COVID lockdowns); the resultant deterioration of public health (especially in terms of the decrease of life expectancy and the spectacular increase of deaths by overdose); the increasing public debt resulting from the enormous amounts of federal spending that will push the budget deficit to $3 trillion for the 2021 fiscal year, as well as the debt of households and enterprises; the deterioration of physical infrastructure, as witnessed regularly by the Association of American civil engineers, and that cannot be fully redressed even if infrastructure spending were to proceed as called for; the increasing inequalities in terms of personal income and access to education and health services; the failure of the decades long war on drugs;[80] the pernicious influence of religious fundamentalism; the appalling level of students' debts; one of the highest incarceration rates in the world (about six times more than in European countries); the constant practice of spying on everybody at home and in the world (including prominent politicians of allies); the increasing limits of freedom of speech by both the government and big tech platforms such as Google, Youtube, and Twitter; the blocking by the U.S. government of foreign TV broadcasting compagnies, and so on. It's not hard to understand why the internal strengths and cohesion of the U.S. have declined during the last decades.

The maneuverability of the U.S. system to address these problems has been greatly restricted by the excessive entry of private money into politics (especially into the electoral and legislative processes) leading to the extraordinary extent of pressure groups' influence over parliament and government. The issue extends beyond the simple concern over corruption to whether this vast array of lobbyists promoting special interests in the fields of taxation, banking, insurance, agro-business, pesticides

---

And the Trump administration is thought to have accelerated the pace of drone killings, though its lack of transparency makes counting difficult. (…) President Joe Biden has a moral obligation to change course in his earliest days in office.' At the time of writing, I have no information about the decision taken by the Biden administration. See also Scahill 2015.

80 See McCoy 2003 and 2021.

and genetically modified organisms, oil, medical drugs, etc. does not in fact have strangleholds that hinder the enactment of significant systemic repairs.

Moreover, recent presidential elections have put into a crude light the extraordinary weakness of the electoral process, which has been increasingly contested with an unbelievable aggressivity whichever is the losing party. Months after the proclamation of the 2016 election, the strategy of the Democratic Party that began well before election day, was to secretly fabricate documents proving a collusion between candidate Trump and the 'existential enemy' of the U.S. establishment: Russia. If Trump had won against all expectations, everything was in place to undermine his election one way or the other. This marked the beginning of the sad spectacle of Russia-gate that lasted practically during the whole 4 years of the Trump presidency, not a positive sign for a mature democracy. The Trump administration in turn showed the extreme politicization in its similar refusal to accept the results of the 2020 election. All these behaviours deteriorate the image of the U.S. democracy both abroad and at home: an important component of a country's comprehensive power. Finally, the Covid-19 crisis has brought to the light the extraordinary polarization of American society reflected in these negative social well-being indicators: the highest rate of poverty in Western countries, one of the highest rates of inequalities (measured by UNDP Gini index), the lack of health insurance for millions of people, serious limits of the coverage for unemployment, very low minimum wage. Last but not least, the discrimination against Afro-Americans across all indicators: revenue, education, health, and rate of imprisonment. The extraordinary vehemence of the conflict between the two major political parties makes it difficult to adopt the radical measures needed to overcome the above-mentioned problems. Some measures that have been taken (e.g. the Covid-19 relief law law), although necessary, are most of the time provisional, whereas more structural reforms seem to be necessary.

Moreover, structural measures, such as the Biden Infrastructure Plan, and the Biden Plan for Climate Change, seem to be confronted by the hostility of important fractions of the establishment. Given these shortcomings one cannot see how it will be possible ... 'to make America Great again' (Trump's slogan, that is not fundamentally different from Biden's slogan: 'America is back'). Perhaps, but what kind of America? There is no polarization for foreign policy: here we have a strong bi-partisan agreement between Democrats and Republicans: fight at all costs the existential enemies: China and Russia. But how well, in fact, will America be able to do so?

International weaknesses

As suggested earlier, power implies the implementation of a mix of military, economic and cultural resources. Moreover, the analysis of competition and conflicts in the international arena shows that there is no real separation between military, economic and cultural resources.[81] In fact, in U.S. foreign policy all its power resources are implemented simultaneously in a mix that can be different from one administration to another, but that operates, in all circumstances, to safeguard the leading role of the U.S. as the sole world super-power. The vast scope of these power resources has given the U.S. an unshakeable confidence in its capacity to continue to impose its will upon others, in spite of the changes in the distribution of power resources that has developed since at least the fall of the Soviet Union. Nevertheless, ever since the Presidency of Ronald Reagan, the mix of power resources the U.S. has implemented has produced the same problems and weaknesses, no matter which party has been in the White House. Let us briefly recall them.

First, the constant increase in spending on military weaponry, wars, military bases and special operations forces have considerably increased the U.S. budget, thus subtracting resources that may (and according to some, should) be spent in other domains, such as the maintenance and upgrade of infrastructure, social security, health and education. Despite this, it has not led to military superiority (witness the preference in the arms market for Russian weapons) nor indeed to lasting success in military engagements.

Second, the negative impact of the domestic problems mentioned above has impacted the capacity of the U.S. to project its power abroad. In fact, these domains are important not only as a contribution to the well-being of the people, but also because they significantly contribute to the strength of a country.

Finally, the excessive U.S. use of military power (both for overt and covert warfare, worsened by the inefficiency of overt warfare) and its frequent use of media, NGOs, and special operation forces for provoking regime changes have the consequence of reducing not only military power, but also considerably reducing its cultural resources as a means of 'attraction and acquiescence' to the country as a whole, and

---

81 Urio 2018, pp. 35–82.

to U.S. foreign policy in particular, hence reducing the overall capacity of the U.S. to impose its will upon others. Moreover, serious problems at home have often redirected U.S. foreign policy towards a more aggressive posture against the rest of the world, which is a fair qualification of Obama and Trump's foreign policy. The Biden administration seems to be trapped into doing similarly, the botched withdrawal from Afghanistan notwithstanding.

Given the analyses presented above, we may conclude that the major weakness of U.S. foreign policy is its incapacity to see, acknowledge and act upon the changes in the distribution of power resources that have occurred since at least the end of the 20th century. The unipolar world that emerged after the collapse of the Soviet Union did not last long. Powerful long-term forces (the 'silent transformations' mentioned in Chapter 2) had been at work for a long time and facilitated the emergence of a multi-polar world, i.e. the emergence of new powers such as China as its most serious competitor, and the re-emergence of Russia, as well as of regional powers that are no longer ready to accept the dictates of the Empire. Clearly, these changes should lead the U.S. to the necessary revision of its foreign policy, in particular the identification of its real national interests: not those of the establishment, but those of the American people. However, the establishment continues to behave as if the U.S. is still the only power in the world capable to impose its will, its values and interests on the rest of the world. The U.S. acts as if these changes have not occurred. But they have, and they should lead the U.S. establishment to a radical revision of its foreign policy. But does the U.S. have the intellectual capacity to do so?

At the turn of the millennium several books were published in the U.S. showing a growing worry about the rise of China. At this time the 'China threat' became a frequent reference in the U.S. mainstream media and university books. At the same time, to comfort the U.S. public and the establishment, several books stressed the fragility of China's development, and the possible (or even inevitable) collapse of China became a frequent leitmotiv.[82]

Later, several books published by renowned Western scholars provided a more in-depth analysis, but basically with the same perspective.

82 See for example: R. Bernstein and R. Munro, *The Coming Conflict with China*, New York, Knopf, 1997;
Bill Gertz, *The China Threat. How the PRC Targets America*, Washington D.C., Regnery Publishing, 2000; Gordon Chang, *The Coming Collapse of China*, New York, Random House, 2001.

For example, a book with a title bearing the troubling question: *Will China dominate the XXI Century*, ends with a final chapter entitled 'China will not dominate the XXI Century.'[83] Some other books have more descriptive titles: *The New Chinese Empire and what it means for the United States*, and *The Chinese Century. The rising Chinese economy and its impact on the global economy, the balance of power, and your job*, or even more disturbing: *In the jaws of the dragon. America's fate in the coming era of Chinese dominance.*[84]

Nevertheless, only recently, when it became clear that the development of China's economy occurred not only in the production of low-value-added goods, but also in high-tech products, and, more worrying, in the military domain, the threat from the Soviet Union, which vanished (or should have vanished) at the beginning of the 1990s, was soon replaced by the 'China threat,' albeit exorcised by the forecast of the 'coming collapse of China'…which did not come. And as the presumed Russia threat did not vanish, nor with it the aggressive U.S. policy and its allies against the Kremlin, inevitably Russia established a *de facto* partnership with China. This really is a massive threat to the U.S., if the U.S. proposes to address it by military means which may not be up to the job. In actuality, it is the American people who should worry, given the unbelievable nonchalance and incompetence of its establishment. Today, renowned scholars have become even more explicit about the decline of the U.S. power in the world. For example: 'America's Longest War Winds Down,' introduced by *TomDispatch* with the title: 'Requiem for the American Century.'[85]

83 Jonathan Fenby, *Will China Dominate the XXI Century?*, Cambridge, UK, Politiy Press, 2017.
84 Among the numerous books on these topics see: Ross Terrill, *The New Chinese Empire and What it means for the United States*, New York, Basic Books, 2003; Oded Shenkar, *The Chinese Century. The Rising Chinese Economy and its Impact on the Global Economy, the Balance of Power, and your Job*, Upper Sadle River, NJ, Wharton School Publishing, 2005; Eamonn Filgleton, *In the Jaws of the Dragon. America's Fate in the Coming Era of Chinese Dominance*, New York, St. Martin Press, 2008; Fred Berngsten et al., *The Balance Sheet. China. What the World Needs to Know Now About the Emerging Superpower*, by the Center for Strategic and International Studies and the Institute for International Economics, New York, Public Affairs, 2006; C. Fred Bergsten et al., *China's Rise. Challenges and Opportunities*, Peterson Institute for International Economics and Centre for Strategic and International Studies, Washington, DC, 2009.
85 Bacevich 2021.

THE FOLLY OF REGIME CHANGE AND SUBVERSIVE ACTIVITIES

I have analyzed above how the U.S. tries to implement regime changes in countries that do not comply with its interests and the many tactics used to obtain this goal. I have further contended that by doing so the U.S. jeopardizes the attraction it might have exerted in countries where opposition movements may look at the American model as the best means to escape from their feudal authoritarian past and actually wish to embrace democracy and capitalism, even if it entails becoming part of the American empire in a subordinate position. This is the case with practically all the Western countries, even though the implementation of neoliberal policies has widened the divide between the 'haves' and the 'have-nots,' and indeed even though their acceptance to participate in U.S. conflicts has created another divide between those favorable or unfavorable to accepting the waves of refugees from Western initiated conflicts, leading to the rise of rightwing nationalist parties. Discontent is even more serious in countries that have embarked on the transition from feudalism to the modernity that the former Western colonies after WW2 have nonetheless regarded as exemplified by the American model. This is what happened in the former Western colonies after WW2. We Westerners have experienced this situation and the violent opposition that has characterized the struggle between the defenders of the old regime and the modernizers. Quite often we tend to forget our troubled past.

The formal liberation of colonized countries went hand in hand with a new configuration of the international system, where the U.S. and USSR tried to incorporate those liberated countries into their sphere of influence. It is here that the U.S. implemented the tactics described in Chapter 3 under 'The American Century and the Development of U.S. Power Resources.' Not only is the list is too long to be dealt with in this book; it suffices to mention the numerous regime changes organized covertly by the CIA, and the later more or less overt 'color revolutions' that followed, organized by pseudo-nongovernmental organizations such as the National Endowment for Democracy (NED). This happened first in Eastern Europe at the moment of the decline of the Soviet bloc, then later in other in-transition countries in North Africa, the Middle East and Asia. China was not spared. But China is not Egypt or Tunisia. It has become too big and too powerful to organize a regime change in China by attacking it frontally. But this does not mean that the U.S. has not tried and is still trying today to use all the opportunities offered by protest movements in Tibet, Hong Kong and Xinjiang to put pressure on

China. The minimal objective is to create obstacles to the rise of China to world power. But the more ambitious goal is to destabilize at least one of these territories that, through a domino effect, would lead to vast protest movements all over China and eventually to a regime change in the country.

The U.S. strategy aiming at a regime change in China

One must not forget that the U.S. has never accepted its loss of China at the end of the 1940s and has acted systematically towards the goal of 'getting China back.' It set up military bases in Taiwan after it allowed its protégé Chiang Kai-shek to retire there in 1949 when he lost the Chinese civil war; it delayed the recognition of the People's Republic of China to 1979; it submitted China to a long series of embargoes and sanctions, especially after the tragedy of Tiananmen in 1989; it build up formidable military forces at the periphery of China; it allowed China to join the WTO (World Trade Organization) hoping thereby to integrate it into the U.S.-led liberal and capitalist order, clearly in a dependent position. Then came Trump's economic war. And now the Biden administration aggressively positions the U.S. and its allies against China and Russia. Nothing has fundamentally changed since WW2, and maybe even earlier.

We have seen in Chapter 2 that China has maintained the authoritarian character of its governance from the Empire to the Nationalist Republic and to the People's Republic, even if under different forms and conditions. Moreover, if we consider that the traditional Confucian political culture has not totally faded away, the right of the people to overthrow the government may still today play its role if the circumstances are favourable. But we have also seen that for the time being, the Chinese people are satisfied with their government and are not in the mood for throwing the Communist Party out of power. But clearly this is not likely to prevent the U.S. from trying to destabilize China.

Insofar as problems do exist in all parts of China, as above indicated, the U.S. has tried by different means to take advantage of these, as it has done in other parts of the world, more particularly so in the three aforementioned areas of the Chinese territory where political, economic, social and identity problems are more acute: Tibet, Xinjiang and Hong Kong. A vast literature is available on these cases, and it is out of the question to analyze them in this short section of this book, taking into consideration all the dimensions that constitute their extreme complexity.

What must be pointed out here is that the mainstream Western narrative not only obscures this complexity but extracts from it the aspects that better suit its ideology—China is a dictatorship, hence it interferes in these areas by brutally imposing its will, and moreover by violating democracy and human rights—leading to a biased narrative in which Western elites, at least, are likely to believe, and feeding into their understanding of how the China issue should be further addressed. Luckily, there are still some mainstream scholars and investigative journalists that help us to have access to information that contradicts the official imperial narrative, cited here.[86] This is not to contend that all their analysis is always accurate. They are dealing with very complex events for which official documents are not fully available to the researchers. Nevertheless, on many occasions they provide empirical evidence proving that the mainstream narrative is not supported by facts, as in the case of the accusation of genocide that China is accused of being in the process of perpetrating on its Uighur minority in Xinjiang.[87]

American and Chinese interests in Tibet, Xinjiang and Hong Kong

These three cases present some differences and some similarities. The main difference is that Tibet and Xinjiang are the homelands of two of the ethnic minorities of China, the Tibetans and the Uighurs. Both were incorporated into China at the end of the 13th century by the Yuan (Mongolian) dynasty. Hong Kong, composed of ethnic Chinese, became part of the Chinese Empire under the Qin dynasty (221–206 BC) and remained part of China until it became a British colony in the 19th century,

---

86 *Tom Dispatch* website: http://www.tomdispatch.com/, with contributions from reliable scholars and serious investigative journalists such as Noam Chomsky, Tom Engelhardt, David Vine, Nick Turse, Alfred McCoy, Dilip Hiro, Nomi Prims and many others. Other alternative websites worth consulting: *Consortium News* (https://consortiumnews.com/), *FAIR* (https://fair.org/), *Naked Capitalism* (https://www.nakedcapitalism.com/), *The GreyZone* (https://thegrayzone.com/), *Investig'Action* (https://www.investigaction.net/en/), *Truthout* (https://truthout. org/), *Global Research* (https://www.globalresearch.ca/), *AntiWar.com* (https:// www.antiwar.com/), *New Eastern Outlook* (https://journal-neo.org/), *Tibetdoc* (http://tibetdoc.org/). the Ron Paul Institute (http://ronpaulinstitute.org/) and the Lew Rockwell (https://www.lewrockwell.com/)

87 Sometimes mainstream scholars arrive basically at the same conclusions as the alternative voices. For example, an article by professors Jeffrey D. Sachs, William Schabas, significantly entitled : 'The Xinjiang Genocide Allegations Are Unjustified' (Sachs and Schabas 2021).

in three stages: 1842, 1860 and 1898. It was returned to China in 1997, under the circumstances explained below.

Although these differences must be taken into account, the similarities are more important in the perspective of a geopolitical analysis. All three areas have been used by the U.S. to destabilize China in its quest for 'getting China back' after it lost it when the Communists won the Chinese civil war in 1949. Nevertheless, in all cases the main publicly declared goal was, and remains today, to allow the inhabitants of these areas to enjoy freedom, democracy and human rights. After the U.S. 'lost China,' it started in its quest for world power to meddle within the country, starting already in 1950 with Tibet, then Xinjiang and Hong Kong. One must recognize that in all cases this was, and still today is, according to international law, an interference within China's territory and an abrogation of its sovereignty.[88]

The three areas have a particular geopolitical importance for China, especially for the Belt and Road Initiative. Several corridors and their interconnections show the centrality of Xinjiang province for the development in north-west China, for the connection to central and western Asia (and thereby to Europe) and to Pakistan's Gwadar port, that enable Chinese transport to avoid the Malacca strait and the U.S. navy. Moreover, Xinjiang is rich in natural resources such as oil and rare earth metals.[89] There is indisputable evidence that U.S. supports separatist Uighur movements in that province and, hardly unexpected, as the U.S. tries desperately to counter China's Belt and Road Initiative that, if and when achieved, will at minimum give China control over large parts of Eurasia. Insofar as American strategists have long considered that whoever controls the Eurasian land mass controls the world, in the context of the increasing partnership between China and Russia, the BRI initiative becomes even more threatening.[90]

---

88 Many U.S. politicians, pundits, mainstream think tanks and journalists accuse China of the worst crimes in Xinjiang against the Uighur minority, as well as in Tibet, and of seeking to kill democracy in Hong Kong. I should like to make it clear that I do not ignore or underestimate the gravity of these concerns, but as a political scientist dealing with the geopolitical dimension of the U.S.-China competition, it is my duty to inform the attentive reader of the importance of the geopolitical context in which this competition takes place. Then he will be able to evaluate the facts using his own values.
89 See below.
90 See above this Chapter 3: The American Century and the development of U.S. power resources, paragraph '*The case for the leading role of the U.S.*'

Criteria for evaluating U.S. and China policies in Tibet, Xinjiang and Hong Kong

In order for the U.S. to make a convincing case that China is really guilty of the many accusations put forward by the West, it needs to provide further corroboration. If this is to be regarded as an actuality rather than a propaganda assault, the U.S. needs to offer China a fair trial, and listen to its defense, without disqualifying it from the outset, and above all, within defined circumstances. This is the accepted behavior when dealing with a crime or a misdemeanor. For that you need an impartial judge, independent from the prosecution and the defense, who will take into consideration the circumstances of the moment and of the past. We do it for criminals. Sometimes we even go back to childhood. For China it would suffice to go back to 1839. Rather, the standard sentence, whether by the mainstream media, the think tanks, or Western politicians, is: 'we are confident that ....' And as such, it joins the long list of evidence-free Western contentions, such as, for example, the Skripals and the Navalny cases.

Moreover, not only do they completely ignore the circumstances. The events that are at stake here, do not take place solely in the reassuring environment of values. Values reassure us, especially if we are certain that we have the best, or even the only valid ones. Obviously, for us Westerners, they are universal. We are reassured, as they tell us that we are on the right side of history, or more exactly at the end of history. However, values are without real value if they are not implemented in the context of real life. Otherwise, they will remain only in the stratosphere of ideology. In fact, for the events we are discussing in this section, values are deployed in the context of international power relations. Ignoring that is a serious mistake.

Second, there is a law of power that applies everywhere, regardless of the nature of the political system (democratic or totalitarian). All governments protect themselves against subversion by all means, even illegally if necessary. It is fear that sets off the process. The fear may be exaggerated, but it is nonetheless real. In note 161 of Chapter 1, I have already referred to the case of Switzerland. During the Cold War, even Switzerland, which I consider to be the world's most democratic country, created a secret army (illegally) and subjected thousands of citizens to police surveillance (equally illegally). From the point of view of democratic values, this is not acceptable, and in fact it has been harshly criticized. But from the point of view of the perception of the threat by the authorities responsible for internal and international security, this is easily understood, especially if one has a good knowledge of these phenomena over the course of history. Certainly, Sinologists know very well the collusion between part of the Chinese elite with the Japanese invader in the 1930s.

Third, speaking of Tibet and Xinjiang, I have the impression that many in the West would like China to retain the cultures of its minorities as they have been for centuries, regarding them as a kind of paradise that risks being lost ... But what remains of European medieval culture, with its 'local' languages (e.g. Welsh in the UK, Catalan in Spain, German in Italy's South Tyrol, etc.), with its lords, its purportedly joyous serfs of the glebe happily working and singing in the domains of the lords, enjoying widespread illiteracy and a life expectancy of 35, almost non-existent medical care, the inquisition, the most delirious superstitions, the witch hunts, and so on? Were these the good old days? In the West today everything looks—as long as you have a good salary—ideally above the average, electricity at home (my father told me about his astonishment when as a child he witnessed the switch from gas lighting to electricity), central heating, running water, cold and hot obviously, indoor toilets at home, a secondary residence in the mountains or by the sea, one or two cars, at least two mobile phones and two televisions, insurance (health, accident, old age, unemployment, maternity leave, paid holidays)—really? It's great, isn't it? Do the prior eras offer something we would wish to return to?

But this development is what China is bringing to its still underdeveloped areas, not only in those inhabited by the Tibetans and the Uighurs, but also in those inhabited by the Han. Have their circumstances improved or have they not? As for the rationale of improving the lives of targeted populations, is this not the U.S. claimed intent in Vietnam, in Iraq, in Afghanistan and in many other parts of the world, including in its own backyard, i.e., Latin America? And did the U.S. achieve its proclaimed goal—or did it leave many of these countries in shambles?

Some claim that the improvements realized in the West, and that China is trying to achieve in its country are fine, under condition that they are achieved while respecting the cultures of origin. Granted. But still, it would be necessary to determine which aspects of these cultures are to be preserved. Obviously not all, for example in Tibet: should the serfs of the glebe remain locked in that era? And does China indeed prevent the Uighurs and the Tibetans from practicing their religion, their language, and their customs? This is not the case.

But there are numerous proofs that in Xinjiang and in Tibet religion has been and is used still today by groups (in fact small minorities) to gain not only more autonomy, but also independence, and that the West has used these efforts in many ways against China. In addition, in Xinjiang these activities have been linked to terrorist acts (very real and numerous), and this has aroused a very real, though probably exaggerated, fear both for the Chinese authorities and the population of Xinjiang. And accordingly, there are restrictions, very real surveillance, and arrests, but not a complete ban on practicing one's customs. There is the same fear in the West which claims to manage terrorism more democratically and with a certain restraint. Nevertheless, the U.S. is not subject to foreign attempts to destabilize our political systems as China is, the bogus threat to U.S. elections notwithstanding.

Moreover, in Xinjiang China has been accused of an impressive list of wrongdoings and crimes such as forced labour, forced sterilizations, sexual assaults, internment in re-education camps, cultural genocide and even genocide. For genocide, Jeffrey Sachs and William Schabas write:

> The genocide charge was made on the final day of Donald Trump's administration by the then Secretary of State Michael Pompeo. (…) Now President Joe Biden's administration has doubled down on Pompeo's flimsy claim, even if the State Department's own layers reportedly share our scepticism. (…) This year Department Country Reports on Human Rights Practices (HRP) follows Pompeo in accusing China of genocide in Xinjiang. Because the HRP never uses the term other than once in the report's preface and again in executive summary of the China chapter, readers are left to guess about evidence.[91]

It is also said that in Xinjiang there are 1 to 1.5 million Uighurs in concentration camps, many others are in prison, and others are reduced to forced labour in the cotton fields. These figures are highly questionable as they are based upon unreliable estimates. Some 'experts' arrive at 2 million, with no proof and without explaining how. Rushan Abbas, founder and Executive Director of the Campaign for the Uighurs, arrives

---

91 Sachs and Schabas 2021.

at 3 million! I will not refer to the ideological profile of people quoted and presented by mainstream media as scholars and experts of China. It would be to easy to disqualify them. Moreover, it has been done by the alternative websites and investigative journalists quoted above. Finally, the conditions that allow the determination of whether a country is guilty of genocide were clearly defined in 1951 in a petition addressed to the United Nations by the Civil Rights Congress (CRC) to the United Nations, titled, "We Charge Genocide: The Crime of Government Against the Negro People." The petition cited the UN's definition of genocide: "Any intent to destroy, in whole or in part, a national, racial, or religious group is genocide." The petition concluded therefore, that 'the oppressed Negro citizens of the United States, segregated, discriminated against, and long the target of violence, suffer from genocide as the result of the consistent, conscious, unified policies of every branch of government.' Clearly, China's policy in Xinjiang province does not match these conditions.[92]

The Hong Kong case

While the situation of Tibet and Xinjiang is very complicated, that of Hong Kong is a little less so and moreover, more rightfully within Chinese jurisdiction because, contrary to Tibet and Xinjiang, it was a UK colony from 1842 to 1997, until the UK was required by international law to hand it back to China. The situation was complicated by the 1984 agreement between the UK and China, through which China accepted to retain for 50 years several features of the former British colony, i.e., from 1997, when China resumed the exercise of sovereignty, to 2047 when the agreement, also known as the Joint Declaration, will expire.

The terms of the declaration, the circumstances in which it was agreed upon, and the events that have made it difficult to implement between 1997 have been elaborated in subsequent publications by the main British negotiator, Percy Cradock, who has written a 1994 book and a 1997 article, as well as by the last British Governor, Chris Patten, who has since published several articles on this subject.[93] The first point

---

92 'Dec. 17, 1951: "We Charge Genocide" Petition Submitted to United Nations,' Zinn Education Project, https://www.zinnedproject.org/news/tdih/we_charge_genocide_petition
93 Cradock 1994, and his 1997 article significantly entitled: 'Losing the plot in Hong Kong.' On Patten: Dimbleby 1997, and by Patten: 2019a, 2019b, 2020, 2021a and 2021b.

to consider is that China could have simply waited until 1997 when it would be free to take over without any international legal restraint on its actions. It was therefore a brilliant achievement by Cradock to have convinced the Chinese that they had a clear interest in cooperating with the UK in order to make the handover as smooth as possible.

Moreover, Cradock succeeded in convincing his Prime Minister, Margaret Thatcher, 'to suppress her original more bellicose instincts.' In fact, he believed that a bellicose stance towards China would be counterproductive and that it was better to try to negotiate. He even informed Thatcher that negotiations would be difficult, as the UK had no cards to play. As a career diplomat, a sinologist with a long experience in China, Cradock knew the way Chinese think and act, and had a clear vision of Chinese interests in Hong Kong and what the goal of the UK strategy should be: 'the long-term welfare of Hong Kong had to be the sole criterion.' Although this laudable posture is a little surprising, given that the UK had governed Hong Kong as a long-time colony (in fact as a colonial dictatorship), it is to the credit of Cradock to have manifested in theory and in practice such a noble long-term priority.

In the Declaration, China makes it very clear that (1) it has decided to resume its exercise of sovereignty over Hong Kong and that it will uphold national unity and territorial integrity; (2) Hong Kong, organized as a Special Administrative Region, will be directly under the authority of the Central People's Government of the People's Republic of China; (3) all the dispositions (to be dealt with below) in the Declaration are elaborated in three annexes, and will be incorporated into a Basic Law of Hong Kong, which is a law promulgated by the People's Republic of China and not by the Hong Kong parliament. Moreover, these dispositions will remain unchanged for 50 years, i.e. until 2047. Thereby China makes it clear that after 2047 it will not be bounded by the Declaration.

The agreement consists of two parts: a political part and an economic part. The political part consists of rules concerning the procedures for electing the local chief executive and the parliament; the economic part enumerates the rights that will be guaranteed by law for 50 years: freedom of the person, of speech, of the press, of assembly, of association, of travel, of movement, of correspondence, of choice of occupation, of academic research, of religious belief and the right to strike. These aspects are dealt with in more details in Annex 1 to the Declaration.

Without entering into too many details, it is clear that the electoral procedures instituted a very limited democratic process, void of universal suffrage. But this is what has been agreed the UK and China, valid for the duration of the agreement. Notwithstanding, many Western pundits, and the Hong Kong protesters, claimed that China had promised to realise full democracy, though in no parts of the Declaration, its annexes and the Basic Law (in fact a mini-Hong Kong constitution) is there an article clearly stipulating this obligation within a precise time framework. Art. 45 of the Basic Law says (emphasis added): '*The ultimate aim* is the selection of the Chief Executive by universal suffrage upon nomination by a broadly representative nominating committee in accordance with democratic procedures.' Similarly, Art. 68 says: '*The ultimate* aim is the election of all the members of the Legislative Council by universal suffrage.'

The articles of the Basic Law are followed by several so-called 'Instruments.' In fact, we can consider them as an interpretation of the articles, especially when they define the circumstances in which it will be possible to implement the articles. Instrument 19 is a decision taken on 26 April 2004 by the Standing Committee of the National People's Congress on the elections of the Chief Executive and the parliament. It confirms the expression 'ultimate aim' and it decides that the methods for selecting the Chief Executive and the Parliament shall be specified *in the light of the actual situation* in Hong Kong and *in accordance with the principle of gradual and orderly progress.* As the Basic law is a Law of the Chinese state, it is clear that after 2049 China would be legally entitled to change the dispositions concerning the political and economic situation of Hong Kong.

The second part of the Declaration concerns Hong Kong's economy between 1997 and 2047. It is repeated twice that it will remain a capitalist economy as it was during the colonial time. This again was quite an achievement for Cradock: a communist country accepts, even if for a limited period of time, that one of its local administrations would keep an economic system in total contradiction with the planned economy it practices all over its territory. Of course, there were some reasons that China did so. China had just begun its reforms by introducing some market mechanisms and opening China to the global economy (see p. 268, 'Economic Development First: Matching U.S. Power'). China's leadership saw the role that a capitalist Hong Kong could play by facilitating financial flows between the Mainland and abroad. But still, that was a brilliant achievement for Cradock. That this was the main objective for Britain is supported by the very precise details concerning the Hong Kong capitalist economy that are further defined in Annex 1, covering practically all the dimensions of a capitalist economy: the guarantee of private property, a free port, independent customs, monetary and financial policies, the permanence of the convertibility of the HK Dollar, etc. Then, what went wrong?

After the signing of the 1984 agreement the implementation proceeded smoothly until the Tiananmen events of June 1989 that threatened to constitute a formidable obstacle to the implementation of the agreement, or even the end of it. In his article, Cradock comments:

> Those tragic events, commented by Britain as by other Western governments, provoked a mood of emotion and revulsion in which rational public discussion of policy towards China and Hong Kong became difficult. There were, for example, calls in the *Times* and the *Spectator* for the government to review, or even denounce, the joint declaration. (…) In particular it was argued that we must have more democracy in Hong Kong, preferably in agreement with China, but, if need be, in disregard of Chinese wishes. In Hong Kong itself there were similar emotions and in the 1991 elections a new policy party emerged under Martin Lee, which saw special merit in a policy of defiance of China.[94]

Notwithstanding, Cradock achieved another miracle: he finalized the 1990 agreement on the number of directly elected seats to the parliament, 'which provided for a partial democratization of Hong Kong. It ensured an immediate increase in indirectly elected seats, with further increase in the future: 18 seats in 1991, 20 in 1997, 24 in 1999 and 30, that is half of the seats, in 2003. The final goal was to form a parliament completely composed of directly elected members.' But the general mood had changed.

In 1992 the successor of Margaret Thatcher, John Major, appointed the last Hong Kong Governor, Chris Patten. Clearly Major was not a politician of the calibre of Thatcher, and Patten had little or no experience of diplomacy, or of China and Hong Kong, except for a formidable

---

94 Cradock, in his 1997 article, written the year of the return of Hong Kong to China, delivers a brilliant analysis of the damages the last Governor had done to the relations between the UK and China, and the devastating consequences that one should have to expect for the future. I must say that the Cradock forecast was confirmed in all its aspects.

and never-ending hatred for communist China. The choice of Patten was clearly a big mistake.

Patten arrived in Hong Kong like a bull in a China shop (no joke!). He brought with him the nostalgia, the illusions and the arrogance of the British Empire. The Empire had faded away after the end of WW2, but Patten had not realised that the time when the British could unilaterally impose their will was over.[95] In his 2021 article, Patten pleads, as Biden has done, for a coalition of liberal democracies that, along with the NATO military alliance, should 'develop policy responses to China's increasingly threatening behaviour in the Indo-Pacific region.'[96] This is but a remake at the global international arena of how he had acted towards China as the last British governor of Hong Kong, but done this time in subordinate position to the U.S., thereby recognizing the end of the British empire.

Patten underestimated the determination and the resilience of the Chinese government. China gave several warnings to the UK, especially concerning possible attempts to further democratize the electoral processes. According to Cradock, 'he decided that he should perform the historic mission to introduce instant democracy in Hong Kong, without discussing with the Chinese.' This is what he did: 'he hoped China would agree to his reforms, if not he was ready to implement them unilaterally.' Moreover, knowing that in any case China would have recovered its sovereignty in 1997 and that the 1984 agreement was to last for just 50 years, Patten's gamble brought on a disaster. Cradock is very severe with the Patten action: he qualified Patten's policy as a fatal miscalculation and did not hesitate to qualify the way Patten interpreted his role as last

---

95 That Patten is a representative of the nostalgia of the British Empire is attested by his positions on several recent events related to the relations between the West and China. I have already quoted his article where he praises the Biden foreign policy towards China (see Chapter 2 section, 'The China threat: The New Cold War is here to stay') (Patten 2021a). Patten was very pleased that the Biden administration 'made clear its determination to work with partners to confront global problems. The Communist Party of China certainly falls into that category.' He did not refer to the country, the People's Republic of China, but to the communist party, panned China's 'appalling behaviour,' and 'the Chinese government's loutish bullying.' China is 'the aggressor, and democracies should seek to restrict its damaging and dangerous behaviour' that 'is also totally untrustworthy, breaking its word whenever doing so suits Xi.' China 'assaults freedom, as it has done so blatantly in Hong Kong, or human life itself as in Xinjiang.'
96 See also Patten 2019a, 2019b, 2020, 2021a and 2021b.

governor of Hong Kong as the 'Patten regime.' A devastating qualification for a politician who claimed to be seeking to introduce liberal democracy in the colony.

In spite of Patten's mistakes, Cradock forecasted that the Hong Kong economy would continue to flourish under the 1984 agreement because 'it is now tied to the booming southern Chinese mainland (...) Business confidence is high, and Hong Kong will continue to provide commercial and financial services for the mainland (...) the Chinese government is determined that the transfer should be a success.' But he warned: the joint declaration is now frayed at the edges and China will reject unilateral additions.

Even more devastating are Cradock's final remarks that still today hold their profound meaning and value, not only for the UK but also for the U.S. and its allies. Let me quote it in full:

> Was it an example of nostalgia in action, an attempted reversion to times when Britain was in a position to impose solutions? Was the failure to read Chinese intentions just another example of that besetting sin of British foreign policy, the incapacity to put ourselves in the shoes of the other side, which has manifested itself in our European as much as our eastern dilemmas? (...) All who look beyond the headlines will wonder why Britain, with its long and rich experience of China, should reserve its biggest mistake for the last act of the play.

Members of the U.S. establishment would be well advised to read and reflect upon Cradock's final comments.

As expected, the Chinese objected to Patten's reforms. Cradock comments: '[the Chinese] saw them as a U-turn in British policy and a breach of the constitutional and political settlement in the joint declaration. (...) The resulting confrontation has bedevilled Sino-British dealings over the colony ever since.' Accordingly, the Chinese in 1997 cancelled Patten's reforms. But nonetheless, for years, they faithfully implemented the 1984 agreement. Then something even more serious went wrong.

Taking advantage of discontent in Hong Kong, the U.S. has intervened at least since the 2010s to support the protest movements, though more likely the support had already begun at the beginning of the 2000s.

Fundamental freedoms and rights (association, expression, media, demonstrations) were widely respected ... to such an extent that after the adoption of the new security law adopted by the Chinese government in June 2020, Western mainstream commentators have found that this law 'kills freedoms in Hong Kong,' indicative of the fact that there indeed had been freedoms before.

Moreover, as we have already seen, the 1984 document contained nothing that could legally require China to accept a reform of the electoral process. On the contrary, China had made it very clear that it would not go any further. It is evident that the demonstrators, with the support of the U.S., were trying to impose reforms that China was not willing to accept. As the protesters did not obtain what they wanted, the demonstrations quickly turned violent —not occasionally, as the Western mainstream narration sustained, but very frequently and often in the absence of police forces, as many clips filmed by the local South *China Morning Post* very well show. Unprovoked violence was taking place against property and people, especially against those who did not share the views of the protesters. Not a clear demonstration of the democratic culture of many protesters. And it went on for several months.

No other state, even a democratic one, would have accepted such behavior. The right to demonstrate in the public domain is not an absolute right, it is subject to authorization. A weighing of interests is carried out between the interest of a group of individuals to manifest on the public domain on the one hand, and the general interest on the other hand. This concerns in particular, the safeguard of private property, integrity of persons, tranquility, and public order. We knew that China had legally regained sovereignty over Hong Kong in 1997, that it would have been equally legally released from the provisions of the 1984 agreement in 2047, and that moreover it made it clear that it would not step back. We knew that article 23 of the Basic Law of Hong Kong, which is seldom quoted in full by mainstream Western media, very clearly states:

> The Hong Kong Special Administrative region shall enact laws on its own to prohibit any act of treason, sedition, subversion against the Central People's Government, or theft of secrets, to prohibit foreign political organizations or bodies from conducting political activities in the Region, and to prohibit political organizations or bodies of the Region from establishing ties with foreign political organizations or bodies.

By 2003, protest movements had already prevented the adoption of such a security law by the local government, which consequently postponed the moment when it would try again to implement such a law. Time went and no security law was adopted. What democratic country would accept to live without a security law?[97] Faced with the worsening violence of the protest movements in 2020, the frequent appeals from several protesters imploring the U.S. to intervene (e.g.: 'Trump Free Hong Kong!') and the blatant and well-documented meddling of the U.S. into Hong Kong, the Central Chinese Government took stock of the failure of the Hong Kong authorities to implement a security law and resorted to the sovereignty it had recovered in 1997 to substitute itself for the failing local government.

This move has been violently criticized by the West. But it should not have been. When private violence manifests itself with no restraint, it is generally mastered by State's violence, independently from the nature of the political system. Given the deteriorating relations between China and the West, and the history of the latter's regime change operations, which governments would not intervene when faced with a situation which could fairly be regarded as being fuelled by foreign support? Indeed, could Western support reasonably have been regarded as being done with the well-being of the Hong Kong population in mind? Would it not be better to prevent such events, instead of allowing a seriously conflictual situation to deteriorate, in the name of the right to manifest on the public domain, with consequences that are not in the interest of anybody, including the protesters?

Why give the protesters, who may well have had good reason to demonstrate peacefully, the assurance that they would have been supported to the end, nourishing their belief that they might achieve an impossible dream, without realizing that they were in fact serving the U.S.'s purpose of destabilizing China? Now they are silenced or exiled. What a

---

97 Switzerland is generally praised for being one of the most liberal democracies in the world. In 1932, in the midst of a serious conflict between the socialists and the fascists, the Geneva authorities refused to ban a meeting organized by the latter, despite the danger of clashes. The police were unable to keep control and the Swiss army was called in to help the police surrounded by hostile demonstrators. In fact, the Swiss army substituted itself for the failing local police. 'In the melee, a trumpet was sounded to warn the crowd to disperse, but it appears that no one understood the signal. An officer then gave the order to fire one shot. Some soldiers obeyed, some did not, some fired into the air, some emptied their magazines. It lasted only a few seconds: 13 people were killed and 65 injured.' Slater 2007.

waste! After the adoption of the security law and the restrictions on the electoral process, Western 'experts' were heard predicting an economic disaster for Hong Kong. But investors do not make decisions based on the nature of the political system, but on its stability, as is clear from the massive investment in China, nor indeed did it restrain American investors from increasing their investments in fascist Italy and Nazi Germany, with the blessing of their democratic state.[98]

Today, the Hong Kong economy, freed from violent protests, is doing well, like that of mainland China. Moreover, focusing on the 'electoral' aspect has allowed commentators to largely ignore the economic terms of the 1984 agreement, and thereby also the primary basis of popular protest. The 1984 agreement establishes (twice in the text) that the Hong Kong economic regime will remain a capitalist economy for the duration of the agreement, i.e. 2047, and indeed, up to 2020, Hong Kong has been ranked first among the capitalist countries. No one in the West has complained about this situation, at most it has aroused jealousy ... But it is precisely its economic regime that has given rise to popular protest in Hong Kong: especially the housing crisis, but also the extreme inequality of income distribution, the highest amongst capitalist countries (Gini at 54 against China at 43.4, the U.S. at 41.4).[99] And here one cannot criticize China for having refrained from intervening in the capitalist regime of Hong Kong. Again, no one in the West has complained, and for good reasons. Western pundits do not have the habit of criticizing a capitalist country that is doing well according to free market economy criteria, even if it is within the territory of Communist China. As the goal was to destabilize China, it was apparently more effective to attack the electoral system ... even if we know (or we should have known) that it would have been very difficult to improve it and that the

---

98 Lacroix-Riz 2014, pp. 31–46; Migone 2015, pp. 141–149, 165–170).

99 The Hong Kong Gini index was 54 in 2016 (it was 45 in 1986) according to the Hong Kong Social Indicator site (http://www.socialindicators.org.hk/en), which is considerably higher than the index of all other capitalist countries, and probably much higher today. According to UNDP Report 2020, China's Gini coefficient was 38.5 for the period covered (2010–2018). For the World Bank database China's Gini was also 38.5 in 2016, but today it is much higher. China's Gini coefficient published by the *China National Bureau of Statistics* was 46.5 in 2019, down from 49.1 in 2008. As we do not have comparable data for the countries, I have taken 43.4 as a personal estimate. In any case this does not contradict the fact that China's Gini is about 2 points above the U.S. index at 41.4 according to UNDP, and approximately 10 points below Hong Kong's index.

governments of Hong Kong and of China had no legal obligation to go in this direction. We have seen with what results.

CHINA'S RESPONSE TO AMERICA: WE ALSO HAVE A DREAM

The 'country's dream' has become a dominant theme in China since Xi Jinping took office in 2013 and made it the central theme of his general approach to China's development for the next 10 years and beyond. The stated goal is to develop the economy as a means to improve the standard of living of the population, to establish a relatively prosperous society in which wealth is equitably distributed, and to restore China as a world power.

The U.S. also developed this theme, indeed arguably from the beginning of the establishment of the Republic. Since then, the U.S. economy enabled a new middle class to achieve a comfortable way of living that became the standard dream of individuals and families, not only in the U.S. but also in many other parts of the World. Indeed, it was a major source of American geopolitical appeal. Moreover, the U.S. was able to develop a variety of power resources that allowed it to become the hegemon of the world.

China has followed a different path. The Empire lagged behind the industrialization and modernization undertaken by Western countries which, taking advantage of this superiority, pursued colonialist and imperialist foreign policies that led to the subjugation of many non-Western countries, including China. At the eve of WW1 more than 80% of the planet was under Western domination, and after WW2 the U.S. took the lead of this two-tier world. When China began to undertake the road to economic development and national independence it chose a different path, an economy that mixes market mechanisms, the leading role of the state, and an authoritarian government contrary to the ideal of liberal democracy. But insofar as China is indeed on the road to succeed and has made a spectacular and recognized improvement in the lives of its people, why should Western countries, and more particularly the U.S., not only fail to understand how this is possible, but also emphatically criticize China for taking a path that works, albeit contrary to the values that the West considers to be universal?

Economic Development First: Matching U.S. Power

Both Western and Chinese researchers consider that China's reforms allowed an astonishing economic growth and a significant improvement of the living conditions of the Chinese people. Thanks to cheap labour, globalization made China the workshop of the world. During the 1990s it became the second receiver of direct foreign investments of the world. Several researchers have already started to talk about the twenty-first century as the Chinese century.

However, this positive evaluation and forecast, must be qualified by the international environment within which China has had to manage its economic development. Since 1839 China has been under significant pressure from the West and Japan which remained ongoing after the victory of the Communists in 1949. On the contrary, this marked the beginning of the U.S. strategy to 'win China back.' Having rightly considered that the first thing to do in order to match the U.S. power was to develop its economy by introducing market mechanisms into its economy, China was nevertheless confronted with the inevitable development of increasing inequalities and environmental damage that occurred during this process, forcing it to manage a balance between economic development and maintaining the cohesion of the nation by limiting the appearance of inequalities and of the environmental impact. Here is how China has managed this dilemma.

China's extraordinary speed of economic development has been indisputable. In its 1997 report the World Bank compared the time needed for doubling the GDP by several countries: the United Kingdom needed 58 years (from 1780 to 1838), the USA 47 years (from 1839 to 1886), Japan 34 years (from 1885 to 1919), South Korea 11 years (from 1966 to 1977), and China only 9 years (from 1978 to 1987). In its 2009 report the World Bank considered that China had already achieved or was well on its way to achieving most of the Millennium Development Goals of the United Nations.[100] In 2021 Xi Jinping proudly announced that China has succeeded in eradicating absolute poverty.

The modernization of China is demonstrated by the changes in the relative contribution of agriculture, industry and services to employment and GDP (see Tables 1a and 1b). In 1952 agriculture still provided 83.5% of China's labour force, with only 7.4% in industry and 9.1 in services. Correspondingly, the agriculture sector contributed 56.6% to GDP,

---

100 World Bank 2009b.

industry 20,6% and services 22.8%. By 2019 the picture had evolved considerably: agriculture engaged only 25.1% of China's labour force, while 27.5% were engaged in industry, and services contribution jumped to 47.4%. The decline of the contribution of agriculture to GDP during the same period has been even more spectacular: it has decreased from 56.6% to 7.1% percent, while the contribution of industry increased from 20.6% to 39%, and that of services from 22.8% to 53.9%.

These changes are reflected into China's increasingly sizeable role in the world economy. Based upon a mix of Chinese and Western values, China has been very skilful in choosing the institutional arrangements that allowed it to build year after year, in the 'long time,' after a careful analysis of the 'situation potential,' the resources that constitute today its Comprehensive National Power—CNP.[101] Let us start with China's place in the world economy, compared to that of the U.S.

U.S. vs. China: Comparing economic strength

The development of China's economy has gone hand in hand with the recovery of its place in the global economy. And here the comparison with the U.S. becomes interesting. First of all, let us look at China's share in the world GDP since 1820 as shown in Table 2. Whereas China GDP (in PPP) was just under one third of world GDP in 1820 (i.e. before its decline during the Qing dynasty), it dropped dramatically to 17.05% a decade after the Second Opium War (1870) and continued to plummet until 1973, during the Cultural Revolution and about five years before the beginning of the reform era, to reach 4.62%, against 22.07 percent for the U.S. Note however that the U.S. is now at the beginning of its decline, compared to its standing of 27.32% in 1950. Moreover, 3 decades after the beginning of reforms, i.e., by the year 2008 (the year of the financial crisis), China's share was already 10.64%, catching up but still behind the U.S. at 18.23%. However, the data shows that the U.S. is continuing its decline. By 2019, four decades after the beginning of reforms China had overtaken the U.S. with 17.33% of global GDP, against the U.S. share of 15.82%. Finally, according to the forecast of the IMF (World Economic Outlook, April 2021) by 2025 China's GDP (measured in 2017 International $) will account for more than 20 percent of the world total, while the U.S. will fall below 15%, equivalent to 75% of that of China.

---

101 Hu Angang and Men Honghua 2004; Urio 2018, Ch 3.

Let us take a further step by using Hu Angang's procedure[102] for determining China's economic strength in the world compared to the members of the G20. This is done first by taking separately China's proportion of GDP (Table 3) and of import-export in the world (Table 4) compared to the G20 countries. Then, in Table 5 China's economic strength is calculated by integrating in a single indicator the GDP and the import-export percentages, giving a 2/3 weight to GDP and 1/3 to import-export.

We see in Table 3 that in 1990, a decade after the beginning of reforms, China's proportion of world GDP was only 3.89% of the world total against 25.09% for the EU, 20.92% for the U.S. and 8.31% for Japan. These three countries, all members of the Trilateral Commission, accounted for more than half of the world total, i.e. 54.32%.[103] At that time, China had a GDP smaller than Germany (5.30%), but not very different from other members of the G20, such as France (3.59%), Italy (3.63%), United Kingdom (3.60%), India (3.49%), and Brazil (3.50%).

Here, too, the finding is that in 2019, four decades after the beginning of reform, China's share of total world GDP had surged to 17.33%, surpassing the U.S. (15.82%), and the EU (15.31%); all the other members of the G20 have a considerably smaller share of world GDP.

---

102 For at least two decades Hu Angang, director of the Institute for Contemporary China Studies at Tsinghua University, has studied the comprehensive power of the U.S. and China. Hu Angang, China-U.S. Comprehensive National Power 2000–2019 (中美综合国力大较量 2000–2019, paper kindly provided by author. See also Hu Angang and Men Honghua (2004), and Hu Angang and Ren Hao (2016).

103 It is interesting to take the Trilateral Commission into consideration, because it was set up by David Rockefeller and Zbigniew Brzezinski in July 1973, to develop cooperation between North America, Western Europe and Japan. The Commission has attracted criticism from both the right and the left. From the right, Republican Senator Barry Goldwater criticized the Commission for being a skilful, coordinated effort to seize control and consolidate the four centres of power: political, monetary, intellectual and ecclesiastical, and to promote the creation of a worldwide economic power superior to the political governments of the nation-states involved. People of the left have been even more critical: Noam Chomsky has described the Trilateral Commission as being the liberal wing of the intellectual elite, i.e. liberal internationalists from Europe, Japan and the United States. [...] [The Trilateral Commission] was concerned with trying to induce what they called 'more moderation in democracy'—return people passivity and obedience so they don't put so many constraints on state power and so on. (https://en.wikipedia.org/wiki/Trilateral_Commission (accessed 12 February 2017).

It is also interesting to remark that the 2019 data represent an unprecedented change in the share of GDP among the 'three worlds.' The G20 countries accounted for 77.88% of the world's total. The 'first world,' headed by the U.S. and the EU comprising Japan, Canada, and South Korea accounted for 38.31% of the GDP world's share. In 2019, this group of countries was overtaken for the first time by the 'second world,' comprising China, India and other emerging economies, accounting for 39.57% of the world's share. The 'third world,' comprising the rest of the other developing countries, accounted for 22.12% of world GDP. It is forecasted that this pattern will become even more prominent by 2050, with the 'second world' further increasing its GDP world's share.

Table 4 shows a similar pattern for import-export percentages in the world total. China's position has dramatically increased in the global economy, if we take its share of exports and imports in the world. In 1990 China had only 1.63% of the world's share of exports and imports, i.e. a decade after the beginning of reforms, while the EU, the U.S. and Germany dominated international trade with 45.60%, 12.89% and 11% respectively. Moreover, the three countries of the Trilateral Commission (U.S., EU and Japan) represented 65.89% of total world trade. But by 2010, 3 decades after the beginning of China's reforms and 9 years after its accession to the WTO, China's share surged to 9.62%, surpassing all the other major G20 players, except the U.S. (10.51%) and the EU (with an astonishing 34.1%) and remained the major economic block for import and exports whereas the share of the three countries of the Trilateral Commission represented a little less than 50% of the world total. In 2019, nine years later with 12.00% China surpassed the U.S. (11.05%), second only to the EU (30%, estimate), whereas the Trilateral Commission for the first time accounted for less than half of the world total with 44.79%.

By combining the share in the world GDP and in the export-import total of the world, we obtain the economic strength of the members of the G20 (Table 5). Remember that this indicator is obtained by giving a 2/3 weight to GDP and 1/3 to import-export. In 1990, China's share of economic power was only 2.39%, far behind the EU (38.76%) and the U.S. (15.57%), whereas the three Trilateral Commission countries accounted for 62.04%. In 2014, China's share soared to 13.07%, surpassing that of the U.S. (12.41%) while still lagging behind the EU (26.99%), whereas the countries of the Trilateral Commission lost 18.58% down to 43.56%. By 2019, four decades after the beginning of reforms, China has further increased its economic power to 14.67% ahead of the U.S. (13.44%) though still behind the EU (22.60%, estimate). As one of the dimensions of the Biden administration policy is to boost the cohesion of U.S. allies, it is interesting to see how the G7 performs. It comprises the U.S., UK, Germany, Canada, France, Italy and Japan. In 1990 the G7 had 47.3% of the world GDP, 51,99% of the world import/export, and 50,43 of the economic strength. This means that in 1990 the economy of the G7 was as strong as that of the rest of the world. By 2019, this position has been considerably eroded by the development of countries such as China and India. The G7 share of world GDP dropped to 31.51%, that of import/export to 30.16%, and that of economic strength to 32.38% i.e., from half to less than one third.

Notably, the share of the BRICS (Brazil, Russia, India, China and South Africa) has also increased considerably, in spite the fact that the cohesion of the group is today being jeopardized by the national situation of Brazil and by the rivalry between China and India. Nevertheless, one should not forget that the data we are discussing here correspond to long term transformations. Rivalries and internal difficulties may change in time, as history very well shows. Moreover, it is the partnership between China and Russia that gives the BRICS its strength. And for the time being, also thanks to the U.S. foreign policy that demonizes both countries, there are no signs that this situation is going to change. On the contrary, China and Russia are strengthening their partnership. In 1990 the BRICS had only 11.7% of world GDP, 3.57% of the world import/expert, and 6.29% of world economic strength. In 2019 its share of GDP had soared to 27.32%, that of import/export to 20.75% and that of world economic strength to 21.53%. Up from less than one-tenth in 1990 to more than one-fifth in 2019 ... still far from the G7, but these countries have a considerable potential, and China's Belt and Road Initiative (to be dealt with below) is also a promising booster for infrastructure and economic development.

These data confirm that, taking into consideration the share in the world economy (GDP, and import/export) China is rising, whereas the U.S., the EU and the G7 are declining, even if the U.S. and the EU retain, along with China, the rank of the three greatest economic powers. Some observers would probably object by saying that economy does not tell the whole story. That is true, but economic development does not occur in a vacuum. It is linked to other features of a country that, together, contribute to its strengths or its weaknesses: education, health, science and technology, the development of social security and strategic public management aimed at improving society in all its dimensions in over the long haul, and its capacity to correct the errors that inevitably occur in these domains, as soon as possible. This is our next concern. Let us start with a comparison of the U.S. and China's comprehensive national power.

U.S. vs. China: Comparing national comprehensive power

Let us turn again to the research of Hu Angang, who has evaluated ten components of a country's power: 1. human resources, 2. economic strength, 3. industrial strength, 4. domestic markets, 5. international markets, 6. technology strength, 7. information resources, 8. infrastructure strength, 9. energy strength, and 10. military strength. In the note below, you will find a brief, non-exhaustive, description of the content of these ten dimensions.[104] The resultant data can be found in Table 6. In summary, the general conclusion is that, if one puts the available data into historical perspective, China has already caught up with the U.S. and, in some domains, it has even surpassed it. Moreover, given the general trend, the forecast is that left unchallenged and unless China in the future makes some major mistakes, it is very likely that it will become a new world power in a not-too-distant future. This does not mean, however, that China will inevitably replace the U.S. as the new hegemon. Rather, it is more likely that its rise will determine the transition from the unipolar international system that emerged at the end of the Cold War, to a multipolar world, comprising the U.S., China, Russia, the European Union, and eventually some other countries such as India, Brazil, Turkey, and South Africa.

---

104 The ten dimensions include: 1. human resources (such as urban population, labor resources), 2. economic strength (such as GDP/PPP, GDP/exchange rate method), 3. industrial resource strength (such as agricultural value-added, industrial value-added), 4. domestic market (final consumption expenditure), 5. Total capital formation, 6. the international market (commodity exports, commodity imports), 7. scientific and technological strength (R&D expenditures, the number of invention patent applications for domestic residents, the number of articles), 8. information resources (mobile phone users, fixed broadband users), 9. infrastructure strength (aviation passenger traffic, port container), 10. energy strength (energy consumption, power generation, renewable energy consumption), and 11. military strength (military expenditure, military personnel).

In 2000, only China's human resources were much higher than those of the U.S., compared to the world total (21.3% against 6.6%). Its industrial strength was almost equal (13.1% for China, 13.9% for the U.S.). The other eight Chinese strategic resources were lower than the U.S. to different degrees. However, the changes that occurred between 2000 and 2019 show that China retained its significant advantage in human resources, while acquiring a significant advantage in industrial strength, technology, infrastructure, and energy. For economic strength China has acquired a small advantage (17.3% against 15.8%), whereas the U.S. and China have an equal strength in the international market. The U.S. keeps a significant advantage regarding domestic markets (21.3% against 9.1%) and for military strength (22.1% against 11.9%). Nevertheless, Hu Angang remarks that even in these domains, China is rapidly increasing its part in the world total, hence its power.

Moreover, looking at the data for 2000, 2010 and 2019, we see that the while China enjoys a 'sustainable rising,' the U.S. is trapped in a 'continuous decline.' In fact, the overall impact of the ten dimensions of strength, shows that between 2000 and 2010 China's overall national strength increased from 8.5% to 20.6%, while that of the U.S. declined from 20.8% to 14.2%. And by 2015, China's overall national power reached 19.39% of world total, whereas the U.S. has declined to 14.14%. One important dimension of strategic power resources is the development of high technology industry. While the majority of the Western observers of China's development still consider that China is behind the U.S.,[105] Hu Augang's research counters this:

> China high-tech industry is catching up and even surpassing the United States in terms of industry added value, exports volume and export added value. This is mainly because the complementarities and mutual benefits between high-tech industry and economic development are reflected by the compatibility of their life-cycles. In addition, high-tech has great externalities, namely promoting high-tech growth of economy and manufacturing industry, facilitating the economic structure transformation, increasing trade growth, accelerating trade structure upgrading, and creating technology spillover effects.[106]

105　Hu Angang and Ren Hao 2016.
106　See for a complementary and different opinion Jost Wübbeke et al., *MADE*

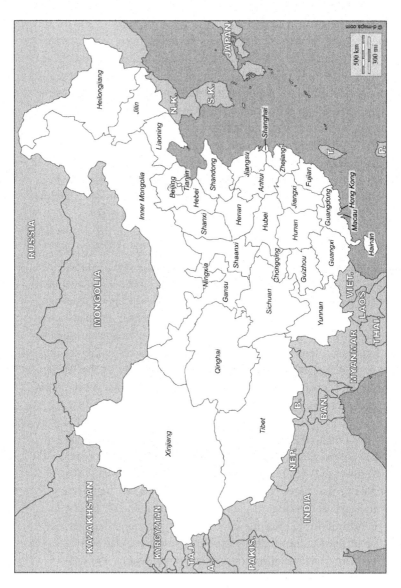

Map 5.1 Map of China's Provinces.

Source: d-maps. URL.: http://d-maps.com/m/asia/china/chine/chine29.pdf

THE NEGATIVE CONSEQUENCES OF ECONOMIC DEVELOPMENT AND THE REBALANCING OF CHINESE SOCIETY

Whereas Deng's reforms produced an impressive improvement of China's economy, nevertheless, their scope and speed resulted in several negative consequences: disparities between regions and provinces, as well as between people within regions, provinces and municipalities. The absence of regulations aiming at protecting the environment resulted in considerable deteriorations of the already precarious conditions of the Chinese environment. The rapid introduction of market mechanisms and competition led state organizations (especially SOEs, but also State bureaucracies) to drastically reduce their staff and to lay off millions of employees and workers. This resulted in a huge rate of unemployment, as well as the emergence of new forms of poverty, that run the risk of counterbalancing the impressive decrease in poverty achieved thanks to the reforms. This trend, and especially the appearance of new forms of poverty, also had an impact on the increase in crime, especially petty crimes.

The transition from a command economy to a new economic system, where market mechanisms (and hence competition among enterprises) were introduced quite rapidly, led the government to free the SOEs from the obligation of providing their workers and employees with the social services they were used to enjoying under the former command economy. This new way of organizing the production process, in conjunction with the one-child policy, was de-structuring both the traditional State and intra-family's solidarities, and moreover was not counterbalanced by a modern safety net.

Finally, the imbalances of society and economy had a negative impact on the realization of the traditional values of harmony, stability and unity. It became therefore necessary to introduce several changes at different levels of the strategy, beginning first of all with the introduction of new values in the ideology of the Party, such as social equity, ruling by law, and innovation.[107]

IN CHINA 2025. The making of a high-tech superpower and consequences for industrial countries, Berlin, Merics, Mercator Institute for China Studies, No. 23, December 2016. We have discussed the strategy China has followed for developing high technology in Chapter 1.
107 I have developed these changes in Chapter 2 in the section 'Economic Development First: Matching U.S. Power.'.

The development of social security in China

In February 2004, Premier Wen Jiabao recognized that China's fast economic development had resulted in the accumulation of the difficulties mentioned above and concluded that China should solve these problems as soon as possible. This strategy strongly suggests that the biggest challenge to China in the twenty-first century is not how to further speed up economic growth, but how to maintain a sustainable and equitable growth by focusing on poverty reduction and human development, the ultimate purpose of development, instead of on development for the sake of development. These policy options were introduced in the 11th Five-year plan (2006–2010) and confirmed at the Party Congress of November 2007. In the framework of the third development strategy, hundreds of billions of yuan have been invested in the poor provinces and regions.

The investments in physical infrastructure needed to be complemented with some parallel investments in human capital. This has been done first by abolishing some of the most irrational decisions taken in the past, and to begin with by eliminating, between 2003 and 2006, the taxes and fees that peasants were obliged to pay that had placed a heavy burden on their already meagre income; second, by abolishing the fees for elementary and junior high school for rural areas of western provinces in 2006, in 2007 for inner and eastern provinces, and in 2008 for urban areas.[108] Then, at the Party Congress of November 2007 President Hu Jintao announced the adoption of China's new health system scheduled to provide universal coverage by the year 2020. Social welfare was regarded as necessary not only by considerations of equity, but also because a well-educated population protected by decent health, unemployment and old age insurances is better armed for contributing to the development of society and for assuring the stability it needs.

The development of a modern social security system to replace the social services enterprises and public bureaucracies provided during the Mao era, is certainly one of the most important tasks China faced to protect its citizens from the debilitations of old age and illness, as well as the unemployment risks inherent in the new economy based upon market mechanisms. It has been clear from the beginning that for a population

---

108 For an authentic account of the difficulties this neoliberal policy caused to poor peasants, one can read the diary of a young schoolgirl of Ningxia province, that describes the situation of peasants' families around the years 2000–2001 (Ma Yan and Haski (2009).

of more than a billion people these social policies would require a colossal expenditure and a long-term strategy. The PRC has undertaken this impressive endeavour in order to serve its people, especially those who have not been able, so far, to fully benefit from the economic development, hardly reflective of claims that it has been 'suppressing its own people,' as then–Vice President Mike Pence, among many others, said on 4 October 2018 in a speech given at the Hudson Institute.[109]

Table 7 summarizes some data on the main social insurances in urban areas of China, indicating how, from 2001 to 2019 the number of people covered by these insurances has increased.

- 3.06 times for old-age insurance
- 5.86 times for work-related injuries
- 5.34 times for maternity insurance (2016 data)
- 1.9 times for unemployment insurance
- 4.31 times for medical insurance for employed people
- Medical insurance for unemployed residents started only in 2007, but by 2019 it had increased 23.9 times.

Even more impressive is the increase in expenditures for these insurances (see Table 8).

Social assistance is a particularly important insurance as it concerns the poor people living in the towns. In 1999, the Chinese government promulgated the 'Regulations on Guaranteeing Urban Residents' Minimum Standard of Living.' It stipulates that urban residents, with non-agricultural permanent residence permits whose family's per capita income is lower than the local urban residents' minimum standard of living, can receive basic subsistence assistance from the local government; those with neither source of income nor working capability, nor legal guardian, supporter or fosterer, can receive in full the minimum living allowance according to the minimum living standard of local urban residents.

By the end of 2018 (the last year when data are available), the minimum living allowance, had increased substantially for all the towns between 3–3.9 times for 8 cities, between 2.5–2.9 times for 13 cities, and between 2–2.4 times for 10 cities. The major big cities such as Beijing, Tianjin, Shanghai and Nanjing enjoyed an increase of about 3.2 times, and Lhasa 3.9 times compared to 2005. In 2018 the minimum living

---

109 Pence 2018.

standard per month was between 449 RMB (Changsha) and 1000 RMB for Beijing. This looks impressive but must be measured against the large increase in the cost of living, especially in China's big cities. Finally, China has also improved social security in rural areas where the rural cooperative medical system has been improved. By the end of 2019, 2856 counties had implemented this insurance, up from 1451 in 2006, to cover 548 million rural residents, up from 410 million in 2006, with a participation rate of 98.8%, thus achieving universal coverage in these areas (according to the *China Statistical Yearbook 2020*). The same can be said for old age insurance in rural areas. The Chinese government began to experiment in the 1990s with an old-age insurance system in accordance with the actual level of local socio-economic development in the rural areas. By the end of 2010, 102.77 million people were covered by the old age insurance. Since 2010 the number of people covered increased every year to reach 532.66 million in 2016, five times more than in 2010, thus again realizing universal coverage in these areas.

The special case of migrant workers

It is well-known that the development of the economy in the urban areas had the consequence of inducing a migration flood from the rural areas to the towns, where a huge number of migrant workers moved, attracted to the better job opportunities in the urban areas. For a long time, migrant workers had not had access to social services and insurances when they migrated to urban areas. This was because their residence permit (the *Hukou*) in their home villages, provided them with access to social service there, but when they migrated to the urban areas, they were forbidden to have access to the same services as the urban residents. This was one of the most important problems China had to deal with. Some commentators calculated that migrant workers contributed to 16% of China's GDP increase during the 1980s and the 1990s, insofar as they represented about 35% of the work force of China, equal to about 245 million in 2016.[110]

It was therefore inevitable that if the Party were truly committed to create a harmonious society, it would have to take measures for alleviating the poor condition of migrant workers. Without entering into too much detail, China did so, started to first tackling this situation seriously in 2010 with the passing of the social security law that requires rural

---

110 ILO 2016.

migrant workers to affiliate under the social insurance regimen for urban workers (SIW), and then by

> the introduction of health and pension schemes for urban and rural residents (SIR) (...) migrant workers and their families are better integrated into urban life with higher levels of consumption and improved health status, all of which are essential for achieving a harmonious society, which is a national strategic objective.[111]

China's safety net has been further improved by the 2008 Labour Contract Law (LCL). Researchers found that 'the implementation of the LCL helped boost migrant workers' chance of social insurance participation consistently and significantly, especially for those who gained a long-term contract. These findings suggest that the LCL at least partly reached its intended policy goal of improving social protection for migrant workers, a disadvantaged group in the Chinese labour market.'[112] That said, the ILO warned that the achievement of basic and universal coverage is only the first step.[113]

While the development of social security in China is quite impressive, the coverage of all insurances is not very high, compared to coverage in the West, albeit in the COVID era in the U.S. is now in flux; in fact, it had been claimed for years that Social Security was running out of money.[114] Nevertheless, it must be stressed that the Chinese effort represents only a first step covering the whole of the population, and within it, more particularly the poor and the lower middle classes, should the Party-State remain faithful to one of its mottos: to build a relatively well-off society where wealth is equitably distributed. As happens in the West, well-to-do and rich people either subscribe to a private insurance or pay out of their own pocket. Developing China's safety net, and then maintaining a satisfactory level of universal coverage and assuring its sustainability in the long term, will not be an easy task, especially in the case of old age and health. In fact, the financing of these insurances is under stress because of the changing structure of the population, in spite of the fact that China has relaxed the one-child policy. Moreover,

---

111 Ibid.
112 Qin Gao & Sui Yang & Shi Li 2017.
113 ILO 2016, China Labour Bulletin 2019.
114 https://www.investopedia.com/ask/answers/071514/why-social-security-running-out-money.asp

whereas China has succeeded in eradicating transmissible diseases typical of an agrarian society, it is now experiencing a dramatic increase in chronic diseases, such as cardiovascular diseases, cancer, obesity and diabetes, all typical of a relatively well-off society, which become more frequent and costly with the aging of the population. Therefore, one can expect that financing social insurances will become increasingly costly in the future.

Rebalancing the income levels of individuals

Let us start with the Gini index, a measure of statistical dispersion intended to represent the income inequality or wealth inequality within a nation, and allows comparison between nations (Table 9). The Gini index varies from zero (complete equality) to 100 (complete inequality). Generally, an index above 40 is considered as a serious warning, as it may signal instability leading to social and political conflicts within society. All 19 Western countries in Table 9 (with Gini indexes between 27 and 35.9) do much better than China (with Gini 43.4) except for the U.S. (with Gini of 41.4) comes close to China. The Western countries can be subdivided into four groups. The first group (with Gini between 27 and 28.8), comprises Northern European countries, joined by Belgium and the Netherlands. The second group (with Gini between 29,7 and 32.8) comprises the Central European countries, joined by Ireland. The countries of these two groups, especially the first, have a strong or fairly performing welfare state and a relatively equitable distribution of income. The third group, with higher income inequalities (between 33.8 and 35.9), comprises 4 of the five Anglo-Saxon countries with a less favourable welfare state, and 3 countries of Southern Europe with a less developed economy, which can explain their higher income inequality. Again, the U.S., a very rich country, has a Gini index standing nevertheless behind the other Western countries.

The Gini index provides an initial insight into a country's inequalities in terms of revenue, but it does not tell the whole story. This is why the United Nations Development Programme (UNDP) has developed the Human Development Index (HDI), that integrates income, health (measured by life expectancy), and education (measured by years of schooling). Here, countries are distributed within four groups: very high development, high development, medium development and low development. Table 10 shows the ranking with the HDI and gender inequality for 2019 for a selection of Western countries, China has been added in the last row. Here, despite the considerable progress realized since the beginning of reforms, China lags far behind the Western countries. Nevertheless, when we take the Gender inequality index China still does better, with rank 39, than the U.S. (rank 46), although still behind the Western countries.[115]

Moreover, taking life expectancy at birth,[116] in 2019 China, placed within the group of 'High Human development' at rank 85 in 2019, and does even better with life expectancy of 76.9 years. This is about the same as 16 other countries (out of a total of 66) ranked in the 'Very high Human Development,' such as Hungary, Argentina, Rumania, Turkey and Uruguay, and not far from Poland, Portugal, and Croatia. Moreover, other data shows that from 1990 to 2019 China's HDI index ranking has constantly improved from a low 0.499 in 1990 to a satisfactory 0.761 in 2019.

Finally, an analysis of the HDI index of the provinces, (based upon the most recently available data for 2015)[117] shows that several provinces were already at the level of Western countries in the Very High development group.

The UNDP 2016 Report, covering 188 countries, shows that in 2015 Beijing occupied the 27th rank (equal to Spain), with Shanghai the 28th rank (equal to the Czech Republic), Tianjin ranking 36th (equal to Poland), Jiangsu at 48th rank (equal to Montenegro), Liaoning at 49th rank (equal to Russia) and Zhejiang at the 50th rank (equal to Romania). It is not surprising that these provinces (except Liaoning) also have the highest provincial Gross National Income, well above the national average. Two other provinces are not very far from the 'Very High Development Group,' in the upper part of the 'High Development Group': Guangdong ranks 54 (equal to Uruguay) and Shandong ranks 59

---

115 *The Gender Inequality Index* measures achievements using the same indicators as the HDI but captures inequalities in achievement between women and men. It is simply the HDI adjusted downward for gender inequality. It takes into consideration: (1) health (maternal mortality ratio, adolescent fertility rate); (2) empowerment (female and male population with at least secondary education, female and male shares of parliamentary seats); (3) labour market (female and male labour force participation rates). The greater the gender disparity in basic human development, the lower the adjusted HDI for gender inequality. *The Inequality adjusted HDI* takes into consideration: (1) long and healthy life, (2) knowledge (mean years of schooling, expected years of schooling); (3) a decent standard of living (GNI per capita in PPP US$).
116 UNDP Report 2020, pp. 343–34.
117 UNDP 2016 Report.

(equal to Malaysia). In addition to Guangdong and Shandong 18 other provinces are placed in the 'High development Group.' Nevertheless, 12 among the latter have an HDI higher than the national average (HDI 0.762). Finally, five provinces are placed in the 'Medium Development Group': Qinghai ranks 107, Gansu ranks 110, Guizhou ranks 118, and Tibet ranks 127. This ranking corresponds to the level of economic development.

The same analysis can be made by taking separately the three components of the HDI. We will take health and per capita income. For health, measured by life expectancy, China's provinces do even better than for the HDI index overall. As for the HDI index, Shanghai (82.8 years), Beijing (82), Tianjin (81.3) rank at the top of China's provinces for life expectancy, at the same level as the countries ranked at the first 26 places of the HDI 'Very High Development Group,' such as Norway, Denmark, Netherlands, New Zealand, France, Germany, etc. With HDI longevity ranking between 75 and 79 years, 20 other provinces also take place in the 'Very High Development Group,' above its last three countries (ranked 49 Russia, 50 Romania and 51 Kuwait); whereas 7 provinces have scores under 75 years (i.e. Shanxi, Guizhou, Gansu, Ningxia, Yunnan, Qinghai, and Xinjiang), and one, Tibet, is under 70. As for the HDI index, life expectancy seems to be linked to the level of economic development, even though the distance between the more performing provinces and the others is less important.

The rebalancing between provinces

Again, revenue per capita is the weakest indicator of China's development.[118] Based upon data in China's Statistical Year Book, it is interesting to distribute provinces into groups labelled according to their level of GDP per capita:

1. Group 1, with provinces in the 'Very High Development Group' with GDP per capita higher than 24.000 USD comprises: Beijing (25.772 USD) and Shanghai (24.349 USD). Only Jiangsu, with 18.996 USD, is not too far from Beijing and Shanghai.

---

118 Data on the GDP per capita of China's provinces are from the *China Statistical Year Book 2020,* converted into USD.

2. Group 2, with 9 provinces with a GDP per capita between 10.350 and 16.541 USD: Tianjin, Inner Mongolia, Zhejiang, Fujian, Shandong, Hubei, Guangdong, Chongqing and Shaanxi;

3. Group 3, with 4 provinces with a GDP per capita between 9085 and 9914 USD: Anhui, Hunan, Sichuan and Liaoning.

4. Group 4, with 7 provinces with a GDP per capita between 8123 and 8890: Jiangxi, Henan, Hainan, Tibet, Yunnan, Ningxia and Xinjiang.

5. Group 5, with 5 provinces with a GDP per capita between 7231 and 7936 USD: Hebei, Shanxi, Jilin, Guizhou and Qinghai.

6. Group 6, with 2 provinces with a GDP per capita between 6664 and 6926: (Heilongjiang and Guangxi).

7. Group 7, with 1 province Gansu with 5621 GDP per capita.

These findings confirm the consensus among experts on China's development that in terms of revenue per capita there are huge differences between provinces. With a few exceptions, the coastal provinces do much better. But, as we have said when examining the inequalities between people by taking the GDP, income inequality does not tell the whole story. But if we take the HDI per provinces to see whether he gap is still as high as with GDP per capita, we will see that there is a process of convergence from Low HDI to the High and even to the Very High HDI. We use here the data from the *China Statistical Year Books*, and we place the provinces in the four HDI levels of the UNDP at five historical moments (1980, 1990, 2000, 2010 and 2015). This will allow us to see what changes have occurred in the distribution of provinces within the four HDI levels: Low, Medium, High, and Very High.[119]

At the beginning of the 1980s, i.e. a few years after the beginning of reforms, all the provinces are in the Low HDI group. This convergence is clearly the result of the Mao era development strategy: provinces, had basically the same level of development measured by the HDI index, in

---

119 The analysis is based upon a table provided by Hu Angang, Tsinghua University.

spite of differences already evident between the coastal and the inner provinces. So, convergence is obtained at the level of the Low HDI.

By 1990, four coastal provinces have jumped to the Medium HDI: Shanghai, Beijing, Tianjin and Liaoning, which may be considered the pioneers of HDI development (i.e. a combination of revenue per capita, health and education). This means that one of the consequences of the strategy focused on economic development focused on the coastal provinces started to produce a divergence movement, as the provinces are now distributed into two HDI categories (Low and Medium HDI). Ten years later, in 2000, the divergence movement accelerates. Provinces are now distributed into three development groups: Low HDI, Medium HDI and High HDI. Only five provinces remain in the Low HDI group: Yunnan, Gansu, Qinghai, Guizhou and Tibet, i.e. Western and North-Western provinces. Three provinces left the Medium HDI group and joined the High HDI group; not surprisingly they are three of the four Municipalities depending on the central government (with a status equivalent to the provinces) Shanghai, Beijing and Tianjin. They are all placed in the coastal area. But at the same time a convergence movement towards the higher HDI groups appears: all the other 23 provinces jumped from the Low HDI to the Medium HDI group.

Ten years later, in 2010, the divergence movement towards the higher HDI groups seems to be confirmed as provinces are distributed, as in 2000, into three HDI groups, although at higher level, i.e. in the Medium, High and Very High groups, instead of the Low, Medium and High in 2000. In fact, not a single province has remained in the Low HDI group. The five provinces that were in the Low HDI in 1990 jumped into the Medium HDI group now comprising 11 provinces: Ningxia, Xinjiang, Jiangxi, Anhui, Guangxi, Sichuan, Qinghai, Gansu, Yunnan, Guizhou and Tibet. Beijing, Shanghai and Tianjin joined the Very High HDI. All the other 17 provinces were within the High HDI group. However, the convergence movement that appeared in 2000 is confirmed, as 25 provinces are now concentrated in the Medium HDI (11 provinces) and the High HDI (14 provinces).

Five years later, in 2015, Liaoning, Zhejiang and Jiangsu joined Beijing, Shanghai and Tianjin in the Very High HDI group. Only Qinghai, Gansu, Guizhou, Yunnan and Tibet remain in the Medium HDI group. All the other 20 provinces are placed within the High HDI group, up from 17 in 2010, thereby confirming an upward convergence movement toward the High HDI group, even if in 2015 provinces are distributed in three HDI groups as in 2010.

The rebalancing between rural and urban areas

Let us see first how China's urban and rural areas compare taking data at the national level. Table 11 shows that the ratio between urban per capita annual disposable income has always been, since the beginning of the reform era in 1978, 1.82 to 3.33 times higher than the rural per capita net income. The ratio has first decreased from 2.57 in 1978 to 1.82 in 1983, very likely thanks to the reforms introduced in the rural areas that boosted rural incomes. But then, the ratio has almost constantly increased to reach 2.86 in 1994. Then, there has been a short period (1994–1999), during the implementation of the first policies to 'open the west,' when the ratio decreased to reach 2.65 in 1999. It is also interesting to note that the ratio started to increase again after the September 1997 Party Congress decided to accelerate market reforms with the goal to bring China within the WTO: the ratio rose from 2.47 in 1997 to 3.33 in 2009 and stayed at about the same level until 2012. Then it started to decrease to reach 2.64 in 2019, very likely thanks to the positive impact of the social policies discussed above.

Let us see now how the provinces compare in terms of the ratio between urban and rural personal income. In the first column of Table 12 you will find the ratios between urban and rural areas personal incomes within the Chinese provinces for 2006. In the second column you will find the ratios for 2019. In the other columns there are the data for disposable income for urban areas and for net income for rural areas, used for calculating the 2019 ratios.

I subdivide the provinces into 6 groups, according to the level of the urban-rural ratio (Table 13). In 2006 there was no single province in the first group with a ratio less than 2. Only five provinces were in the second group with ratios 2 to 2.5. Not surprisingly, they were: Tianjin, Shanghai, Beijing, Jiangsu and Zhejiang, i.e. all coastal provinces. In the third group, with ratios 2.5 to 3, we find 9 coastal provinces, except Jiangxi and Hubei; but the latter are very close to the coastal provinces. In the fourth group, with ratios 3 to 3.5, we have 10 provinces, a mix of coastal provinces (Guangdong and Guangxi), one inner province close to the coastal ones (Anhui), and seven inner or northern provinces (Hunan, Shanxi, Henan, Ningxia, Inner Mongolia, Sichuan, and Xinjiang). Two northwestern provinces were in the fifth group with ratios 3.5 to 4 (Tibet and Qinghai); finally, five provinces were in the sixth group (with ratio higher than 4), two central (Chongqing and Shaanxi), one southern with no sea access (Guizhou), one northern (Gansu) and one southern

(Yunnan). This distribution is not surprising as it reflects the different level of development, and confirms the hypothesis, many times put forward, that the smallest difference between urban and rural areas is to be found in the most developed provinces.

Between 2006 and 2019 many interesting changes have occurred (Table 12). First, at the national level, the gap has been reduced from 3.27 in 2006 to 2.64 in 2019. Second, comparing the provinces, the difference between the highest and the lowest scores has been reduced: 2.03 in 2006 (Guizhou 4.59 divided by Shanghai 2.26); 1.81 in 2017 (Gansu 3.36 divided by Tianjin 1.86). More generally, all the provinces have reduced the gap, except Beijing, but only by very little, with an increase from 2.41 to 2.55. The most spectacular change occurred in Chongqing that passed from 4.02 to 2.51, and from the sixth group to the second, reflecting the impact of the policies implemented since the mid-2000s in favour of peasants and migrant workers. Third, leaving aside the exceptional case of Tianjin, which constitutes a group on its own, there is a clear convergence movement. First, within the provinces the gap between urban and rural personal income has decreased. Second, there is a convergence between provinces: in 2006 provinces were distributed into 5 groups, in 2019 into only three, with ratios between 2 and 3.44, whereas no provinces are to be found in groups 5 and 6, defined by the highest inequality between urban and rural personal incomes. Finally, whereas in 2006 groups 2 and 3 comprised 14 provinces, in 2017 they comprise 28 provinces, and only two provinces are in the less favourable group 4. We can conclude that there is a remarkable convergence of provinces towards a smaller ratio between personal income of their urban and rural areas.

The reasons for these positive changes are to be found first in the new fiscal policy that since the mid-1990s gave more financial means to the central government for investing in the development of the inner and northern provinces; second, in the new regional integration and coordinated development strategy adopted in 1995 at the 5th Plenum of the 14th CCP Central Committee, which includes the *Development of the West Regions Strategy* (2001), *Rejuvenation of Old Industrial Bases in Northeastern China* (2004) and *Rise of Central China Strategy* (2006); third, to the social policies implemented and developed especially since 2002; and fourth, to the massive migration of workers from the poor inland rural areas to the rich urban coastal areas which contributes to reducing inter-regional disparities.[120] The overall result is that China is improving the living conditions of all strata of its society, thus realizing a satisfactory level of social cohesion, stability, unity and harmony, in spite of the persistence of disparities. However, the latter are contained to acceptable levels, as attested by the support that Chinese citizens continue to manifest towards the Party-State.[121]

This is not to say that there are not protest movements. Official records show an increasing number of protest movements throughout the country, mainly targeting the negative consequences of economic development and the difficulties the Chinese leadership have had in countering those who seek to profit excessively and ruthlessly from the opportunities (i.e. more freedom from constraint) offered by the market-oriented reforms and by the difficulties of managing the transition process. Corruption, the illegal sale of land to real estate speculators and consequent destruction of old habitations and the displacement of the tenants, the non-payment of wages to migrant workers, etc. Local citizens look to the Party-State to intervene to put an end to these practices. In spite of these problems, which the Party-State is taking very seriously today, the majority of the Chinese people seem to support the development strategy it has set up. There are not throughout the country the kind of vast protest movements that many naïve Western observers have predicted throughout the life of the PRC. Protest movements contesting the leadership of the Party-State exist in areas where parts of the local elites have developed independentist movements, especially in Xinjiang, Tibet and Hong Kong, which have been supported by foreign Western countries, more particularly the U.S., as we discussed above.

THE DEVELOPMENT OF CHINA'S POWER RESOURCES

In the previous section we have seen that China has managed to develop not only its economic power but also the other power resources such as energy, science and informatics that together constitute the comprehensive national power. Here I will comment upon these resources

---

120 This conclusion had also already been partially confirmed by research conducted by Albert Keidel in the mid-2000s that proved that migrant workers, by sending back money to their families in the rural areas, contributed to the improvement of their standard of living for both income and consumption: Keidel 2007.

121 Cunningham et al (2020).

and show how they converge into China's grand strategy: the Belt and Road Initiative.

Internal and international strengths: An overview

The recovery of full sovereignty was the first and fundamental resource that the People's Republic of China recovered during the Mao era, following one century of foreign interventions that reduced China to a semi-colonial status.[122] In that era, despite the damages of the Great leap Forward and of the Cultural Revolution, China considerably improved the health and the literacy of its population and started the modernization of its industry even at the cost of environmental damages. It is thanks to these achievements that Deng Xiaoping was able to further develop China's economy and society by introducing market mechanisms and by opening up China to the global economy. The improvement realized thereby, allowed Deng to further realize the four modernizations that would help China to reclaim world power status: agriculture, industry, science and technology, and national defence. I remind the reader that these modernizations had already been defined by Zhou Enlai in 1993. During this period, Chinese leaders abstained from implementing assertive foreign policies that could have given rise to hostility from other countries, recognizing that a peaceful international environment was necessary to allow China to focus on the improvement of its national power resources.

As we have already seen above, Deng's reforms also had several negative consequences that China tried to overcome by investing heavily in the infrastructure the Inner and Northern provinces and in social safety nets. Despite serious problems yet to be overcome, it seems that overall, the Chinese people of all social classes (and not only those of the middle class) appreciate the improvements of their standard of living, as it is attested by reliable surveys.[123]

The West has witnessed the implementation of these policies with some sense of superiority: granted, China had become the workshop of the world, but only for low value-added goods. In the West the declarations of Chinese leaders to improve the economy and the well-being of Chinese society have long been taken as the propaganda the Party

---

122 This is the opinion shared by practically every Chinese intellectual. See for example Wang Hui 2009, pp. xii-xxxiii. See also on the important question of China's transition from Empire to State: Wang Hui (2014).

123 Cunningham, Shaikh and Turiel 2020.

needed to maintain its hold on power. In particular, convinced that China was only good at imitating Western technologies, the West has not taken seriously the declarations of Chinese leaders who insisted that China must undertake the road of 'independent innovation' (as Hu Jintao declared at the Party Congresses of October 2007). Today, as addressed above, China has caught up with practically all the technology domains, including several sectors of military equipment.

Having consolidated its internal power resources, China was ready to 'go out' during the leadership of Hu Jintao. This became a necessity. As China became more and more imbedded into the global economy, restoring national power by isolating itself as it had done in the past was no longer possible. Inevitably, China had to cope with the 'transformations' at work since the 19th century in the international system. Under pressure from the traditional colonial European countries, then from the U.S., the Chinese economy had become more and more open. If China was to benefit from the global market, it had to comply with the international rules established by the West. Hence the accession of China to the WTO in December 2001. As the Chinese economy did not cease to grow, it became important to assure access to the global market not only for selling goods, but also for importing the raw material and energy resources necessary for sustaining China's growing economy.

Moreover, China had accumulated funds to start to invest abroad, in particular to buy shares of high-tech enterprises, real estate, ports, etc. This trend finally led China to become more active in international organizations, to establish commercial agreements with other countries, to contribute to instituting regional organizations, such as the Shanghai group, and to improve its national defence both quantitively and qualitatively. As relations with the U.S. become more and more tense, and because the U.S. dollar is becoming a source of instability, China started to develop a strategy to become progressively independent from the U.S. dollar, and eventually to transform the RMB into a new international currency. As we shall see, this is a long-term strategy, progressing step by step, taking advantage not only of the growing strength of the Chinese economy, but of the declining power of the U.S., and the favourable opportunities afforded by the strategy of other countries, such as Russia and Iran, also eager to escape from the dominant role of the U.S. based upon the U.S. dollar as the major reserve and payment currency in the international economic system.

Given the massive military presence of the U.S. in the Far East, its pretence to unilaterally assure freedom of navigation in the China Sea, its aggressive attitudes (together with those of its European allies) in Europe and in the Middle East led China to develop a grand strategy to confront the U.S. and to assure its political and economic security. This strategy is generally known as the Belt and Road Initiative (BRI) that has been viewed in the West in the terms expressed by a leading Western newspaper, the *Financial Times*: 'China encircles the world with One Belt, One Road strategy.'[124] In fact, BRI (sometimes OBOR) may be interpreted as China's response to U.S. strategy to retain the status of sole world super-power by encircling Russia and China, intervening massively in the Middle East, keeping Latin America under its control, increasing its interventions in Africa, and maintaining the USD as the major international currency.

Let us now see how China has been able to achieve these results. I will deal with the build-up of several power resources: China's economy and its share in the world and the development of its investments abroad; the challenge to the U.S. dollar; the development of bilateral agreements and the implication in global and regional organizations; the diffusion of Chinese culture; and the development of military resources.

The development of China's economy and its place in the world

Whereas China remained isolated from the global economy until the end of the Mao Era, the development of its economy, based upon Deng's reforms (competition and opening to the world) inevitably led China to increase its exports and imports to and from the rest of the world. We have already seen above (Tables 3, 4, and 5) how China's development has been very rapid since the beginning of Deng's reform. Between 1990 and 2019 its share in the World GDP leapt from 3.89% to 17.33% (greater than the U.S. at 15.82%), as did its share of important-export from 1.63% to 12% (greater than the U.S. at 11.05%).

Towards the beginning of the third millennia China started to seriously invest abroad, thus confirming the analysis of Fernand Braudel: '… capital and credit have always been the surest way of capturing and controlling a foreign market. Long before the twentieth century the exportation of capital was a fact of daily life, for Florence as early as

---

124 Hancock 2017.

the thirteenth century.'[125] Derek Scissors of the American Enterprise Institute (AEI) regularly reports on the evolution of China's investments abroad.[126]

The analyses by Derek Scissors give a synthetic idea of the scope of China's investments abroad and allow us to appreciate China's worldwide reach.[127] From 2005 to 2018 the combined value of China's investment and construction exceeded $1.9 trillion globally, with a significant increase from $1.6 trillion in 2017. This amount is distributed among the following areas as follows: $385.1 billion to Europe ($291.9 in 2017), 299.1 to Sub-Saharan Africa ($272.1 in 2017), $275.1 to West Asia ($240.4 in 2017), $266.4 to East Asia ($214 in 2017), $182.6 to the U.S. (172.4 in 2017), $182.2 to Arab Middle East and North Africa ($149.8 in 2017), $169.4 to South America (144.7 in 2017), $111.6 to Australia ($100.8 in 2017), and $69.8 to North America, excluding U.S. ($66.7 in 2017).

Moreover, Scissors shows the great variety of China's construction and investment sectors abroad, energy and power being the most important, followed by transport, metals, real estate, finance, agriculture, technology, tourism, entertainment, logistics, and health. Finally, he also shows the relative importance of the share of private investment (as opposed to SOEs). From 2010 to 2018 the share of private investment rose from 9.5% to 47.4% in 2016, decreased sharply to 31.5% in 2017, but increased again to 44.3% in 2018. Even if private investments may again increase after 2019, it is very probable that China will not diminish SOEs investments in the strategic sectors, as they are easier to orient and control than private investments. This is part of the general CPC strategy to keep in its hands the management of China's development strategy. Finally, even though Scissors has reported on the decrease China's foreign investments due to the Covid-19 crisis, in a 2021 report he was obliged to forecast that 'a powerful recovery will materialize at some point this year and likely continue into 2022.' In my opinion this is because China has been able to overcome the crisis well before Western countries, and especially the U.S.[128]

Demonstrably, China invests all over the world. By 'going out' to the global economy, China is following in some respects the same

125 Braudel 1979, pp. 113–14.
126 Scissors 2019 and 2021.
127 Scissors 2019.
128 Scissors 2021.

trajectory as the West has implemented at least since the beginning of the industrial revolution. An economy whose development leads to the production of goods and capital that cannot be absorbed by the national demand, inevitably leads to a search for external markets where one can sell excess goods and invest excess capital. This explains the inevitable trajectory of China's foreign investment.

And this is the source of Western countries' concern. They see China as 'invading' the economies of countries where they have been used to selling goods and investing money for a very long time. Should China start to move from the production of low-value goods to goods with a high technological content (such as artificial intelligence, quantum computing, and the maglev train based upon magnetic levitation technology) one can understand that the concerns not only of the U.S. but also of the EU would inevitably reach a climax. And this is exactly what happened at the beginning of the 21st century. The West has always considered the intrusion of other countries into its 'exclusive influence zones' as an unacceptable threat to its interests, especially in Africa and in Latin America. So, in its view, the development of China's investments all over the world must be dealt with in conjunction with practically all the other dimensions of the relationship between China and the West, and especially those with the U.S.[129] And this is exactly what happened between the end of the 20th and the first decades of the 21st centuries. In Chapter 1 ('The Myth that China Is Only Able to Imitate the West') we have seen how China planned, in the long time, its transition from goods with low-added value to high tech.

The challenge to the international role of the U.S. dollar

As is well understood, the two most important power resources of the U.S. are the military and the international status of the U.S. dollar. Whereas improving the military resources is a relatively independent endeavour (provided has the technology and the money), contesting the supremacy of the U.S. dollar necessitates a complex strategy, as it is almost impossible to proceed immediately to a frontal attack. So, China

---

129 For the moment it suffices to remind the reader of the critiques the West has addressed to China's investments abroad that we have already discussed above in Chapter 1 ('The Myth that China Is Today Implementing an Imperial Foreign Policy'): the risk of the so-called 'debt trap' and the fact that Chinese companies bring with them their employees and workers, instead of employing the local manpower. We have seen that these critiques are not valid.

has progressively explored several ways to diminish, and even to escape, dependence on the U.S. dollar for its economic development both internally and internationally, by initiating and supporting what is generally called a strategy of 'de-dollarization' of the global economy. These measures include the creation of international banks as competitors to the international financial institutions dominated by the U.S. and its allies; obtaining a better position within international financial organization more in conformity to the economic weight of China; setting up bilateral agreements allowing the contracting countries to pay for their trade in their local currencies instead of the U.S. dollar; developing an alternative to the petro-dollars, i.e. the petro-yuan; setting up new institutions enabling the transmission worldwide of financial transactions in a secure, standardized and reliable environment, independent from the SWIFT system that is dominated by the U.S.; setting up international trade and investment partnerships that exclude the U.S. as a response to the partnerships planned by the U.S. to exclude, isolate and contain China, such as the Trans-Pacific-Partnership (see Chapter 1), that has failed so far; and preparing for a possible return to a new gold-standard totally or partially independent from the U.S. dollar, by buying important quantities of gold, and encouraging its domestic population to also do so.[130]

The creation of the Asian Infrastructure Investment Bank (AIIB), an international bank initiated by China, was the first clear response to U.S. obstruction of China's proposed reforms of the financial institutions such as the World Bank and the International Monetary Fund. AIIB is directly connected to China's investment strategy, and is also an important support for the Belt and Road initiative, both of which will be dealt with below.

This announcement was made at the same time as the announcement of the second part of the BRI (the maritime road), the first part (the continental silk road) having been announced a month before, on 7 September 2013. Immediately, the AIIB attracted many countries, including the closest U.S. allies, in spite of very strong U.S. opposition, as well as the BRICS countries (Russia, India, Brazil and South Africa).

---

130 In addition to Hudson 2003 that explains the U.S. strategy for establishing world dominance since the end of the Second World War, see for the recent development of this strategy the brilliant articles by Michael Hudson (Hudson 2019a and 2019b).

Today, the AIIB has 86 members and 17 prospective members around the world.[131] China has started to use different means for avoiding using the U.S. dollar and for increasing the use of the RMB. The first means is the use of bilateral swap agreements that China has concluded with several countries and economic organizations, e.g., Russia, Brazil, and South Africa (i.e., the BRICS countries, but not India), Pakistan, Australia, Brazil, UK, Canada, the EU and even Switzerland. Bilateral Swap agreements allow the contracting countries to pay for their trade exchanges in their own currency instead of in USD.

These agreements and the success of the BRI initiative show the growing attractiveness of China's economy, which today is the only large country that is increasing its GDP at an annual rate of just below 7%.[132]

The trend to use national currencies instead of the U.S. dollar has been growing. This is due essentially to the aggressive policy of the U.S. against countries that do not comply with its national interests. It is necessary here to remind the reader that many countries have been attacked by the U.S. through economic embargo and/or military interventions, because they manifested the will to sell their petrol in another currency, namely the Euro instead of the USD. As of June 2021, countries or regions subject to U.S. sanctions (either unilaterally or in part) include the Balkans, Belarus, Burma, Burundi, Central African Republic, Cuba, Democratic Republic of Congo, Hong Kong, Iran, Iraq, Lebanon, Libya, Mali, Nicaragua, North Korea, Somalia, Sudan, South Sudan, Syria, Ukraine/Russia, Venezuela, Yemen, and Zimbabwe.[133]

---

131 Here is a non-exhaustive list. European countries: Australia, Canada, Denmark, Finland, France, Georgia, Germany, Italy, Netherlands, New Zealand, Norway, Poland, Portugal, Russia, Spain, Sweden, Switzerland, United Kingdom); Asian: Azerbaijan, Bangladesh, Brunei, Cambodia, India, Indonesia, Kazakhstan, Laos, Malaysia, Mongolia, Myanmar, Nepal, Pakistan, Philippines, Singapore, Sri Lanka, Tajikistan, Thailand, Uzbekistan, and Vietnam), as well as other countries from other continents, in particular the other BRICS countries (Brazil and South Africa, in addition to China, Russia and India), and Egypt, Ethiopia, Iran, Israel, Jordan, South Korea, Kuwait, Oman, Qatar, Saudi Arabia, Turkey, and United Arab Emirates (Wikipédia under Asian Infrastructure Investment Bank).

132 Prasad 2017.

133 U.S. Department of the Treasury. "Sanctions Programs and Country Information." Accessed June 16, 2021. Cited in Investopedia, Joseph Elmerraji. 'Countries Sanctioned by the U.S. and Why,' https://www.investopedia.com/ financial-edge/0410/countries-sanctioned-by-the-u.s.—-and-why.aspx

It is interesting to note that the two main competitors of the U.S., China and Russia, had already signed in 2014 an agreement of 400 billion equivalent of U.S. dollars to use their own currencies to finance the exchange of their goods, especially petrol. Moreover, another important deal has been signed between China and Iran on 16 March 2021, to be dealt with below under *'Bilateral agreements and implication in global and regional organizations.'*

Indeed, China, as well as other countries such as Russia, Iran, Venezuela and the member-states of the EU have today additional good geo-political reasons for avoiding the use of the U.S.-dominated SWIFT for their international payments and to resort to alternative institutions.[134] Under the SWIFT system, thanks to the information thus acquired, the U.S. can block the transactions, seize money being transferred to countries under U.S. sanctions, threaten to exclude the companies concerned from the U.S. market, and eventually charge them with very severe fines, as it has done habitually in the past. This U.S. policy is particularly dissuasive as employed, e.g., for forbidding countries to do business with Iran and for hindering the construction of the Nord Stream 2 pipeline between Russia and Germany.

Accordingly, an additional move to avoid U.S. dominance in the international financial domain was put forward. In January 2019, the UK, Germany and France announced their decision to set up the instrument (called *INSTEX, Instrument In Support of Trade Exchanges*) that they will use instead of SWIFT, thus avoiding U.S. sanctions. Although it is not clear, at the time of writing, if INSTEX will actually work, it was nevertheless a strong sign that these EU members, which the U.S. claims to be its privileged allies within the NATO military alliance, were

---

134 SWIFT was created in 1973 in order to facilitate financial transactions through a secure means. Since the attack on the Twin Towers on 11 September 2001, which led to the U.S. using the pretext of the war against terrorism to take military action against numerous countries, the U.S. also set up a strategy to use SWIFT as an economic lever, forcing SWIFT (in furtherance of its sanctions regime) to allow it to gain access to information allowing the U.S. to determine the origin and the destination of financial transactions. Several U.S. public bodies have been implicated in this strategy, such as the Treasury, the CIA and the National Security Agency (NSA). Information about these moves were made known by the Danish newspaper *Berlingske* and the German *Der Spiegel*, as well as by the documents leaked by Edward Snowden, that revealed that the NSA spied on SWIFT using a variety of methods, including reading SWIFT printer traffic from numerous banks.

eeking a way around their treatment as vassals by the U.S.[135] Not only are European states dissatisfied with SWIFT, but Russia and China too have been seriously envisaging setting up alternatives to SWIFT.

An additional move to contest the supremacy of the U.S. dollar came on Mary 27, 2018 when China, the biggest oil buyer, announced the opening of its crude-futures contract in the Shanghai International Energy Exchange (SIEE), that will allow trading oil in yuan. This has given birth to a new expression, the 'petro-yuan' that may constitute a challenge to the petro-dollar, i.e., the dollar-denominated oil benchmarks Brent and West Texas Intermediate.[136] After China's having waited for 25 years before launching it, the SIEE had an impressive start with over 10 billion Yuan notional trade within the hour, and in spite of the alarms expressed by the Western media, six months later (beginning of October 2018) the oil markets continue to function, and China's futures had established themselves and overtaken in volume the dollar-denominated oil futures traded in Singapore and Dubai. Nevertheless, this constitutes a small fraction of the amount traded in U.S. dollars.

Moreover, influential Western media still today express their doubts about the future of the SIEE. Their remarks are valid in the very short run. China's moves must be considered in the framework of its long-term strategy, implemented within the changing structure of the international system that very clearly shows that the West, and especially the U.S., are losing their dominant position from which they have been accustomed to benefit. This is not to say that the RMB will replace the U.S. dollar. It simply means that the changing structure of the international power balance is changing in favour of China, and this means that the U.S. dollar will not remain the unique international currency through which the U.S. has dominated the world since WW2 and more so since the end of the Cold War. Another regimen for governance of the international economic and financial system is coming sooner than several influential pundits have today foreseen or feared.[137]

---

135 Irish 2019.
136 Bloomberg 2018; Park 2018.
137 The time of the end of the domination of the U.S. dollar in international finance is also suggested by the phenomenal amount of gold bought recently by several countries, such as China and Russia. This seems to suggest that even if today there is no other currency to replace the U.S. dollar, it is likely that we may evolve towards the establishment of regional payment systems, based upon a regional basket of currencies, possibly sustained by gold, pending an international agreement between the major economic blocs on the establishment

To conclude this section on the role China may play in the future in the international financial system, it remains the case that the internationalization of the RMB may represent a danger for the independence of China's development strategy. This is likely to happen if China opens its capital account, considered by experts in these matters to be a necessity should China want to play a leading role in international finance. This means freeing the flow of capital to and from China, thus allowing international investors (American, but also European and Japanese) to operate within the China market, putting a huge pressure on China's central bank and its State-owned banks. I should like to remind the reader that China had been able to overcome the Asian financial crisis of 1997 and the global crisis of 2008, thanks to its capital account being closed. It is no secret that the West, and especially the U.S. and its major banks and multi-national companies, are pressing the Chinese government to open its capital account. For the time being, China is very keen on safeguarding its control over the movements of capital and thereby on its development strategy.

Bilateral agreements and engagement in global and regional organizations

Several Western pundits claim that one of China's weaknesses compared to the U.S. is that it does not possess by far the same number of allies both within international organizations, such as the U.S.-led NATO alliance, or through bilateral cooperation. Their inevitable conclusion is that China is isolated within the international system as it is about Russia. Nothing is farther from the real situation. China was certainly isolated during the Mao era. But this was due to an autonomous decision China took to isolate itself, taken at the end of the Chinese civil war that came after more than one century of foreign aggressions. China had decided then that it needed to reconstruct its polity, economy and society autonomously, without foreign interferences. International cooperation, for example with Russia, was established and eventually terminated according to an autonomous evaluation.

Moreover, we have here another example of how Chinese culture differs, still today, from the West on many counts. Interpersonal relations are still important, and even if the signing of formal agreements is becoming the rule, this is preceded by taking time for establishing mutual respect and understanding. Mutual respect and understanding are

---

of a new international currency, that would replace the unstable U.S. dollar.

also very important because the rise of China has worried its neighbouring countries. But one must also understand that the rise of China also constitutes a powerful attraction for its neighbouring countries due to opportunities its massive economy represents. So, if China wants to play a leading role in Asia, thereby limiting and in the end eventually excluding the U.S., it has to make it clear to its neighbours that it does not want to dominate them but wants to set up win-win cooperation, as it has been claiming to do so for a long time. The U.S. is aware of these factors. and has been trying by every means to persuade China's neighbours that it represents a more reliable and stable partner that much better guarantees their security and independence. Hence, the U.S. is trying to attract intro its orbit countries like India, a serious competitor to China. Here again, it is up to China to persuade India that a win-win cooperation is possible. The U.S. should understand that Asian countries have not forgotten the aggressions the West, including the U.S., has perpetrated at their expense during more than three centuries. Rivalries do not exclude cooperation forever, as is borne out by the multiple levels of European cooperation that followed WW 2.[138]

Given these premises, it is enough here to mention the numerous bilateral cooperation projects China has established with Eurasian countries, in particular those related to the Belt and Road Initiative. The U.S. committed a devastating strategic mistake at the end of the Cold War by continuing to implement toward Russia the containment strategy adopted at the end of WW 2 against the Soviet Union against what was in the 1990s a vastly weakened Russia. Stuck within its ideology analysed at the beginning of Chapter 2, and incapable still today of changing strategy, the U.S. has ignored the warnings of some of its own strategists that it should avoid the emergence of a world power in Eurasia, as this power will inevitably dominate the world, given the weight and the centrality of this continent. By continuing to attack Russia after the end of the Cold War, by expanding NATO and the EU eastward, thereby betraying the promise made to Gorbachev, the U.S. has practically pushed Russia into the arms of China. The foreign policy of the Biden administration shows

---

138 Let me just give an example concerning India, which the majority of experts cite as to the positive heritage left by the British colonization, thereby making India a 'natural' ally of the West. Shashi Tharoor, former Under-Secretary General of the UN and Congress MP in India and former Minister writes in his book significantly entitled *Inglorious Empire. What the British Did to India*: 'Indians can never afford to forget the conditions in which they found our country after two centuries of colonialism.' (Tharoor 2016, p. 216).

that the U.S. is going back to the usual imperial stance that has been implemented by the Clinton-Bush-Obama (Biden) administrations. But has the U.S. today enough power resources to simultaneously contain Russia and China? Or is the U.S. inevitably moving towards the 'coming American collapse'?[139]

In addition to its excellent cooperation with Russia, which is already well-known and does not need further elaboration, China has established good to excellent cooperation with a variety of countries in Asia, Africa, Latin America, the Middle East and even in Europe. In particular, cooperation with countries of de facto or potential strategic importance includes relations with Turkey, Iran, Syria, the Philippines, and the countries situated along the Belt and Road Initiative (BRI) project, the 'Grand Chinese strategy,' to be dealt with hereafter.

Amongst these agreements, the one signed on 26 March 2021 between China and Iran has a particular importance for several reasons. First, it should be evaluated within the triangular partnership between China, Russia and Iran, as it is bound to constitute one of the main backbones of the BRI. This agreement, the Iran-China Comprehensive Strategic Partnership, began negotiations after Xi Jinping visited Teheran in 2016. Historically and geopolitically, it follows the same logic as the partnership between China and Russia, i.e., the imperial U.S. foreign policy.

U.S. policy targeting Iran began in 1953 when the CIA organized the regime change that rendered destitute the democratically elected Prime Minister, Mohammad Mossadegh, and replaced him with a dictatorship under the so-called Shah of Persia, Mohammad Reza Pahlavi. Later, the Obama administration imposed severe sanctions on Iran with the purpose of forcing it to negotiate a deal by which Iran would limit the development of his nuclear energy programme to civil activities, excluding nuclear energy for military uses. The deal, the Joint Comprehensive Plan of Action (JCPOA), was signed in 2015 by the five permanent members of the United Nations Security Council (China, France, Russia, United Kingdom, United States—plus Germany) together with the European Union. In May 2018 the Trump administration withdrew the U.S. from the deal and dramatically increased the sanctions on Iran with the clear purpose of making the Iranian 'economy scream' (as Nixon had asked his staff for preparing the Chili regime change in 1973), i.e. making the living conditions of the Iranian people so desperate, that they would

---

139 It is the subtitle of Martyanov 2021.

finally rebel against the government and call the U.S. to 'liberate them from the tyranny of the Ayatollahs.' That was as successful as the same policy and rationale had been when used against Iraq. Iran was practically forbidden to have trade and investment deals with foreign countries, including U.S. allies, including selling its main source of revenue: oil. A wonderful example of democratic behaviour and of respect of human rights. While nonetheless remaining within the confines of the JCPOA, Iran responded in kind and by looking for alternative avenues to sustain its economy. Quite naturally it established contacts and discussions with countries similarly targeted by the imperial U.S. foreign policy. Hence, the establishment of a triangular partnership with Russia and China.

From a geopolitical point of view, the Iran-China partnership is a 25-year strategic partnership that takes place within the framework of the Belt and Road Initiative. Iran is one of the destinations of the BRI to the Middle East and Europe. It's projected that high-speed trains will connect China's North-West Xinjiang Province to Iran, through Kazakhstan, Kyrgyzstan, Uzbekistan and Turkmenistan, then through Iraq and Turkey all the way to Europe. The deal plans to increase bilateral trade over 10-fold to 600 USD billion and covers everything from political and cultural ties to security, defence, and regional and international cooperation. China envisages to invest as much as 400USD billion in Iran's' oil, gas, petrochemicals, renewable energy and nuclear energy infrastructure. In turn Teheran has committed to becoming a major reliable source of energy for China. While several aspects of the deal will have to be discussed and agreed upon, the deal must nevertheless be evaluated in the framework of China's strategy: first define the general purpose of the deal in its major dimensions, then in the making of the deal problems are discussed and solutions are mutually agreed upon, taking into consideration the evolving 'situation potential' both within Iran and China and the international system. No wonder that this deal has already been considered by reliable mainstream observers as a challenge to the Biden administration, as noted in an article published 27 March 2021 by *Bloomberg* with the significant title: 'China Signs 25-Year Deal With Iran in Challenge to the U.S.'[140]

In addition to the pursuit of bilateral cooperation, China's strategy has developed an increasing engagement in international, regional and global organisations through which it can acquire additional power resources. China has been a member of the Security Council of the UN

---

140 Shala 2021.

since 1971, and its role has increased through use of its veto power, generally with Russia, to oppose U.S. initiatives concerning, inter alia, Georgia, Ukraine and Syria. More recently China has increased its contribution to UN peacekeeping operations, of which it has been, since the beginning of the 2010s, one of the major contributors.[141]

More significantly, China has contributed to the creation of international regional organizations that are in fact an obstacle to the U.S. leadership in some parts of the world, such as the BRICS and more importantly, the Shanghai Cooperation Organization (SCO), a political, economic, and security organization, the creation of which was announced in 2001 in Shanghai by the leaders of China, Kazakhstan, Kyrgyzstan, Russia, Tajikistan, and Uzbekistan. With the admission of India (the other economic giant with China) and Pakistan, the SCO is today the most populous organization in the world, with more than 3 billion people. If we add the 125 million of the four countries with an observer's status (Iran, Afghanistan, Mongolia and Belarus), and five other countries presently in dialogue for membership, of which Turkey is the most significant,[142] the SCO encompasses more than 42% of the world population. It is also the biggest land mass in the world, with more than 60% of Eurasia. Its GDP (in PPP) is more than $37.200 billion, almost as much as that of the U.S. and the EU combined.

The SCO has combined military forces of 5.6 million and a combined military budget of $370 billion, compared to the more than $900 billion of the NATO countries. Over the years, the SCO has developed cooperation in many domains, and more particularly exerted its diplomatic strength as it relates to security, resolving border issues, initiating military cooperation, intelligence sharing, countering terrorism and countering American influence in Central Asia, where it plays the role of an eastern counterbalance to NATO. This is important since NATO is also planning to become more engaged in Asia, as we have seen above. Here again, in contributing to the activities and increasing strength of the SCO, China has acquired additional resources useful for the realization of its national and international interests.[143]

---

141 Perlez 2015.
142 https://en.wikipedia.org/wiki/Member_states_of_the_Shanghai_Cooperation_Organisation
143 Other organizations with which China is cooperating include the Asia-Pacific Economic Cooperation (APEC), the Association of Southeast Asian Nations (ASEAN) and the Eurasian Economic Union.

The BRICS is the other notable organization of which China is one of the founding members. Created between 2006 and 2009, it comprises five of the major countries in the world: Brazil, Russia, India, China and South Africa, all members of the G-20 and has been meeting annually at formal summits since 2009. In 2015, the five BRICS countries represented over 3.6 billion people, or about 40% of the world population and with a share of 30.38% of the world GDP (see Table 3 in the Statistical Annex).

The BRICS deal with economic, financial and global governance issues. In 2013, the member countries agreed to create the New Development Bank (NDB) with the purpose of rivalling with the Western-dominated IMF and World Bank, with an initial capital of US$100 billion. In March 2014, the BRICS foreign ministers issued a communiqué that 'noted with concern the recent media statement on the forthcoming G20 Summit to be held in Brisbane in November 2014 [and reminded those concerned that] the custodianship of the G20 belongs to all Member States equally and no one Member State can unilaterally determine its nature and character.' It was a clear reference to the habit of the U.S. to unilaterally determine the G20 agenda and the writing of its final communiqué. Moreover, referring to the Ukraine crisis, the BRICS ministers remarked that 'the escalation of hostile language, sanctions and counter-sanctions, and force does not contribute to a sustainable and peaceful solution, according to international law, including the principles and purposes of the United Nations Charter,' a clear critique of the U.S. regime change in that country, and beyond.[144]

Again, some observers warn that the development of the BRICS cooperation may be endangered by the economic difficulties experienced recently by Brazil and South Africa, as well as by disagreements between China and India, over territorial disputes, and between Russia and China because of competition between the Russia-led Eurasian Economic Union and the China-led BRI. All things considered, it is clear that if the BRICS countries succeed in solving these difficulties, they may continue to pose their organization as a competitor, if not an alternative, to the U.S.-led international order.

Furthermore, China and Russia, which are developing their partnership, constitute the core of the BRICS and that relationship itself can counterbalance the weaknesses of the other members. Several countries

---

144 https://en.wikipedia.org/wiki/New_Development_Bank, accessed 24 July 2017.

have expressed strong interest in full membership of the BRICS, such as Afghanistan, Argentina, Indonesia, Mexico, Turkey, Egypt, Iran, Nigeria, Sudan, Syria, Bangladesh and Greece. The great variety of members and interested countries explains why China is very keen to contribute to the development of inter-BRICS cooperation, as it has a clear link with the China-led One Belt One Road Initiative (OBOR/BRI).

At last in 2020, after years of negotiations, China has succeeded in achieving the signing of two international agreements, one comprising Asian countries, the other with the EU. This is a remarkable proof of the attraction the Chinese economy is exerting all over the world, and places China as a very serious competitor of the U.S. These provide further examples of how China has implemented its strategy to become a major player in the international arena. The time span over which these agreements have been finalized, i.e., during the transition period from the Trump to the Biden administrations, shows that China acts very quickly when the 'situation potential' enables it to seize the opportunity to finalize agreements that have been in negotiations for a long time and with considerable difficulties. This choice of the moment facilitated the avoidance of the likely opposition of the U.S., as had happened already, for example at the moment of the creation of the Asian Infrastructure Investment Bank (AIIB). Clearly, the technical aspects of the two agreements must be further discussed, and obstacles may occur. Moreover, after the beginning of the Biden administration, the EU Parliament has blocked the ratification of the China-EU agreement, in the hysterical anti-China (and also anti-Russia) climate fomented by the U.S. Nevertheless, as we have seen above, several influential American observers have considered that the two agreements having even reached such a point constitute a defeat for the new Biden administration.[145] No wonder that the U.S. will do everything it can to make their implementation difficult or even impossible, not least, insofar as, in addition to the traditional U.S. allies within the EU, the AIIB agreement comprises several of the U.S. allies and partners in Asia.

The Regional Comprehensive Economic Partnership (RCEP) is a free trade agreement presently encompassing 15 countries: 10 members of the ASEAN (Brunei-Darussalam, Cambodia, Indonesia, Laos, Malaysia, Myanmar, Philippines, Singapore, Thailand and Viet Nam) and five regional countries with which ASEAN has existing free trade agreements (Australia, China, Japan, South Korea, and New Zealand).

---

145 Shala 2021 and Barfield 2021.

RCEP was concluded and signed in November 2020. India had withdrawn from negotiations in November 2019, leading to a fast-track accession process being established, should India wish to re-join RCEP in future. The 15 countries within RCEP represent: a population of 2.3 billion, 30% of the world's population, and a total gross domestic product (GDP) of around $38,813 billion or 30% of global GDP. Moreover, five RCEP countries (Australia, China, Indonesia, Japan and South Korea) are members of the Group of 20 (G20), the international forum for global economic cooperation among the world's 20 largest economies. If and when finalized, this agreement will pull the economic centre of gravity back towards Asia, with China poised to take the lead in writing trade rules for the region, leaving the U.S. behind in economic and political affairs. The RCEP has been criticized for ignoring labour, human rights, and environmental sustainability issues.

The China-EU Comprehensive Agreement on Investment (CAI), has the goal of facilitating investments between these two important economic zones, that with the U.S. constitute the three biggest economies of the world. Its importance goes without saying. If finalized, it would represent a serious challenge to the leadership of the U.S. not only in the Atlantic area and in the Euro-Asian continent. Here again, U.S. diplomacy is highly likely to push its European allies to remain faithful to the North-Atlantic vision of the world. Nevertheless, already today several European countries are not ready to cut economic relations with Asia. Germany and France have already expressed their doubts about the foreign policy of the new Biden administration insofar as it is clear that the new administration remains faithful to the traditional U.S. foreign policy that divides the world between GOOD and the EVIL where, in George W. Bush's blunt assessment, 'you are either with us or against us.'[146]

The diffusion of Chinese culture abroad

Another dimension of China's strategy is the diffusion of its culture abroad. This is realized mainly thanks to two initiatives. The first is by the creation abroad of many Confucius Institutes. Their main role is to make the Chinese language and culture accessible to foreign audiences through the teaching of Chinese to young university students, but also through public conferences for larger audiences. In some cases, the Institutes may also support research activities between Chinese and local

---

146 https://www.washingtonpost.com/wp-srv/nation/specials/attacked/transcripts/bushaddress_092001.html

scholars. The Institutes have been criticized as being a propaganda tool in the hands of the Communist Party of China. If so, then the same can be said of Western countries' proliferation of similar institutions such as the German Goethe Institutes, the French 'Institut Français,' the American Cultural Centres, and the British Councils. All such institutes seek to improve the mutual understanding between different cultures. It is only when they are used to support ideas and protest movements inside the hosting country that their activity may be criticized. This does not appear to be the case as yet with the Confucius Institutes.

The other means to diffuse language, culture and ways of thinking and of analysing problems and issues, is by the broadcasting of news and the analysis of political, economic and social issues. China is trying to reach people of other cultures by developing a worldwide broadcasting network, China Global Television Network (CGTN) available in English and in French, as well as in other languages. Since its beginning (as the CCTV—China Central Television) China's international channel has considerably improved its offering with a variety of cultural programmes and news covering all the continents. A choice of several excellent journalists is enabling the presentation of news in a more balanced way than some Western (mainly American) channels, such as CNN and BBC. Moreover, the debates organized by CGTN bring together debaters coming from different perspectives (generally one Chinese and one or two participants from other countries). CGTN is an invaluable source of information to understand how China sees and analyses national and international issues. Of course, the critical reader knows that in order to acquire a balanced view of an issue, it is necessary to have access to different sources of information, i.e., to several channels from different countries and, maybe more important to have access to a mix of mainstream and alternative media.

The development of military resources

One cannot understand the development of China's military power without taking into account that its encounter with the West has led it to a continuous race to catch up with Western military superiority.[147] It is this gap that first enabled the West (mainly by European powers in the

147 This part is based upon the reports to Congress on the U.S.-China Economic and Security Review Commission (USA 2016–20); USA 2018b; USA 2020; PRC (2015a); Nuclear Threat Initiative (2015); an evaluation of China's military power (U.S. 2019); and articles by the *South China Morning Post,* 2016–21.

mid-19th century to force China to open itself to the global economy, and enabled the U.S., after the end of World War II, to establish near the Chinese territory a set of military alliances and bases for safeguarding its national interests as well as those of its allies. This unequal relationship has put some serious limits on China's freedom to safeguard its own national interests and on its efforts to contribute to the revision of the rules of the international system. The U.S. has consistently attempted to re-enforce such limits.

Still today, military resources remain the primary domain where China clearly lags behind the U.S. Nevertheless, the gap is narrowing, as China has massively invested in science and technology, especially artificial intelligence, where innovations have led to the improvement of the quality of its weaponry.[148] It is evident that, thanks to the build-up of its military resources, China has been able to develop a more assertive (for some aggressive) foreign policy in its immediate neighborhood, e.g., in the China Sea.

One way to evaluate China's military would be to discover how its major competitor assesses it. While the U.S. leadership has an unfailing confidence in the U.S. military, it also takes the 'China military threat' very seriously. While it is difficult to tell whether this evaluation is based upon an objective analysis of the threat or is exaggerated in order increase its funding from the federal budget, it is nevertheless clear that the consequence has been the increasing U.S. investments in the military, especially with the intention of improving the quality of U.S. air and sea weaponry, and its nuclear arsenal. The most important question for both China and the U.S. is to determine whether their respective military resources constitute a deterrent sufficiently powerful to discourage aggression.

Several official U.S. documents show an increasing concern about what we may label 'the Chinese military threat,' such as the *Military and Security Developments Involving the People's Republic of China 2018* (Secretary of Defence), or the *China Military Power. Modernizing a Force to Fight and Win* (Defence Intelligence Agency). Here I will refer to the biannual *China Economic and Security Review Commission Reports to Congress*.[149] These reports present a remarkable analysis of

---

148 Feng 2017, Chan 2017.
149 USA 2016–20. Also, I have analysed in greater detail how the U.S. sees the development of China's military resources in my 2018 and 2019 books (see bibliography).

the increasing power of China and the threats it poses to the supremacy of the U.S. and to the 'world America made.' They cover not only the military, but all aspects of China's growing power resources. However, the reports insist heavily on military resources, thus confirming my analysis that considers military resources to be at the core of power, either as a threat or by their actual use, without which power could not exist.[150] The 2016 Report considers, and seems to regret, that

> China's actions in the economic, foreign policy, and military realms suggest China's leaders have decided the time has come for China to leave behind its long-held strategy, espoused by Deng Xiaoping, of "hide your strength, bide your time." China is showing itself to the world now, and the outcome is not what many had hoped for 15 years ago when the country was welcomed into the WTO and the global economic system. Our Report and recommendations reflect *the China that is, not the China for which some have hoped.*[151]

What, then, in the U.S. view, went wrong?

The 2016 Report very strongly criticizes China's behaviour in the international system:

> China continues to violate the spirit and the letter of its international obligations by pursuing import substitution policies, imposing forced technology transfers, engaging in cyber-enabled theft of intellectual property, and obstructing the free flow of information and commerce. China is also becoming a less welcoming market for foreign investors.[152]

More particularly, the report complains that China does not comply with the rules of the free market economy:

> Despite repeated pledges to let the market play a "decisive role" in resource allocation, Beijing continues to use State-owned enterprises (SOEs) as a tool to pursue social,

---

150 Urio 2018, Ch. 2

151 *China Economic and Security Review Commission Reports to Congress*, 2016, p. viii, quotations are from the Executive summary. My emphasis has been added to the succeeding quotations from it.

152 p. vii.

industrial, and foreign policy objectives, offering direct and indirect subsidies and other incentives to influence business decisions and achieve state goals.[153]

It is in this context that the report takes stock of the modernization (both for quantity and quality) of China's military, especially for the navy and air forces. Consequently, it considers:

The military capabilities China is developing and [sic] will expand or improve the ability of the People's Liberation Army *to conduct a range of externally focused operations* (...) Improvements in these areas can also strengthen China's traditional warfighting capabilities *against weaker neighbours.* Given its enhanced strategic lift capability, strengthened employment of special operations forces, increasing capabilities of surface vessels and aircraft, and more frequent and sophisticated experience operating abroad, *China may also be more inclined to use force to protect its interests.*[154]

Moreover,

the PLA Navy's underway replenishment capability, which will improve its *ability to sustain long-distance operations,* will be augmented by China's first overseas military support facility in Djibouti. China's pursuit of expeditionary capabilities, coupled with the aggressive trends that have been displayed in both the East and South China seas, are compounding existing concerns about China's rise among U.S. allies and partners in the greater Asia.[155]

Also, the report takes stock of the fact that

China operates an increasingly sophisticated and extensive array of intelligence, surveillance, and reconnaissance assets *capable of monitoring U.S. forces deployed to the Western Pacific.* (...) Chinese intelligence collection operations

153 p. 4.
154 p. 12
155 P. 12

against the United States pose *a large and increasing threat to U.S. national security.*[156]

Quite rightly, the report establishes a clear link between China's willingness to project its power abroad with the BRI initiative, to be dealt with below:

> China's willingness to reshape the economic, geopolitical, and security order to accommodate its interests are of great concern as China's global influence grows. This influence has been manifesting most recently with China's "One Belt, One Road" initiative aimed at connecting China with great portions of the rest of the world via a wide range of investments and infrastructure projects.[157]

Nevertheless, the authors of the 2016 Report did not think it necessary to devote a full section to BRI, whereas the 2018 Report deals with BRI in a new section of more than 30 pages (pp. 259–291). Notably, it also introduced a new chapter entitled 'China High-Tech Development,' indicating that its analysis of China's power resources has become more sophisticated, taking stock of two of the most important dimensions of its power (military and technology) as well as their mutual strengthening impact.

The 2018 Report confirms and exacerbates its criticisms. As in 2016, the 2018 Report regrets the good old days of Deng Xiaoping's motto: 'hide your capabilities and bide your time,' that unfortunately 'faded into history.' In fact, in 2017, at the 19th National Congress of the CPC, 'Xi Jinping announced a "new era" that sees China "moving closer to the world's centre stage" and offering "a Chinese approach" to solving problems.' The 2018 Report further explains that

> the CCP has used economic growth to strengthen its own grasp on authority, advance its state-capitalist model, buttress authoritarian governments abroad, leverage its market against other nations, and fund *a massive buildup of Chinese military power to intimidate and silence its neighbours.* (all references are from the Executive summary).

---

156 P. 13.
157 p. vii.

Even more worrying, China

views [this] strong military as essential for supporting its global ambitions, with the ultimate goal of becoming a world-class force. In the Indo-Pacific China is intensifying preparation for combat and enhancing its capabilities to deter and defeat the U.S. military should it be required to do so in a future conflict.[158]

The Report also criticizes China's behaviour within the BRI. China

engages in predatory economic practices. Rather than providing development finance in line with established rules, China provides loans and investment in non-transparent ways on projects that do not always meet global governance standards and pass tests of commercial viability. Rather than respecting other countries' sovereign rights, China is altering the status quo in the Indo-Pacific and has publicly congratulated itself on its militarization of the South China Sea.

Inevitably then comes the existential question: is Xi Jinping's *pursuit of structural changes in the global order to facilitate Chinese ambitions,* compatible with the existing order or is it creating a new era of persistent competition? The U.S. answer comes immediately: China's attempt to seize leadership has undoubtedly *put at risk the national security and economic interest of the U.S., its allies and partners.*

The last available Report of the *China Economic and Security Review Commission Reports to Congress* (2020) confirms the analyses of previous reports. Notably, the tone overall is much more assertive (some would say: aggressive). Here is how the report analyses the 'China threat' (summarized from the executive summary, emphasis added). The Report recognizes that PRC's ambitions as neither new nor secret. However, the Communist Party is aggressively asserting its interests both domestically and globally. Moreover, *it envisions itself atop a*

---

158 Let us note that 'the Commission's work this year led to a lively, yet unfinished, debate on China's status as a "peer" to the U.S. military. In the coming year we will explore the accuracy of such claims, the qualifications under which such a title is warranted, and the implications for U.S. national security of facing a "peer competitor" with self-described competing national security interests.' (p. vii).

new hierarchical global order in which the world acquiesces to China's worldview while supplying it with markets, capital, resources and talent. Moreover, the Party accelerates its aggressive pursuit of global power leadership with *the goal of building a new, Sinocentric world order.* This is evident as China's army is evolving into a formidable and increasingly modern force, *capable of projecting power globally*, far away from China's shores.

The above summary confirms the analysis provided by the evaluation made in 2019 by the U.S. Defence Intelligence Agency, significantly entitled: *China Military Power. Modernizing a Force to Fight and Win.*[159] In the Preface of this document, the Director of the Defence Intelligence Agency, Robert P. Ashley, Jr., Lieutenant General, U.S. Army, explains:

China's double-digit economic growth has slowed recently, but it served to fund several successive defence modernization Five-Year Plans. As international concern over Beijing's human rights policies stymied the PLA's search for ever more sophisticated technologies, China shifted funds and efforts to acquiring technology by any means available. Domestic laws forced foreign partners of Chinese-based joint ventures to release their technology in exchange for entry into China's lucrative market, (…) The result of this multifaceted approach to technology acquisition is a PLA on the verge of fielding some of the most modern weapon systems in the world. *In some areas, it already leads the world.* (…) For example, China's technological advancement in naval design has begun to approach a level commensurate with, and *in some cases exceeding, that of other modern navies.*[160] [Emphasis added]

And this, in turn, will lead China to *'achieve great power status.'* Indeed, China is building a robust, lethal force with capabilities spanning the air, maritime, space and information domains which will enable China to impose its will in the region. As it continues to grow in strength and confidence, Ashley reports, *'our nation's leaders will face a China insistent on having a greater voice in global interactions, which at times may be antithetical to U.S. interests.'* And he concludes:

159 USA 2019.
160 p. 70.

This report offers insights into the modernization of Chinese military power as it reforms from a defensive, inflexible ground-based force charged with domestic and peripheral security responsibilities to a joint, highly agile, expedition-ary, and *power-projecting arm of Chinese foreign policy that engages in military diplomacy and operations across the globe.*[161]

Coming back to the 2020 *China Economic and Security Review Commission Reports to Congress*, its conclusion is clear: the past 20 years are littered with the Communist Party's broken promises. In China's intended new order, there is little reason to believe the Party promises of 'win-win' solutions, mutual respect, and peaceful coex-istence. Therefore, *China threatens the vital interests of the U.S.* and the security and vitality of an increasing number of countries around the world. Just let me rephase this: China is threatening the U.S.-led-liberal-rule-based international order in which the U.S. has played, and still today tries to play a leading role. But is this *aggressive analysis* of China's rise as a global power a reasonable (or even rational) reaction to the increasing power of China and the partnerships it has been able to establish with countries such as Russia, Iran and many others as we have seen above?

Again, the 2020 Report very aggressively refers to China's pol-icy in its territories of Hong Kong, Tibet and Xinjiang. In its 'Key Recommendations' the report suggests that U.S.-China relations should be based upon the following principles: (1) the ability of journalists and online media to operate without undue restrictions; (2) the ability of non-governmental organizations to conduct meaningful engagement with civil society; (3) access for social media and mobile apps from U.S. companies; (4) access for diplomatic personnel, including but not limit-ed to diplomats' freedom of travel and ability to meaningfully exchange views with the host country's public. It is not necessary to be an expert in the analysis of the means the U.S. uses for conducting regime change operations in countries that do not comply with American interests as elaborated above to see the full meaning of these recommendations.

In spite of this alarmistic analysis, the U.S. still retains the most powerful army, at least on paper, even if we take into consideration the

---

161 p. 5.

numerous failures in overt warfare since the end of World War II, and in particular the most recent debacle in Afghanistan (to be commented upon below). How does China stack up with regard to this military and geopolitical environment? China has only one military base abroad (Djibouti). It is true that it has militarized several isles in the China seas, and may transform ports it has acquired for civil operation into dual civil-military operations ports. But it is miles away from the roughly 800 military bases the U.S. has all over the world, especially those close to China. And China does not have any military bases in the Gulf of Mexico or near the coasts of California. The U.S. military budget is more than three times that of China. China has developed its navy and air forces, but overall, it still does not match the U.S. Finally, China has only about 280 nuclear warheads, against more than 1700 for the U.S.

Moreover, one should take into consideration the fact that, contrary to the U.S., China does not have a global policy based mainly upon the aggressive use of military power. It is building military resources to protect its land. And here, its navy is already superior to that of the U.S. forces based in the Far East. But in addition, one should take into consideration the changes in warfare, especially since the development of hypersonic weapons (missiles) that are very difficult (even impossible) to intercept. Here China is making considerable progress, also thanks to the transfer of technology from Russia. These medium range missiles are the perfect choice for China's defensive policy, as they are for Russia, which also does not base its foreign policy on the aggressive global projection of military power. The superiority of the U.S. Navy overall is based upon its aircraft carriers. But now, as Martyanov sustains, hypersonic missiles can sink or at least considerably damage aircraft carriers, impacting assessments of their military significance.[162] While the U.S. has 11 carriers, and China only two, which do not match the quality of U.S. ones, hypersonic missiles cost a fraction of the cost of a carrier, and without carriers, the U.S. navy would lose a significant part of its power.

Let me conclude this section by referring again to the evaluation of the Defence Intelligence Agency (*China Military Power. Modernizing a Force to Fight and Win*). Quite rightly the report establishes a clear link between military transportation and the BRI initiative:

transportation is also at the heart of the Belt and Road Initiative (BRI), which consists of establishing roads, railways, and

---

162 Martyanov 2018, 2019, 2021.

ports to connect to countries from Asia to Africa and Europe. Although the BRI is marketed as primarily an effort to increase trade and development, China's improved domestic transportation infrastructure and access to transportation infrastructure abroad also would benefit the PLA by enhancing PLA access to transportation hubs and road systems.[163]

THE BELT AND ROAD INITIATIVE, OR CHINA'S GRAND STRATEGY

It is not surprising that President Xi Jinping used this sentence (already quoted in Chapter 1) when on 7 September, 2013 he announced for the first time China's project to build an 'economic belt along the Silk Road' in his speech in Astana:

> Over 2100 years ago during China's Han Dynasty, a Chinese envoy, Zhang Qian, was sent to Central Asia with a mission of peace and friendship. His journey opened contacts between China and Central Asian countries, as well as the Silk Road linking East and West, Asia and Europe.[164]

Referring to the already ongoing cooperation with Russia, Xi Jinping clearly stated the objectives of the initiative: to expand regional cooperation, improve policy communication, promote unimpeded trade, enhance monetary circulation, and increase understanding between peoples. This announcement came less than one year after Xi Jinping had been voted by the Party Congress to be the next Secretary General of the CPC. Less than a month later, Xi Jinping proposed to add a New Maritime Road in a speech given in Jakarta on 2 October 2013. These new roads were later referred to as the 'Belt and Road Initiative (BRI).' Clearly, such a vast project must have been in preparation for a long time beforehand, and in any case, it is the logical consequence of integration and rationalization of the previous moves made by China to recover world power status.

A lot of factual information is now available on the BRI thanks to several serious sources.[165] Therefore, I will focus my analysis on the core

---

163 P. 104.
164 Xi Jinping 2013a, se also 2013b.
165 E.g., Swaine 2015, Leverett et al. 2015). Information about BRI from the Western point of view can be found in the *Financial Times*; in the publications of

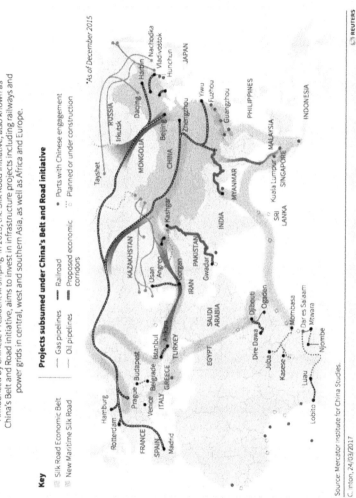

Reviving the Silk Road

Announced by Chinese President Xi Jinping in 2013, the Silk Road initiative, also known as China's Belt and Road initiative, aims to invest in infrastructure projects including railways and power grids in central, west and southern Asia, as well as Africa and Europe.

Key

Projects subsumed under China's Belt and Road initiative

Silk Road Economic Belt
New Maritime Silk Road

— Gas pipelines
— Oil pipelines
— Railroad
▬ Proposed economic corridors

● Ports with Chinese engagement
○ Planned or under construction

*As of December 2015

Source: Mercator Institute for China Studies.

C. Inton, 24/03/2017

REUTERS

of the BRI, and show to what extent it represents a serious challenge to U.S. leadership not only in Asia, but also all over the world.

The way toward the Belt and Road strategy

As we have seen in Chapter 2, China's strategy takes advantage of the 'situation potential.' At times this may give the impression of being chaotic. However, the goal still orients the actions, and actions are implemented when and where the 'situation potential' suggests that their chances of success are reasonably favourable. Moreover, if the situation potential is not favourable, or in case of failure, China does not act or retreat, but waits for the long-term 'silent transformations' to change the 'situation potential' to its advantage. Then, it sees it as important to act with no hesitation, otherwise the favourable moment may be lost. This is what China has done in order to arrive at the implementation of its Grand Strategy, the Belt and Road Initiative (BRI). As André Chieng has very well explained: the essence of the strategy is on the one hand to gradually trap the competitor into a fixed position upon which the strategist can act, and on the other hand, to constantly change one's position in order to make its own strategy incomprehensible to the competitor.[166] The following analysis shows that China is applying this approach. Some of the actions I will analyze were implemented simultaneously, others in sequence. But the ultimate strategic goal remains to reclaim world power status.

In summary, the starting point of China's strategy has been the development of its domestic economy, thanks to the introduction of market mechanisms, and also to the opening of the economy to the rest of the world, that allowed China to export its goods and to benefit from foreign investment in the Chinese economy. This allowed it on one hand to improve the living conditions of the Chinese people, and on the other hand to develop an increasingly positive balance of trade, and the acquisition

---

the Centre for Strategic and International Studies; the China Leadership Monitor of the Hoover Institution at Stanford University; the American Enterprise Institute; the Council of Foreign Affairs (its journal *Foreign Affairs*); and Mercator Institute for China Studies (MERICS). For Chinese sources, in addition to those quoted below, see the official Chinese news agency, Xinhua (http://www.news.cn/english/); the *South China Morning Post* (https://www.scmp.com/frontpage/international); the Caixin magazine (http://www.caixinglobal.com/); a book by a professor at Renmin University: Wang Yiwei 2016; and a collective of Chinese scholars and officials: Wei Liu 2018.

166 Chieng, 2006, p. 210, Jullien 1995, Ch. 1.

of monies by both private and SOEs that could be used for investing in the global market. This also allowed the government to acquire an astonishing number of foreign currencies that could also be invested in the global market, either directly or through new financial institutions promoted by China. Moreover, this strategy allowed the acquisition of technology through joint ventures with foreign companies. The consequence has been the development of Chinese investment in many countries on all the continents, including in the U.S. China started this development first by making low-added values products, hence the myth of China as the factory of the world (see Chapter 1), that has been regarded with some condescendence by the West, which saw the Chinese as good at eventually producing low value-added products by stealing Western technologies they were not able to invent by themselves. Then in 2007 came the announcement made by the General Secretary of the CPC, Hu Jintao, that China would develop autonomous innovation in many strategic sectors. The following year, China published the 'Thousand Talents' project, whose goal was to attract to China top-level scientists from abroad, and to repatriate Chinese scientists educated abroad. These announcements were confirmed twice in 2006 and 2011 by the State Assets Supervision and Administration Commission (SASAC).

Two years later, in 2013, the newly appointed Party Secretary, Xi Jinping, announced the launching of a vast project, the Belt and Road initiative, that would link China's economy to the rest of the world, this time in a leading position. Then later in October 2013, China announced the creation of the Asian Infrastructure Investment Bank (AIIB), immediately seen by the U.S. as a competitor of the financial institutions it dominates (IMF and WB). Consequently, the U.S. and its allies turned down China's proposals to reform the international financial organisations dominated by the U.S., EU and Japan. China considered that the architecture of these institutions did not reflect its economic weight. The Chinese proposals had also sought to diminish China's dependence upon the U.S. dollar that dominates the international finance. Confronted with the hostility of the U.S., China has progressively implemented a strategy to become less dependent on the U.S. dollar. These measures, that together constitute what is often called the 'de-dollarization' of the global economy, include the signing of bilateral swap agreements, that allow the contracting countries to pay trade in their currencies instead of the U.S. dollar; the launch in March 2018 of a yuan-denominated crude oil futures market based in Shanghai; initiatives to create, alone or with some other countries, a new society for enabling financial institutions worldwide to send and receive financial transactions in a secure, standardized and reliable environment, instead of the U.S.-dominated *Society for Worldwide Interbank Financial Telecommunication* (SWIFT) system.

In May 2015, less than two years after the announcement of the AIIB, the Prime Minister made public the 'Made in China 2015' project, thereby making it clear that this time the projection of Chinese manufacturing abroad was going to be based upon its first-class high-tech competencies. At the same time, China started to buy enormous quantities of gold, giving the impression that it was preparing for a change in the international financial system that could be based upon gold. China also started to develop its military resources, thus making it clear to the U.S. that it was prepared to face the massive military presence of U.S. and its allies in the vicinity of its borders.

Simultaneously to these initiatives, China has increased its presence within international organizations, both global and regional, and established cooperation with countries which are also eager to diminish their dependency on the U.S. dollar. This cooperation has also the purpose of ensuring the security of the countries concerned in their region. Finally, China started to develop instruments not only for diffusing its culture all over the world, but also, and maybe mainly, for making accessible to people outside China its position on the many problems that are at stake in the international system. Last but not least, during this period China continued to improve its military resources, as we have seen above. Let me start with the development of China's economy.

China's strategy transition towards an internationalization of its development strategy integrating its national territory and the international territory could have been anticipated by analysing the changes at work in the global economy since at least the end of the 20th century. This trend persisted and even accelerated in 2014 when, during the Ukraine crisis, the U.S. and its European allies put heavy economic sanctions on Russia, thus contributing to the already ongoing development of China-Russia cooperation.

In May 2017, an HSBC briefing note observed that

> the One Belt One Road is an infrastructure initiative conceived and promoted by the Chinese Government to connect more than 65 countries and 4.4 billion people worldwide

corresponding to 40% of world GDP (...) Although potential investment opportunities are very heterogeneous by sector and geographic location, HSBC has highlighted how they tend to focus on areas of strong economic interest for Chinese companies, such as Thailand, Malaysia, Singapore and Indonesia, and sectors such as transport, energy, renewables and industrials through the creation of new and important railway networks, highways, pipelines and electricity networks. (...) the opportunities [for foreign investors] do not come only from the infrastructure side. By 2050 there will be 3 billion people joining the middle class in emerging markets entailing a huge explosion of service demand, including technology but also entertainment or healthcare. HSBC's analysis also points out that most of the projects are now at an early stage of planning and tendering and that is the reason why for European businesses and states this could be a perfect opportunity to join one of the largest economic initiatives in the world.[167]

Despite the criticisms that appeared in the Western media immediately after the announcement of the BRI in September-October 2013, and that persist today, pointing to the imprecisions, difficulties and uncertainties of the project, some attentive observers of the development of China's strategy have understood right from the beginning the importance of the initiative and the threat that it poses to U.S. primacy in Asia, and have tried to anticipate China's 'pivot to the West.'[168] For example, the *Washington Post* had already commented on 24 October 2013:

[Xi Jinping] has eclipsed an American vision of a New Silk Road that was advanced with much fanfare by the then-Secretary of State Hillary Rodham Clinton two years ago and was supposed to revitalize Afghanistan as the link between Central and South Asia. The contrast between the two visions —one with huge sums of money on the table, the other struggling to get off the ground—only underlines how China's

---

167 HSBC 2017, Rapoza 2017.
168 Bao et al. 2013.

ever-growing clout in Asia is challenging the influence of the Unites States.'[169]

There has been an increasing number of acknowledgments by Western media of the success of the BRI since its announcement in 2013, such as a 9 September 2016 article in which *Forbes* recognizes:

> Unfortunately this bold plan [i.e. Clinton's New Silk Road] appears to have flopped before it even got started. Now China is making good of this ambition by integrating Afghanistan in with their BRI initiative (…) As part of this endeavour, a pair of cargo trains departed from two Chinese cities at the end of August bound for Afghanistan.[170]

The Belt and Road Initiative: Encircling the world

What, then, is the real meaning of the BRI initiative? In the West, the policy framework most frequently associated with BRI is geopolitics, meaning that through BRI China is developing its geopolitical strengths to achieve its national goals all over the world.[171] Chinese officials reply that the BRI is not about politics, but about economic cooperation based upon a 'win-win' strategy. Nevertheless, history shows that economic resources have been very frequently used (together with military means, discussed above) to achieve geopolitical goals. An article by the influential *South China Morning Post* of June 2017 says: 'The initiative is supported by US3$ trillion of foreign currency reserves and state-owned enterprises. The new Silk Road also reflects geopolitical ambitions; it shows how the Chinese leadership wants to shape the order of an area that represents more than half the world.'[172] We will see in the future whether China will have been able to avoid this historically demonstrated causal link between economic and military resources and geopolitical ambitions. At minimum, BRI can be considered as China's reaction to U.S. presence in the Far East.[173]

169 Denyer 2013.
170 Shepard, 2016
171 Donnan 2014, Smith Yves 2015, Smith Jeff 2015.
172 Clauss 2017.
173 Two official Chinese documents are worth reading, even if they have been acknowledged with some sarcasm and criticisms by some Western observers: PRC (2015b), 'Vision and Actions on Jointly Building Silk Road Economic Belt and XXI century Maritime Road,' and PRC (2017), *Building the Belt and Road:*

In order to understand the meaning and scope of the BRI, I will first rely again upon Hu Angang's analysis of the strategies implemented by the Chinese leadership to develop the country since 1949 as cited above. In fact, the progression from the first strategy to the fourth help us to understand that the first three strategies led inevitably to the fourth, which projects China abroad, and in fact all over the world.[174] These strategies take into consideration the diversity of the Chinese territory and the human activities developed on it during the 19th century and first half of the 20th century. Hu considers that there have been four successive versions of the regional development strategy corresponding to different development stages. To summarize:

- The first strategy (1949–1978) organized a balanced development thanks to the planned economy but had serious negative consequences, such as poor economic performance, limitation of personal freedom, few incentives for innovations, environmental damages, as well as suffering the catastrophic impact of the Great Leap Forward and the Cultural Revolution.

- The second (1979–1998) prioritized rapid economic development focused on the coastal and western regions thanks to the introduction of market mechanisms and the progressive opening to the global economy; nevertheless, while it developed the economy and reduced poverty, it also increased disparities between regions, provinces and people.

- The third strategy (1999–2013) was based upon a regional balanced development and the reduction of disparities, thanks to investments in the inner and western regions, and the beginning of the development of a modern social security system.

- The fourth strategy (2013–....) 'will not only continue to reduce regional disparity and promote collaborative development among different economic blocks [to be explained below], but also contributes to reshape the world economic geography, innovate international development

---

Concept, Practice and China's Contribution.
174 Hu Angang 2016, Wong et al. 2017.

mode, and construct a new international political and economic order toward the future.'[175]

So, after three stages of development strategy addressed to the
Chinese territory, with the aim of developing the economy (first and second strategies) and to reduce inter-regional disparities (third strategy),
China's fourth development strategy aims at further reducing disparities
and building a developmental bridge between the country and its global
environment.

We now understand that the worries expressed by U.S. politicians,
academics and think tanks were and still are today quite understandable.
While some commentators have defended President Obama's efforts to
keep the U.S. in charge of defining the rules of the international system,
as indicated in his 2016 State of the Union Address where he stated 'with
TPP, China does not set the rules in that region; we do. You want to
show our strength in this new century? Approve this agreement. Give
us the tools to enforce it. It's the right thing to do.'[176] This might well be
regarded as already too late. As I have noted on several occasions, the
changes, i.e. the 'silent transformations,' have been at work since at least
the end of the Cold War, little by little have weakening the dominant
position of the U.S.

The move from internal to external development, which is one of
the main aspects of the BRI, is the logical consequence of these changes
as well as of the development of China's economy. Through the selling
of its products abroad China has accumulated a lot of money that can
be invested in the global economy, has developed over-production in
several sectors that may be sold overseas, and now it needs to import raw
material and energy resources necessary to its economic development.
Therefore, the acceleration and expansion of the trend to 'go out' appears
to be the only rational, and hopefully reasonable and peaceful, move to
sustain a steady, balanced economic development, thus guaranteeing the
traditional Chinese values of stability, unity and harmony.

The fourth development strategy, that establishes for the first time
a clear link between internal regional development and its projection to
the outside world, was included in the 13th Five-year Plan (2016–2020,
adopted March 2016). This overall strategy integrates three regional
development strategies (the Beijing-Tianjin-Hebei, the Yangtze River

175 Hu Angang 2016, p. 1.
176 Obama 2016a.

Economic Zone, and the BRI) in combination with four economic regional blocks, i.e. Northeast, Central, East, and West.[177] The three strategies and the four economic regional blocks are inter-connected to form China's grand strategy, that should reshape China's economic geography. In addition to this, China formulated a special planning for urbanization development for 2014–2020.

Moreover, the fourth strategy aims at further improving the reduction of regional development gaps already started during the third stage (1999–2013) by realizing full coverage of social security in both urban and rural areas (see Chapter 3 subsection, 'The Negative Consequences of Economic Development and the Rebalancing of Chinese Society'). The BRI strategy notably involves all four economic blocks, comprising 25 provincial-level administrative units out of a total of 31,[178] i.e., for the Belt Road: Heilongjiang, Liaoning, Jilin, Henan, Jiangsu, Shaanxi, Gansu, Qinghai, Ningxia, Sinkiang, Chongqing, Sichuan, Yunnan, Guangxi, Tibet, and Inner Mongolia; and for the Maritime Road: Zhejiang, Fujian, Guangdong, Shanghai, Hainan, Liaoning, Tianjin, Shandong, and Guangxi.

So, one can understand the importance China attributes to the BRI strategy not only for its projection abroad but also for the development of its provinces. The fourth Chinese development strategy,

> in particular the BRI, will extend domestic regional development to neighboring countries through strengthening the infrastructure construction with relevant countries and enhance the cooperation in investment, trade, and finance, therefore reshaping world economic geography (…) and more importantly emphasizes the coordinated development among different [Chinese] economic blocks.[179]

---

177 The four blocks are: Northeast (comprising the provinces of Liaoning, Heilongjiang, and Jilin), Central (Shanxi, Henan, Hubei, Hunan, Jiangxi, Anhui), East (Beijing, Tianjin, Hebei, Jiangsu, Zhejiang, Shanghai, Fujian, Guangdong, Hainan, Shandong), West (Inner Mongolia, Sichuan, Chongqing, Yunnan, Guizhou, Shaanxi, Gansu, Qinghai, Ningxia, Sinkiang, Tibet, Guangxi). Source: Hu Angang 2016, p. 16.

178 China has 33 provincial-level administrative units: 22 provinces, 4 municipalities (Beijing, Tianjin, Shanghai and Chongqing), 5 autonomous regions (Guangxi, Inner Mongolia, Tibet, Ningxia, and Xinjiang) and 2 special administrative regions (Hong Kong and Macau). The Hu Angang analysis does not include Hong Kong and Macau.

179 Hu Angang 2016, p. 15.

Therefore, the novelty and the force of the BRI reside not only in the projection of China's economic power abroad, but also as a means to strengthen and coordinate the internal economic and social development of the different parts of China (blocks, provinces, and regions). The analysis of China's four development strategies shows that the Chinese leadership does not rely upon theoretical models defined prior to action, thereby following the traditional Chinese way to understand and implement strategy. On the contrary, action is evaluated upon results, and then, when results are not only positive, but also and inevitably present some important negative aspects (e.g., the increase of disparities of Deng Xiaoping's reforms), then some new steps are defined and implemented (i.e., institutions and policies). And so forth. In Hu Angang's words:

> It needs to be emphasized that no regional development strategy can accomplish its aims in one move. (…) each stage experiences the process of adjustments and upgrading, reflecting the feature of 'learning by doing.' By the same token, the fourth strategy will also experience the process from 'strategy proposal' to 'policy implementation,' 'policy adjustment,' and 'policy maturity' to cope with new opportunities and challenges [i.e., resulting from the evolution of the 'situation potential' from domestic and external development.[180]

There are no *a priori* ideological choices: institutions and policies are not viewed as possessing an intrinsic value, but rather are evaluated on the basis of their capacity to realize the policy goal, i.e. the recovering of world power status, which is the only element of the strategy that does not change, in addition to the safeguard of domestic harmony. Also, China intervenes where and when it has a reasonable chance to succeed. Moreover, insofar as everything is bound to change over time, the Chinese leadership waits until the 'silent transformations' have changed the 'situation potential' to its advantage, in this case instance the distribution of power resources in the international system. Then, it acts within the context of the new situation, e.g. Trump's retreat from the Trans-Pacific Partnership.

It is not necessary to go into too many details inside the BRI to show why this strategy constitutes a serious threat to the 'world America

180 Hu Angang 2016, p. 24.

made' not only in Asia but all over the world. The following information is enough for seeing the scope of the initiative. China has defined five routes for the BRI: three routes for the Road Belt and two for the Maritime Road.

The first route of the Road Belt goes from Northeast China to Northwest China and Europe and the Baltic Sea via Central Asia and Russia; the second goes from North-west China to the Persian Gulf and the Mediterranean Sea, passing through Central Asia and West Asia; and the third from Southwest China through the Indochina Peninsula to the Indian Ocean.

The first route of the Maritime Road starts at coastal ports of China, crosses the South China Sea, passes through the Malacca Strait, and reaches the Indian Ocean, extending to the Mediterranean Sea and Europe; and the second starts at coastal ports of China, crosses the South China Sea, and extends to the South Pacific.[181]

Within the framework of the five routes China has proposed six corridors:

1. the New Eurasian Land Bridge Economic Corridor,
2. the Russia Economic Corridor,
3. the China-Central Asia-West Asia Economic Corridor,
4. the China-Indochina Peninsula Economic Corridor,
5. the China-Pakistan Economic Corridor, and
6. the Bangladesh-China-India-Myanmar Economic Corridor.

Within the corridors the projects are mainly related to infrastructure development in transport (highways, railways), energy (electricity grids, power plants, pipelines, such as the Russia-China pipeline), ports, mining, IT and communications infrastructure, but also cover industrial parks, Special Economic Zones (SEZ), tourism and urban development. Many of the BRI projects had already commenced before 2013 but gained momentum under the Initiative.

Moreover, the project also envisages the interactions and intersections between corridors, and therefore their strategic meaning. For example:

---

181 For the importance of BRI for Europe and the Mediterranean countries see: Putten et al. 2016, and Fardella et al. 2016.

1. The China-Pakistan corridor connects the Road Belt (from Kashgar—Xinjiang Autonomous region) to the Maritime Road in Gwadar, a port city on the southwestern coast of Baluchistan, Pakistan, thus avoiding the Malacca strait.[182]

2. The New Eurasian Land Bridge Economic Corridor connects the China-Mongolia-Russia Economic Corridor.

3. The China-Central Asia-West Asia Economic Corridor that runs through central and eastern Eurasia, connects the economically-dynamic East Asian economic circle and the developed European economic circle, while also building a smooth cooperation channel from the Persian Gulf to the Mediterranean and the Baltic Sea. They make it possible for establishing an efficient and smooth Eurasian market, and create opportunities of development for countries in the hinterland of Eurasia and along the Belt and Road.

4. The China-Indochina Peninsula Economic corridor connects the China-Pakistan Economic Corridor and the Bangladesh-China-India-Myanmar Economic Corridor.

The last two connections run through eastern and southern parts of Asia, the world's most densely populated areas, connecting major cities and populations and industrial clusters along the Belt and Road. The Lancang-Mekong River international sea-lane and regional railways, highways, and oil and gas networks link the Road Belt with the Maritime Silk Road, whose economic radiation effects cover South Asia, Southeast Asia, the Indian Ocean, the South Pacific and other regions.[183] Several corridors and their interconnections show the centrality of Xinjiang province for the development of north-west China, for the connection to central and western Asia (and thereby to Europe) and for the connection

---

182 The importance of the Malacca strait has been stressed by Peter Navarro: '... whoever controls the South China Sea's gateway to the Indian Ocean, through the narrow and perilous Malacca Strait, also controls South Asia—and perhaps East Asia too, given that much of the oil that lights lamps in Japan and South Korea must first pass through the South China Sea.' Navarro 2016, p. 14. See also Navarro 2015. Peter Navarro is an American economist who served as the Assistant to President Trump, Director of Trade and Industrial Policy, and the Director of the White House National Trade Council.

183 Navarro 2015, pp. 11–12.

to Pakistan's Gwadar port, thereby allowing to avoid the Malacca strait and the U.S. Navy to be sidestepped. Moreover, Xinjiang itself is rich in natural resources such as oil and rare earth metals. As we have seen above, the U.S. supports separatist Uighur movements in that province. The withdrawal of the U.S. from Afghanistan, taking place at the moment of writing in a climate of chaos, recriminations and disillusionment about how the U.S. establishment has conducted American foreign policy for several decades, has brought into the open the heightened importance of the China-Pakistan Economic Corridor, already foreseen as proposed by Hillary Clinton's (failed) New Silk Road.[184] The announcement of the U.S. withdrawal has accelerated the cooperation between China, Pakistan and Afghanistan, which has been ongoing for a long time. The importance of this cooperation for China is twofold. First, it will make it possible to better control the transfer of jihadists to Xinjiang. Second, it will complete the development of the China-Pakistan corridor (that avoids the Strait of Malacca) to Afghanistan, which will become a *de facto* part of the China-Pakistan corridor. China's offer to provide what countries such as Afghanistan desperately need, i.e. roads, electricity, medical care, telecommunications and education within the framework of 'win-win' agreements will sharply contrast with the vague promises of democracy and human rights that the U.S. has been unable to deliver during its astonishing 20 years-long failed war. Another blowback for the U.S.

The U.S. withdrawal from Afghanistan has often been qualified as a debacle even by the U.S. mainstream media. Some even do not hesitate to consider it as a neocolonialist war.[185] Nevertheless, while

---

184 For a short and reliable history of the U.S. interventions in Afghanistan see the article by John Pilger, 'The Great Game of Smashing Countries,' *Global Research,* 25 August 2021. Pilger goes back to the 1978 Afghan revolution against the monarchy, which instituted a secular government that introduced equal rights for women and minorities, free medical care and a mass literacy campaign. As a result, women made up half of university students, 40% of doctors, 70% of teachers and 30% of civil servants. For the U.S., the problem was that the Soviet Union supported that government. This was the beginning of an American policy that financed the Afghan mujahedin that it later developed to spread radical Muslim terrorism in pursuit of its interests.

185 The *New York Times* has long been one of the more faithful supporters of the U.S. imperial policy. Its response to the Afghanistan events was reflected in the article it published by Adam Nossiter, 'America's Afghan War: A Defeat Foretold?,' 21 August 2021: 'The war the Americans thought they were fighting against the Taliban was not the war their Afghan allies were fighting. That made

sending a serious clear message to the U.S. bi-partisan leadership, this debacle is not likely to fundamentally reorient the U.S. foreign policy in the foreseeable future. The industrial-military complex, i.e. the core of the U.S. establishment, will not disappear because of the Afghanistan debacle. There are many other parts of the world where the U.S. intervenes by overt and covert warfare, by proxies, and by selling weapons. The good days of the industrial-military complex are far from being over.[186] Moreover, within the framework of the U.S. imperial policy, Afghanistan is (or should we say 'was'?) important not so much for the conduct of the 'war on terrorism,' as for the policy of containment of China. The loss of Afghanistan in 2021 is far from as devastating as the loss of China in 1949. Certainly, the Afghanistan debacle has come after a long series of debacles starting from Korea (1949) that was not recognized as such, thanks to an efficient propaganda orchestrated by the U.S. establishment. Certainly, it will make things more difficult for the U.S., and some American pundits have already started to revise not so much the fundamental goal of containing China, but the means for doing so, as we shall see below. Faced with the negative reactions to these events by a large spectrum of American observers and actors responsible for the U.S. foreign policy, it is necessary for the moment to recognize that two of the major characteristics of the present international system are not likely to fundamentally change in the foreseeable future. First, the fundamental objective of U.S. foreign policy (China containment), as well as the economic, military and diplomacy means for achieving it will remain at the disposal of the U.S. What may change is the admission by the American establishment that the unipolar world the U.S. has dominated since the end of the collapse of the Soviet Union is over, and therefore that containment of China should be implemented within a new strategy.

---

the American war, like other such neocolonialist adventures, most likely doomed from the start. Recent history shows it is foolish for Western powers to fight wars in other people's lands, despite the temptations. Homegrown insurgencies, though seemingly outmatched in money, technology, arms, air power and the rest, are often better motivated, have a constant stream of new recruits, and often draw sustenance from just over the border.'

186 See, for example, the article by Prof. Karl Grossman, 'Insane U.S. Plan to spend Billions on Weaponizing Space Makes Defense Contractors Jump for Joy—But Rest of World Cowers in Horror at Prospect of New Arms Race Leading to World War III,' Global Research, 26 August 2021. Interestingly, the author mentions that while the U.S. has developed this policy for decades (strengthened by President Trump and confirmed by President Biden), China, Russia and Canada have always been in favor of a weapons-free space.

Moreover, the U.S. may start to address some of the major aspects of its weakness, i.e. its internal contradictions: income inequality, poverty, racism, education system, infrastructure. Second, neither will China's objective to become again a world power change, nor its means to realize it, i.e. the Belt and Road grand strategy. We have already seen that this strategy is very complex and goes well beyond the consequences that the positioning of Afghanistan with the U.S. or with China may have.

Clearly, as it stands today, the BRI is beyond the stage of a project. The BRI website[187] provides updated information about dozens of projects approved and in implementation phase. Several features of BRI are clearly intended to challenge the U.S. power in Asia and in the rest of the world. Again, the China-Pakistan Corridor is meant to avoid the passage through the Malacca strait where the U.S. Navy may forbid Chinese trade with its suppliers of raw material and energy resources, in case of serious disagreements with China;[188] similarly, the numerous railways from China to Europe permit China to trade with Europe by land, thus avoiding the shipment of goods by sea, where the U.S. so far has a clear superiority that may be used to block trade between China and Europe. Moreover, the corridors to Europe, as well as its investments in European ports, e.g. the Port of Piraeus, make it possible for China to compete with the U.S. on the territory of its traditional European allies. The same is true for the roads to the Middle East. Finally, the maritime road from China to the Pacific region may open the Americas to China, where it has already invested heavily.

Let us note that China is planning yet another route, i.e., an Arctic shipping channel. There are multiple strategic reasons for sustaining this project: to avoid the geopolitical risk deriving from the competition with the U.S. when passing through the already existing maritime routes; to avoid passing through politically unstable regions (e.g. for the Road Belt); and to avoid the difficulty of passing though regions with different religions and cultures; all thereby avoiding energy security risks, already mentioned regarding the competition with the U.S., as is the case for the BRI Maritime Road. This new route

> refers to the Arctic shipping channel which is the ocean shipping channel connecting the Pacific Ocean and the Atlantic Ocean via the Arctic Ocean, including the North-east channel

---

187 http://english.www.gov.cn/beltAndRoad/
188 Navarro 2016, p.14.

(also known as the Northern channel) and the North-west channel. As the shortest sea route connecting North-east Asia and Western Europe, the North-east channel starts from the northern waters of north-west Europe in the west and reaches Vladivostok at the east, passing through Barents Sea, Kara Sea, Rapp Jeff Sea, Novosibirsk Sea and the Bering Strait. The North-east channel is currently navigable for 2–3 months, and the entire route reaches Sweden, Iceland, Finland, Russia and other countries.[189]

The BRI has attracted much criticism and fears from Western official public bodies, pundits and mainstream media.[190] However, many Western influential observers consider that the BRI is on its way to becoming the greatest economic and geo-political endeavor ever. For example, the first page of the HSBC site dealing with the BRI (dated 9 March 2018) says that

> China's Belt and Road is now gaining greater impetus with 67 countries partnered with China. (…) Trade between countries that link the officially named 'One Belt, One Road' project, already exceeded USD 3 trillion between 2014 and 2016, with China's investment in these nations surpassing USD 50 billion. (…) Already BRI is extending beyond China's immediate neighbours and into regions and countries not traditionally known for their economic links with Beijing. The Asian Infrastructure Investment Bank (AIIB), Silk Road Fund and the New Development Bank have also already committed roughly USD1.1 trillion to develop infrastructure under the banner of the BRI.

The *South China Morning Post* (*SCMP*) has admitted that the BRI 'may have its flaws, but some critics are taking it too far,' such as then U.S. Vice-President Mike Pence 'who launched a savage attack

---

189 Hu Angang et al. 2017, see also PEN Charitable Trust 2017.
190 In addition to the U.S. official documents analysed above (especially the U.S. Intelligence Agency report), one can consult the reports by the European Union and of the Mercator Institute for China Studies (MERICS), the HSBC bank's site, the Belt and Road Portal of the Chinese government, The BRI website, and the analyses by influential media such as the *Financial Times*, the *Caixin*, and the *South China Morning Post.*

on Chinese "debt trap" tactic during the APEC summit last November [2018].' According to the *SCMP* Pence declared: '"we don't drown our partners in a sea of debt [and] we don't coerce or compromise your independence."' The *SCMP* then observed with regard to Pence's ridiculous claim that: 'this was a bit rich given the way that U.S. banks lent billions of dollars to Latin America causing a huge debt crisis there in the 1980s. Ditto at the time of the Asian Debt Crisis [1997].'[191]

On its site devoted to the BRI, the *SCMP* informs its readers of the progress of five major projects within the BRI that have strong symbolic, economic and political impacts:

- the railways to London,
- the Gwadar Port in Pakistan (that allows China to avoid the Malacca Strait), the railway to Iran,
- the Asian gas pipeline, and
- the Khorgos Gateway, that it qualifies as 'a new Dubai in China.'[192]

The analysis of the development of U.S. foreign policy does seem to be different from that of Trump-Pence administration (addressed above, and in Chapter 2).

More recently, the most influential U.S. think tank on foreign policy, the Council on Foreign Relations (CFR) has set up an impressive Independent Task Force to evaluate the implications of the BRI for the U.S., comprising no fewer than 29 members and 9 observers. Its 79th Report (2021) allows one to see the extent to which the BRI is considered as a threat to the leading role of the U.S., and to the preservation of the world America made.[193]

The Executive Summary to the Report considers that

the BRI, the world's largest infrastructure programme, poses a significant challenge to U.S. economic, political, climate change, security, and global health interests. The initiative has since outgrown the original corridors outlined by Xi

---

191 SCMP, 20 January 2019.
192 The U.S. government has officially identified the ten largest BRI projects for a total of $US 90 billion, of which 4 under construction, 2 constructions expected 2019/19, 2 MOU signed, 1 feasibility study completed, and 1 under review (U.S. 2019, p. 13).
193 Council on Foreign Relations 2021.

and become a globe-spanning enterprise encompassing 139 countries (although not every country that has formally signed on to BRI hosts BRI projects), with Latin America (the traditional—since the 1823 Monroe Doctrine as the exclusive back-garden of the U.S.) added as a 'natural extension of the 21st Century Maritime Silk Road.' BRI's scope has also grown, becoming a more amorphous undertaking, with China adding a Digital Silk Road (DSR), Health Silk Road (HSR), and Green Belt and Road, which are unbounded geographically. (This quotation is from the main Report, all the other quotations are from the Executive Summary).

How has this been possible? The Report explains, not without reasons (emphasis added):

U.S. inaction as much as Chinese assertiveness is responsible for the economic and strategic predicament in which the United States finds itself:

• *U.S. withdrawal helped create the vacuum that China filled with BRI.*

• Although the United States long ago identified an interest in promoting infrastructure, trade, and connectivity throughout Asia (...) it has not met the inherent needs of the region.

• Its *own lending to and investment in many BRI countries was limited and is now declining.*

• *Its cutbacks in research and development and investments in advanced technologies* have allowed China to move ahead in the development and sale of fifth generation (5G) technology, the installation of high-speed rail, the production of solar and wind energy, the promulgation of electronic payment platforms, the development of ultra-high-voltage transmission systems, and more.

• Despite enjoying a leading role in the World Bank and regional development banks, the United States *has watched those institutions move away from backing significant infrastructure projects.*

- Washington has not joined regional trade and investment agreements that would have enhanced U.S. economic ties to Asia.

The CFR thus recognizes one of the main features of China's strategy: when the potential in the international environment is favourable, it acts as quickly as possible. If you wait, the situation is likely to change, and you will, have lost the 'magic' moment. The CFR goes on to say that

> if BRI meets little competition or resistance, Beijing could become the hub of global trade, set important technical standards that would disadvantage non-Chinese companies, lock countries into carbon-intensive power generation, have greater influence over countries' political decisions, and acquire more power-projection capabilities for its military. The United States has a clear interest in adopting a strategy that both pressures China to alter its BRI practices and provides an effective alternative to BRI—one that promotes sustainable infrastructure, upholds high environmental and anticorruption standards, ensures U.S. companies can operate on a level playing field, and assists countries in preserving their political independence.

The U.S. response has been: 'America is back.' But what can be done in deeds and not only in words? The CFR recognizes that the U.S.' means to implement such a policy are limited:

> *The United States cannot and should not respond to BRI symmetrically,* attempting to match China dollar for dollar or project for project. Instead, the United States should focus on those areas where it can offer, either on its own or in concert with like-minded nations, a compelling alternative to BRI.

The CFR recommends:

- *leading a global effort* to address emerging BRI-induced debt crises and to promote adherence to high-standards lending practices;

- enhancing U.S. commercial diplomacy to promote U.S. high-quality, high-standards alternatives to BRI and to *raise public awareness in host countries of the environmental and economic costs of certain BRI projects*;

- *offering technical support to BRI countries* to help them vet prospective projects for economic and environmental sustainability; and embarking on a robust *anticorruption campaign*

- Several measures to improve U.S. competitiveness

- To strengthen the multilateral response to BRI, [in particular] *working with allies and partners to re-energize the World Bank so that it can offer a better alternative to BRI.*

Finally, the CFR takes stock of the success of the BRI:

> Though principally aimed at developing countries, with Pakistan, Malaysia, Bangladesh, Myanmar, and Sri Lanka among the largest recipients of BRI funds, BRI also includes developed countries, with numerous U.S. allies participating.

And the CFR warns that:

> if these U.S. allies were to turn to BRI to build critical infrastructure, such as power grids, ports, or telecommunications networks, this could complicate U.S. contingency planning and make coming to the defence of its allies more difficult.

Although the strategy suggested by the CFR report recognizes that the U.S. *cannot and should not respond to BRI symmetrically*, attempting to match China dollar for dollar or project for project, it nevertheless remains in line with the traditional U.S. foreign policy: criticise China for wrongdoings, many of which the U.S. has itself practised for a long time; place itself as the only possible leading country able to save the world from 'China's aggressions'; for this purpose, work with same-minded liberal democracies with capitalist economy in a leading position, it goes without saying; work with international organizations such as the World Bank, the International Monetary Fund and multilateral development banks to support worthy development projects, i.e. with organizations that have lost their credibility not only with developing countries, but also with U.S. allies including several European countries. Not really a brilliant alternative to the BRI. But then, the question is: what *can* be done?

Two articles published by two leading mainstream media give an idea of the overall alternatives to address the dilemma in which the U.S. are stuck: either continue the traditional imperial policy or change perspective. An article by the *Wall Street Journal* seems to support the dominant position represented by the CFR.[194] It complains about China's strategy to become the world's most powerful country, in particular through the BRI. It then casts this glimmer of hope: 'much of the world is becoming uneasy with China's unremitting aggression on its home turf in Asia,' which it supported by the inevitable references to China's actions, the taking

> down of democracy in Hong Kong; started military spats with India, disrupted life for tens of millions by damaging the headwaters of the Mekong River; conducted what the U.S. government now deems a campaign of genocide against Muslim Uighurs; escalated tensions with Japan over the Senkaku Islands; made repeated bellicose gestures designed to test the international community's resistance to 'unifying' the 'renegade province' of Taiwan.

What else?

More in tune with the real situation of the relations between the U.S. and China and their respective power resources, an article published by Eyck Freymann in the no less influential *Fortune*, starts by confirming, almost word for word, the statement of the CFR mentioned above: 'The U.S. does not need to match China dollar for dollar, project for project. But it should at the very least be in the arena, working with the private sector, the World Bank, International Monetary Fund, and multilateral banks to support worthy development projects.'[195] But then, he elaborates somewhat on the mainstream's evaluations when taking stock of the development of the BRI project:

---

194 Webb 2021.
195 Freymann 2021. Eyck Freymann is Indo-Pacific director at Greenmantle, an investment strategy firm, and author of *One Belt and Road: Chinese Power Meets the World*, Harvard University.

[the BRI] is expanding conceptually. China is now pushing a Polar Silk Road [the Arctic shipping channel mentioned above] to link China to the Arctic and Antarctic; a Digital Silk Road of underseas cables, data centres, and 5G telecommunications systems; a Health Silk Road to promote Chinese Covid vaccines; a green Silk Road for exporting subsidized Chinese renewable technology; and [the BRI] space information corridor to supplant GPS as the world's leading satellite navigation system.

Then Freymann quite rightly mentions the positive aspect of China's BRI strategy that it will be difficult to ignore:

China is not preying on victims; it is attracting willing partners. This is because China is offering a suite of economic, political, and technological perks that the U.S. does not. That include the intangible but hugely significant ability to trust that China will deliver in a moment of crisis.

Then comes the reasonable question:

If BRI is actually so dangerous and predatory, why does China keep finding so many willing partners? The U.S. cannot stop the inexorable expansion of Xi's massive project without making a better counteroffer to countries considering alignment with China. In other words, America needs to stop criticizing and start competing.

But can the U.S. compete?

The Council on Foreign Relations report, as well as the official U.S. documents analysed above, show the frequent tendency of the U.S. experts to attribute to China several negative aspects of its foreign policy that the U.S. itself has implemented for several decades, in fact for centuries: from the Indian Wars to the Second Cold War of today. If this were only irritating and also ridiculous, those following world events could certainly put up with it. Unfortunately, it is also very dangerous as it runs the risk of maintaining the world in a perpetual state of war (cold or warm, overt or covert) where the U.S. establishment tries by all means to impose upon others an organization of the world that satisfies the realisation of its own economic and power interests. And doing so under the cover of diffusing democracy and human rights. The BRI is a long-term project, extending over 25 to 30 years. Time will tell if it succeeds and how. The analysis of the foreign policies of China and the U.S. in the changing world system presented in this book, do not allow us to forecast that China will replace the U.S. as the sole superpower. Nevertheless, China is irrefutably already becoming a world power, and if it does not commit major mistakes (and it has not made any since 1978) it will certainly become, in a not-too-distant future, a new world power on equal footing with the U.S. So far, China is achieving this objective without using its military power (that is not even mentioned in the official BRI documents), except as a means to deter the type of aggressions it suffered during the 19th century.

It's true that the BRI initiative looks like a grandiose project, many parts of which are still to be defined, accepted and implemented. Nevertheless, it has already achieved remarkable results, including the contribution (with some other emerging and re-emerging powers) of awakening in American leaders the feeling (and maybe for some even the certitude) that the U.S. is no longer the sole superpower.

That said, the BRI should be regarded as a contemporary mani-festation of the Chinese traditional way of defining and implementing strategy. The general framework is described in general, but in meaning-ful terms. It is during the 'practice' of its implementation that actual deci-sions, international agreements, and formal projects are chosen, accepted by other countries, and implemented, depending upon the actual oppor-tunities that the evolving 'situation potential' presents to the Chinese leadership. The difference with the first three development strategies (ex-plained above), especially with the second one of Deng Xiaoping, is that the general objective is expressed more openly and transparently. China is today strong enough to publicly declare its objectives and ambitions.

It suffices to add to this, taking into consideration the grandiose presentation of the project, that the BRI is not simply a new 'economic geography' of China, nor a simple 're-shaping of the world economic geography.' BRI is above all a geo-strategic project that, if fully realized, will allow China to reclaim its status as a world power, thereby putting an end to the unipolar 'world America made.'

CONCLUSION

If America is Back, What Kind of America Is It?

America is back, we are told. But just as for all things there is a season, so too is there for empires. Both are born, develop, reach the apex of their vibrancy and power, then decline, and finally disappear. At which point is America, given this reality encoded in humanity's historical evolution? An answer came when, at the moment of finalizing the writing of this conclusion, protest movements exploded in Cuba. Immediately American mainstream media, right-wing politicians and right-wing Cuban expats rushed to support the Cuban people who, it was claimed, were 'demanding freedom from the Communist dictatorship.' President Biden was also quick in publicly declaring his support. On 12 July 2021 the White House published his statement (emphasis added):

> We stand with the Cuban people and their clarion call for *freedom* and relief from the tragic grip of the pandemic and from the *decades of repression* and economic suffering to which they have been subjected by *Cuba's authoritarian regime*. The Cuban people are bravely asserting *fundamental and universal rights*. Those rights, including the *right of peaceful protest* and the right to freely determine their own future, must be respected. The United States calls on the Cuban regime to hear their people and serve their needs at this vital moment rather than enriching themselves.

As it is well known that the U.S. has tried on several occasions to kill Fidel Castro and to invade the country, and moreover has imposed upon Cuba cruel embargos and sanctions for more than 60 years despite annual UN near-unanimous votes to rescind them, it is not possible to refrain from qualifying Biden's statement as hypocritical, demagogic and cynical. The U.S. blames the Cuban government for the problems the country is presently facing, despite the fact that U.S. sanctions have devastated the lives of the Cuban people. And in spite of this, Cuba, a small country of 11 million people, has succeeded in resisting for such a long time, developing in particular an efficient and globally respected health system. Cubans are experiencing serious difficulties, but they are not starving. The goal of sanctions is to make the living conditions of the people so desperate that they would finally rebel against the government and call upon the U.S. to 'liberate them from the tyranny of a dictatorial regime.' One cannot but recall President Nixon telling his staff to impose sanctions on Chile in 1973, with the clear purpose of making the Chilean 'economy scream' in preparation for the regime change that followed. The U.S. strategy has not changed, as sanctions are used for the same purpose against Iran, Venezuela, Syria as for a multitude of other countries, and but for unfortunate Chile, appear to have had contrary effect.

China is a particular case of the U.S. addiction to imposing sanctions on countries who do not comply with its interests, the use of using internal problems (that are real) in an attempt to destabilize the country and, most optimistically in its view, to produce a regime change. As we have seen in Chapter 3, under 'The Folly of Regime Change and Subversive Activities,' the U.S. targets China by interfering in three very sensitive regions: Hong Kong, Xinjiang and Tibet.[1] This happens in the midst of a surge in anti-China propaganda embedded into the U.S. Cold War mentality, with the usual mix of sanctions, military build-up in the China Seas, and support to subversive activities within China. Moreover, the U.S. is trying to convince its allies in Europe and in Asia to unite against the purported existential threat represented by China. The same aggressive policy is also directed against Russia. Taking stock of the various policy initiatives taken by the U.S. and its allies, some U.S. columnists do not hesitate to qualify this war against China and Russia as a fight of the civilized nations to deter the non-civilized ones.[2] It is

---

1 Several U.S. federal laws have been approved by the U.S. Senate with an overwhelming majority concerning these three areas: The Hong Kong Human Rights and Democracy Act, The Uyghur Human Rights Policy Act, The Uyghur Forced Labour Prevention Act, The Tibet Policy and Support Act.

2 George F. Will: 'Opinion: Civilized nations' efforts to deter Russia and China are starting to add up,' *Washington Post*, July 16, 2021: 'It is, therefore, well to notice how, day by day, in all of the globe's time zones, civilized nations are, in word and deed, taking small but cumulatively consequential measures that serve deterrence.' George F. Will writes a twice-weekly column on politics and domestic and foreign affairs. He began his column with the Post in 1974, and he received the Pulitzer Prize for commentary in 1977. His latest book, The Conservative Sensibility, was released in June 2019.

therefore not surprising that China and Russia have formed a *de facto* alliance.

The U.S. foreign policy of President Biden clearly demonstrates a shift towards the globalization of the NATO alliance.[3] Thus, contrary to its original *raison d'être*, the containment of Soviet Russia, NATO is on track to become a global alliance for the perpetuation of the U.S. empire. In chapter 3.1, I have shown that, based upon the first months of the Biden administration, there will be no changes in the U.S. foreign policy despite the verbal announcements that the U.S. foreign policy of President Trump will undergo a fundamental change: diplomacy is back. Unfortunately, the Biden administration has made it clear that the military build-up will continue, as well as the demonization of the enemy. But the contradictions between the declared U.S. priority to diplomacy and the persistence of U.S. sanctions, overt and covert military actions, and subversive activities against countries that do not comply with the interests of the establishment of the U.S. Empire are becoming ever more evident to global publics and elites, who may finally start getting the bigger picture

This zero-sum perspective on conducting international relations, based upon the opposition between WE with our values, and THEM against our values, is reminiscent of the famous 'We against Them' of President George W. Bush, or his father's four-word implicit threat, 'What We Say, Goes.' This is making the traditional U.S. foreign policy even more sclerotic. The U.S. is in reality beginning the first stages of an undeclared war against the existential threat China is representing for its liberal democracy and capitalism model.

THE IMPORTANCE OF VALUES FOR THE IMPLEMENTATION OF U.S. FOREIGN POLICY

Biden's foreign policy is based upon the primacy of values—which may seem paradoxical, given U.S. actual actions. Values are not valid if they remain stuck in the stratosphere of ideology. In order to acquire real value, they must be implemented in reality, both at home and abroad. Now, for five centuries the European countries first, and then the U.S., have manifested the habit of *not* implementing those values abroad. While the U.S. liberated Germany, Italy, Japan and South Korea from dictatorship at the end of WW2, the liberation was immediately followed by military occupation and the stationing of military bases. Moreover,

---

3 Mahdi Darius Nazemroaya , The Globalization of NATO, Clarity Press, 2012.

that liberation was conditional: the liberated countries were not only to change to democracy and capitalism, but they above all they had to become the allies of the Empire, obviously in a subordinate position. The manner in which Biden has called upon U.S. allies to unite against China and Russia leaves no doubt about how the U.S. sees its role in the world, and its relations with its allies—in fact as its vassals. This is reminiscent of Jefferson's statement referred to in Chapter 2: 'We are destined to be a barrier against the return of ignorance and barbarism. Old Europe will have to lean on our shoulders, and to hobble along by our side.'[4]

As for the implementation of values domestically, not only is the U.S. a non-democracy, it is, more precisely, a plutocracy. There is sufficient empirical evidence indicating that European countries have been following the same pattern. It is true that President Biden has put forward several initiatives for improving the living conditions of the American people: the American Rescue Plan, healthcare, taxes (i.e., a taxation system more in tune with the fiscal capacity of the taxpayers), student debt, workers' rights, 'made in all of America,' infrastructure and climate change, rural America, and the American middle class. Very commendable—if in fact they proceed from campaign rhetoric and even manage to achieve legal enactment! Two *caveats* with a negative prognosis. First, many of these initiatives go contrary to the traditional way the establishment has managed its relationship with the American people, giving priority to the interests of its component sectors, with the support of those who make their living by so doing, e.g., mainstream scholars, journalists, and think tanks. Second, and equally important, these values must also be implemented in the international arena, when in fact the U.S. is already trying to engage the world in a new Cold War.[5]

It must be said that this type of behaviour does not find its origin with the U.S. After all, Americans came out of Europe, as Eve came out from Adam's rib. And they took with them the main features of the European

---

4 Jefferson 1816. It is interesting to note that 'old Europe' has been used on 22 January 2003 by Secretary of Defence Donald Rumsfeld, two centuries after Jefferson used it.

5 President Biden delivered a self-congratulatory speech to commemorate his achievements during the first six months in office ('The White House: Remarks by President Biden Before Cabinet Meeting to Mark Six Months in Office,' 20 July 2021). But even *The Guardian*, that for several years has become a supporter of the U.S.-led crusade against China and Russia, has been less optimistic (*The Guardian:* 'Joe Biden: six months on, cold, hard reality eclipses early euphoria,' 18 July 2021).

culture. Certainly, it can be argued that the U.S. has brought several features of the European culture close to perfection. Unfortunately, those it perfected were not the best ones. If the West really wants to develop a constructive relationship with the rest of the world, it must first look unflinchingly at the years of its troubled past. Especially if it wants to promote itself as a model that the rest of the world should embrace. Western civilisation is indeed a great one. It developed through at least two and a half millennia to reach today's form: Greek philosophy, Roman law, Christianity, the scientific revolution, the passage from the slave and serf-based economy of the Middle Ages (using a form of slavery, the serfs of the glebe) to a new form of economy—market economy (albeit with wage slavery), the industrial revolution, the liberal revolution with its ideas of democracy, human rights, freedom and individual responsibility, and the socialist counter-revolution with its idea of collective responsibility. It is a great civilization, especially because of the ideas and values it has developed for itself and promoted to the rest of the world. It is much less great (to say the least) for its deeds.

THE BETRAYAL OF VALUES BY WESTERN COUNTRIES' FOREIGN POLICY

European countries first and then the U.S., have invaded the rest of the world since the discovery of the Americas. Since the beginning this has been done in the interests of the elites, who launched an unending series of aggression and conquest wars, including among themselves. Most people do not want to go to war. They want to live peacefully and have a reasonable income in order to lead a decent life. But the Western establishment (European first, then the American) out of greed devastated the Americas, committing one of the worst genocides ever through the centuries-long wars against indigenous peoples in the northern and southern hemispheres, and by organizing a large-scale trade of African slaves. In the U.S. slavery lasted from 1619 (arrival of the first slaves) to the end of the civil war (1865), followed by a century of apartheid. Meanwhile, the Europeans (soon joined by Americans) were busy in submitting the whole of Africa, large parts of the Middle East and of Asia to the dictatorship and exploitation of the colonial powers. Many Western pundits take pride in referring to the fact that after independence their former colonies introduced several features of liberal democracy, e.g., India. But the West should not be too proud of this achievement. Just read the statement by Shashi Tharoor in his book significantly entitled

Inglorious Empire. What the British Did to India: 'Indians can never afford to forget the conditions in which they found our country after two centuries of colonialism.'[6] The era of colonialism and the struggle between Western (mainly European) countries for the conquest of the colonies ended with the apotheosis of the two world wars they themselves had started. The argument that WW2 was for the good cause notwithstanding, it led to tens of millions of deaths on battlefields and elsewhere, including the slaughter of hundreds of thousands of Japanese and German people guilty of having not been able to oppose the rise of Nazi-fascism in their countries.

Then came the glorious time of decolonization—unfortunately only in words, as many of the 'liberated' colonies were soon submitted to neocolonialism under the yoke of the so-called Washington Consensus, through which the Western countries continued to exploit their former colonies. The U.S. was quick to step in, using the economic international organizations it set up to serve its economic and power interests (World Bank, International Monetary Fund). Both Europeans and Americans hypocritically hid their real motives under the pretence of helping these countries to develop their economy. Ha-Joon Chang quite rightly qualified these new colonizers as 'bad Samaritans.'[7] Real emancipation from the colonial era became an impossible mission for the great majority of these countries. Only countries that had already started the transition to modernization, such as Japan and South Korea, were able to develop their economies thanks to a strategy based upon the leading role of their governments, which was permitted and even encouraged by the U.S., providing they accepted its dominant role, in order to project them as a developmental competitor to Asian Communism, much as occurred with Germany and the USSR in Europe.

During the immediate post-WW2 era, the U.S. established an astonishing number of military bases in the liberated countries: 119 in Germany, 44 in Italy, 25 in the UK, 119 in Japan, 80 in South Korea. How can a country be free under such circumstances? Then came the time of the regional wars (warm and cold) with their deaths, mutilations, displacements and massacres: Korea, Vietnam, Iraq, Afghanistan, Syria, Libya—not counting more or less violent regime changes in Latin America, and elsewhere. Add to this the frequent use of sanctions, should the targeted countries not comply with the U.S. dictates, most of

---

6 Tharoor 2016, p. 216.
7 Chang, Ha-Joon 2008.

the time with the willing or coerced support of its European and Asian allies. Moreover, during this era the U.S. set up several secret armies in European countries during the Cold War, launched 13 illegal wars during and after the Cold War, attempted at least 81 meddlings in other countries' elections during and after the Cold War, and at least 59 attempts at regime change during and after the Cold War, while setting up numerous illegal prisons where torture of U.S. enemies could be secretly practiced.

THEN CAME THE TIME OF BLOWBACKS TO U.S. FOREIGN POLICY

Then came the time of the blowbacks or, as they are sometimes called, the historical nemesis that comes in the wake of hubris. Some countries developed enough power resources to be able to resist the dictates of the Empire. Already during the Trump Administration, the U.S. witnessed several 'blowbacks.' To begin with, North Korea resisted the explicit menace in the form of bombastic language that it would be 'obliterated' from the earth by the U.S. military power, should it fail to comply with the U.S. demand to de-nuclearize. Then, the attempted regime changes in Syria, Venezuela and Iran failed. Moreover, these countries have been supported by the existential enemies of the U.S.: China and Russia. Even more worrying, not only Russia and China have been cementing their *de facto* alliance, but China and Iran have concluded a mega-agreement covering a large number of strategic domains.

Two more important blowbacks came during the transition from the Trump to the Biden administrations. On 15 November 2020, 15 countries, led by China, signed the Regional Comprehensive Economic Partnership (RCEP), the world's largest trade bloc, comprising 2.3 billion people and covering 30% of global trade. An influential mainstream think-tank did not hesitate to qualify this agreement as 'a geopolitical win for China.'[8] Then another important 'blowback' came, as Europe gave a clear message to the U.S. on 30 December 2020 by signing an important trade and investment deal with China: the China-EU Comprehensive Agreement on Investment (CAI). A few days later, another mainstream think-tank qualified this deal as a Biden defeat.[9] It is true that the approval of this agreement has since been suspended by the European parliament, very likely under pressure from the U.S. Nevertheless, the fundamental reasons that explain why the EU signed it will not vanish in

8 Ward 2020; see also the *Financial Times*: Brunsden 2020 et al.
9 Barfield 2021.

the foreseeable future. France, Italy, and above all Germany, as well as other European countries, have clear economic interests in cooperating with China. This does not mean that they approve of China's political system. In fact, contrary to the U.S., their analysis of the international situation is not based exclusively upon values but is closer to reality than that of the U.S., which is stuck in its foreign policy that gives prominence to values. More worrying, the U.S. establishment does not seem to understand the meaning of these 'clear messages' and has embarked on a crusade against China and Russia, while trying to gain the support of its European and Asian allies, albeit against their interests.

At the beginning of the Biden Administration, several additional clearer messages have been delivered to the U.S. establishment. First at the Alaska meeting between American and Chinese top diplomats (19 March 2021), and second at the Geneva meeting between Biden and Putin (16 June 2021). During these meetings, top leaders of the two 'existential threats' made it very clear that they were not going to kowtow to the U.S. When accused of violating universal values, they both fought back, reminding the U.S. of its troubled past, as well to its current violations of these same values, both at home and abroad.

Then, July 1, 2021, at the anniversary of the foundation of the Communist Party of China, President Xi Jinping made China's message even clearer. He started his speech by reminding the audience and the world that after the Opium War of 1840, China had been gradually reduced to a semi-colonial, semi-feudal society and suffered greater ravages than ever before. The country had endured intense humiliation, the people were subjected to great pain, and the Chinese civilization was plunged into darkness. Since that time, national rejuvenation has been the greatest dream of the Chinese people and the Chinese nation. Then, he implicitly referred to Mao's 1949 statement:

> Ours will no longer be a nation subject to insult and humiliation,' and confirmed it: 'through tenacious struggle, the Party and the Chinese people showed the world that the Chinese people had stood up, and that the time in which the Chinese nation could be bullied and abused by others was gone forever.

These three events constitute an epochal change in the relations between the U.S. and China and Russia. They are visible and audible manifestations of the 'silent transformations' that have changed the balance of power since the collapse of the Soviet Union, and in fact had already started to be visible and audible at the end of WW2. Mao's statement was certainly at that time a cry of hope for a better future more than a reality. In fact, the bullying of China went on for several decades after 1949. But Xi Jinping's statement stands, without doubt, as a very serious warning to China's enemies, and above all the U.S.: It was China's 'Yes, we can!'

Xi Jinping's statement should be taken very seriously, and not as a simple variation in Chinese rhetoric. The first event that showed the reality of this statement occurred in August 2021, a few weeks after Xi Jinping's speech: the chaotic and humiliating withdrawal of the U.S. from Afghanistan. As explained above,[10] Afghanistan is one of the dimensions of the Belt and Road Initiative (BRI), i.e. China's grand strategy, through which China 'is encircling the world,' as the influential *Financial Times* had already asserted in 2017.[11] One of the most important components of the BRI, the China-Pakistan corridor, connects the Road Belt (from Kashgar–Xinjiang Autonomous region) to the Maritime Road in Gwadar, a port city on the southwestern coast of Pakistan, thus avoiding the Malacca Strait and the U.S. navy. For several years China has been negotiating with the Taliban, offering to build what Afghanistan desperately needs: roads, railways, electricity, medical care, telecommunications and education. In exchange China asks the Taliban to control the transfer of jihadists to Xinjiang where they act as U.S. proxies destabilizing this province situated on the BRI. Put more plainly, China is planning for Afghanistan to become a *de facto* part of the China Pakistan corridor: the U.S. out, China in.

It is my view that the loss of Afghanistan has been exaggerated by all the components of the U.S. establishment. One can understand their reaction, given the shock of the humiliation delivered by a 'bunch of peasants' wanting to retake control of their underdeveloped country—and this after 20 years of war with the most sophisticated weaponry, billions of USD of American taxpayers' money, and devastating consequences for Afghan civilians. Yet, Afghanistan is only one piece of the puzzle of the Asian chessboard on which China and the U.S. are competing.

A more significant consequence is the impact that this defeat may have on the morale of the U.S. establishment and its allies. Already

10 Chapter 3, 'The Belt and Road Initiative: Encircling the world.'
11 Hancock, (2017).

China has warned Taiwan not to count on the faithfulness of the U.S. to its allies when it considers that its national interests are no longer at stake.[12] Even more particularly worrying for the American people and the rest of the world is the possibility that the U.S. establishment might succumb (again) to the temptation of using even more military means in order to recover confidence in the U.S. ability to impose its will. As this book has suggested on several occasions, doing otherwise would entail a radical revision of the way the U.S. sees the world and its role within this world, towards a more cooperative attitude toward the countries it considers as its existential threats: China and Russia. But is the U.S. establishment ready to at least explore this path? The problem for the U.S. is that not only is China back, but it has been back for a couple of decades since its accession to the WTO, without the U.S. recognizing its rise as a world power. China, it is not likely to be intimidated. So, yes, China can!

YES, CHINA CAN!

That China can, is first confirmed by how China has implemented its strategy for making Mao's statement come true. China has been successful, thanks to a long series of actions, when it had a reasonable chance to succeed, and non-actions, waiting for the 'silent transformations' to change the 'situation potential' to its advantage, both nationally and internationally. By doing so it succeeded in trapping the U.S. into a fixed position from which it seems unable to escape, i.e., continuing to implement a foreign policy based upon the threat, and eventually the actual use of economic and military resources. During the same period of time, China has given the impression of being all the time on the move, evolving from one stage to the other: from the economy to the military, technology, investments abroad, training of talents, and the diffusion of Chinese culture; from copying the West to innovating autonomously; from opening up its economy to the world to protecting its national market from predatory capitalists; from pursuing bilateral agreements to establishing new multilateral organizations; from asserting local interests (the China Seas, Taiwan) to developing global interests in Eurasia, Africa, Latin America, and the Arctic; from criticizing traditional enemies (e.g. Japan and India) to negotiating with them, and so on. Thereby,

---

12 All the commentators have inevitably referred to the humiliating evacuation of the U.S. embassy in Saigon in 1975.

China has confirmed François Jullien and André Chieng's assessment of the essence of strategy:

> the essence of strategy is on the one hand to gradually trap the competitor into a fixed position [i.e. from which it cannot escape] upon which the strategist can act, and on the other hand to constantly change its position in order to make its own strategy incomprehensible to the competitor' ... and when it starts to understand it, it is too late.[13]

Not being able to take stock of one's mistakes is clearly the foolish habit of the U.S. establishment. As the Chinese calligrapher Lei Pingyang would say: 'foolishness is like bamboo, empty inside but unshakable (*chǔn zhě ruòzhú: zhōngkōng ér bù dǎo*).'

That China really can, is further attested to by the analysis of official documents, especially those written by the U.S. military agencies, that shows that today the U.S. is not ready to envisage its relations with the rest of the world, and more particularly with China and Russia, in a constructive and cooperative way. These countries are considered as *revisionist powers* that constitute the central challenge to U.S. prosperity and security. These documents regard it as increasingly clear that China and Russia want to shape a world consistent with what is regarded as *their authoritarian model*. The consequence that is put forward is the need to accelerate modernization programmes of the U.S. military resources by investing more money in a sustained effort 'to solidify our competitive advantage.' In particular, this requires, among other measures, the modernization of key capabilities as it concerns nuclear forces; space and cyberspace as warfighting domains; artificial intelligence, surveillance, and reconnaissance; and missile defence.

A HISTORY OF THREATS, FROM THE INDIANS TO THE CHINESE

Clearly, this returns us the beginning of this book, i.e., to the Indian threat and the fear it produced: *the savage Indians are attacking us!* This threat and the related fear have been followed by a long list of other fears caused by countries that did not conform to the U.S. model and the interests of its establishment: the Mexicans, Latin Americans, Bolsheviks, Germans, Japanese, North Koreans, Vietnamese, Syrians, Libyans, and finally Chinese and Russians. In fact, the essence of the fear is not that

13 Chieng, 2006, p. 210, Jullien 1995, Ch. 1.

these countries intend to harm what is now called the Homeland and the American people, but rather that these countries want to put an end to the world America made and to downgrade it from the position of No. 1 that it has enjoyed since the end of WW2.

Today the U.S. is not what it was between the end of WW2 and the end of the 20th century. Then, the balance of power in terms of economic, military and cultural resources was largely in favour of the U.S. But today the U.S. has lost large parts of its economic, military and cultural (i.e., values) advantage.

It seems that the Biden administration has not understood that it is the economic and not military values that will decide the alignment of secondary powers with the superpowers. This is another law of history that the U.S. establishment should have learned from its own historical experience. It was the extraordinary development of the U.S. economy that attracted countries into the U.S. orbit, *volens nolens.* while its military resources served mainly to force the liberated countries, as well as the recalcitrant ones, to remain in the U.S. Empire. Most of the time, cultural resources have been used as a 'window dressing attraction'; it is clear that they alone would not have been able to attract secondary powers. Indeed, their very appeal is more likely to have been due to the U.S. economic and military standing.

Today, China's attraction is a confirmation of this historical law: despite its weaker cultural resources, and the negative evaluation of its political system by liberal democratic countries, its power of attraction based upon its booming economy speaks volumes. Here, as shown in this book, the U.S. is declining on almost all accounts (both in absolute and relative terms) while China is increasing its power resources at a pace that has been recognized, with fear, by outstanding official U.S. circles.

The consequence is that the U.S. and its allies are distraught. They continue to define their problem as an existential fight between democracy and autocracy, ignoring the fact that today the U.S. is not what it was between the end of WW2 and the end of the 20th century when the balance of power in terms of economic, military and cultural resources largely favoured the U.S. But today, the U.S. has lost large parts of its economic, military and cultural (i.e., values) advantages. We have seen what has happened between the time when the U.S. could advertise itself as a dream model and impose its will, and this present time when it is experiencing serious difficulties in imposing choices upon others, whether by economic and military actions and/or by cultural attraction.

Why does the U.S. fear to be domestically destabilized and internationally dethroned by interferences from China and Russia? Is it because the U.S.' establishment has lost its faith in the superiority of its model? Or maybe is it because the U.S. establishment has at last realized that it has not been able to satisfy its own citizens and has failed to convince them of the benefits of democracy, at least the type of democracy it has practiced for a long time. But was it a real democracy? Or is it because those in charge of developing capitalism have diverted it from industrial capitalism, that creates real wealth, to financial capitalism, that creates, out of greed, the astonishing enrichment of a small minority of speculators, as brilliantly sustained by Michael Hudson?[14] Given this reality, one can have little hope of seeing non-democratic countries enthusiastically embracing liberal democracy and capitalism.

Then comes the even more worrying question: will China be satisfied to have put an end to the world America made, or will it want to replace the U.S. as the new hegemonic power? But is this even possible? Can this really serve as a U.S. catalyst for fear?

Again, Chinese history and culture suggest that China never had an imperial strategy such as that of the Western powers, who dreamt of conquering the world and imposing their rule. Contrary to the West's clear manifestation of its intent, China has never invaded or colonized America, Africa, the Middle East, and large parts of Asia. It could have done so well before the discovery of the Americas by the West. Already during the 14th and the first half of the 15th centuries China had the economy, the military, and the technological resources to project its power all over the world as the West has done.[15] Nevertheless, the Chinese Empire has always remained limited to the periphery of the 'Chinese space.' Even when China had the technological capacity to conquer the world, it did not. Even when its vessels were much bigger and better performing than the feeble caravels Christopher Columbus used to discover the Americas, China limited its excursions abroad to establishing cultural and trade relations, and in any case, they were not motivated by the will to conquer foreign countries.[16]

Moreover, today's situation is quite different. After the discovery of the Americas Western powers had developed, especially since the

---

14 Hudson 2003 and 2005.
15 Sun, Jayaram and Kassiri 2017.
16 Nevertheless, for excursion to Europe and America, see the analysis of the expedition of the eunuch admiral Zheng He by Levathes 1994, Menzies 2003 and 2008.

Industrial Revolution, such a formidable economic and military strength that no other country has been able to resist them. Driven by economic interests, and by the missionary dream to diffuse its culture in all its dimensions (political, economic, social, and religious), the West has dominated the world for several centuries. But should China today try to impose its will on the rest of the world, it would face a formidable opposition, first of all from the U.S. and its allies, but then also from regional powers, as no one wants to be the vassal of anybody else. Certainly, if China does succeed in putting an end to the international system as dominated by the U.S., it will weaken the U.S., but it will not be able to destroy America's power resources, especially if the U.S. renounced behaving as if it were the master of the world because of the superiority of its culture, and instead adopted a more cooperative stance.

Unfortunately, the U.S. has neither done so nor seems unlikely to do so. Today China faces U.S. propaganda that demonizes its foreign policy and its leaders, starting with Xi Jinping. Moreover, the Trump administration launched a trade war against China supported by a variety of sanctions that the Biden administration does not seem to want to abandon. Finally, the U.S. is continuing its strategy of promoting subversive activities implemented by its self-defining nongovernmental organizations, in fact organizations funded by the U.S. government. History shows that all forms of power (democratic, authoritarian or totalitarian) protect themselves against subversion by all means, even illegally if necessary.

THE IMPORTANCE AND LIMITS OF IDEOLOGY AS A GUIDE TO U.S. FOREIGN POLICY

To explain the difficulties that the U.S. and China have experienced for a long time in establishing relationships based upon cooperation, mutual understanding and respect, I have foregrounded the influence of the ideologies the U.S. and China have developed through time (Chapter 2).

The competition between the U.S. and China derives from the very special role ideology plays in forging the implementation of both countries' foreign policies. Chinese culture is particularly flexible and has changed through time under pressure from the West. Moreover, China does not decide with whom to cooperate, according to the nature of whichever country's political, economic and cultural system. Implementing the principles of sovereignty and of non-intervention into a country's internal affairs, China does not seek to impose changes in the internal organization of a country as a precondition for establishing cooperation. Rather, the idea of mutual benefits guides the choice, hence the slogan: 'win-win.' Despite its appearance of openness, the U.S. in fact has a more rigid culture. It tends to establish cooperation with countries that share its values, as the Biden foreign policy clearly shows. Of course, there are exceptions based upon the geopolitical evaluation made by U.S. administrations. The U.S. empire has often cooperated, and it is still cooperating today, with authoritarian countries, such as Saudi Arabia. and has even replaced democratically elected governments with dictatorships, such as in Iran in 1953 and in Chile in 1973. Moreover, it has accepted to cooperate with non-democratic countries on matters such as climate change and terrorism. But in all these cases the cooperation does not mean an acceptation of those countries' political organizations, nor that the cooperation will last forever. The criterion is the U.S. evaluation of its geopolitical interests. For example, after the attack on the Twin Towers in New York and the development of Islamist resistance that followed the U.S. assaults on Iraq and Afghanistan, the U.S. accepted to cooperate with Russia and China, which similarly faced Islamist movements. But as soon as the U.S. evaluated that the geopolitical situation had changed, the U.S. ceased to regard these countries as partners in this struggle. For example, as the competition with China had reached new heights, the U.S. not only changed its policy towards terrorist attacks in Xinjiang but even started to support separatist Islamist movements in Xinjiang that are accused of cooperating with terrorist groups.[17]

The U.S. ideology as reconstructed in Chapter 2 constitutes a formidable and coherent set of interrelated beliefs. It has become a way of thinking such that, when it is embedded into the human mind, it is practically impossible not to follow by analysing the world and giving meaning to one's position and action inside that world. Only the grip of an ideology that considers the U.S. to be the exceptional, virtuous, indispensable Republic chosen by God to lead the world towards the end of history, can explain the vigour, determination and even the sincere sense of justice (based upon U.S. values) that has accompanied the U.S. expansion over vast territories occupied by other peoples. That ideology has been the major driver of the U.S. foreign policy, albeit undoubtedly

---

17 The U.S. even deleted one of the latter from the list of terrorist organizations it had established for a long time. The goal is to deploy destabilizing activities within China's territories, as we have seen in Chapter 3—a clear violation of the principles of sovereignty and non-intervention within a foreign country.

amplified by economic interests, the development of political power, and messianic and religious motives that have tended over time to reinforce each other. This ideology has been used throughout history as the guide and a permanent justification of U.S. foreign policy that in fact has operated since the foundation of the American republic, and still operates today. If one looks at the implementation of this ideology since the foundation of the U.S. republic, one cannot help considering that this ideology has become a formidable Weapon of Mass Destruction.

It has destroyed the capacity of the American establishment to conceive of any other world in which the U.S. could play a different role. By implementing that ideology, the U.S. has thought it to be its duty and its right (in practice of God's imperative) to embark on a long series of mass destructions all over the world, many of which could hardly be justified by an existential threat of an enemy ready to defeat and destroy the 'people chosen by God' and with it the values it claimed to defend.[18] On the contrary, by doing so the U.S. has invariably ended up justifying its own operations of mass destruction (and those of its allies), even as it condemns alleged mass destructions perpetrated by its enemies, hardly approximating its own in scale. This corresponds to the well-known use of double standards exhibited by both the U.S. and the EU.

Thanks to this ideology, the U.S. has been able to achieve remark-able power results, at least until recently. It is also because of the U.S. two-century long success story, both at home and abroad, that this ide-ology has left the U.S. mired in the nostalgia of its purported 'glorious past' despite its numerous betrayals of those values, both at home and abroad. When a culture gets to the point that it has the absolute certitude of having gotten everything right (values) and sees no need to change, it is a dead culture or in the process of dying.

Would it not have been better to consider an encounter with oth-er civilizations instead of a clash? Would it not be better to take ad-vantages of the resources every culture possesses and work towards a

---

18 Ganser 2016 and 2020, Blum 2013-14. For example, the napalm bombing of 67 Japanese towns (spring of 1945), followed by the atomic bombing of Hiroshima and Nagasaki (August 1945), which according to former Secretary of State McNamara would have ended by the condemnation of the U.S. for war crimes, should the U.S. have been defeated in World War II (McNamara 2009). Then followed a long series of attempted and very often succeeded mass destructions: Korea, Vietnam, Iraq, Afghanistan, Syria, Libya, Iran, to quote just a few.

354 OF THE CHINA THREAT

cross-fertilization between cultures, instead of imposing one's culture on the rest of the world as a condition for developing cooperation, inevitably in a subordinate position, as the history of the West very well demonstrates? Joseph Chan has shown that while Confucianism may possess some values that are not compatible with those of other cultures (e.g. liberal democracy), it is also holds many that not only are compatible, but can improve the implementation of the values of the encountering culture.[19]

Nevertheless, ideology and values are not enough to provide the means of power. Without science and technology, economic and military means, the U.S. would not have been able to become the world power it has been for a long time. Similarly, nor would China have been able to become strong enough to resist the dictates of the U.S. empire. The decline of the U.S. is not only due to the sclerosis of its ideology, but also to the decline of its power resources. The traditional foreign policy that served so well the realization of the interests of the U.S. establishment, cannot be implemented any more. The balance of power resources has undergone a dramatic change since at least the end of the Cold War.[20] Today, it is clear that the U.S. government lacks not only the means to unilaterally impose its will in the international system, but it also lacks the administrative and economic means to satisfy the needs of its own citizens, especially in health, education, and infrastructure. Unless one considers that the economic means are there but are diverted in favour of the upper 1% so strongly denounced by Joseph Stiglitz.

Is the U.S. Capable of Adapting Its Ideology and Foreign Policy to the New Multi-Polar World?

Considering the probability of the persistence of China's political and economic system into the foreseeable future and its growing power in the international arena, has the U.S. the capacity to revise its national interests and to reorient its foreign policy accordingly? In this respect, the fundamental question is: is the U.S. ready to abandon its traditional

---

19 Chan 2014, and Chapter 2 (see 'Bridge Values and Today's Ideology of the PRC').

20 This is a beautiful demonstration of the validity of the analysis of power Max Weber put forward a century ago. Charisma, tradition and respect of legality are not enough to obtain acceptance of the decisions taken by the government, both nationally and internationally. For Weber, governments need administrative and economic means, to which we can add military means to impose one's will in the international arena.

messianic posture based upon the indisputable superiority of the Western model? To abandon its strategy of meddling in other countries' internal affairs, of seeking regime changes, as well as other types of aggressions both verbal and factual for the purpose of curtailing their perceived 'threats' to U.S. national interests? This will only be possible if one accepts the right of 'national sovereignty' as the fundamental guiding principle orienting states' behaviour in an international system based upon mutual understanding and respect.[21]

Or will the U.S. inevitably lead the world not to peace and prosperity but to an armed conflict with China, which could turn nuclear with devastating consequences for humanity? Has the U.S. leadership the capacity to understand the fundamental change in contemporary warfare as explained by Andrei Martyanov? The U.S. has been able to develop the Jeffersonian dream of world expansion while protected by two vast oceans. Even the formidable Nazi army did not represent an existential threat to America. It was not even able to conquer the UK separated from continental Europe by only 21 miles. But today the U.S. homeland must face the possibility of missile strikes on its Atlantic coasts by Russia and on its Pacific coast by China—or even North Korea. None of these countries is so foolish as to risk a nuclear war with the U.S., but should a conventional conflict evolve to a nuclear war, it is clear that China and Russia will have the means to strike back.

Certainly, from the point of view of Western values, one may regret and strongly criticize China's evolution towards an increasingly author- itarian state. But in doing so, we forget that we have done our part of pushing China in this direction, and were we not pushing so hard, China might not have felt it necessary to protect itself by such means. No won- der China developed its power resources following Mao and Zhu Enlai's four modernizations: agriculture, economy, science and technology, and defence. Napoleon is famous for having forecasted: 'When China wakes, she will shake the world.' In fact, she did not wake, the West woke her, and what a rude awakening!

The U.S. and the West wanted a liberal democratic China imbedded into global capitalism, obviously in a dependent position. We forget the time we took from the first idea of democracy that appeared in Ancient Greece to the time when the West started to implement the features of a very partial liberal democracy in the 18th and 19th centuries. We have

---

21 See in this sense the article by Stephen M. Walt of Harvard University, significantly entitled: 'Countries Should Mind Their Own Business' (Walt 2020).

taken a lot of time, but we are impatient to see other countries and cultures to adopt our values and societal organization. We tend to impose our historical time upon others. We claim that we have democracy now, and we do not understand why other countries are not willing to adopt democracy immediately. We also tend to forget our frequent violations of our own values, both at home and abroad. The West has integrated the other countries in its globalizations, the British first, then the American, in a position of inferiority. Why doesn't it accept that a great civilization such as the Chinese cannot indefinitely accept this type of subordinate relationship? Is the West ready to make its culture evolve? Neither the U.S. nor the European countries seem to be ready to go in this direction. Indeed, history shows that this type of behaviour is today not only very difficult to implement but is also followed by blowbacks that harm the real interests of the American people

THE TRAGEDY OF AMERICAN FOREIGN POLICY

The tragedy of the Western and specifically American imperial foreign policy and the mounting aversion to it all over the world (including by some U.S. allies) is that the world still needs the U.S.—not as an exceptional and indispensable nation, nor as a hegemon that considers the rest of the world as a territory to be conquered, entrusted with the right and even the duty to lead humankind toward an end of history based upon a parochial and provincial 'manifest destiny.'

Americans, I mean the American people, possess a lot of qualities, that probably existed already before they left Europe and were later cemented by the struggle they were forced to go through in order to survive during the troubled history of their new fatherland.[22] Unfortunately, they have not been served well by their establishment. Given the ideology mentioned above, when did it go wrong? Was it during the four decades of the neoliberal revolution that increased the already existing inequalities, the rate of poverty, the unequal access to services such as health and education? Or was it during the post WW2 era of unending wars starting with Korea? Or was it at the beginning of the 20th century when an extraordinary propaganda campaign was orchestrated by the establishment to convince the American males to enlist into the U.S. army to join the Europeans in 'their' WW1? In a war the majority of Americans did not see as an American war? Or was it during the era of the Robber Barons in

---

22 Howard Zinn, significantly entitled *A People's History of the United States* (Zinn 1999). See also Sjursen 2021.

the last decades of the 19th century when unscrupulous industrialists and financiers made fortunes exploiting workers? Was it the rush to enrich oneself by all means, as happened right at the beginning of the U.S.' long march toward China, when several Americans made fortunes in the opium trade?

Or was it already embedded into the ideology that took form at the beginning of the exemplary Republic I analysed in Chapter 2? I have sustained there that the internal rift between ordinary Americans and the elite (today, the establishment) was already present at the moment of the Declaration of independence. We have here another dimension of the rift between WE and the OTHER. Those who signed this historical document were members of the upper class, and above all proprietors of plantations, where slavery was legally practiced. And here we find one of the main features of the motives of the American elite. The exploitation of the cotton fields needed a cheap manpower, that ideally was to last forever, thanks to the racial laws that forbade intercourse between Blacks and Whites. Not only the lords of the plantations exploited a manpower deprived of all rights, but the financiers of the North made fortunes by investing in the slave trade needed by the agriculture of the South. And it has never changed since. Fortunately, today there is a new generation of politicians who try to awake the country from its lost dream. But will the establishment surrender, given its extraordinary power to write and impose its narration of the U.S. past, present and future?

Will the U.S. be able to accept to act within a multipolar world, seeking cooperation in all domains? For it is by accepting that it is possible to cooperate with countries that are organized upon different values and principles without interfering in their domestic affairs, and by implementing a real democracy at home, that the U.S. will be able to persuade these countries of the superiority of the Western Model.

To conclude, for Americans who may still today be opposed to changing the U.S. foreign policy as suggested in this book, here is a message upon which they may reflect.

Let us return to Percy Cradock's evaluation of the UK policy towards Hong Kong between 1992 and 1997 with regard to relinquishing its hold on Hong Kong,[23] paraphrased here as an excellent summary of questions to be put to today's U.S. foreign policy establishment with regard to its possible future policy towards China and the rest of the world. It goes like this:

---

23 See 'The Hong Kong case' in Chapter 3.

Is it an example of nostalgia in action, an attempted reversion to times when America was in a position to impose solutions? Was the failure to read Chinese intentions just another example of that besetting sin of U.S. foreign policy, the incapacity to put itself in the shoes of the other side, which has manifested itself in its European as much as its eastern dilemmas? All who look beyond the headlines will wonder why America, with its long and rich experience of China, should reserve its biggest mistake for the last act of the play.

Clearly, there are several similarities between the UK policy towards Hong Kong and the U.S. policy towards China. Both are based primarily on values, that moreover have been used for hiding or justifying economic and power objectives. In 1992 Hong Kong should have turned democratic instantaneously by the magic hand of the UK, as China should today do the same under the magical hand of the U.S. Finally, I am sure the world will appreciate it if the final act of the U.S. foreign policy will not be war against China, which would be a catastrophe not only for the American people, but also for all humanity.

Statistical Annex

TABLE 1A.

CHANGES IN EMPLOYMENT OF THE THREE ECONOMIC SECTORS (1952–2019)

Unit: %

	1952	1978	2003	2006	2008	2016	2019
Agriculture	83.5	70.5	49.1	42.6	39.6	27.7	25.1
Industry	7.4	17.3	21.6	25.2	27.2	28.8	27.5
Services	9.1	12.2	29.3	32.2	33.2	43.5	47.4
Total	100.0	100.0	100.0	100.0	100.0	100.0	100.0

Source: National Bureau of Statistics of China 2020

TABLE 1B.

CHANGES IN GDP OF THE THREE ECONOMIC SECTORS (1952–2019)

	1952	1978	2003	2006	2008	2016	2019
Agriculture	56.6	27.7	12.3	10.0	10.2	8.1	7.1
Industry	20.6	47.7	45.6	47.6	47.0	39.6	39.0
Services	22.8	24.6	42.0	41.8	42.9	52.4	53.9
Total	100	100	100	100	100	100	100

Source: National Bureau of Statistics of China 2020

TABLE 2.

THE PROPORTION OF GDP (PPP) IN THE TOTAL OF THE WORLD (1820–2019)

	1820	1870	1913	1929	1950	1973	2000	2008	2015	2019
China	32.88	17.05	8.83	7.37	4.50	4.62	6.43	10.64	15.28	17.33
U.S.	1.80	8.84	18.94	22.70	27.32	22.07	20.88	18.23	16.47	15.82
US/China	0.05	0.52	2.14	3.08	6.07	4.78	3.25	1.71	1.08	0.91
Japan	2.98	2.28	2.62	3.45	3.02	7.76	6.68	5.31	4.45	4.05
U.K.	5.21	9.00	8.22	6.76	6.53	4.22	3.31	2.94	2.57	2.41
Germany	3.86	6.48	8.69	7.06	4.98	5.90	5.21	4.25	3.68	3.45
Russia	5.42	7.52	8.50	6.42	9.57	9.44	3.16	3.86	3.29	3.06
India	16.02	12.12	7.48	6.52	4.17	3.09	4.01	4.83	6.28	7.05

Data source for (1820–1973): Angus Maddison, *Historical Statistics of the World Economy: 1–2008 AD.*

Data source for (2000–2019): World Bank Database.

Based upon by the *IMF World Economic Outlook* (April 2021), we forecast that by 2025, China's GDP (2017 International $) will account for more than 20% of the world's total, while the United States' will fall below 15%, which is equivalent to 75% of China.

TABLE 3.

G20's GDP (PPP) PROPORTION IN THE WORLD
(1990–2019)

Unit: %

Country	1990	1995	2000	2005	2010	2014	2019
Argentina	NA	NA	NA	NA	NA	NA	0.76
Australia	1.04	1.04	1.05	1.02	0.97	0.95	0.97
Brazil	3.50	3.58	3.29	3.14	3.17	3.01	2.38
Canada	1.95	1.87	1.86	1.78	1.54	1.44	1.42
China	3.89	6.13	7.65	10.08	13.98	16.59	17.33
France	3.59	3.37	3.29	2.94	2.64	2.37	2.38
Germany	5.30	5.16	4.55	4.06	3.66	3.41	3.45
India	3.49	3.94	4.37	5.01	6.08	6.80	7.05
Indonesia	1.84	2.36	2.02	2.11	2.27	2.46	2.46
Italy	3.63	3.41	3.15	2.63	2.33	1.96	1.97
Japan	8.31	7.86	6.83	5.95	4.89	4.26	4.05
South Korea	1.29	1.66	1.77	1.78	1.70	1.60	1.71
Mexico	1.80	2.06	2.20	2.03	1.96	1.98	1.94
Russia	4.16	2.28	2.08	2.60	3.31	3.45	3.06
Saudi Arabia	1.31	1.33	1.24	1.31	1.38	1.48	1.24
South Africa	0.82	0.76	0.72	0.72	0.68	0.65	0.56
Turkey	0.84	0.87	1.22	1.20	1.32	1.34	1.82
UK	3.60	3.35	3.36	3.20	2.55	2.36	2.41
US	20.92	20.95	21.37	20.04	16.93	16.04	15.82
EU	25.09	23.75	22.87	21.06	18.96	17.00	15.31
Total*	80.25	80.44	80.54	79.83	79.14	79.05	77.88

Source: 1990-2014 data are calculated according to constant international dollar of 2011 GDP (PPP); 2019 data are calculated according to constant international dollar 2017 GDP (PPP) provided by World Bank database.

*Note: The data for UK, Germany, France and Italy has been deducted from the total, as they belong to EU.

TABLE 4.

G20'S IMPORTS AND EXPORT VOLUME PROPORTION IN THE WORLD (1990-2019)

Unit: %

Country	1990	1995	2000	2005	2010	2014	2019
Argentina	0.23	0.39	0.39	0.32	0.40	0.36	0.30
Australia	1.16	1.09	1.03	1.08	1.34	1.26	1.29
Brazil	0.76	0.96	0.86	0.92	1.27	1.22	1.07
Canada	3.55	3.45	3.95	3.19	2.56	2.49	2.39
China	1.63	2.69	3.59	6.64	9.62	11.30	12.00
France	6.38	5.65	5.05	4.52	3.67	3.32	3.20
Germany	11.00	9.44	7.95	8.16	7.49	7.17	7.14
India	0.59	0.62	0.71	1.13	1.87	2.04	2.12
Indonesia	0.67	0.82	0.83	0.76	0.95	0.93	0.89
Italy	4.99	4.20	3.63	3.54	3.02	2.63	2.64
Japan	7.40	7.45	6.51	5.19	4.74	3.96	3.74
South Korea	1.91	2.49	2.52	2.55	2.89	2.88	2.74
Mexico	1.19	1.47	2.62	2.07	1.97	2.13	2.44
Russia	0.00	1.36	1.14	1.72	2.10	2.11	1.76
Saudi Arabia	0.97	0.75	0.82	1.12	1.16	1.36	1.09
South Africa	0.59	0.56	0.45	0.53	0.61	0.56	0.52
Turkey	0.50	0.55	0.62	0.89	0.97	1.05	1.03
UK	5.78	4.83	4.80	4.25	3.26	3.13	3.04
US	12.89	12.96	15.47	12.30	10.51	10.59	11.05
EU	45.60	41.26	37.73	38.49	34.01	31.98	30 (est.)
Total*	79.64	78.87	79.24	78.9	76.97	76.22	74.43

Source: World Bank and WTO database.

*Note: The data for UK, Germany, France and Italy has been deducted from the total as they belong to EU.

TABLE 5.

G20's Economic Strength Proportion in the World (1990–2019)

unit: %

Country	1990	1995	2000	2005	2010	2014	2019	2010-2019 Variance
Argentina	NA	NA	NA	NA	NA	NA	0.53	
Australia	1.12	1.07	1.03	1.06	1.22	1.15	1.13	-0.09
Brazil	1.67	1.84	1.67	1.66	1.91	1.81	1.73	-0.19
Canada	3.02	2.92	3.25	2.72	2.22	2.14	1.91	-0.32
China	2.39	3.83	4.95	7.79	11.08	13.07	14.67	3.59
France	5.45	4.89	4.46	3.99	3.33	3.00	2.79	-0.54
Germany	9.10	8.01	6.82	6.79	6.21	5.92	5.30	-0.92
India	1.56	1.73	1.93	2.42	3.27	3.63	4.59	1.32
Indonesia	1.06	1.34	1.22	1.21	1.39	1.44	1.68	0.29
Italy	4.53	3.94	3.47	3.24	2.79	2.41	2.31	-0.49
Japan	7.71	7.58	6.62	5.44	4.79	4.06	3.90	-0.90
South Korea	1.70	2.21	2.27	2.29	2.49	2.45	2.23	-0.27
Mexico	1.40	1.67	2.48	2.05	1.97	2.08	2.19	0.22
Russia	1.39	1.66	1.45	2.01	2.50	2.56	2.41	-0.09
Saudi Arabia	1.08	0.94	0.96	1.18	1.23	1.40	1.17	-0.07
South Africa	0.67	0.63	0.54	0.59	0.63	0.59	0.54	-0.09
Turkey	0.61	0.65	0.82	0.99	1.09	1.15	1.44	0.34
UK	5.05	4.34	4.32	3.90	3.02	2.87	2.73	-0.30
US	15.57	15.62	17.43	14.88	12.65	12.41	13.44	0.79
EU	38.76	35.42	32.78	32.68	28.99	26.99	22.6 est.	--
Total*	79.71	79.11	79.4	78.97	77.43	76.93	76.16	-1.28

Source: World Bank Database

*Note: The data for UK, Germany, France and Italy has been deducted from the total as they belong to EU.

TABLE 6.

OVERALL COMPARISON OF POWER RESOURCES OF CHINA AND THE U.S. IN % OF WORLD TOTAL

	2000	2005	2010	2015	2020	2000–2015
Economic Resources						
China	7.43	9.83	13.99	17.21	19.9	9.78
US	20.57	19.33	16.72	15.67	14.6	-4.90
US/China	2.78	1.97	1.20	0.91	0.74	
Human Capital						
China	27.04	29.26	30.27	28.36	26.60	1.32
US	9.46	8.93	8.43	7.94	7.49	-1.52
US/China	0.35	0.31	0.28	0.28	0.28	
Energy Resources						
China	10.68	16.40	20.42	22.92	25.74	12.24
US	24.63	21.48	18.76	17.35	16.04	-7.28
US/China	2.31	1.31	0.92	0.76	0.62	
Capital Resources						
China	5.31	8.49	18.11	30.29	40.00	24.98
US	30.60	27.17	17.43	20.06	23.07	-10.54
US/China	5.76	3.20	0.96	0.66	0.57	
Scientific Resources						
China	3.97	9.29	15.78	24.17	29.31	20.20
US	25.63	24.58	22.64	19.66	17.06	-5.97
US/China	6.46	2.65	1.43	0.81	0.58	
Government Resources						
China	7.45	8.67	10.38	13.23	16.85	5.78
US	18.61	18.35	16.24	12.73	9.98	-5.88
US/China						
Military Resources						
China	7.30	7.95	8.60	9.92	11.12	2.62
US	21.95	22.29	22.65	21.01	19.51	-0.94
US/China	3.01	2.80	2.63	2.12	1.75	
International Resources						
China	2.99	5.56	7.98	10.67	14.26	7.68
US	16.21	13.03	11.31	12.03	14.26	-4.18
US/China						
Information Resources						
China	8.40	14.20	19.32	19.95	19.92	11.55
US	22.03	14.33	8.15	6.98	5.87	-15.04
US/China	2.62	1.01	0.42	0.35	0.29	

Source: Data source: mainly from World Bank database, and estimates by Hu Angang for 2020.

TABLE 7.

PEOPLE INSURED BY THE MAJOR SOCIAL INSURANCES
IN URBAN AREAS (2001–2019)

millions

| year | old-age insurance | medical insurance | | work-related injury insurance | maternity insurance | unem- ployment insurance |
		for employed	for urban and rural residents*			
2001	141.83	76.3	--	43.45	34.55	103.55
2002	147.36	94	--	44.06	34.88	101.82
2003	155.06	109.02	--	45.75	36.55	103.73
2004	163.53	124.04	--	68.45	43.84	105.84
2005	174.87	137.83	--	84.78	54.08	106.48
2006	187.66	157.32	--	102.68	64.59	111.87
2007	201.37	180.20	42.91	121.73	77.75	116.45
2008	218.91	199.96	118.26	137.87	92.54	124.00
2009	235.50	219.37	182.10	148.96	108.76	127.15
2010	257.07	237.35	195.28	161.61	123.36	133.76
2011	283.91	252.27	221.16	176.96	138.92	143.17
2012	304.27	264.86	271.56	190.10	154.29	152.25
2013	322.18	274.43	296.29	199.17	163.92	164.17
2014	341.24	282.96	314.51	206.39	170.39	170.43
2015	353.61	288.93	376.89	214.33	177.71	173.26
2016	379.30	295.32	448.60	218.89	184.51	180.89
2017	402.93	303.23	873.59	227.24		187.84
2018	419.02	316.81	1027.78	238.74		196.44
2019	434.88	329.25	1024.83	254.78		205.43

Source: Official Website of National Bureau of Statistics of China, *China Statistical Yearbook (2020)*.

*Note: The medical insurance system for urban residents was introduced in 2007.

TABLE 8.

Fund Revenues of the Old-age Insurance, Basic Medical Insurance (2001–2019)

Unit: billion yuan

| Year | Fund Revenues | | | | |
	Old-age insurance	Basic medical insurance (in urban areas)	Unemployment insurance	Work-related injury insurance	Maternity insurance
2001	248.9	38.4	18.7	2.8	1.4
2002	317.2	60.8	21.3	3.2	2.2
2003	368.0	89.0	25.0	3.8	2.6
2004	425.8	114.1	29.1	5.8	3.2
2005	509.3	140.5	34.0	9.3	4.4
2006	631.0	174.7	40.2	12.2	6.2
2007	783.4	225.7	47.2	16.6	8.4
2008	974.0	304.0	58.5	21.7	11.4
2009	1149.1	367.2	58.0	24.0	13.2
2010	1387.3	430.9	65.0	28.5	16.0
2011	1800.5	553.9	92.3	46.6	22.0
2012	2183.0	693.9	113.9	52.7	30.4
2013	2473.3	824.8	128.9	61.5	36.8
2014	2762.0	968.7	138.0	69.5	44.6
2015	3219.6	1119.3	136.8	75.4	50.2
2016	3799.1	1308.4	122.9	73.7	52.2
2017	4661.4	1793.1	111.2	85.4	64.3
2018	5500.5	2138.4	117.1	91.3	78.1
2019	5702.6	2442.1	128.4	81.9	

Source: *China Statistical Yearbook 2020.*

TABLE 9.

UNDP Gini Index for 19 Western Countries and China (2010–2018)

Countries	Gini UNDP	Rank	Countries	Gini UNDP 2015	Rank
Norway	27	1	Canada	33.8	12
Finland	27.4	2	Portugal	33.8	12
Belgium	27.4	2	Australia	34.4	14
Netherlands	28.5	4	Greece	34.4	14
Denmark	28,7	5	Spain	34.7	16
Sweden	28.8	6	UK	34.8	17
			Italy	35.9	18
Austria	29.7	7			
France	31.6	8	US	41.4	19
Germany	31.9	9			
Switzerland	32.7	10			
Ireland	32.8	11	China	43.4	20

Source: UNDP Human Development Report.

According to UNDP, China's Gini coefficient was 38.5 for the period covered (2010-2018). For the World Bank database China's Gini was also 38.5 in 2016, but today it is much higher. China's Gini coefficient published by the *China National Bureau of Statistics* was 46.5 in 2019, down from 49.1 in 2008. As we do not have comparable data for the countries in the table, I have taken 43.4 as a personal estimate. In any case this does not contradict the fact that China's Gini is about 2 points higher than the US, and much higher than the index of the other countries in the table.

TABLE 10.

HDI, GENDER INEQUALITY INDEX, AND RANKING IN 20 WESTERN COUNTRIES AND CHINA (2019)

Countries	HDI 2015	HDI Rank	Gender Inequality Index	Gender Inequality rank
Norway	0.957	1	0.045	6
Australia	0.944	8	0.097	25
New Zealand	0.931	14	0.123	33
US	0.926	17	0.204	46
Ireland	0.955	2	0.093	23
Netherlands	0.944	7	0.043	4
Canada	0.929	16	0.080	19
Sweden	0.945	7	0.039	3
Germany	0.947	6	0.084	20
Switzerland	0.955	3	0.025	1
France	0.901	26	0.049	8
Finland	0.938	11	0.047	7
Belgium	0.931	14	0.043	4
Denmark	0.940	10	0.038	2
Spain	0.904	25	0.070	16
Greece	0.888	32	0.116	29
Italy	0.892	29	0.069	14
Austria	0.922	18	0.069	14
United Kingdom	0.932	13	0.118	31
Portugal	0.864	38	0.075	17
China	0.761	85	0.168	39

Source: UNDP Human development report 2020.

TABLE 11.

CHINA'S URBAN PER CAPITA ANNUAL DISPOSABLE INCOME AND RURAL PER CAPITA NET INCOME (1978–2020)

	Ratio [1]/[2]	Urban Per Capita Annual Disposable Income (Yuan) [1]	Rural Per Capita Net Income (Yuan) [2]
1978	2.57	343	133
1979	2.53	405	160
1980	2.50	477	191
1981	2.24	500	223
1982	1.98	535	270
1983	1.82	564	309
1984	1.84	652	355
1985	1.86	739	397
1986	2.13	900	423
1987	2.17	1002	462
1988	2.17	1180	544
1989	2.28	1373	601
1990	2.20	1510	686
1991	2.40	1700	708
1992	2.58	2026	784
1993	2.80	2577	921
1994	2.86	3496	1221
1995	2.71	4283	1577
1996	2.51	4838	1926
1997	2.47	5160	2090
1998	2.51	5425	2162
1999	2.65	5854	2210
2000	2.79	6280	2253
2001	2.90	6859	2366
2002	3.11	7702	2475
2003	3.23	8472	2622
2004	3.21	9421	2936

	Ratio [1]/[2]	Urban Per Capita Annual Disposable Income (Yuan) [1]	Rural Per Capita Net Income (Yuan) [2]
2005	3.22	10493	3254
2006	3.27	11759	3587
2007	3.33	13785	4140
2008	3.31	15780	4760
2009	3.33	17174	5153
2010	3.23	19109	5919
2011	3.13	21810	6977
2012	3.10	24565	7916
2013	2.98	26467	8896
2014	2.92	28844	9892
2015	2.90	31195	10772
2016	2.72	33616	12363
2017	2.71	36396	13432
2018	2.69	39251	14617
2019	2.64	42359	16021
2020	2.56	43834	17131

Source: the data of 1978-2008 are from: *China Compendium of Statistics 1949-2008*, compiled by Department of Comprehensive Statistics of National Bureau Statistics. The data of 2009-2019 are from the National Bureau of Statistics of China.

TABLE 12.

PER CAPITA ANNUAL INCOME OF URBAN AND RURAL HOUSEHOLDS IN CHINA'S PROVINCES (2006–2019)

		Urban Areas		Rural Areas	
Ratio (2)/(1)*	Ratio (2)/(1)*	Regions	Disposable income (2)	Regions	Net income (1)
2006 3.27	2019 2.64	National average	42358.8	National Average	16020.7
2.41	2.55	Beijing	73848.5	Beijing	28928.4
2.29	1.86	Tianjin	46118.9	Tianjin	24804.1
2.71	2.32	Hebei	35737.7	Hebei	15373.1
3.15	2.58	Shanxi	33262.	Shanxi	12902.4
3.10	2.67	Inner Mongolia	40782.5	Inner Mongolia	15282.8
2.53	2.47	Liaoning	39777.	Liaoning	16108.3
2.68	2.16	Jilin	32299.2	Jilin	14936.0
2.58	2.07	Heilongjiang	30944.6	Heilongjiang	14982.1
2.26	2.22	Shanghai	73615.3	Shanghai	33195.2
2.42	2.25	Jiangsu	51056.1	Jiangsu	22675.4
2.49	2.01	Zhejiang	60182.3	Zhejiang	29875.8
3.29	2.44	Anhui	37540.0	Anhui	15416.0
2.84	2.33	Fujian	45620.5	Fujian	19568.4
2.76	2.31	Jiangxi	36545.9	Jiangxi	15796.3
2.79	2.38	Shandong	42329.2	Shandong	17775.5
3.01	2.26	Henan	34201.0	Henan	15163.7
2.86	2.29	Hubei	37601	Hubei	16390.9
3.09	2.59	Hunan	39841.9	Hunan	15394.8
3.15	2.56	Guangdong	48117.6	Guangdong	18818.4
3.10	2.54	Guangxi	34744.9	Guangxi	13675.7
2.88	2.38	Hainan	36016.7	Hainan	15113.1

Ratio (2)/(1)*	Ratio (2)/(1)*	Regions	Urban Areas Disposable income (2)	Rural Areas Regions	Net income (1)
3.11	2.46	Sichuan	36153.7	Sichuan	14670.1
4.59	3.20	Guizhou	34404.2	Guizhou	10756.3
4.47	3.04	Yunnan	36237.7	Yunnan	11902.4
3.67	2.89	Tibet	37410.0	Tibet	12951.0
4.10	2.93	Shaanxi	36098.2	Shaanxi	12325.7
4.18	3.36	Gansu	32323.4	Gansu	9628.9
3.81	2.94	Qinghai	33830.3	Qinghai	11499.4
3.32	2.67	Ningxia	34328.5	Ningxia	12858.4
3.24	2.64	Xinjiang	34663.7	Xinjiang	13121.7

Data Sources: *China Statistical Yearbook 2020.*
*Author's calculation.

TABLE 13.

SIX GROUPS OF PROVINCES WITH DIFFERENT URBAN-RURAL PERSONAL INCOME RATIOS (2006 AND 2019)

2006

Group 1 < 2	Group 2 2.0–2.5	Group 3 2.5–3	Group 4 3–3.5	Group 5 3.5–4	Group 6 > 4
	Tianjin Shanghai Beijing Jiangsu Zhejiang	Hebei Liaoning Jilin Heilongjiang Fujian Jiangxi Shandong Hubei Hainan	Hunan, Shanxi Inner Mongolia Anhui Henan Guangdong Sichuan Guangxi Ningxia Xinjiang	Tibet Qinghai	Chongqing Gansu Guizhou Yunnan Shaanxi
N = 0	N = 5	N = 9	N = 10	N = 2	N = 5

2019

Group 1 < 2	Group 2 2.0–2.5	Group 3 2.5–3	Group 4 3–3.5	Group 5 3.5–4	Group 6 > 4
Tian- jin(1.9)	Liaoning Jilin Shanghai Jiangsu Anhui Fujian Jiangxi Shandong Henan Hubei Guangxi Hainan Chongqing Sichuan Heilongjiang Zhejiang Hebei	Beijing Shanxi Inner Mongolia Hunan Guang- dong Yunnan Xizang Shanxi Qinghai Ningxia Xinjiang	Gansu Guizhou		
N = 1	N = 17	N = 11	N = 2		

Source: Table 12

Bibliography

Alford, Matthew and Tom Secker (2017). *National Security Cinema: The Shocking New Evidence of Government Control in Hollywood.* Drum Roll Books.

Almond, Gabriel A. and Powell, G.B. (1966). *Comparative Politics: A Developmental Approach.* Boston: Little, Brown & Co.

Almond, Gabriel A. and Verba, Sidney (1963). *The Civic Culture.* Boston: Little, Brown & Co.

Andersen, Kurt (2017). *Fantasy Land. How America Went Haywire. A 500-year History.* London: Penguin.

Anderson, P. (2015). *American foreign policy and its thinkers.* London: Verso.

Angell, Marcia (2005). *The Truth About the Drug Companies: How They Deceive Us and What To Do about It.* New York: Randon House.

Bacevich, Andrew (2008). *The Limits of Power. The End of American Exceptionalism.* New York: Henry Holt.

Bacevich, Andrew (ed.) (2012). *The Short American Century: A Postmortem.* Cambridge, Mass.: Harvard University Press.

Bairoch, Paul (1993). *Economics and World History: Myths and Paradoxes.* New York: Harvester Wheatsheaf.

Bandow, Doug (2020a). 'President Joe Biden Plans a World of Endless Intervention and Probably War,' *AntiWar,* 28 October, https://original.antiwar.com/doug-bandow/2020/10/27/president-joe-biden-plans-a-world-of-endless-intervention-and-probably-war/ (accessed 2 January 2021).

Bandow, Doug (2020b). 'When Washington Sends a Massage by Threatening War. Other Countries Hear 'Build Nukes!,'' *AntiWar,* 30 December, https://original.antiwar.com/doug-bandow/2020/12/29/when-washington-sends-a-message-by-threatening-war-other-countries-hear-build-nukes/ (accessed 2 January 2021).

Bao, Beibei, Charles Eichacker, and Max J. Rosenthal (2013). 'Is China pivoting to the Middle East?' *The Atlantic*, 28 March, https://www. theatlantic.com/china/archive/2013/03/is-china-pivoting-to-the-middle-east/274444/.

Barfield, Claude (2021). 'Biden's forts defeat: The China-EU trade agreement,' *American Economic Institute*, 4 January, https://www.aei.org/economics/bidens-first-defeat-the-china-eu-trade-agreement/ (accessed 10 January 2021).

Barton, Dominic, Yougang Chen, and Amy Jin (2013). 'Mapping China's middle class,' *McKinsey Quarterly,* June 1, 2013.

Beinart, Peter (2018). 'The U.S. Needs to Face Up to Its Long History of Election Meddling,' *The Atlantic,* 22 July, https://www.theatlantic.com/ideas/archive/2018/07/the-us-has-a-long-history-of-election-meddling/565538/ (accessed 25 August 2018).

Bell, Daniel (2006). *Beyond Liberal Democracy. Political Thinking for an East Asian Context.* Princeton, NJ: Princeton University Press.

Bell, Daniel (ed.) (2008). *Confucian Political Ethics.* Princeton, NJ: Princeton University Press.

Bell, Daniel, and Chaibong Hahn (eds.) (2003). *Confucianism for the modern world.* Cambridge: Cambridge University Press.

Bell, Kurt M. and Ely Ratner (2018). 'How Beijing Defied American Expectations,' *Foreign Affaires*, 13 February.

Benjamin, Medea and Marcy Winograd (2020). 'Why Senators Must Reject Avril Haines for Intelligence,' *Common Dreams*, 29 December.

Bergère, Marie-Claire (1986). *L'âge d'or de la bourgeoisie chinoise.* Paris: Flammarion.

Bergère, Marie-Claire (2007). *Capitalisme et capitalistes en Chine.* Paris: Perrin.

Bernays, Edward (1928). *Propaganda.* New York: Ig Publishing (reprinted 2005).

Beveridge, Albert J. (1900). In Support of an American Empire. *Record, 56* Cong., I Sess., 1900, pp. 704–712. Retrieved December 15, 2018, from https://www.mtholyoke.edu/acad/intrel/ajb72.htm.

Biden, Joseph R., Jr. (2020). 'Why America must lead again,' *Foreign Affairs,* March-April.

Biden, Joseph (2021a). Inaugural Address by President Joseph R. Biden, Jr., 20 January, The White House

Biden, Joseph (2021b). Remarks by President Biden on America's Place in the World, The White House, 4 February.

Biden, Joseph (2021c). Remarks by President Biden in Press Conference, The White House, 25 March.

Biden, Joseph R., Jr. and Michael Carpenter (2018). 'How to Stand Up to the Kremlin,' *Foreign Affairs,* January/February.

Billeter, François (2006). *Contre François Jullien.* Paris: Allia.

Blackwill, Robert D. and Ashley J. Tellis (2015). 'Revising US grand strategy toward China,' Council on Foreign Relations, Council Special Report no. 72, March 2015.

Blackwill, Robert D. and Kurt Campbell (2016). 'Xi Jinping on the global stage: Chinese foreign policy under a powerful but exposed leader,' *Council on Foreign Relations,* Council Special Report No. 74, February 2016.

Blinken, Anthony J. and Kagan, Robert (2019). '"America First" is not only making the world worse. Here's a better approach,' *Washington Post,* 1 January 2019.

Blinken, Anthony (2021). A Foreign Policy for the American People, U.S. Department of State, 3 March, https://www.state.gov/a-foreign-policy-for-the-american-people/ (accessed 24 April 2021).

Blomberg, David R. Baker and Ari Natter (2021). 'Biden moves to rapidly adopt climate policies, stunning the oil and gas industry,' Fortune, 28 January 2021, https://fortune.com/2021/01/28/biden-climate-oil-and-gas/ (accessed 20 February 2021).

Bloomberg (2018). 'China Ends 25-Year yait as Yuan Oil Futures to Start Trading,' *Bloomberg News,* 9 February, https://www.bloomberg.com/news/articles/2018-02-09/china-ends-25-year-wait-as-yuan-oil-futures-set-to-start-trading (accessed 15 March 2018).

Blum, William (2014a). *Killing Hope. US Military and CIA Interventions since World War II.* Monroe, ME: Common Courage Press.

Blum, William (2014b). *Rogue State. A Guide to the World's Only Superpower*. London: Zed Books.

Blum, William (2014c). Overthrowing other people's governments: The Master List, https://williamblum.org/essays/read/overthrowing-other-peoples-governments-the-master-list (accessed 26 September 2018).

Blum, William (2016). 'What can go wrong? The brighter side of Trump's election,' *Foreign Policy Journal*, 2 December 2016, http://www.foreignpolicyjournal.com/2016/12/02/what-can-go-wrong-the-brighter-side-of-trumps-election (accessed 19 December 2016).

Bovard, James (2020). 'The Korean War's Forgotten Lessons on the Evil of Intervention,' *Counterpunch*, 17 November 2020, https://www.counterpunch.org/2020/11/17/the-korean-wars-forgotten-lessons-on-the-evil-of-intervention/ (accessed 15 November 2020).

Bradley, James (2009). *The Imperial Cruise. A Secret History of Empire and War*. New York: Little, Brown & Co.

Bradley, James (2015). *The China Mirage. The Hidden Story of American Disaster in Asia*. New York: Little, Brown & Co.

Brands, Hal and Zack Cooper (2021). 'U.S.-Chinese Rivalry Is a Battle Over Values. Great-Power Competition Can't Be Won on Interests Alone,' *Foreign Affairs*, 16 March.

Braudel, Fernand (1972). 'Fernand Braudel et les différents temps de l'histoire,' interview published by *Jalons*, ORTF (Collection: Signes des temps), 30 October, http://fresques.ina.fr/jalons/ fiche-media/InaEdu04649/fernand-braudel-et-les-differents-temps-de-l-histoire.html (accessed 21 March 2004).

Braudel, Fernand (1979a). *Civilisation matérielle, économie et capitalisme (XVe–XVIIIe siècle)*. Paris: A. Colin (*vol. 1: Les structures du quotidien; vol. 2: Les jeux de l'échange; vol. 3: Le temps du monde)*. English translation: *Civilization and Capitalism: 15th–18th Century, vol. 1: The Structure of Everyday Life; vol. 2: The Wheels of Commerce; vol. 3: The Perspective of the World*. Berkeley: University of California Press, 1992.

Braudel, Fernand (1979b). *Afterthoughts on Material Civilization and Capitalism* (The Johns Hopkins Symposia in Comparative History). Baltimore, MD: Johns Hopkins University Press.

Braudel, Fernand (1992). *On History*. Chicago: University of Chicago Press.

Brunsden, Jim Mehreen Khan and Michael Peel (2020). 'EU and China agree new investment treaty,' *Financial Times*, 30 December, https://www.ft.com/content/6a429460-4bfb-42d4-9191-73ba97dde130 (accessed 3 January 2021).

Brzezinski, Zbigniew (1997a). A geostrategy for Eurasia. *Foreign Affairs*, September 1. Retrieved December 6, 2016, from https://www.foreignaffairs.com/articles/asia/1997-09-01/geostrategy-eurasia.

Brzezinski, Zbigniew (1997b). *The grand chessboard: American primacy and its geostrategic imperatives*. New York: Basic Books.

Brzezinski, Zbigniew (2016). 'Toward a global realignment. As its era of global dominance ends, the United States to take the lead in realigning the global power architecture,' *The American Interest*, 17 April 2016.

Buckley Ebrey, P. (1999). *The Cambridge illustrated history of China*. Cambridge: Cambridge University Press.

Butman, John and Simon Targett (2018). *New World Inc., The Making of America by England's Merchants Adventurers*, New York: Little, Brown & Company.

Cabestan, Jean-Pierre (1994). *Le système politique de la Chine populaire*. Paris: Presses Universitaires de France, first edition.

Campbell, Kurt M. and Ely Ratner (2018). The China Reckoning. How Beijing Defied American Expectations, *Foreign Affairs*, 13 February, https://www.foreignaffairs.com/articles/united-states/2018-02-13/china-reckoning?cid=nlc-fa fatoday-20180214 (accessed 15 February 2018).

Canfora, Luciano (2002a). *L'imposture démocratique. Du procès de Socrate à l'éléction de G.W. Bush*. Paris: Flammarion.

Canfora, Luciano (2002b). *Critica della retorica democratica*. Bari: Laterza.

Canfora, Luciano (2006). *Democracy in Europe. A History of an Ideology*. New York: Wiley.

Canfora, Luciano (2008). *Exporter la liberté: Echec d'un mythe*, Paris: Ed. Desjonquères.

Canfora, Luciano (2010). *La nature du pouvoir*. Paris: Les Belles Lettres.

Canfora, Luciano (2017). *La schiavitù del capitale*. Bologna: Il Mulino.

Canfora, Luciano and Gustavo Zagrebelsky (2014). *La marchera democractica dell'oligarchia*. Bari: Laterza.

Cartier, Michel (ed.) (2004). *Giuseppe Castiglione dit Lang Shining, 1688–1766, Jésuite italien et peintre chinois*. Paris: Favre.

Cashill, Jack (2020). 'Media Firemen Scramble to Save Biden Candidacy,' *Lew Rockwell*, 28 October.

Chan, Joseph (1999). 'A Confucian Perspective on Human Rights For Contemporary China,' in Bauer, Joanne R. and Daniel A. Bell, *The East Asian Challenge for Human Rights*. Cambridge: Cambridge University Press.

Chan, Joseph (2014). *Confucian Perfectionism: A Political Philosophy for Modern Times*. Princeton: Princeton University Press.

Chang, Gordon C. (2001). *The Coming Collapse of China*. New York: Random House, 2001.

Chang, Gordon C. (2006). 'Halfway to China's collapse,' *Far Eastern Economic Review*, June, pp. 25–8.

Chang, Ha-Joon (2008). *Bad Samaritans. The Myth of Free Trade and the Secret History of Capitalism*. New York: Bloomsbury.

Chayes, Sarah (2020a). *On Corruption in America. And What is at Stake*. New York: Knopf.

Chayes, Sarah (2020b). 'The strategies are Foreign, but the Corruption is American,' *Foreign Affairs*, November/December 2020.

Chen Yali (2016). *Confucianisme et Démocratie Libérale : une étude comparative*, Master dissertation in Political Science, University of Geneva.

Chernova, Anna, Zahra Ullah and Rob Picheta (2021). 'Russia reacts angrily after Biden calls Putin a 'killer,'' CNN, 18 March.

China Briefing (2019). 'China's Middle Class in 5 Simple Questions' (From Dezan Shira & Associates), 13 February 2019, https://www.china-briefing.com/news/chinas-middle-class-5-questions-answered/ (accessed 20 February 2019).

China Labour Bulletin (2019). China's social security system, *China Labour Bulletin*, First published 2012, last upadated (in part) March 2019, https://clb.org.hk/content/china%E2%80%99s-social-security-system (accessed 3 April 2019).

China Power Report (2018). 'How well-off is China's middle class?,' https://chinapower.csis.org/china-middle-class/ (accessed 25 July 2019).

Chinese People's Political Consultative Conference, September 21, 1949, https://china.usc.edu/Mao-declares-founding-of-peoples-republic-of-china-chinese-people-have-stood-up.

Chollet, Derek, et al. (2017). 'Building "situations of strength": A national security strategy for the United States,' *Brookings,* February.

Chomsky, Aviva (2018). 'The DNA Industry and the Disappearing Indian. DNA, Trace, and Native Rights,' *TomDispatch,* 29 November, https://tomdispatch.com/aviva-chomsky-making-native-americans-strangers-in-their-own-land/ (accessed 7 June 2021).

Chow, Gregory C. (2002). *China's Economic Transformation.* Oxford: Blackwell.

Chung, Cynthia (2019). 'On Churchill's Sinews of Peace,' *Strategic Culture*, 24 November.

Chung, Cynthia (2020a). 'On Roosevelt and Stalin: What Revisionist Historians Want Us to Forget,' *Strategic Culture*, 18 September.

Chung, Cynthia (2020b). 'The Enemy Within: A Story of the Purge of American Intelligence,' *Strategic Culture*, 14 June.

Chung, Cynthia (2020c). 'The Day the World Stood Still: A Story of the First Atomic Bomb and Our Perpetual Cold War,' *Strategic Culture*, 1 October.

Chung, Cynthia (2021). 'Return of the Leviathan: The Fascistic Roots of the CIA and the True Origin of the Cold War,' *Strategic Culture*, 7 May.

Clauss, Michael (2017). 'Why Europe and the US cannot afford to ignore China's belt and road,' *South China Morning Post*, 16 June, http://www.scmp.com/comment/insight-opinion/article/2098527/why-europe-and-us-cannot-afford-ignore-chinas-belt-and-road (accessed 8 August 2017).

Conway-Lanz, Sahr (2006). *Collateral Damage: Americans, Noncombatant Immunity, and Atrocity after World War II*. London: Routledge.

Council on Foreign Relations (2021). Independent Task Force for the evaluation of the implications of the BRI for the U.S., 79th Report.

Cradock, Percy (1994). *Experiences of China*. London: Trafalgar Square.

Cradock, Percy (1997). 'Losing the plot in Hong Kong,' *Prospect*, 20 April.

Craig, David (2015). *Rip-Off! The Scandalous inside story of the management consulting machine*. London: The Original Book Company.

Craven, Mattew (2015). 'Between law and history. The Berlin Conference of 1884–1885 and the logic of free trade,' *London Review of International Law*, Vol 3. Issue 1, pp. 31–59.

Creel, G. (2012). *How We Advertised America: The First Telling of the Amazing Story of the Committee on Public Information That Carried the Gospel of Americanism to Every Corner of the Globe Corner*. Forgotten Books (Classic Reprint). Retrieved from https://www.forgottenbooks.com/en (first edition 1920).

Cumings, Bruce (2005). *Korea's Place in the Sun. A Modern History*. New York: Norton.

Cumings, Bruce (2011). *The Korean War. A History*. New York: The Modern Library.

Cumings, Bruce (2017). 'A murderous history of Korea,' *London Review of Books,* 18 May 2017. Retrieved May 20, 2017, retrieved May 20, 2017 from https://www.lrb.co.uk/v39/n10/bruce-cumings/a-murheroushistory-of-korea.

Cunningham, Edward, Tony Saich and Jessie Turiel (2020). 'Understanding CCP (Chinese Communist Party) Resilience: Surveying Chinese Public Opinion Through Time,' *Ash Center Programs for Democratic Governance, Harvard University*, July.

Democracy Now (2013). 'Make the Economy Scream': Secret Documents Show Nixon, Kissinger Role Backing 1973 Chile Coup, *Democracy Now*, 10 September, https://www.democracynow. org/2013/9/10/40_years_after_chiles_9_11 (accessed 25 October 2016).

Deng Xiaoci and Fan Anqi (2020). 'Chang'e-5 lands on moon, lays foundation for manned mission,' Global Times, https://www. globaltimes.cn/content/1208681.shtml, 01 December 2020 (accessed 4 December 2020).

Denyer, Simon (2013). 'China bypasses American "New Silk Road" with two of its own,' *The Washington Post*, 14 October, https://www. washingtonpost.com/world/asia_pacific/china-bypasses-american-new-silk-road-with-two-if-its-own/2013/10/14/49f9f60c-3284-11e3-ad00-ec4c6b31cbed_story.html?utm_term=.058ccff83b09 (accessed 24 June 2015).

Dickson, Bruce J. (2003). *Red capitalists in China: The party, private entrepreneurs, and prospects for political change*. Cambridge: Cambridge University Press.

Dickson, Bruce J. (2008). *Wealth into power: The communist party's embrace of China's private sector*. New York: Cambridge University Press.

Dimbleby, Johnathan (1997). *The Last Governor. Chris Patten and the Handover of Hong Kong*. London: Little, Brown and Company.

Dlouhy, Jennifer A. (2021a). 'Biden's plan to cut US oil production becomes clearer,' *World Oil*, 23 January 2021, https://www.worldoil. com/news/2021/1/22/biden-s-plan-to-cut-us-oil-production-becomes-clearer (accessed 20 February 2021).

Dlouhy, Jennifer A. (2021b). 'Keystone XL Oil Pipeline Is Terminated After Years of Climate Activism,' *Insurance Journal*, 11 June, https://www.insurancejournal.com/news/international/2021/06/11/618209.htm (accessed 14 June 2021).

Dlouhy. Jennifer and and Robert Tuttle (2021). 'Keystone XL protestors want Biden to revoke more pipeline permits,' *World Oil,* 13 June, https://www.worldoil.com/news/2021/6/11/keystone-xl-protestors-want-biden-to-revoke-more-pipeline-permits (accessed 14 June 2021).

Dollar, David, et al. (2017). 'Avoiding containment, competition, and Cooperation in U.S.-China Relations,' *A Brookings Interview,* November.

Donnan, Shawn (2014). 'Geopolitics cast shadow over New Silk Road,' *Financial Times,* 17 October (accessed 24 February 201).

Dower, John (2017). *The Violent American Century. War and Terror since World War II.* Chicago: Haymarket Books.

Easton, Ian (2017). *The Chinese Invasion Threat: Taiwan's Defense and American Strategy in Asia.* Arlington, VA: Project 2019 Institute

Eberhardt, Pia (2016). 'The Zombie ISDS. Rebranded as ICS, rights for corporations to sue states refuse to die,' *Corporate Europe Observatory.*

Economist (2018). 'China wants to reshape the global oil market,' *The Economist,* 28 March, https://www.economist.com/finance-and-economics/2018/03/28/china-wants-to-reshape-the-global-oil-market (accessed 15 April 2018).

Edelman, Murray (1985). *The Symbolic Uses of Politics.* Chicago: University of Illinois Press.

Eisenhower, Dwight (1961). Transcript of President Dwight D. Eisenhower's Farewell Address, https://www.ourdocuments.gov/doc.php?flash=false&doc=90&page=transcript (accessed 22 April 2021).

Engdahl, F. William (2014). *Target China. How Washington and wall street plan to cage the Asian dragon.* San Diego: Progressive Press.

Engelhardt, Tom (2014). *Shadow Government. Surveillance, Secret Wars, and Global Security State in a single-Superpower World.* Chicago: Haymarket Books.

Esfandiary, Dina and Tabatabai, Ariane (2018). *Triple Axis. Iran's Relations with Russia and China.* London: I.B. Tauris.

European Chamber (2017). China Manufacturing 2015, Putting Industrial Policy Ahead of Market Forces, available at http://www.europeanchamber.com.cn.

Fang, Alex, Marrian Zhou and Francesca Regaldo (2020). 'Team Biden says America is back. But is Asia ready to welcome it?' *Nikkei Asia*, 2 December, https://asia.nikkei.com/Spotlight/The-Big-Story/Team-Biden-says-America-is-back.-But-is-Asia-ready-to-welcome-it (accessed 18 December 2020).

Fannin, Rebecca (2019). *Tech Titans of China.* Boston: Brealey.

Fardella, Enrico, et al. (2016). La Belt and Road Initiative: la globalizzazione secondo Pechino, *Rivista bimestrale di politica, relazioni internazionali e dinamiche socio-economiche della Cina contemporanea*, Vol. 7, No.6, December.

Farrell, Diana, Ulrich A. Gersch and Elisabeth Stephenson (2008). 'The value of China's emerging middle class,' *The McKinsey Quarterly*, 2008 Special Edition.

Farrow, Anne, Joel Lang and Jenifer Frank (2006). *How the North Promoted, Prolonged and Profited from Slavery.* New York: Ballantine Books.

Fassihi, Farnaz and Steven Lee Myers (2020). 'Defying U.S., China and Iran Near Trade and Military Partnership,' *New York Times,* 11 July 2020 (accessed 29 March 2020).

FBI (2015). Chinese Talent Programs. *Federal Bureau of Investigation (FBI)*, Counterintelligence Strategic Partnership, Intelligence not (Spin), September. Retrieved 25 January 2019 from https://info.publicintelligence.net/FBI-ChineseTalentPrograms.pdf

Fenby, Jonathan (2014). *Will China Dominate the XXI Century?,* Cambridge, UK: Polity Press.

Flounders, Sara (2020). 'China's global vaccines – A game changer,' *Workers World,* 8 December, https://www.workers.org/2020/12/53125/ (accessed 25 January 2021).

Forsythe, Michael (2015). 'Tony Saich on what Chinese want from their leaders,' *Sinosphere*, 11 September. Retrieved October 18, 2015, from https://sinosphere.blogs.nytimes.com/2015/09/11/anthony-saich-china-communist-party/.

Freymann, Eyck (2021). 'The USA can't keep waiting for China's Belt and Road Initiative to fail,' *Fortune*, 24 March.

Friedberg, Aaron L. (2020). 'An Answer to Aggression,' *Foreign Affairs*, September/October.

Friedman, Milton (1982). *Capitalism and Freedom*. Chicago: The University of Chicago Press, preface to the second edition (1st edition 1962).

Fukuyama, Francis (1989). 'The end of history?,' *The National Interest*, Summer, No. 16, pp. 3–18.

Fukuyama, Francis (1992). *The End of History and the Last Man*. New York: Free Press.

Galbraith, James (2008). *The Predator State. How conservatives abandoned the free market and why liberals should too*. New York: Free Press.

Ganser, Daniele (2005). *NATO's secret armies. Operation gladio and terrorism in western Europe*. New York: Frank Cass.

Ganser, Daniele (2016). *Les guerres illégales de l'OTAN. Comment les pays membres de l'OTAN sapent l'ONU*. Plogastel Saint-Germain (France): Editions Demi-Lune.

Gernet, Jacques (1991). *Chine et christianisme: La première confrontation* (2nd edition). Paris: Gallimard.

Gordon-Reed, Annette (2018). 'America's original Sin,' *Foreign Affairs,* January/February.

Green, Michael J. (2017). *By More than Providence. Grand Strategy and American Power in the Pacific Since 1783*. New York: Columbia University Press.

Griffin, David R. (2018). *The American trajectory. Divine or demonic?* Atlanta: Clarity Press.

Grundvig, James Ottar (2016). *Master Manipulator, The Explosive True Story of Fraud, Embezzlement, and Government Betrayal at the CDC*. New York: Skyhorse.

Guyer, Jonathan (2020). 'How a Biden Adviser Got a Gig With Uber,' *Prospect.org*, 8 July.

Hancock, Tom (2017). 'Silk Road: China encircles the world with One Belt, One Road strategy,' *Financial Times*, 4 May, http://www.ft.com/content/0714074a-0334-11e7-aa5b-6bb07f5c8e12 (accessed 22 July 2017).

Hanley, Charles J, Sang-Hun Choe, and Martha Mendoza (2001). *The Bridge at no Gun Ri. A Hidden Nightmare From The Korean War.* New York: Holt & Company.

Harding, Robin and John Reed (2020). 'Asia-Pacific countries sign one of the largest free trade deals in history,' *Financial Times*, 15 November.

Harris, Stewart (2014). *China's Foreign Policy.* Cambridge, UK: Polity Press.

HM Government (2021). Global Britain in a competitive age. The Integrated Review of Security, Defence, Development and Foreign Policy, March 2021

Ho, Johnny, et al. (2019). China Consumer Report 2020, McKinsey, December.

Ho, Matt (2021). 'Is the Chinese prototype the shape of maglev train tech to come?,' *South China Morning Post*, 13 January.

Hobson, John M. (2004). *The Eastern Origins of Western Civilisation* (chapters 3 and 9 on Chinese influence on the West). Cambridge, Mass.: Cambridge University Press.

Houska, Tara (2021). 'Enbridge's Greenwashing Will Not Stand,' *Common Dreams*, 8 March 2021, https://www.commondreams.org/views/2021/03/08/enbridges-greenwashing-will-not-stand (accessed 22 March 2021).

HSBC (2017). 'One Belt One Road briefing note,' 12 May, http://www.lmfinternational.com/index.php/news/560-trends/40553-hsbc-one-belt-one-road-briefing-note (accessed 20 May 2017).

Hsü Immanuel C.Y. (1995). *The Rise of Modern China.* New York: Oxford University Press.

Hu Angang (2014). *China's Collective Presidency.* Heidelberg and Beijing: Springer.

Hu Angang (2016). 'One Belt One Road: Reshaping Chinese economic geography,' paper kindly provided by author. Beijing: Institute of Contemporary China Studies, Tsinghua University, April.

Hu Angang and Men Honghua (2004). 'The Rising of Modern China: Comprehensive National Power and Grand Strategy,' paper presented at the international conference on 'Rising China and the East Asian Economy,' Seoul, 19–20 March 2004, kindly provided by authors. The original Chinese version was published in *Strategy & Management*, No 3, 2002. This article is available on *Wikipedia*, under 'Comprehensive National Power.'

Hu Angang and Ren Hao (2016). 'How can China's high-technology industry catch up with United States.' *Strategy and Policy Decision Research* (Vol. 31, pp. 1355–1364), Proceedings of Chinese Academy of Sciences, 1355 Phase 12.

Hu Angang, Wang Yi, et al. (1992). *Survival and Development: A Study of China's Long-Term Development*. Beijing and New York: Science Press.

Hu Angang, Zhang Xin, and Zhang Wei (2017). 'Strategic connotation and conception of the development of the Belt, Road and Channel (Arctic Shipping Channel) Initiative,' paper kindly provided by main author. Beijing, School of Public Policy and Management, Tsinghua University, 12 April.

Hu Angang and Zou Ping (1991). *China's Population Development.* Beijing: China's Science and Technology Press.

Huang, Kristin and Kinling Lo (2019). As China and US spar over tech, scientists would rather not talk about their talent awards, *South China Morning Post*, 14 January.

Hudson, Michael (2003). *Super Imperialism. The Origin and Fundamentals of US World Dominance*. London: Pluto Press, Second edition with a new preface (first edition 1972).

Hudson, Michael (2005). *Global Fracture. The New International Economic Order*. London: Pluto Press, Second edition with a new introduction (first edition 1977).

Hudson, Michael (2019a). Trump's Brilliant Strategy to Dismember US Dollar hegemony, Hudson Website, 1 January, https://michael-hudson.com/2019/02/trumps-brilliant-strategy-to-dismember-u-s-dollar-hegemony/accessed 2 January 2019.

Hudson, Michael (2019b). Venezuela as the pivot for New Internationalism?, Michael Hudson Website, 6 January, https://michael-hudson.com/2019/02/venezuela-as-the-pivot-for-new-internationalism/ (accessed 8 January 2019).

Huntington, Samuel P. (2011). *The Clash of Civilizations and the Remaking of World Order*. New York: Simon & Schuster

IHEP (2018). CEPC (Circular Electron Positron Collider) Design Report Released, Institute of High Energy Physics, Chinese Academy of Sciences, 11 November, http://english.ihep.cas.cn/doc/3229.html (accessed 29 January 2019).

Immerwahr, Daniel (2020). 'You Can Only See Liberalism From the Bottom. Why Pankaj Mishra sees the ideology's limits more clearly than its moist powerful fans, *Foreign Policy*, 21 September.

ILO (2016). Extending social protection to rural migrants. People's Republic of China, September, http://www.social-protection.org/gimi/RessourcePDF.action?ressource.ressourceId=53859 (accessed 20 June 2017).

Irish, John (2019). 'Skirting US sanctions, Europeans open new trade channel to Iran.' *Reuters*, 31 January. Retrieved 10 February 2019, from https://www.reuters.com/article/us-iran-usa-sanctionseu/skirting-u-s-sanctions-europeans-launch-trade-mechanism-for-iran-idUSKCN1PP0K3.

Jäcklein, Wolf (2014). 'Transatlantic Trade and Investment Partnership: ten threats to Europeans,' *Le Monde Diplomatique*, 14 2014, http://mondediplo.com/2014/06/11ttip (accessed 23 May 2017).

Jacobs, Ben (2015). 'The Donald Trump doctrine: "Assad is bad" but U.S. must stop "nation-building,"' *The Guardian*, 13 October, https://www.theguardian.com/us-news/2015/oct/13/donald-trump-foreign-policy-doctrine-nation-building (accessed 15 December 2016).

Jayaman, Kartik, et al. (2017). 'The closest look yet at Chinese economic engagement in Africa,' *McKinsey&Company*, Report, June

Jefferson, Thomas (1801). 'From Thomas Jefferson to James Monroe,' 24 November, National Archive, Founders Online, https://founders. archives.gov/documents/Jefferson/01-35-02-0550 (accessed 18 August 2018).

Jefferson, Thomas (1816). 'To John Adams from Thomas Jefferson,' 1 August 1816, National Archive, Founders Online, https:// founders.archives.gov/documents/Adams/99-02-02-6618 (accessed 18 August 2018).

Jie Chen (2013). *A Middle Class Without Democracy: Economic Growth and the Prospects for Democratization in China.* Oxford: Oxford University Press .

Jie Chen and Chunglong Lu (2006). 'Does China's Middle Class Think and Act Democratically? Attitudinal and Behavioral Orientations Towards Urban Self-Government,' *Journal of Chinese Political Science*, Fall, pp. 1–19.

Jie Chen and Bruce J. Dickson (2008). 'Allies of the state: Democratic support and regime support among China's private entrepreneurs,' *China Quarterly*, December 2008, pp. 780–804.

Johnson, Chalmers (2000). *Blowback. The Costs and Consequences of American Empire.* New York: Henry Holt.

Johnson, Chalmers (2004). *The Sorrows of Empire. Militarism, Secrecy, and the End of the Republic.* New York: Henry Holt.

Johnson, Chalmers (2006). *Nemesis. The last days of the American Republic.* New York: Henry Holt.

Johnson, Chalmers (2010). *Dismantling the Empire. America's last Best Hope.* New York: Henry Holt.

Johnson, Jake (2020). 'Biden Quietly Adds Goldman Sachs, Big Tech Officials to Transition,' *Consortium News*, 22 December 2020.

Johnstone, Caitlin (2021a). 'Boot Coming Down Hard and Fast on Social Media,' *Consortium News*, 10 January.

Johnstone, Caitlin (2021b). 'Les médias mainstream utilisent déjà l'émeute du Capitole pour exiger davantage de censure sur le Net,' *Investigaction,* 8 January.

Johnstone Diana (2016). *Queen of Chaos: The Misadventures of Hillary Clinton*. Petrolia, Calif.: Counterpunch.

Jones, Owen (2017). 'Americans can spot elections meddling because they've been doing it for years,' *The Guardian*, 5 January, https://www.theguardian.com/commentisfree/2017/jan/05/americans-spot-election-meddling-doing-years-vladimir-putin-donald-trump (accessed 13 June 2017).

Jullien, François (1989). *Procès ou création. Une introduction à la pensée chinoise*. Paris: Seuil, 1989

Jullien, François (1995). *The Propensity of Things. Towards a History of Efficacy in China*. New York: Zone Books.

Jullien, François (1999). *The Propensity of Things. Towards a History of Efficacy in China*. New York: Zone Books, 1999

Jullien, François (2004). *A Treatise on Efficacy. Between Western and Chinese Thinking*, Honolulu, University of Hawai'i Press, 2004.

Jullien, François (2005a). *De l'être au vivre. Lexique euro-chinois de la pensée*. Paris: Gallimard, 2015, pp. 8–10.

Jullien, François (2005b). *Conférence sur l'efficacité*. Paris: Presses Universitaires de France.

Jullien. François (2006). 'Postface,' in André Chieng, *La pratique de la Chine, en compagnie de François Jullien*. Paris: Grasset.

Jullien, François (2008). *In Praise of Blandness. Proceedings from Chinese Thought and Aesthetics*. New York: Zone Books, 2008.

Jullien, François (2011). *The Silent Transformations*. London: Seagull.

Jullien, François (2015a). 'Du commun à l'universel,' in Le Huu Khoa (dir.), *Le dialogue entre cultures, du commun à l'universel*. Paris: Les Indes savantes, pp. 9–55.

Jullien, François (2015b). *Le dialogue entre cultures, du commun à l'universel*. Paris: Les Indes savantes.

Jullien, François (2017). *Il n'y a pas d'identité culturelle*. Paris: L'Herne.

Kagan, Robert (2003). *Of Paradise and Power. America and Europe in the New World Order*. New York: Vintage Books.

Kagan, Robert (2008). *The Return of History and the End of Dreams*. London: Atlantic Books.

Kagan, Robert (2012a). 'Not fade away: Against the myth of American decline,' *Brookings Institution*, 17 January.

Kagan, Robert (2012b). *The World America Made*. New York: Alfred A. Knopf.

Kagan, Robert (2012c). 'Why the World Needs America,' *Wall Street Journal*, 11 February, https://www.wsj.com/articles/SB1000142405 2970203646004577213262856669448 (accessed 25 January 2021).

Kagan, Robert (2014). 'Superpowers don't get to retire. What our tired country still owes to the world,' 27 May, *New Republic*, https://newrepublic.com/article/117859/superpowers-dont-get-retire (accessed 20 March 2017).

Kagan, Robert (2017a). 'The twilight of the liberal world order,' *Brookings Report*, 24 January, https://www.brookings.edu/research/the-twilight-of-the-liberal-world-order/ (accessed 27 January 2017).

Kagan, Robert (2017b). 'Backing into World War III,' *Brookings Institution*, 6 February, https://www.brookings.edu/research/backing-into-world-war-iii/ (accessed 14 February 2017).

Kagan, Robert (2021). 'A Superpower, Like it or Not: Why Americans Must Accept Their Global Role,' *Foreign Affairs*, March-April.

Kania, Elsa B. (2018). 'China's Quantum Future. Xi's Quest to Build aHigh-Tech Superpower.' *Foreign Affairs*, 26 September. Retrieved 20 October, https://www.foreignaffairs.com/articles/china/2018-09-26/chinas-quantum-future.

Karp, Walter (1979). *The Politics of War: The Story of Two Wars which Altered Forever the Political Life of the American Republic (1890–1920)*. New York: Harper Colophon Books.

Keidel, Albert (2007). *The Causes and Impact of Chinese Regional Inequalities in Income and Well-Being*. Carnegie Endowment for International Peace, December 2007.

Kramer, Michael (2001). 'Rescuing Boris.' *Time*, 24 June. Retrieved June 10, 2017, from http://content.time.com/time/printout/0,8816,136204,00.html.

Kelsey, Jane (2011). 'International civil society demands end to secrecy in TPPA talks,' media release, 16 February 2011, http://tppwatch.org (accessed 29 March 2011).

Kelstrup, Jesper Dahl (2016). *The Politics of Think Tanks in Europe.* London and New York: Routledge.

Kendall, Brent and John D. McKinnon (2020). 'Facebook Hit With Antitrust Lawsuits by FTC, State Attorneys General,' *Wall Street Journal,* 9 December.

Kendall-Taylor, Andrea and David Shullman (2021). 'China and Russia' Dangerous Convergence. How to Counter an Emerging Partnership,' *Foreign Affairs*, 3 May 2021.

Kendall-Taylor, Andrea, Erica Frantz, and Joseph Wright (2020). 'The Digital Dictators. How Technology Strengthens Autocracy,' *Foreign Affairs*, March-April.

Kennan, George (1947). The sources of soviet conduct, *Foreign Affairs*, July issue, https://www.foreignaffairs.com/articles/russian-federation/1947-07-01/sources-soviet-conduct (accessed 15 May 2017).

Kennedy, Robert F. Jr. (2016). 'Why the Arabs don't want us in Syria. They don't hate "our freedoms." They hate the fact that we've betrayed our ideals in their own countries.' *Politico*, 16 September 2016. Retrieved December 18, 2016, from http://www.politico.eu/article/why-the-arabs-dontwant-us-in-syria-mideast-conflict-oil-intervention/.

Kingston, Reif and Shannon Bugos (2021). 'U.S., Russia Extend New START for Five Years,' *Arms Control Association,* March, https://www.armscontrol.org/act/2021-03/news/us-russia-extend-new-start-five-years (accessed 15 March 2021).

Kinzer, Shephen (2017). *The True Flag. Theodore Roosevelt, Mark Twain, and the Birth of American Empire.* New York: Henry Holt.

Klein, Kent (2012).'Obama: US "The one indispensable nation in world affairs,"' *Voice of America News*, 28 May, http://www.voanews.com/content/obama (accessed 18 April 2016).

Kluth, Andreas (2020). 'The China-EU Investment Deal Is a Mistake,' *Bloomberg*, 30 December, https://www.bloomberg.com/opinion/articles/2020-12-30/europe-s-big-investment-deal-with-china-is-a-mistake (accessed 2 January 2021).

Koepke, Logan, et al. (2020). 'Mass Extraction: The Wide-spread Power of U.S. Law Enforcement to Search Mobile Phones,' *Forensic Resources, Upturn Towards Justice in Technology*, October.

Kuzmarov, Jeremy and John Marciano (2018). *The Russians are Coming, Again: The first cold war as tragedy, the second as farce*. New York: Monthly Review Press.

Kyle Crossley, Pamela, et al. (2017). 'How does China's imperial past shape its foreign policy today?,' *A ChinaFile Conversation*, 15 March, http://www.chinafile.com/conversation/how-does-chinas-imperial-past-shape-its-foreign-policy-today (accessed 19 March 2017).

Kynge, James (2009). 'The West miscasts Tiananmen protesters,' *Financial Times*, 3 June.

La Feber, Walter (1994). *American Age. U.S. Foreign Policy at Home and Abroad: 1750 to the Present*. New York: W.W Norton (2nd edition).

La Feber, Walter (1998). *The New Empire: An Interpretation of American Expansion 1860–1898*. Ithaca and London: Cornell (Thirty-fifth Anniversary Edition).

La Feber, Walter (2012). 'Illusions of an American Century,' in Bacevich, Andrew (ed.) (2012), *The Short American Century: A Postmortem*. Cambridge, Mass.: Harvard University Press, pp. 158–186.

Las Casas, Bartolomé de (1974). *The Devastation of the Indians. A Brief Account* (translated by Herman Briffault). Baltimore, Md.: Johns Hopkins University Press, 1974 (first published in Spanish 1552).

Las Casas, Bartolomé de (1992). *In Defense of the Indians* (translated and edited by Stafford Poole, with foreword by Martin Marty). DeKalb, IL, Northern Illinois University Press.

Lacroix-Riz, Annie (1985). *Le choix de Marianne. Les relations franco-américaines 1944-1948*. Paris: Messidor/Editions sociales.

Lacroix-Riz, A. (2014). *Aux origines du carcan européen 1990–1960.* Paris: Delga.

Lauria, Joe (2021). 'Capitol Incident a Dress Rehearsal. The storming of the Capitol may just be a harbinger of things to come,' *Consortium News,* 7 January.

Le Bon, Gustave (1905). *Psychologie des foules.* Paris: Felix Alcan.

Le Corre, Philippe and Jonathan Pollack (2016). 'China's global rise: can the EU and US pursue a coordinated strategy?,' Brookings Institution, October.

Lee, Kai-fu (2018). *AI Superpowers. China, Silicon Valley, and the New World Order.* Boston: Houghton Mifflin Harcourt.

Lee, Matthew (2021). 'Biden fills out State Department team with Obama veterans,' *Associated Press,* 16 January 2021, https://apnews.com/article/joe-biden-donald-trump-biden-cabinet-antony-blinken-foreign-policy-e7026ce218735c9faec9c7349aefb51e (accessed 26 January 2021).

Leebaert, Derek (2011). *Magic and Mayhem. The Delusions of American Foreign Policy from Korea to Afghanistan.* New York: Simon and Schuster.

Levathes, Louise (1994). *When China Rules the Seas. The Treasure Fleet of the Dragon Throne, 1405–1433.* New York: Oxford University Press.

Levin, Dov H. (2016). 'Sure, the US and Russia often meddle in foreign elections. Does it matter?,' *The Washington Post,* 7 September 2016, https://www.washingtonpost.com/news/monkey-cage/wp/2016/09/07/sure-the-u-s-and-russia-often-meddle-in-foreign-elections-does-it-matter/?utm_term=.ca54b59ff042 (accessed 13 June 2017).

Litovsky, Alejandro (2017). 'China plans super-grid for clean power in Asia,' *Financial Times,* December, https://www.ft.com/content/e808a542-d6c6-11e7-8c9a-d9c0a5c8d5c9 (accessed 20 December 2018).

Lofgren, Mike (2016). *The Deep State. The Fall of the Constitution and the Rise of a Shadow Government.* New York: Penguin Books.

Longling Wei (2020). 'China Eyes Shrinking Jack Ma's Business Empire,' *Wall Street Journal,* 29 December, https://www.wsj.com/articles/china-eyes-shrinking-jack-mas-business-empire-11609260092?mod=djemalertNEWS (accessed 29 December 2020).

Losurdo, Domenico (2011). *Liberalism: A Counter-History.* London: Verso, 2011.

Losurdo, Domenico (2007). *Il linguaggio dell'Impero: Lessico dell'ideologia americana.* Bari: Laterza, 2007.

Ma Yan and Pierre Haski (2009). *The Diary of Ma Yan: The struggle and hopes of a Chinese schoolgirl.* New York: Harper Collins.

MacLeod, Alan (2021). 'Trump's Twitter Ban May Be Justified, but that Doesn't Mean Tech Giants' Power Isn't Scary,' *Fair.org,* 15 January.

Mao Zedong (1949). 'The Chinese People Have Stood Up!' Opening address by the Chairman of the Chinese Communist Party, at the First Plenary Session of the Chinese People's Political Consultative Conference, 21 Sept., https://china.usc.edu/Mao-declares-founding-ofpeoples-republic-of-china-chinese-people-have-stood-up.

Marguerat, Daniel and Junod, Eric (2010). *Qui a fondé le christianisme?* Genève: Labor et Fides.

Marty, Dick (2018). *Une certaine idée de la justice. Théchénie, Kosovo, CIA, Drogue.* Lausanne: Favre.

Martyanov, Andrei (2018). *Losing Military Supremacy. The Myopia of American Strategic Planning.* Atlanta: Clarity Press.

Martyanov, Andrei (2019). *The Real Revolution in Military Affairs.* Atlanta: Clarity Press.

Martyanov, Andrei (2021). *Disintegration. Indicators of the Coming American Collapse.* Atlanta: Clarity Press.

Maupin, Caleb (2020). *Kamala Harris and the Future of America: An Essay in Three Parts.* Center for Political Innovation.

McCoy, Alfred W. (2003). *The Politics of Heroin: CIA Complicity in the*

Global Drug Trade. Atlanta: A Cappella Books.

McCoy, Alfred W. (2015). 'Grandmaster of the Great Game: Obama's geopolitical strategy for containing China,' *Tom Dispatch*, 17 September 2015, http://www.tomdispatch.com/post/176044/ tomgram:_alfred_ mccoy, maintaining_American_supremacy_in_ the twenty-first century (accessed 18 September 2015).

McCoy, Alfred W. (2021). 'America's Drug Wars,' *TomDispatch*, 6 July.

McFaul, Michael (2021). How to Contain Putin's Russia, *Foreign Affairs*, 19 January.

McGovern, Ray (2020). 'Catapulting Russian-Meddling Propaganda,' *Consortium News*, 21 August.

McNamara, Robert (2005). Apocalypse Soon, *Foreign Policy*, May-June, reprinted 21 October 2009, https://foreignpolicy.com/2009/10/21/ apocalypse-soon/ (accessed 15 January 2019).

Menzies, Gavin (2008). *1434: The Year a Magnificent Chinese Fleet Sailed to Italy and Ignited the Renaissance*. New York: HarperCollins.

Menzies, Gavin (2003). *1421: The Year China Discovered America*. New York: Harper Collins, 2003.

Migone, Gian Giacomo (2015). *The United States and Italy. The rise of American finance in Europe*. New York: Cambridge University Press.

Mishra, Pankaj (2020). *Bland Fanatics. Liberals, Race and Empire*. New York: Verso.

Mishra, Pankaj (2013). *From the Ruins of Empire. The Revolt Against the West and the Remaking of Asia*. London: Penguin Books.

Mitter, Rana (2121). 'The World China Wants,' *Foreign Affairs*, January/ February.

Montanino, Andrea and Earl Anthony Wayne (2016). *The Arguments for TTIP and the Concerns to Address*, Atlantic Council, Global Business and Economic Program, April.

Mosbergen, Dominique (2019). 'Joe Biden Promises Rich Donors He Won't "Demonize" The Wealthy if Elected President,' *Huffpost,* 19 June, https://www.huffpost.com/entry/joe-biden-wont-demonize-the-rich_n_5d09ac63e4b0f7b74428e4c6 (accessed 15 January 2021).

Munene, G. Macharia (1990). 'The United States and the Berlin Conference on the partition of Africa, 1885–1885,' *Transafrican Journal of History*, Vol. 19, 1990, pp. 73–79.

Napolitano, Andrew P. (2020). 'From the Streets of Portland to the NSA, U.S. Government Spying on Everyone Proceeds Unabated,' *Washington Times*, 19 August.

NATO (2021). *Brussel Summit Communiqué,* 14 June, https://www.nato.int/cps/en/natohq/news_185000.htm (accessed 15 June 2021).

Navarro, Peter (2015). *Crouching Tiger. What China's Militarism Means for the World.* New York: Prometheus Books.

Navarro, Peter (2016). 'Introduction: Crouching Tiger—China Acts, America Dithers,' in Fred Fleitz (ed.) (2016), *Warning Order: China Prepares for Conflict and Why We Must Do the Same.* Washington: Center for Security Policy Press.

Needham, Joseph (1954-2004). *Science and Civilisation in China.* Cambridge: Cambridge University Press.

Needham, Joseph (1969). *The Grand Titration: Science and Society in East and West.* London: Allen & Unwin.

Norton, Ben (2020a). 'Twitter Spreads Paid US Gov't Propaganda With Falsely Claiming it Bans State Media Ads,' *The Grayzone*, 10 August.

Norton, Ben (2020b). 'Leaked Docs Expose massive Syria Propaganda Operation by Western Govt Contractors & Media,' *Consortium News*, 13 October.

Nuclear Threat Initiative (2015). China Nuclear, April. Retrieved May 26, 2016, from http://www.nti.org/learn/countries/china/nuclear/.

Nuland, Victoria (2020). 'Pinning Down Putin,' *Foreign Affairs*, July/August.

Nye, Joseph S. (2004). *Soft Power. The Means to Success in World Politics*. New York: Public Affairs.

Nye, Joseph S. (2008). *The Powers to Lead*. Oxford: Oxford University Press.

Nye, Joseph S. (2011). *The Future of Power*. New York: Public Affairs.

Nye, Joseph S. (2015). *Is the American Century Over?* Cambridge: Polity.

Obama, Barack (2012). 'President Obama commencement speech at the U.S. Air Force Academy,' The White House, Office of the Press Secretary, 23 May 2012.

Obama, Barack (2014). 'Remarks by the President at the United States Military Academy Commencement Ceremony, U.S. Military Academy-West Point,' The White House, Office of the Press Secretary, 28 May.

Obama, Barack (2015). 'Remarks by President Obama on the Iran Nuclear Deal,' The White House Office of the Press Secretary, For Immediate Release, August 05, 2015, American University, Washington, D.C., https://obamawhitehouse.archives.gov/the-press-office/2015/08/05/ remarks-president-iran-nuclear-deal (accessed 7 march 2016).

Obama, Barack (2016a). 'Remarks of President Barack Obama: State of the Union Address as Delivered,' 16 January 2016, https://www. whitehouse.gov/the-press-office/2016/01/12/remarks-president- barack-obama-%E2%80%93-prepared-delivery-state-union- address (accessed 27 January 2016).

Obama, Barack (2016b). 'Remarks by the President in Commencement Address to the United States Air Force Academy,' The White House, Office of the Press Secretary, For Immediate Release, June 02, https://obamawhitehouse.archives.gov/the-press-office/2016/06/02/ remarks-president-commencement-address-united-states-air-force- academy (accessed 20 January 2017).

O'Brien, Robert C. (2020). 'How China Threatens American Democracy: Beijing's Ideological Agenda Has Gone Global,' *Foreign Affairs*, 21 October.

Osborne, Andrew and Tom Balmforth (2021). 'Putin offers Biden public talks after US president says he is a killer,' *Reuters,* 18 March 2021

Park, Sungwoo (2018). 'How China Is About to Shake Up the Oil Futures Market,' *Bloomberg*, 8 March, https://www.bloomberg. com/news/articles/2018-03-08/how-china-is-about-to-shake-up-the-oil-futures-market-quicktake (accessed 15 March 2018).

Parramore, Lynn (2020). 'How Corruption is Becoming America's Operating Sytem,' *Naked Capitalism*, 2 October (originally published by *Institute for New Economic Thinking*).

Patten, Chris (2019a). 'Unforgettable Tiananmen,' *The Asian Post*, 31 May.

Patten, Chris (2019b). 'China's Hong Kong Problem,' *Project Syndicate*, 30 September.

Patten, Chris (2020). 'The China "Constrainment" Doctrine,' *Project Syndicate*, 25 June.

Patten, Chris (2021a). 'Biden's Good Start on China,' *Project Syndicate*, 22 February.

Patten, Chris (2021b). 'China's One-Way Diplomacy,' *Project Syndicate*, 1 June.

Peerenboom, Randall (2002). *China's Long March Toward Rule of Law*. Cambridge: Cambridge University Press.

Peerenboom, Randall (2006). 'A government of laws. Democracy, rule of law, and administrative law reform in China,' in Zhao 2006, pp. 58–78.

Peerenboom, Randall (2007). *China modernizes. Threat to the west or model for the rest?* Oxford: Oxford University Press.

PEN Charitable Trust (2017). 'The Integrated Arctic Corridors Framework. Planning for Responsible Shipping in Canada's Arctic Waters,' a report of the *PEN Charitable Trusts*, April 2016, available at http://www.pewtrusts.org/en/research-and-analysis/reports/2016/04/the-integrated-arctic-corridors-framework (accessed 10 June 2017).

Pence, Mike (2018). 'Vice President Mike Pence's remarks on the administration's policy towards China.' *Hudson Institute*, 4 October. Retrieved November 15, 2018, from https://www.hudson.org/events/1610-vice-president-mike-pence-s-remarks-on-the-administration-s-policy-towardschina102018m.

Pfaff, William (2010). *The Irony of Manifest Destiny*. New York: Walker & Co.

Pillsbury, Michael (2015). *The Hundred-Year Marathon. China's Secret Strategy to Replace America as the Global Superpower*. New York: Henry Holt & Co.

Pike, John (2020). 'Donald Trump The Manchurian Candidate?,' *Globalsecurity*, 25 November.

Pimpaneau, Jacques (2011). *Les chevaux célestes. L'histoire du Chinois qui découvrit l'Occident*. Arles, France: Philippe Picquier.

Pirazzoli-T'Serstevens, Michèle (2007). *Giuseppe Castiglione, 1688–1766, peintre et architecte à la cour de Chine*, Paris: Thalia.

Planetary (2020). 'Chang'e-5: China's Moon Sample Return Mission,' *Planetary Society*, December 2020, https://www.planetary.org/space-missions/change-5 (accessed 4 January 2021).

Platt, Stephen (2018). *Imperial Twilight. The Opium War and the End of China's Last Golden Age*. London: Atlantic Books.

Polanyi, Karl (2001). *The Great Transformation. The Political and economic Origins of Our Time*. Boston: Beacon Press (1st edition 1944).

Ponsonby, Arthur (1928). *Falsehood in War-Time: Propaganda Lies of the First World War*. London: George Allen and Unwin.

Porter, Patrick (2018a). 'Why America's Grand Strategy Has Not Changed. Power, Habit, and the US Foreign Policy Establishment,' *International Security*, Vol. 42, No. 4 (Spring), pp. 9–46.

Porter, Patrick (2018b). 'A World Imagined: Nostalgia and Liberal Order,' *Cato Institute,* Policy Analysis No. 843, June 5.

PRC (2015a). The Information Office of the State Council of PRC, 'China's Military Strategy,' May, Beijing, http://www.chinadaily.com.cn/china/2015-05/26/content_20820628.htm (accessed 25 March 2017).

PRC (2015b). Vision and Actions on Jointly Building Silk Road Economic Belt and XXI century Maritime Road, 28 March, issued by the National Development and Reform Commission, http://en.ndrc.gov.cn/newsrelease/201503/t20150330_669367.html (accessed 15 July 2015).

PRC (2015c). *The National Medium- and Long-Term Program for Science and Technology Development (2016–2020)* known as '*Made in China 2025.*' The State Council. Retrieved September 26, 2016, from http://english.gov.cn/2016special/madeinchina2025/.

PRC (2017). *Building the Belt and Road: Concept, Practice and China's Contribution*, Office of the Leading Group for the Belt and Road Initiative. Beijing: Foreign Language Press, May 2017.

Prins, Nomi (2011). 'Debt from bailouts didn't pan out,' 10 August, http://www.nomiprins.com/articles/ (accessed 27 October 2011).

Prins, Nomi (2018). *Collusion: How Central Bankers Rigged the World*. New York: Nation Books.

Putten, Franz-Paul van der, et al. (eds.) (2016). *Europe and China's New Silk Roads*, The European Think-tank Network on China (ETNC), December Report.

Qin Gao & Sui Yang & Shi Li (2017). 'Social insurance for migrant workers in China: impact of the 2008 Labour Contract Law,' *Economic and Political Studies*, Taylor & Francis Journals, vol. 5(3), pages 285-304, July.

Raphaël, René and Ling Xi (2019). Bons et mauvais chinois. Quand l'Etat organise la notation de ses citoyens, *Le Monde Diplomatique*, Janvier.

Rapoza, Kenneth (2017). 'Why HSBC Loves China's Silk Road,' *Forbes,* 17 May, https://www.forbes.com/sites/kenrapoza/2017/05/17/why-hsbc-loves-chinas-silk-road/#201c2faf697e (accessed 29 May 2017).

Rashish, Peter S. (2014). '*Bridging the Pacific: The Americas' New Economic Frontier?*, Atlantic Council, Global Business and Economic Program, July 2014.

Rastrick, Crhistopher J, (2018). *Think Tanks in the US and EU. The Role of Policy Institutes in Washington and Brussels*. London and New York: Routledge.

Reevell (2021). 'Putin challenges Biden to debate after president calls him a 'killer,' NBC News, 18 March 2021.

Renewable Energy Institute (undated). About 'Asia Super Grid (ASG).'

Tokyo. Retrieved December 25, 2018, from https://www.renewable-ei.org/en/asg/about/.

Reuters Staff (2020). 'Sinopharm says may be able to make over 1 billion coronavirus vaccine doses in 2021,' *Reuters*, 20 October, https://www.reuters.com/article/health-coronavirus-china-vaccine-int-idUSKBN2750WM (accessed 25 January 2021).

Richard, H. (2018). 'Lonely Russia: No room for Moscow in "common European home."' *Le Monde Diplomatique*, English edition, October.

Rojansky, Matthew (2016). George Kennan is still the Russia expert America needs. *Foreign Policy*, 22 December. Retrieved May 16, 2017, from http://foreignpolicy.com/2016/12/22/why-georgekennan-is-still-americas-most-relevant-russia-expert-trump-putin-ussr/.

Sachs, Jeffrey and William Schabas (2021). 'The Xinjiang Genocide Allegations Are Unjustified,' *Project Syndicate*, 20 April.

Saich, Tony (2016).'How China's citizens view the quality of governance under Xi Jinping,' *Journal of Chinese Governance*, 7 April (online), pp. 1–20

Salazar Torreon, Barbara (2020). *Instances of Use of United States Armed Forces Abroad, 1798–2020.* U.S. Congressional Research Service, 7–5700, R42738, 20 July 2020.

Sanderson, Henry (2019). 'Hydrogen power: China backs fuel cell technology. Producers are buying foreign tech but industry must build for future after subsidies.' *Financial Times*. Retrieved January 15, 2019, from https://www.ft.com/content/27ccfc90-fa49-11e8-af46-2022a0b02a6c.

Saunt, Claudio (2020). *Unworthy Republic: The Dispossession of Native Americans and the Road to Indian Territory.* New York: Norton.

Schadlow, Nadia (2020). 'The End of American Illusion—Trump and the World as It Is,' *Foreign Affairs,* September/October, https://www.foreignaffairs.com/articles/americas/2020-08-11/end-american-illusion (accessed 25 November 2020).

Schweizer, Peter (2020). *Profiles in Corruption: Abuse of Power by America's Progressive Elite.* New York: Harper, 2020.

Science Alert (2020). 'China Just Switched on Its "Artificial Sun" Nuclear Fusion Reactor,' *Science Alert*, 7 December.

Scissors, Derek (2019). 'Chinese Investments: State-Owned Enterprises Stop Globalization, for the Moment,' *American Economic Institute*, 17 January

Scissors, Derek (2021). 'China's Coming Global Investment Recovery: How Far Will It Go?,' *American Economic Institute*, January.

Scott, Peter Dale (2017). *The American deep state. Big money, big oil, and the struggle for U.S.* New York: Rowman & Littlefield.

Shala, Arsalan (2021). 'China Signs 25-year Deal with Iran in Challenge to the U.S.,' *Bloomberg*, 27 March, https://www.bloomberg.com/news/articles/2021-03-27/china-signs-25-year-deal-with-iran-in-challenge-to-the-u-s (accessed 30 June 2021).

Shane, S. (2018). 'Russia Isn't the Only One Meddling in Elections. We Do It, Too,' *The New York Times*, 17 February. Retrieved March 25, 2018, from https://www.nytimes.com/2018/02/17/sunday-review/russia-isnt-the-only-one-meddling-in-elections-we-do-it-too.html.

Shepard, Wade (2016). 'China's "New Silk Road" picks up where Hillary Clinton's flopped,' *Forbes, Asia, Foreign Affairs*, 9 September, https://www.forbes.com/sites/wadeshepard/2016/09/09/chinas-new-silk-road-picks-up-where-hillary-clintons-flopped-in-afghanistan/#61af395963f9 (accessed 28 July 2017).

Singh, Ajit (2020). 'U.S. Pushes Conspiracy Theory on China's Coronavirus Death Toll to Deflect from Trump Administration Failures,' *The Grayzone*, 1 April.

Sjursen, Daniel (2020). *Patriotic Dissent: America in the Age of Endless War*, Berkeley, Heyday.

Sjursen, Daniel (2021). A *True History of the United States: Indigenous Genocide, Racialized Slavery, Hyper-Capitalism, Militarist Imperialism and Other Overlooked Aspects of American Exceptionalism*, Truth to Power.

Slater, Julia (2007). 'When the Army Killed Civilians,' *SWI - SwissInfo. ch*, 9 November, https://www.swissinfo.ch/eng/when-the-army-killed-civilians/6239400 (accessed 10 July 2021).

Smith, Jeff M. (2015). 'Beware of China's Grand Strategy,' *Foreign Affairs*, 20 May, https://www.foreignaffairs.com/articles/china/2015-05-20/beware-chinas-grand-strategy (accessed 13 June 2015).

Smith, Yves (2015). 'How the China's New Silk Road is Shifting Geopolitics,' 27 May, *Naked Capitalism*, https://www.nakedcapitalism.com/2015/05/how-the-chinas-new-silk-road-is-shifting-geopolitics.html (accessed 27 May 2015).

Smith, Yves (2017). 'Newly-Declassified Documents Show Western Leaders Promised Gorbachev that NATO Would Not Move "One Inch Closer" to Russia.' *Naked Capitalism,* 15 January 3, 2018, fromwww.nakedcapitalism.com/2017/12/newly-declassified-documents-showwestern-leaders-promised-gorbachev-nato-notmove-one-inch-closer-russia.html.

Solis, Myreya (2016). 'The Trans-Pacific Partnership: the politics of openness and leadership in the Asia-Pacific,' Brookings Institution, October 2016

Sorman, Guy (2008). *The Empire of Lies: The Truth about China in the XXI Century*. New York: Encounter Books.

Starr, Paul (2019). 'The New Masters of the Universe,' *Foreign Affairs,* November-December.

Starr, Evan, Prescott, and Bishara (2018). 'Noncompetes in the U.S. Labor Force,' *University of Michigan Law & Econ Research Paper No. 18-013*, 74 Pages, Posted: 3 Jul 2015 Last revised: 13 Sep 2018, https://papers.ssrn.com/sol3/Papers.cfm?abstract_id=2625714 (accessed 16 December).

Stelzenmüller, Constance (2020). 'Stronger together: A strategy to revitalize trans-Atlantic power,' *Brookings*, 14 December.

Stephanson, Anders (1995). *Manifest Destiny: American Expansion and the Empire of Right*. New York: Hill & Wang.

Stephanson, Anders (2010). 'The Toughness Crew,' *New Left Review*, July-August 2013, pp. 145–52. Review of Peter Beinart, *The Icarus Syndrome: A History of American Hubris*. New York: Harper & Collins, 2010.

Stiglitz, Joseph E. (1998). 'More instruments and broader goals: Moving toward the Post-Washington consensus,' in *Wider Annual Lectures 2*. Helsinki: UN World Institute for Development Economics Research.

Stiglitz, Joseph E. (2002). *Globalization and its Discontent*. New York: W.W. Norton.

Stiglitz, Joseph E. (2010). *Freefall: America, Free Markets, and the Sinking of the World Economy*. New York: Norton.

Stieglitz, Joseph E. (2013). 'The free-trade charade,' *Project Syndicate*, 14 July, https://www.project-syndicate.org/commentary/transatlantic-and-transpacific-free-trade-trouble-by-joseph-e--stiglitz (accessed 25 September 2013).

Stiglitz. Joseph E. (2016). 'Monopoly's new era,' *Project Syndicate*, 13 May, https://www.project-syndicate.org/commentary/high-monopoly-profits-persist-in-markets-by-joseph-e--stiglitz-2016-05 (accessed 16 May 2016).

Stiglitz, Joseph E. (2018a). 'American Democracy on the Brink,' *Project Syndicate*, 29 June, https://www.project-syndicate.org/onpoint/american-democracy-on-the-brink-by-joseph-e--stiglitz-2018-06 (accessed 15 July 2018).

Stiglitz, Joseph E. (2018b). 'Can American Democracy Come Back?,' *Project Syndicate,* 6 November, https://www.project-syndicate.org/commentary/american-democracy-under-attack-midterms-by-joseph-e-stiglitz-2018-11 (accessed 11 November 2018).

Stone, Deborah (1997). *Policy Paradox. The Art of Political Decision Making*. New York: Norton (2nd edition).

Stone, Isidor F. (1952). *The Hidden History of the Korean War* (with a preface by Stephen E. Ambrose added to the paperback edition of 1970). New York: Monthly Review Press.

Sun, Irene Yuan, Kartik Jayaram and Omid Kassiri (2017). *Dance of the lions and dragons: How are Africa and China engaging, and how will the partnership evolve?* McKinsey&Company, June 2017.

Swanberg, W.A. (1972). *Luce and His Empire*. New York: Dell Books.

Takian, Amirhossein, Azam Raoofi and Sara Kazempour-Ardebili (2020). 'COVID-19 battle during the toughest sanctions against Iran,' *Lancet*, 18 March 2020, Correspondence, https://www. thelancet.com/journals/lancet/article/PIIS0140-67362030668-1/ fulltext (accessed 26 February 2021).

Temple, Roberts (1998). *The Genius of China. 3,000 Years of Science, Discovery and Invention* (with introduction by Joseph Needham). London: Prion.

Tharoor, S. (2016). *Inglorious Empire: What the British did to India.* London: Penguin.

Todd, Emmanuel (1979). *The Final Fall: An Essay on the Decomposition of the Soviet Sphere.* New York: Karz Publishers.

Tournès, Ludovic (ed.) (2010). *L'argent de l'influence. Les fondations américaines et leurs réseaux européens* [Money of Influence. American Foundations and Their European Networks]. Paris: Editions Autrement.

Truman, Harry (1963). 'Limit CIA Role To Intelligence,' *Washington Post*, 22 December, http://www.maebrussell.com/Prouty/Harry%20 Truman%27s%20CIA%20article.html (accessed 25 September 2021).

Trump, Donald (2017). *National security strategy of the United States of America.* The White House: Washington, DC.

Trump, Donald (2018). Remarks by President Trump in Briefing at Al Asad Air Base Al Anbar Province, Iraq, 26 December. Washington DC: The White House. Retrieved 14 January 2019, from https:// www.whitehouse.gov/briefings-statements/remarks-president- trump-briefingal-asad-air-base-al-anbar-province-iraq/.

Tuchman, Barbara W. (2017). *Stilwell and the American Experience in China: 1911–1945.* New York: Random House.

Turse, Nick (2012a). 'The new Obama doctrine: a six-point plan for global war – special ops, drones, spy games, civilian soldiers, proxy fighters, and cyber warfare,' *Tom Dispatch*, 14 June, http:// www.tomdispatch.com/blog/175557nick_turse_changing_face_of_ empire (accessed 10 June 2016)

Turse, Nick (2012b). *The Changing Face of the Empire: Special Ops, Drones, Spies, Proxy Fighters, Secret Bases, and Cyberwarfare.* Chicago: Haymarket Books and Dispatch Books.

Turse, Nick (2015). *Tomorrow's Battlefields: U.S. Proxy Wars and Secret Ops in Africa.* Chicago: Haymarket Books.

Turse, Nick (2016). 'Commands without borders: America's elite troops partner with African forces but pursue US aims,' *TomDispatch,* 18 December, http://www.tomdispatch.com/blog/176223/tomgram%3A_nick_turse%2C_washington%27s_america-first_commandos_in_africa (accessed 3 January 2017).

Turse, Nick (2017a). 'The year of the commando,' *TomDispatch,* 5 January, http://www.tomdispatch.com/blog/176227/tomgram%3A_nick_turse,_special_ops,_shadow_wars,_ and_the_golden_age_of_the_gray_zone (accessed 5 March 2017). that gives several maps on which you can locate the location of the operations.

Turse, Nick (2017b). 'America's war-fighting footprint in Africa: secret U.S. military documents reveal a constellation of American military bases across that continent,' *TomDispatch,* 27 April, http://www.tomdispatch.com/post/176272/tomgram%3A_nick_turse%2C_the_u.s._military_moves_deeper_into_africa (accessed 28 April 2017).

Turse, Nick (2018). 'Commando sans frontières,' *TomDispatch,* 17 July 2018. Retrieved August 15, 2018, from http://www.tomdispatch.com/blog/176448/tomgram%3A_nick_turse%2C_special_ops%3A_133_countries_down%2C_17_to_go.

Turse, Nick (2020). 'America's Commandos Deployed to 141 Countries. And "Criminal Misconduct" Followed,' *TomDispatch,* 19 March, https://tomdispatch.com/nick-turse-america-s-commandos-what-did-they-do-and-where-did-they-do-it/ (accessed 2 January 2021).

Urio, Paolo (1999). 'La gestion publique au service du marché.' In M. Hufty (ed.). *La pensée comptable. Etat, néolibéralisme, nouvelle gestion publique* (pp. 91–124). Paris: Presses Universitaires de France, Collection Enjeux, Cahier de l'IUED, Genève.

Urio, Paolo (1984). *Le rôle politique de l'administration publique.* LEP: Lausanne.

Urio, Paolo (2010a). *Reconciling state, market and society in China, the long March towards prosperity.* London and New York: Routledge.

Urio, Paolo (ed.) (2010b). *Private partnerships. Success and failure factors in transition countries.* Lanham, Md., and New York: UPA (University Press of America).

Urio, Paolo (2012). *China, the west, China, the west, and the myth of new public management. Neoliberalism and its discontents.* London and New York: Routledge.

Urio, Paolo (2013). 'Reinventing Chinese society, economy, and polity. A very short history and interpretation of China's reforms.' *Politics and Society* (Vol 1, No. 2, pp. 1–37). Central China Normal University.

Urio, Paolo (2016). 'The emergence of NGOs in China and the changing role of the Party-State: assessment and future prospects,' *The China Non-Profit Review*, no. 8, 2016, pp. 188–214.

Urio, Paolo (2018). *China reclaims world power status. Putting an end to the world America made.* London and New York: Routledge.

Urio, Paolo (2019). *China 1949-2019, From Poverty to World Power.* Singapore, Springer Nature

Urio, Paolo and Yuan Ying (2014). *L'émergence des ONG en Chine. Le changement du rôle de l'Etat-Parti.* Bern: Peter Lang.

U.S. Chamber of Commerce (2017). Made in China 2015: Global Ambitions Built on Local Protections. Retrieved March 15, 2018, from https://www.uschamber.com/sites/default/files/final_made_in_china_2025_report_full.pdf.

'U.S. CONGRESS (1976). July 4, The unanimous Declaration of the thirteen United States of America', http://www.ushistory.org/declaration/document (accessed 22 May 2017).

U.S. Department of State (2017). Office of the Historian, *A Short History of the Department of State, Milestones in the History of U.S. Foreign Relations, Key Milestones 1750–2000,* https://history.state.gov/milestones (accessed 18 April 2017).

USA (2016). Office of Naval Intelligence, 'The PLA Navy: new capabilities and missions for the 21st century', http://www.dtic.mil/docs/citations/ADA616040 (accessed 27 July 2016).

USA (2016–20). *US–China Economic and Security Review Commission, 2016–2020 Reports to Congress.*

USA (2018a). *Summary of the National Defense Strategy of the United States of America. Sharpening the American Military's Competitive Edge.* Department of Defense.

USA (2018b). *U.S.-China Economic and Security Review Commission, 2018 Report to Congress.* November. Retrieved January 12, 2019, from https://www.uscc.gov/Annual_Reports/2018-annual-report.

USA (2018c). *Military and Security Developments Involving the People's Republic of China 2018.* Office of the Secretary of Defense.

USA (2019). *China's Military Power. Modernizing a Force to Fight and Win.* Defense Intelligence Agency. Retrieved January 15, 2019, from http://www.dia.mil/News/Articles/Article-View/Article/1732500/defense-intelligence-agency-releases-report-on-china-military-power/.

Valentine, Douglas (2017). *The CIA and organized crime. How illegal operations corrupt America and the world.* Atlanta: Clarity Press.

Van Den Berghe, Pierre (1967). *Race and Racism. A Comparative Perspective.* New York: Wiley.

Vidal, Gore (2003). *Inventing a Nation: Washington, Adams, Jefferson.* New Haven: Yale University Press.

Vine, David (2015). *Base Nation: How U.S. Military Bases Abroad Harm America and the World.* New York: Metropolitan Books.

Vine, David (2017). 'Most countries have given up their colonies. Why hasn't America?', *Washington Post*, 28 September.

Vine, David, et al. (2020). 'Creating Refugees: Displacement Caused by the United States' Post-9/11 Wars.' Watson Institute, Brown University, 21 September.

Vinton, Kate (2016). 'These 15 Billionaires Own America's News Media Companies,' *Forbes,* 1 June, https://www.forbes.com/sites/katevinton/2016/06/01/these-15-billionaires-own-americas-news-media-companies/?sh=26ce41f5660a (accessed 17 May 2017).

Vohra, Anchal (2020). 'Assad's Syria Is Starving Like Saddam's Iraq. How sanctions against the Syrian regime are forcing the country into famine,' *Foreign Policy,* December 2, https://foreignpolicy.com/2020/12/02/bashars-assads-syria-is-starving-like-saddams-iraq/?utm_source=PostUp&utm_medium=email&utm_campaign=28099&utm_term=Editors%20Picks%20OC&?tpcc=28099 (accessed 3 December 2020).

Vos, Elisabeth (2020). 'The Revelations of WikiLeaks: No. 6 – U.S. Diplomatic Cables Spark "Arab Spring" Expose Spying at UN & Elsewhere,' *Consortium News,* 14 January.

Walker, Chris (2020). 'NSA Surveillance Program Exposed by Snowden Was Illegal, Rules Appeals Court,' *Truthout,* 2 September.

Wall, Mike (2019). 'China Makes Historic 1st Landing on Mysterious Far Side of the Moon.' *Scientific American,* 3 January. Retrieved January 15, 2019, from https://www.scientificamerican.com/article/china-makes-historic-first-landing-on-mysterious-far-side-of-the-moon/.

Wallach, Lori (1998). 'A dangerous new manifesto for global capitalism,' *Le Monde Diplomatique,* English edition, February 1998, http://mondediplo.com/1998/02/07mai (accessed 23 May 2017).

Wallach, Lori (2013). 'The corporation invasion,' *Le Monde Diplomatique,* English edition, December 2013, http://mondediplo.com/2013/12/02tafta (accessed 22 May 2017).

Wallach, Lori (2014). 'Transatlantic Trade and Investment Partnership: ten threats to Americans,' http://mondediplo.com/2014/06/10ttip (accessed 23 May 2017).

Wallach, Lori (2017). 'The choice is not between TPP or no trade,' *Huffington Post,* 25 March, http://www. huffingtonpost.com/lori-wallach/the-choice-is-not-between_b_9541300.html (accessed 15 May 2017).

Wallerstein, Immanuel (2006). *European Universalism. The Rhetoric of Power*. New York: The New Press.

Walt, Stephen M. (2020). 'Countries Should Mind Their Own Business,' *Foreign Policy*, 17 July.

Wang Hui (2003). *China's New Order. Society, Politics, and Economy Transition*. Cambridge, Mass.: Harvard University Press.

Wang Hui (2009). *The End of the Revolution: China and the Limits of Modernity*. London: Verso.

Wang Hui (2011). *The Politics of Imagining Asia*. Cambridge, Mass.: Harvard University Press.

Wang Hui (2014). *China from Empire to Nation-State*. Cambridge, Mass.: Harvard University Press.

Wang Hui (2016). *China's Twentieth Century. Revolution, Retreat and the Road to Equality*. London: Verso.

Wang Shaoguang, Hu Angang (1993). 'Strengthen the role of the Central Government during the transition towards a market economy,' report on China's state capacities. Shenyang: Liaoning People Press, 1993.

Wang, Xiaoying (2002). 'Post-Communist Personality: The spectre of China's capitalist market,' *The China Journal*, no. 47, January 2002, pp. 1–17.

Wang Yanan, (1949). *Zhong guo guan liao zheng zhi yan jiu* (The Study of Chinese Bureaucracy). Shanghai: Contemporary Culture Editions (Shi dai wen hua).

Wang Yiwei (2016). *The Belt and Road Initiative. What Will China Offer the World in Its Rise*. Beijing: New World Press.

Wang Zhaogang (2004). *Guo min dang xun zheng ti zhi yan jiu* (Study of the Driving Role of the National Party). Beijing: Social Sciences Edition of China.

Ward, Robert (2020). 'RCEP Trade Deal: A geopolitical win for China,' *The International Institute of Strategic Studies*, 25 November.

Washington Blog (2015). 'America Has Been At War 93% of the Time—222 Out of 239 Years—Since 1776,' 20 February. Retrieved March 18, 2016, from https://washingtonsblog.com/2015/02/america-war-93-time-222-239-years-since-1776.html.

Watkins, Eli (2018). 'Trump blames Putin, Obama for "Animal Assad," tweets "big price" after reports of Syrian chemical attack,' *CNN*, 9 April, https://edition.cnn.com/2018/04/08/politics/donald-trump-syria-assad/index.html (accessed 20 September).

Webb, Jim (2021). 'An American Belt and Road Initiative?,' *Wall Street Journal,* 17 February.

Weber, Max (1978). *Economy and society* (Vol. 1 and 2). Berkeley: University of California.

Wei Liu (ed.) (2018). *China's Belt and Road Initiatives. Economic Geography Reformation*. Singapore: Springer.

Wolton, Thierry. *Le grand bluff chinois. Comment Pékin nous vend sa « révolution » capitaliste*. Paris: Laffont, 2007.

Wong, Erebus, Lau Kin Chi, Sit Tsui and Wen Tiejun (2017). 'One Belt One Road: China's Strategy for a New Global Financial Order,' *Monthly Review*, 1 January, https://monthlyreview.org/2017/01/01/one-belt-one-road/ (accessed 15 May 2017).

Wood, Tony (2017). 'Eat Your Spinach,' *London Review of Books*, Vol. 39 No. 5, 2 March, https://www.lrb.co.uk/v39/n05/tony-wood/eat-your-spinach (accessed 15 March 2017).

World Bank (2012). *China 2030. Building a modern, harmonious and creative society*, officially dated 2013, but already available on line Spring 2012.

Wübbeke, Jost, et al. (2016). *Made in China 2025. The making of a high-tech superpower and consequences for industrial countries.* Berlin: MERICS, Mercator Institute for China Studies, No. 23, December.

Xi Jinping (2013a). Speech of 7 September, Astana. Retrieved June, 14, 2015, from http://www.fmprc.gov.cn/ce/cebel/eng/zxxx/t1078088.htm.

AMERICA AND THE CHINA THREAT

Xi Jinping (2013b). Speech of 2 October, Jakarta. Retrieved July, 22, 2017, from http://www.aseanchina-center.org/english/2013-10/03/c_133062675.htm.

Yip, Georges S., and Bruce Mickern (2016). *China's next strategic advantage. From imitation to innovation.* Cambridge: MIT Press.

Zakaria, Fareed (1997). 'The rise of illiberal democracy,' *Foreign Affairs*, vol. 76, no. 6, November–December, pp. 22–43.

Zakaria, Fareed (2019). 'The New China Scare: Why America Shouldn't Panic About Its Latest Challenger,' *Foreign Affairs*, 6 December.

Zhang, Wei Wei (1996). *Ideology and Economic Reform under Deng Xiaoping.* London and New York: Kegan Paul International.

Zhao, Suisheng (ed.) (2006). *Debating Political Reform in China: Rule of Law vs. Democratization.* New York: M.E. Sharpe.

Zheng, Chuxuan and Shaochun Liu (2004). 'Dandai zhon xi zhengzhi zhidu bijiao' (comparisonbetween the Chinese political system and the Western contemporary political systems). *People Editions of Guangdong*, 2004.

Zheng Yongnian (2004). *Globalization and State Transformation in China.* Cambridge: Cambridge University Press.

Zinn, Howard (1999). *A People's History of the United States.* New York: Harper Collins (1st edition 1980).

Zuboff, Shoshana (2019a). 'Un capitalisme de surveillance,' *Le Monde Diplomatique*, January.

Zuboff, Shoshana (2019b). *The Age of Surveillance Capitalism. The Fight for a Human Future at the New Frontier of Power.* London: Profile Books.

Zuboff, Shoshana (2021). 'The Coup We Are Not Talking About,' *The New York Times*, 29 January, https://www.aei.org/economics/bidens-first-defeat-the-china-eu-trade-agreement/ (accessed 5 February 2021).

Zufferey, Nicolas (2008). Introduction à la pensée chinoise, Pour mieux comprendre la Chine du XXIe siècle. Paris: Hachette.

Index

Z

Printed by Printforce, United Kingdom